ANTISEMITISM
IN CANADA

*History
and
Interpretation*

ALAN DAVIES, EDITOR

Wilfrid Laurier University Press

Canadian Cataloguing in Publication Data

Main entry under title:

Antisemitism in Canada : history and interpretation

Includes bibliographical references.
ISBN 0-88920-221-4 (bound)   ISBN 0-88920-216-8 (pbk.)

1. Antisemitism – Canada – History.   2. Jews –
Canada – Social conditions.   I. Davies, Alan T.

DS146.C2A78 1992   305.892'4071   C92-094903-7

Copyright © 1992

Wilfrid Laurier University Press
Waterloo, Ontario, Canada
N2L 3C5

Cover design by Connolly Design Inc.

Cover photographs: Synagogue at St. Marguerite (Lac Casson),
Quebec, 1938; and some of the fascist newspapers available
in Canada in the 1930s. Both from the Canadian
Jewish Congress National Archives.

Printed in Canada

To

Emil Fackenheim

Contents

Contributors

Pierre Anctil is Associate Professor of Jewish Studies, McGill University, and Director of the McGill French Canada Studies Programme.

Michael Brown is Associate Professor of Humanities, Vanier College, York University.

Alan Davies is Professor of Religion, Victoria College, University of Toronto.

Richard Menkis is Assistant Professor of Religious Studies, University of British Columbia.

Marilyn F. Nefsky is Associate Professor of Religious Studies, University of Lethbridge.

Howard Palmer, who died on March 15, 1991, was Professor of History, University of Calgary.

Manuel Prutschi is Executive Director, Canadian Jewish Congress, Ontario Region.

Phyllis M. Senese is Assistant Professor of History, University of Victoria.

Stephen Speisman is Director of the Archives of the Jewish Community, Toronto Jewish Congress.

Harold Troper is Professor of History, The Ontario Institute for Studies in Education.

Gerald Tulchinsky is Professor of History, Queen's University.

Morton Weinfeld is Associate Professor of Sociology and Chairman of the Department of Sociology, McGill University.

Introduction

While various studies have touched on the question, or dealt with some of its aspects,[1] a comprehensive history of antisemitism in Canada has never been written. This book does not fill the lacuna. However, it does supply some of the materials for such a history and some suggestion of its range. The essays reflect the saga of the nation itself, beginning with the colonial period and ending with the final decades of the twentieth century. They also reflect the saga of the Canadian Jewish community and its fortunes and misfortunes in the land of the north. To be sure, there are many gaps: the Atlantic provinces, for example, have been omitted, not because they are unworthy of attention, but because I was unable to find anyone to examine this facet of the subject. No doubt, on another occasion, and in another book, someone will make good this omission. On the other hand, Ontario and Quebec have received ample attention, perhaps more than their due, but size and centrality have made these two old 'Canadas' a centre of gravity; moreover, the majority of Canadian Jews dwell within their bounds. Quebec, with its Catholic culture and its nationalistic ethos, is a complicated case in addition, and requires more than a cursory glance. As far as western Canada is concerned, Alberta, with its 'funny money' politics and its Texas-style religion, is another complicated case in need of special examination. I fear that Saskatchewan, Manitoba and British Columbia, while they have not been ignored entirely, have not received equal treatment. This is unfortunate, since Manitoba in particular contains a significant urban Jewish population, and even a rural one as well.[2] Again, I trust that someday someone will study the ethnic press on the prairies with this question in mind. Despite these regional deficiencies, however, the fare is rich, and the danger of disappointment is not great. The reader is invited to test this claim. Since the essays have been arranged in a more or less chronological fashion, it is advantageous to read them in sequence.

Notes for the Introduction are on pp. 8-9.

1

But one need not be a slave to chronology; each essay is autonomous, and can be read independently. If variety is the spice of life, this book is well flavoured.

Antisemitism is a complex and contentious subject. The term itself, a coinage of the German Second Reich, bestowed respectability for a time on an ancient animosity because of its vagueness and its crypto-scientific character.[3] Today, of course, it has completely lost this aura. Both because of its modern connotations, and because the compound never had any integrity in the first place, its continued usage is often criticized. Are not the German words *Judenhass* or *Judenfeinschaft* (hatred of Jews, enmity toward Jews) more exact descriptions of the age-old antipathy that has engaged our attention in this volume? Perhaps. But for better or worse, *Antisemitismus* has entered our language in its English form, and we must live with it. As long as we remember its dubious origins, and what it does *not* mean (i.e., hatred of Arabs), it is not a barrier to communication. Like the later words 'racism' and 'sexism', antisemitism introduces a chain of associations that can be regarded as common coin. Animosity toward Jews, whether cultural, racial, religious, social, economic or political, or a combination of all of these motivations, falls under its rubric. So do its manifold expressions, ranging from personal insult to public discrimination and physical persecution. Antisemitism can be mild or severe; it can be polite and genteel, rude and vulgar. It can be covert or overt; it can arise in conjunction with both power and powerlessness, and it can attach itself to other ideologies, notably national, racial and class myths current at given times in given societies. It can even attach itself to political liberalism, as Gerald Tulchinsky demonstrates in his study of Goldwin Smith. In the case of Canada, the two myths of Anglo-Saxondom (in English Canada, including the west) and the pre-conquest mystique of the French-Canadian nation (in Quebec) are both significant in this respect; so, incidentally, is Ukrainian nationalism. In the case of Canada, also, the historical friction between the major ethnic and cultural communities that compose the Canadian mosaic, quite apart from their respective myths, has always carried its own dangers, notably a climate of mutual suspicion and distrust that can easily be changed into something worse when times are bad. Not infrequently, in both Canadian and European history, the Jews have been trapped in the middle of other rivalries. To study antisemitism, therefore, is to expose the soul of the social order. If, as Irving Greenberg has written,[4] antisemitism is an "early warning system" of dangerous currents in the body politic, much as canaries once warned miners of poisonous fumes in coal mines, it must be brought under microscopic inspection for the sake of the collective good. In large measure, this is the purpose of our inquiry. How sound is Canada's social health? The past illumines the present, and the present, in turn, casts light on the probable future.

For obvious reasons, it was the Second World War and its aftermath that made the investigation of the roots of antisemitism in Western civilization a matter of general concern. Prior to the mass destruction of the European Jews at Nazi hands, few non-Jewish scholars were interested in the subject, although there were some notable exceptions;[5] antisemitism was seen as a Jewish problem. Since 1945, however, this attitude has changed, especially among Christian historians, theologians and ethicists. The Holocaust did not occur in a temporal and spatial vacuum; it occurred in Christian time and Christian space, and its instigators were either Christians or ex-Christians. Christendom, as a consequence, has been faced with an intellectual, moral and spiritual crisis of unprecedented proportions, requiring the utmost soul-searching and self-critical examination. According to the American church historian Franklin H. Littell, the Holocaust constitutes an "alpine event" in Christian as well as in Jewish history, albeit for different reasons.[6] He is undoubtedly correct in this designation. Another American writer has made the same point by describing himself as a "post-Auschwitz Christian."[7] This is not to say that Christian anti-Judaism is solely or mainly responsible for the fate of the Jews at the hands of Nazi Germany; such a conclusion is far too simplistic, and ignores a host of other factors associated with modernity, as well as the special circumstances of European history that allowed Hitler to rise to power. It also ignores the vagaries of the human spirit. Nevertheless, the crisis is genuine and serious. For at least the past 20 years, a growing number of Christian theologians have engaged in a radical critique of traditional Christian ideas about Jews and Judaism, and in their revision.[8] The deicide and malediction myths, for example, as well as the belief that the Jews are conspirators against Christendom in league with the devil, have wreaked havoc for centuries. Moreover, the antisemitic 'classics' that preserve these myths, such as the late nineteenth-century *Protocols of the Elders of Zion*, appear and reappear in new contexts and new forms, feeding each generation of antisemites with the same poison as their predecessors. As various essays in the book make evident, this poison has infected Canadian society from time to time, especially Catholic Quebec and fundamentalist Alberta. However, as the contributions show, one must not draw facile equations between conservative forms of Christianity and antisemitism. James Keegstra, whose head is full of both old and new anti-Jewish obsessions, does not represent Protestant fundamentalism as it exists for the most part today. To examine the religious patterns of Christian society in Canada in the light of the Holocaust, and with the wisdom of hindsight, is to realize that antisemitism has often been a potent force in the public policies of our nation — sometimes visible, sometimes invisible. After all, Canada, although not a Christian society in the homogeneous sense, is certainly a society strongly coloured by Christian values, and one in which the churches have played no minor role. What they believe and say about Jews, therefore, can cause both good and ill.

Not only has classical Christian theology been subjected to post-Holocaust reconsiderations in recent years, but the moral conscience of the Christian West has been scrutinized as well. When confronted with the actual spectacle of persecution and violence inflicted on Jews, how have Christians responded? How have Canadian Christians responded? The ritual murder trials in Hungary and Russia, the Dreyfus affair in France, the pogroms in turn-of-the-century Russia, the mounting storms of the 1930s, and the more terrible deeds of the 1940s, all started seismic waves that reached the Americas, largely through the media of the press. Jewish refugees, moreover, soon followed these tales, especially during the later period, and Canada was forced to face an unprecedented situation. The hard-heartedness of the federal government of the day, as well as the Ottawa bureaucracy, has been documented by Irving Abella and Harold Troper in their exposé *None Is Too Many*. According to these authors, with some notable exceptions, the Canadian churches and their leadership did little or nothing to raise the voice of public outcry: "As long as the churches remained silent—which they did—the government could dismiss the (Canadian National Committee on Refugees) members as well meaning but impractical idealists to be patronized but not taken seriously."[9] How silent, in fact, were the churches? Did antisemitism mute their voices, or did the plight of the Jews prick the conscience of Christian Canada more than Abella and Troper indicate? This question is worthy of a more detailed investigation than is possible in this volume; however, in Marilyn Nefsky's essay, a beginning has been made. The manner in which a country treats the refugees that come to its shores from zones of pillage and murder is still an important test of the intrinsic morality of its culture, whether Christian or non-Christian. If the chilling predictions of Richard L. Rubenstein in his studies of social triage and the fate of surplus people in the modern world are accurate,[10] it will become more important than ever. In the case of the Jews, Canada (as well as Great Britain and the United States) has encountered already the tragic configurations of an age in which no lines of escape are allowed. Ideology, the evidence suggests, is largely responsible.

At the end of the Nazi chapter in European history, it was difficult to imagine any society ever again being tempted by an antisemitic madness of such grotesque proportions: the Nuremberg trials and the death camps were irrefutable testimonies of its terrible harvest. Astonishingly, however, these testimonies have been challenged in more recent decades by the new school of historical revisionism, a movement of both European and American origin.[11] Its thesis is simple: Germany is innocent, Hitler has been maligned, the Jews were never murdered, the Holocaust is (another) Jew-

ish fraud, and if any crimes were committed, the allies were fully as implicated as Hitler's legions. This new line of thought, which has been promoted extensively in recent years, has not failed to make its début on
Canadian soil. It is the shape of the characteristic antisemitism of our day.
In one sense, it is as ancient as Apion of Alexandria, since it rests on the
conviction of a Jewish hatred for the rest of humanity, and of Jewish lies
from time immemorial; in another sense, it is as modern as modern can
be. It emerged in Keegstra's classroom in Alberta, but its most notorious
Canadian representative is the Toronto propagandist and pamphleteer
Ernst Zündel, who, in fact, is a German, not a Canadian, citizen. Ironically
during Zündel's first trial, the Holocaust itself was placed in the dock,
along with the veracity of its victims. Had Zündel been acquitted, historical revisionism (Holocaust denial) would have been vindicated, at least in
the public mind, and antisemitism would have scored an important victory. For this reason, his two trials, and Keegstra's, possess a significance
greater than the two men themselves; indeed, both courtrooms became
the setting of a debate about more than legal issues, since, beyond the narrow parameters of the Criminal Code, stretch a host of wider questions
regarding freedom of speech, defamation and slander, and the proper values of civilized existence. Keegstra and Zündel are small fry, but it would
not be an exaggeration to describe their trials as constituting a kind of
morality play in which the contours of good and evil are clearly etched. If
one views antisemitism as intrinsically evil, as only an antisemite would
not, these courtroom dramas afford an extraordinary glimpse into its
depths, a glimpse rendered all the more profound by the fact that both
Keegstra and Zündel have cast themselves as heroes while casting the Jews
as villains. In this respect, the Canadian trials resemble the older and more
famous Dreyfus trials in France, although, of course, the French military
officer was a victim of antisemitism, not its propagator. However, despite
the reversal of roles, the Dreyfus affair was also a morality play of the first
order.

Another morality play in the form of another trial and series of possible
trials has been in the public eye: that of Imre Finta (recently acquitted)
and other suspected Nazi war criminals, although, in two cases, Stephan
Reistetter and Michael Pawlowski, the charges have been dropped by the
Crown for lack of sufficient evidence and other difficulties. Not the least
of the scandals of the immediate post-war era is the ease with which such
individuals were able to enter Canada as respectable immigrants, and to
begin their lives afresh, as if nothing untoward had ever happened. The
account of their date with destiny, and the innumerable difficulties in its
path, including the subtle arts of antisemitism, supply the book with a fitting climax. Throughout its pages, a profile of the Canadian nation can be
discerned. From colony to dominion, from a bicultural to a multicultural

society, from a Christian to a religiously pluralistic community, Canada has changed steadily and is still changing in its relatively brief but highly eventful history. The Meech Lake constitutional crisis and its unresolved aftermath is the latest symptom of this fact. Canada's definition of itself has also changed, shattering what the sociologist Evelyn Kallen has called the "cherished Canadian myth of Canada the Good — the tolerant, peaceful and above all 'just' society."[12] This transformation is recent, and one brought about not only by latter-day revelations concerning the King government and the Jewish refugees, but also by a dawning public awareness of the harsh treatment meted out to the wartime Japanese Canadians for reasons of race,[13] and by other violent racial incidents directed against newly arrived immigrants, especially blacks and East Indians. 'Canada the Good' has not disappeared completely; peace, order and good government are still our happy lot, in spite of some things to the contrary, and in spite of present uncertainties, and the attendant social unrest. Nor have tolerance and justice fled our domain altogether. But the proud complacency implied in the phrase has suffered a mortal blow; our national self-righteousness has been left in tatters. The vile odour of old hatreds still lingers in the air, and antisemitism is not the least of their acrid fumes. Interestingly, the war crimes trials do not appear to have attracted universal public support; in fact, traces of sympathy for their subjects can be found in certain sectors of Canadian society, and not merely in the ethnic communities from which they derive. Are not bygones better forgotten, and should not these sad old men — model citizens and good neighbours in their adopted country — be left to live out the rest of their lives in peace? Much conventional wisdom argues in this fashion, but such conventional wisdom forgets both the enormity of past crimes and the possibility of future ones. Morality plays are still necessary.

There is a further point. As the final essay (by Harold Troper and Morton Weinfeld) shows, antisemitism does not stand alone; more often than not, it is deeply entangled with other feelings, notably rival nationalisms and sacred histories in which roles are transposed, and definitions of oppressor and victim sometimes have opposite connotations. Not only does Jewish historiography see its past as a vale of tears; Ukrainian historiography does the same, implicating Russian Jews in the crucifixion of the Ukrainian nation. Complex questions emerge immediately: what is fable and what is reality? who defines antisemitism: is antisemitism in part a matter of individual or communal perception? By analogy, the same questions apply to other ethnic conflicts involving Jews and non-Jews, both in Canada and elsewhere, since the objective and subjective components of life can never be separated completely. Jews, therefore, and non-Jews will never agree fully about antisemitism, even when they agree in large measure. The three essays on Quebec in this volume illustrate this dictum. Moreover, as far as Canada is concerned, the anti-immigrant, anti-refugee policies of the federal government and bureaucracy during the King years were rooted in blindness as well as hard-heartedness: a blindness arising from the complacent assumptions of an ethnocentric pride — "White Canada Forever," as Peter Ward has called it[14] — that simply did not detect its own prejudice. Its actions, consequently, were reflex actions, in defence of preconceived and precious values. Because nativism and its attendant fears were embedded in both English and French Canada *a mare usque ad mare*, it cannot be said that the federal policies of the day were out of joint with the greater segment of contemporary public opinion. On the contrary, it was pressure from the provinces, including Quebec, that caused the prime minister, his cabinet and his bureaucrats to intern the Japanese Canadians and to exclude the Jews. The British Columbia delegation at the Conference on Japanese Problems (Ottawa, January 8, 1942) was adamant in its insistence on the Japanese menace in Canada and, according to one observer, spoke of the Japanese Canadians in exactly the same fashion as "the Nazis would have spoken about Jewish Germans."[15] At the time of the Bermuda Conference on the international refugee crisis (April 19, 1943), the Canadian government was castigated by the Quebec press for its failure to demand an invitation in order to make certain that the "Jewish problem" was not solved at Canada's expense![16] Racism and antisemitism? Yes, indubitably. But it is surely erroneous to reduce these evil actions to evil for evil's sake. Myths, sacred stories, misconstrued ideals, misreadings of the signs of the times, misunderstandings of the stakes, all contributed to the tragedy.

It only remains to thank the various contributors to this volume. I regret, however, that I cannot thank Howard Palmer, since death has intervened, and removed a distinguished social historian from our midst. Each has worked independently, although in full awareness of the others; each has supplied his or her own perspective. I have served as mediator, conciliator and interlocutor: in short, as intermediary in a rather protracted process. The essayists were selected according to their special qualifications vis-à-vis each other and the larger design. No attempt has been made on my part to disguise differences of opinion or to harmonize the findings unduly. I have even allowed the chapters to overlap on occasion for the sake of a rounded discussion, and there are many inner connections; however, some editorial surgery has been performed as well. My invisible hand shows mainly in the construction of the whole. The essays are both substantial and original, although some, or parts of some, have been published elsewhere in other forms. This does not mean that our book is a rehash of other books; new material and new interpretations are abundant throughout. Pierre Anctil's analysis of Judeo-Christian relations in Quebec during the interwar period has appeared in a book-length

French version entitled *Le Rendez-vous manqué*, a fact that in no way undermines the novelty or importance of this text. Several of the essays — for example, Gerald Tulchinsky's study of the eminent Victorian Goldwin Smith, Phyllis Senese's analysis of the western-Canadian press during the Dreyfus scandal, and Manuel Prutschi's account of Ernst Zündel — venture into uncharted seas. In any case, a great many loose ends have been drawn into a larger, if still imperfect, pattern. Perhaps some future Canadian historian will correct its defects.

The Canadian Jewish Congress kindly supplied the photographs used on the cover from its National Archives. Every effort has been made to trace the ownership of all copyright material reprinted in the text. The author and publisher regret any errors, and will be pleased to make necessary corrections in subsequent editions.

Thanks are also due to the Canada Council and to Multiculturalism and Citizenship Canada, both of which provided funds for the publication of this book.

As always, I am deeply indebted to June Hewitt for her tireless assistance and inexhaustible skills.

Victoria College, Toronto   Alan Davies

Notes

1 Notably Irving Abella, *A Coat of Many Colours: Two Centuries of Jewish Life in Canada* (Toronto: Lester & Orpen Dennys, 1990); Irving Abella and Harold Troper, *None Is Too Many: Canada and the Jews of Europe* (Toronto: Lester & Orpen Dennys, 1982); Pierre Anctil, *Le Rendez-vous manqué: Les Juifs de Montréal face au Québec de l'entre-deux guerres* (Montreal: Institut Québécois de recherche sur la culture, 1988); Lita-Rose Betcherman, *The Swastika and the Maple Leaf: Fascist Movements in Canada in the Thirties* (Toronto: Fitzhenry & Whiteside, 1975); Michael Brown, *Jew or Juif? Jews, French Canadians, and Anglo-Canadians, 1759-1914* (Philadelphia: Jewish Publication Society, 1987); Erna Paris, *Jews: An Account of Their Experience in Canada* (Toronto: Macmillan, 1980); Stuart A. Rosenberg, *The Jewish Community in Canada*, 2 vols. (Toronto: McClelland & Stewart, 1970-71); and Stephen Speisman, *The Jews of Toronto: A History to 1937* (Toronto: McClelland & Stewart, 1979).

2 As a resident of rural Manitoba (the interlake area) during 1957-59, I recall knowing at least one Jewish farmer in the vicinity of the town of Eriksdale.

3 Cf. Moshe Zimmermann, *Wilhelm Marr: The Patriarch of Antisemitism* (New York: Oxford University Press, 1986), pp. 112-13.

4 Irving Greenberg, "Cloud of Smoke, Pillar of Fire: Judaism, Christianity, and Modernity after the Holocaust," in Eva Fleischner, ed., *Auschwitz: Beginning of a New Era? Reflections on the Holocaust* (New York: Ktav, 1977), p. 37.

5 Cf. James Parkes, Conrad Moehlmann.

6 Franklin H. Littell, *The Crucifixion of the Jews: The Failure of Christians to Understand the Jewish Experience* (New York: Harper & Row, 1975), p. 16.

7 Harry James Cargas, *Reflections of a Post-Auschwitz Christian* (Detroit: Wayne State University Press, 1989).

8 Especially significant in this respect are A. Roy Eckardt, John T. Pawlikowski, Paul van Buren, Rosemary Radford Ruether, Jürgen Moltmann, et al.

9 Abella and Troper, *None Is Too Many*, p. 264.

10 Richard L. Rubenstein, *The Cunning of History: Mass Death and the American Future* (New York: Harper & Row, 1975; Beacon Press, 1983), and *The Age of Triage: Fear and Hope in an Overcrowded World* (Boston: Beacon Press, 1983).

11 For a good recent discussion, see Deborah E. Lipstadt, "The Evolution of American Holocaust Revisionism," in *Remembering for the Future: The Impact of the Holocaust and Genocide on Jews and Christians*, International Scholars' Conference (Oxford: Pergamon Press, 1988), pp. 269-83. See also Gill Seidel, *The Holocaust Denial: Antisemitism, Racism and the New Right* (London: Beyond the Pale Collective, 1986).

12 Evelyn Kallen, *Ethnicity and Human Rights in Canada* (Toronto: Gage, 1982), p. 20.

13 Cf. Ann Gomer Sunahara, *The Politics of Racism: The Uprooting of Japanese Canadians during the Second World War* (Toronto: James Lorimer, 1981).

14 W. Peter Ward, *White Canada Forever: Popular Attitudes and Public Policy Toward Orientals in British Columbia*, 2nd ed. (Montreal-Kingston: McGill-Queen's University Press, 1990).

15 Cited in Sunahara, *The Politics of Racism*, p. 33.

16 Abella and Troper, *None Is Too Many*, p. 142.

1

Antisemitism and Anti-Judaism in Pre-Confederation Canada

Richard Menkis

The history of the Jews in Canada prior to Confederation has been unjustly ignored. Certainly, the relative size of the Jewish population was small; in 1871, the Jews constituted less than .03 percent of the total population.[1] However, the significance of this period of Canadian-Jewish history is greater than this number suggests. By the mid-nineteenth century, Jews had wandered into many areas, from the Maritimes to Vancouver Island, of what eventually would become Canada,[2] and, by the 1970s, the early loosely organized settlements had evolved into visible and viable Jewish communities in Montreal, Toronto, Hamilton and Victoria.[3] By the 1870s, the Jews were treated *legally* as full citizens, with the right to vote and hold office; in short, they had achieved emancipation. For these two reasons alone, early Canadian Jewish history must be explored in greater detail than hitherto has been the case.[4] Thus far, only David Rome, in a variety of writings, and Michael Brown, in his book *Jew or Juif*, have undertaken the task of synthesizing the broad range of materials pertaining to public attitudes toward Jews and Judaism. Brown has argued that a major reason why Jews identified with English Canada rather than French Canada was because of the hostility inspired by French right-wing thought and French Catholicism. English Canada, with its roots in a more tolerant British and Protestant society, held them in greater esteem. While anti-Jewish sentiments were undeniably present in both parts of pre-Confederation Canada, I shall argue that the Jewish question was not central politically or religiously in either. Moreover, while it is clear that French Canada did sustain more overt hostility toward Jews and Judaism than

---

Notes for Chapter 1 are on pp. 29-38.

English Canada, a nuanced appraisal of each in the colonial era reveals more shading than has been acknowledged.[5]

Anti-Judaism and antisemitism, however defined, are phenomena with a variety of causes, numerous modes of expression and varying degrees of intensity.[6] The distance between the prejudice of an individual and a prejudice embodied in law is not small. Both, however, occupy points on the same continuum, although the latter is far more dangerous because it has the force of societal institutions behind it.[7] Similarly, hostility to the Judaic tradition draws from various roots, and can be expressed in various ways.[8] Some anti-Jewish Christians believe that Judaism has been superseded by Christianity, whereas others reject Judaism on more general grounds, as part of a rejection of all non-Christian religions. Those who believe in the inferiority of Judaism may or may not be motivated to engage in missionary activity and work for the conversion of the Jews. Any analysis must take these different types and degrees of hostility into account, placing them in a larger context and noting the extent to which they have found legitimacy in Canadian society.

From New France to Quebec

The first European settlers in what is now Canada brought with them a host of assumptions regarding Jews and Judaism. The policy in New France was that Jews should not settle there, and the clergy attempted to ensure that this policy was not challenged. In 1738 Esther Brandeau,[9] a young Jewish woman originally from the large Sephardic community of St. Esprit, a suburb of Bayonne, arrived in Quebec on the ship *Le Saint Michel*. According to her own testimony, she successfully disguised herself as a boy on the crossing from La Rochelle after living away from home for several years. Had she been willing to convert to Catholicism, she could have remained in Quebec. Despite the best efforts of the local clergy, she refused; in the words of the *intendant* Hocquart, in response to his superior, the Minister of the Marine: "Her conduct is so fickle, that at different times she has been as much receptive as hostile to the instructions that zealous ecclesiastics have given her; I have no alternative but to send her away."[10]

The legal reasoning behind the decision was not stated explicitly, but can be surmised. From its earliest history, settlement in New France was officially restricted to Catholics. In 1627, the Cardinal de Richelieu, Louis XIII's first minister, moved against the powerful Huguenot merchants of La Rochelle, granting a charter for the exploitation of the colony to the newly formed Company of One Hundred Associates. In return for certain economic benefits, the company agreed to settle New France, but only Catholics were to be allowed entry.[11] Further justification for Brandeau's expulsion could have been drawn from the laws of other French colonies.

While the *Code Noir* — a series of laws which, *inter alia*, prohibited Jews and Protestants from settling in the French islands of the Caribbean — had not been registered in Quebec (as in Louisiana), it was influential nonetheless. Certain stipulations were followed, such as that involving the baptism of children of slaves,[12] and it would not be surprising to find that the exclusion of the Jews had some impact, as promoted by a zealous clergy. Moreover, Sephardic Jews, such as Esther Brandeau, were permitted to reside only in southwestern France, where they were granted certain privileges and protection. Outside this region, defined as the *généralités* of Bordeaux and Auch, they were subject to imprisonment; if they died outside of the permitted areas, they lost the right to transmit property to their families, and their belongings could be confiscated by the Crown.[13]

Had a persistent economic interest been demonstrated by the Jews in New France, matters may have been different. Trade often served as the wedge by which non-Catholics opened the restrictive legislation of the French colonies. Jewish merchants managed to set up their relatives in the French West Indies in the eighteenth century, despite the provisions of the *Code Noir*. Although their status was tenuous — they were likely to have their property seized at death by the Crown under the *droit d'aubaine* unless they converted — they remained settled there, either undergoing a superficial conversion or challenging the law on various grounds.[14] However, with the notable exception of the shipping firm *David Gradis et fils*, French Jewry showed little interest in the French colonies outside the Indies.[15] Protestants, in contrast, whose presence was also forbidden in Quebec (as elsewhere on French colonial soil), managed to settle against the wishes of the clergy. François Bigot, the last *intendant* of New France, defended the Huguenot merchants in 1749, claiming that in no way did they disrupt the religious and civil life of the colony, and believing that the economic benefits derived from their presence more than compensated for a "zeal for religion [which] appeared a little exaggerated."[16] Clearly, the clergy did not have the only, or necessarily the most powerful, voice in New France. But, whatever the reason, there was no legal Jewish presence, and the one attempt by a professing Jew to remain in the colony was met with expulsion. The policy that Jews were not allowed was scarcely tested.[17]

After the conquest, however, matters were different. Legal regulations surrounding the British colonies differed dramatically from the French regime, and Jewish settlers were permitted. Hence, they began to enter the former French, now British colony, where they encountered no continuous tradition of political hostility among the *Canadiens*. In the early nineteenth century, French-Canadian politicians of note did not look back on the pre-conquest era as idyllic; many, in fact, appreciated the British system of government, especially after the Constitution Act of 1791. No evidence suggests that anyone regarded the French colonial situation, in which there were no Jews, as ideal. There were, however, a few incidents proving the existence of some antisemitism in the political arena, most notably *L'Affaire Hart*.[18] In 1807, the voters of Trois-Rivières elected a scion of a pioneer Jewish family, Ezekiel Hart, to sit in the Legislative Assembly of Lower Canada. In preparation for taking up his seat on January 29, 1808, Hart took the oath which Jews were accustomed to swearing in courts of law,[19] "on the Bible, his head being covered." The next day an objection was raised by the attorney general, Jonathan Sewell, that the oath was not taken in the manner required for sitting in the assembly — an oath of abjuration, which would have required Hart to swear "on the true faith of a Christian." Sewell moved that the assembly pass a resolution to this effect, and that Ezekiel Hart be provided with a copy of the resolution, "to the end that he may thereupon pursue such further course in the premises as the law of Parliament may be found to require."[20] Shortly after, Thomas Coffin, the runner-up in the election in Trois-Rivières, petitioned the assembly, calling for the removal of Hart because, as a Jew, he was not "capable of being elected to serve in the House of Assembly, or of taking the oaths required, or sitting or voting in the Assembly," and asking that the election be considered null and void and that Coffin be given the seat for Trois-Rivières in his place.[21] Another petition came from Hart himself, saying that, while he believed that he was justified in law in taking a seat by means of the oath used by Jews in the courts, he was willing to swear the oaths used for those elected to the assembly.[22] After some deliberation, however, the assembly decided that "Ezekiel Hart . . . professing the Jewish religion, cannot take a seat, nor sit, nor vote, in this House."[23]

The matter was not resolved. In 1808, new elections were held, and once again Trois-Rivières returned Hart as one of its two representatives. This time, Hart took the oath in the same fashion as a Christian, and when the assembly finally reconvened in 1809, sat as a member for Trois-Rivières for several days. But the issue was raised again, and, after ascertaining that Hart had been expelled the previous year, the assembly voted to expel him again. One resolution declared that the member "professing the Jewish Religion" had taken the oath "on the Holy Evangelist, which could not bind him, and did therefore profane the Religious institution thereof. . . ." This was amended to state simply that "Ezekiel Hart, Esquire, professing the Jewish faith, cannot sit, nor vote in this house," and, in this form, it was passed. The vote was divided along ethnic lines; all 18 votes in favour came from French Canadians, and all but one of the votes against came from the English.[24] Soon after, Governor Craig dissolved the assembly, and, when finally it was reconvened, the issue of whether or not a Jew could sit in Parliament was no longer paramount, as Hart did not run again.

Some scholars have argued that the Hart affair should not be treated as an antisemitic episode. The French Canadians were anxious to remove him because he was perceived correctly as aligned with the English side, although the latter, especially the governor, had no great love for either Hart personally or for the Jews. Craig only wished to use the controversy as a means of undermining the French Canadians, who were becoming more strident in their demands for an increased role for the legislative assembly. Others have interpreted this affair as proof of a tradition of ongoing hostility toward Jews among French Canadians, reflecting the appropriation of political antipathy from liberal circles in France, as well as religious fanaticism. Ezekiel Hart himself stated that, with only one exception, his opponents were Catholics, and he assumed they were encouraged in voting against him by their priests.[25]

This 'either-or' approach has clouded the issue. There was definitely an antisemitic component to the incident. When Hart was elected for the first time, *Le Canadien*, the mouthpiece of the Canadian party, published a scurrilous poem decrying the choice of a Jew for a seat as even more foolish than Caligula's appointment of his horse as a Roman consul.[26] In the same issue, a more ideologically explicit attack was launched. A letter to the editor argued that the electors of Trois-Rivières should be reprimanded for electing a Jew to office. In language akin to that used by conservative European opponents of emancipation — there are references to an unnamed "writer of our time" — the author argued that Jews tend to be concerned only with other Jews. In fact, he continued, it is a principle of Judaism that Jews should separate themselves from their surroundings. How then, could they be expected to look after the interests of the people as a whole?[27]

In his presentation to the assembly in 1808, Pierre Bédard, the leader of the *Canadiens*, argued against granting Hart a seat in the assembly. In addition to addressing the question on legal grounds, he used language similar to that used in the aforementioned letter. Bédard claimed that no Christian nation had granted Jews the rights of citizens,[28] not for unjust reasons, but because they themselves do not wish to be part of any country. They may make a country their residence to pursue their business dealings, but never their home. This state of affairs, Bédard continued, is a result of the Jewish tradition, which requires Jews to wait for the messiah, their prince; while waiting, they cannot pledge allegiance to any other prince.[29] It would be specious, therefore, to suggest that the *Canadiens* did not draw on antisemitic arguments in arguing for Hart's ejection. At the same time, it is too simple to treat the incident as reflecting a persistent and deep-seated anti-Jewish hostility. Antisemitic arguments were not the focal point of the debate, nor were religious motivations dominant. The resolution referring to the "profanation" that had occurred when Hart swore on

Christian scriptures was dropped, and, when one member moved that Hart could not sit "until he proved that he had embraced the Christian religion," his motion was defeated 20 to two, indicating that the *Canadiens* were against this type of religious pressure.[30] In fact, the church was not impressed with these early nationalists; Bishop Plessis disliked their newspaper, *Le Canadien*, intensely.[31]

The antisemitism was instrumental. The *Canadiens* were anxious to remove Hart, and drew from a well of antisemitic charges then current in Europe. Once Hart decided not to run, however, the Jewish issue was not pursued to its potential limits, e.g., if Jews could not be expected to be loyal to their country, why should they be allowed to vote? The inconsistency of the members of the *parti canadien* in the assembly, including Bédard, their leader, was a reflection of the selective liberalism characteristic of these early nationalists. On the one hand, they appreciated the parliamentary system that had come with the English, and gravitated toward positions designed to maximize the power of the legislative assembly. According to some historians, they even developed an early argument for ministerial responsibility in order to limit the power of the colonial officials and their appointees. On the other hand, they had an adversary in the English merchants, who were perceived to be in alliance with the colonial administration, thus threatening the assembly. They were willing to utilize all devices and rationales—many of them markedly non-liberal—to preserve their control, including the marshalling of anti-Jewish arguments to prevent a pro-English Jew from taking his seat.[32]

The events of 1807-1809 did not become a model for subsequent French-Canadian nationalists, as a later sequel would prove. On July 26, 1830, another Hart, Samuel Becancourt, was asked by the colonial secretary, on behalf of the governor, whether he would be willing to serve as a magistrate for the district of Trois-Rivières. Two days later, Hart replied in the affirmative. On October 19, however, the colonial secretary notified him that both the attorney general and the executive council had advised the governor that a Jew could not take the oath of qualification, and therefore could not fill the proposed commission. This set off a train of events that included petitions to both the legislative assembly and the legislative council by members of the Jewish community and by Hart himself. The ultimate result was a bill that passed in both houses and was given royal approval in 1832 as Act 1 Wm. IV, cap. 57, "An Act to declare persons professing the Jewish Religion entitled to all the rights and privileges of the other subjects of His Majesty in this Province."[33] The political manoeuvering surrounding this bill and the ideological context of the discussions have not been explored to the same extent as the Hart affair, but several facts are apparent. The virulence of the earlier controversy found no echo in 1832 in the assembly, the council or the press; it was simply treated in a factual manner by both English and French.[34] One of the petitions on behalf of the Jews of Lower Canada was presented to the legislative council by the nationalist Denis-Benjamin Viger. In February 1831, Hart decided that, rather than merely present his case to the governor, it was best to petition the assembly and council as well.[35] Apparently, he was confident that he could raise the issue without heated controversy, and in this he was correct. The French-Canadian liberals of the 1830s were firmer and more consistent in their liberalism than the earlier nationalists. When questions arose about the efficacy of the law several years later — raised by two Jews, incidentally — a commission headed by René Kimber was appointed, and the matter was again discussed calmly by all sides. The committee ultimately decided that the law had not been questioned by a competent authority, and that 1 William IV, cap. 57 was indeed sufficient to safeguard the political liberties of the Jews, and that "Under these circumstances, Your Committee does not deem it fitting or necessary to recommend any additional Legislative enactments on the subject referred to them."[36]

Even after anti-Liberal forces became powerful in French Canada in the aftermath of the rebellion of 1837, writers of the period considered the events of 1807 to 1809 an aberration, and the law passed in 1832 as the true reflection of the sentiments of the French population.[37] While there was a definite unwillingness to recognize the virulence of some of the early attacks, their apologetic motif indicates that the preservation of Jewish political rights was not debatable. The reasons must be understood in the context of the political and religious climate of the mid-nineteenth century. Before we turn to this crucial era, however, it is necessary to explore some religious images.

Unlike the sporadic outbursts of political hostility, a steady stream of theological anti-Judaism ran throughout the pre-Confederation era. Although, with the remarkable exception of Esther Brandeau, Jews themselves apparently did not migrate to New France, religious ideas about Judaism did make the trans-Atlantic voyage. Traditional anti-Judaic notions found expression in one of the earliest works that had as its aim the improvement of the educational level of the Christian population of Quebec, the *Catéchisme du Diocèse de Québec* of Monsignor de Saint-Vallier (1653-1727). Published as the *Grand Catéchisme* for Quebec in 1702, it remained a backbone of Catholic education until the 1750s.[38] The first section was a catechism on sacred history from the creation of the world to the early church,[39] where Saint-Vallier described the character of ancient Israel and the role of the Jews in the crucifixion. He promoted a traditional Christian view of the old Israel as obstinate, and post-biblical Jewry as without divine favour. His text emphasized the sins of Jews and the temporary nature of the old covenant; after Sinai, Israel rebelled against God 10 times in the desert, and frequently abandoned God for idols even in the Promised Land.[40] God subsequently established a more noble alliance with the Christians.[41] The rejection of the Jews occurred with their rejection and murder of Jesus; Jerusalem was destroyed as a consequence. Moreover, Saint-Vallier linked the situation of the Jews in antiquity to the situation of the Jews in his own time:

> *And what happened to them then? [after the destruction of Jerusalem]*
> They were reduced to servitude, and dispersed throughout the world.
> *What has happened to them since?*
> They are still in the same state? (*sic*)
> *For how long?*
> Sixteen hundred years.[42]

Thus the Catholic educator succinctly conveyed the notion that the Jews were under divine punishment, and would continue in this state until their conversion. Saint-Vallier had appropriated this Christian super-sessionist attitude toward Judaism from the earlier model of the Abbé Fleury in France, who, despite his positive view of Judaism in *Les Moeurs des Israélites*, was very much the Christian traditionalist in his catechism.[43] The harshness of Saint-Vallier's appraisal was somewhat mitigated by his rigorous moralism. In fact, he so emphasized the sins of the individual in his reluctance to administer the sacrament of absolution that he was accused of Jansenism by his adversaries. A recent major study claims that pastoral psychology rather than theology determined his outlook as he confronted hostile civil authorities and a flock reluctant to live Christian lives.[44] Whatever the case, Saint-Vallier used the story of the punishment of the Jews rejecting Jesus as a warning to Christians:

> *What do we learn from this lesson?*
> That if the city of Jerusalem and the Jews were punished with so much severity for having put Jesus to death just once, what punishments ought we not to expect having killed him so many times by an infinite number of sins. . . .[45]

His flock should identify with the Jews rather than the persecuted Jesus, focusing on the weakness of all humanity.[46] Christians, however, have an opportunity of redeeming themselves — by being good Christians. Jews, on the other hand, must cease to observe Judaism if they are to escape their fate. In fact, in a later section of the catechism, Jews are catalogued as infidels who, along with atheists, idolators and the impious, violate the first commandment by not submitting to Christ.[47]

Popular suspicions also appeared in Quebec. In 1742, Havard de Beaufort, a soldier stationed in the garrison in Montreal, caused a great stir when he agreed to the request of a shoemaker to perform an act of divina-tion to discover the identity of a local thief. Havard performed his magic

with a large crowd in attendance, using as one of the "ingredients" a crucifix. The rumour spread that the crucifix had been profaned by stabbing,
and that Havard was of Jewish origin.[48] (Jews, like Protestants, were associated with witchcraft,[49] as well as with the devil, gladly committing outrages against Christian religious symbols.)[50] Subsequently, the crucifix
became an object of veneration after being handed over to the sisters of
the Hôtel-Dieu, especially after 1782, when Pope Pius VI granted a full
indulgence to all who came on the first Friday of October; however, there
is no indication that an anti-Jewish motif persisted.[51]

Before the end of the French regime, a new *Grand Catéchisme* had found
its way into French Canada, replacing that of Saint-Vallier. The *Catéchisme
du diocèse de Sens* was used in New France in 1750, and was published in
Quebec in 1765 — the first volume in French ever published in the colony — and it quickly sold out, becoming the catechism of Quebec until
1890, with only minor changes.[52] The author of this work was a strong
anti-Jansenist, and his catechism did not contain the same rigorous moral
viewpoint. The sections referring to Jews reflect this fact; in the discussion
of Palm Sunday, for example, Jesus was put to death "by the malice of the
Jews" without Christians being asked to reflect on their own sins.[53]
Another motif was the notion that all salvation comes from Jesus alone;
even Abraham and Moses did not enter heaven until Jesus had escorted
them there.[54] This theological anti-Judaism was variously modified, reinforced and propagated by related instruction and sacred history, as well as
by legend and popular devotions. Ancillary works to guide the young believer included Fleury's historical catechism, which was published in
Quebec in 1807.[55] This text draws a sharp distinction between 'Jews of the
spirit' and 'Jews of the flesh'; the former honour God for the sake of the
divine power, whereas the latter fear God for material reasons and read
Scriptures in a literal fashion.[56] The history of the Jews came to an effective end with the Jewish rejection of Jesus; as a result, Jerusalem was destroyed and the Jews were chased from the land and "reduced to the miserable state in which they have been for the past 1700 years."[57] A later historical catechism declared that the Jews have a false idea of the messiah,
and that Jewish history really concluded with the birth of Jesus.[58]

The theological teaching of the punishment of the Jews for the crucifixion became embodied in the popular legend of the wandering Jew, in
which a Jew who had taunted Jesus on the way to his death was condemned to roam the earth forever. This legend had its origins in the
Middle Ages, but was disseminated widely after first appearing in pamphlet form in the early seventeenth century.[59] From the seventeenth to the
twentieth centuries, numerous individuals reported meeting the wandering Jew. By the 1870s, the legend had found its way to Quebec. Narcisse
Faucher Saint-Maurice, a recorder of folk tales of the countryside, told of

meeting a captain who claimed to have encountered the wandering Jew in Kamouraska. After describing this mysterious personage (an old man with a remarkably long beard), the captain added that he and several of his crew saw the Jew resume his travels at night, finding, on the next day, drops of dried blood on his path: "These [drops of blood] came from the pained feet of he who, encountering Jesus on the route to Calvary, took to laughing at the latter when he fell, and to ridiculing his step weighted by the sins of man, and as a result was condemned, *he and his race*, to circle the world without end."[60] The image of the Jew as tormentor of Jesus, and of subsequent Jewish history as punishment, thus found concrete expression in Quebec. According to Saint-Faucher, the legend was widespread in the countryside.

The representation of the Jew as the tormentor of Christ was featured in some of the pietistic literature associated with the devotion of the Way of the Cross. This devotion, in which a pilgrim stops and reflects on the various stages of the suffering of Jesus on his way to crucifixion, also became highly popular in Europe in the seventeenth and eighteenth centuries. In late 1822, Monsignor Plessis, armed with a pamphlet he had acquired in Rome on the subject, declared himself ready to set up the devotion and, by the 1830s, it was already present in Quebec, with Montreal clamouring for locations.[61] Various manuals providing background on the devotion, as well as reflections for each of the stations, were published; the first was a translation of the Roman pamphlet, as well as an introductory letter by Plessis, which was reproduced several times in the 1830s.[62] Most of these early manuals were, in fact, rather benign, and did not develop any explicit anti-Judaic themes. In two volumes of the early 1840s, however, both published in Montreal, and both drawing on European models, a subtle shift can be detected. In 1841, the reflections of the Way of the Cross of Alphonse de Liguori — a popular eighteenth-century Italian ecclesiastic, well known for his exuberant advocacy of Catholic traditions — were published, one of the many imports from Italy that informed popular piety in nineteenth-century Quebec.[63] At the fifth station, which represents the place where the Cyrene, Simon, was pressed into service to carry Jesus's cross (Matt. 27:32), the pilgrim is asked to consider "how the Jews, seeing that Jesus was so weak that with each step he seemed about to give up his soul, and fearing that he would die on the road, those who wished to see him die on the ignominious punishment of the cross, forced Simon the Cyrene to carry the cross behind Jesus Christ." This was markedly more hostile than the earlier version published in Quebec, which simply exhorted the pilgrim to imitate Simon.[64] In the second manual, also published in Montreal,[65] there is a similar negative tone. At the first station, where Jesus is condemned to die, the Jews are portrayed as crying out for his death "like ferocious beasts"; at the second, where Jesus is forced to carry the cross, the Jews are portrayed as crying with joy, "as they are finally the masters of Jesus."[66]

These two volumes, in which the Jews are cast as the enemies of Christ, were imported as part of the new ultramontane religiosity taking hold in Quebec.[67] The first bishop of Montreal, Jean-Jacques Lartigue, had been greatly influenced by French ultramontanism and attempted, with limited success, to introduce it into Quebec. However, the social and political environment changed dramatically when Ignace Bourget assumed the office of Bishop of Montreal in 1840. Monsignor Bourget correctly sensed that the time was ripe for new policies. The church, for example, could promote civil obedience, thereby appealing to those who had despaired in the wake of the rebellion of 1837. This meant an advantageous alliance with politicians who, frightened by the radicalism of Papineau, had embraced political conservatism, seeing the church as a valuable ally in preventing further insurrections. Bourget also perceived the need to build a powerful Catholic bulwark against the Protestants. Although Lord Durham was not particularly interested in religious conversion, many evangelical Protestants elaborated on the assimilationist mentality of Durham's report and established the pan-Protestant French-Canadian Missionary Society in 1839.[68] In his struggles, Bourget was aided by large numbers of French clerics who, imbued with ultramontanism, had settled in Quebec.[69]

One French cleric in particular sparked a great deal of enthusiasm for this new piety. In 1840-41, Monsignor Charles de Forbin-Janson, Bishop of Nancy, visited Quebec and delivered a number of highly successful sermons, creating a revivalist mood among Quebec Catholics, and assisting the less colourful Bourget in enhancing the place of ultramontane Catholicism in the diocese of Montreal.[70] His visit, which was carefully followed in the French-language press, concluded with a trip to the newly established pilgrimage site on Montagne de St. Hilaire. There he induced the large and exuberant crowds to cry out "vive la Croix, vive Jésus, vive Marie, vive le Canada toujours catholique," and delivered a sermon in which he called on his listeners to behave militantly and "defend, everywhere, at the risk of one's life, this flag of Catholicism."[71] Liguori's manual of the Stations of the Cross was published as an appendix to a reprint of these events from the ultramontane newspaper *Mélanges religieux*; thus, a hostile theological image of the Jew was placed at the centre of a great wave of religious exuberance.

The other edition of the Stations of the Cross published in Montreal was also appended to an interesting text, the description of a pilgrimage of a G. Labbé, first published in Le Mans in 1837.[72] This pilgrimage text called for Catholics to be careful lest they turn to impiety, and the Montreal edition included the warning specifically for the benefit of Canadians;[73] it clearly fitted into the ultramontane cry to work for a Catholic

Quebec. In this volume, the image of the Jew is harsh. The destruction of Jerusalem was total because the behaviour of Israel was so abysmal: God sent the prophets, Jews stoned them; God sent His beloved son Jesus, they crucified him.[74] The sins of the Jews were a warning, not for the individual to repent, as with Saint-Vallier, but rather to guard against allowing non-Catholic ideals to take hold in Catholic society. The sin of the Jews in rejecting Jesus is parallel to the sin of those who resist the Catholicization of their lands. Such persons will suffer the same fate as the Jews: "What will be the punishment of nations which, like the Jews, are crying in our days: 'We do not want God to rule over us'. . . . In the (French) Revolution of '93, did one not see the heads of those who had voted for the death of Christ the Lord under the hatchet of the executioner?"[75] To chart the parallels:

Actors	Crime	Punishment
Jews	Crucifixion	Jerusalem destroyed in 70
Jacobin leaders	Anti-Christian revolution in France	Executed in 1794

In France, the association between liberals and Jews became still more explicit in the 1870s. The Jews were not merely analogous to the Jacobin leaders of the French Revolution, but were actually among those elements determined to destroy Christendom. The origins of this doctrine are found in French ultramontane ideology at a relatively early date. After 1832, when the converted Jew Simon Deutz was implicated in the Duchesse de Berry's plot to overthrow King Louis Philippe, the Jews were regularly included among the segments of the population who created upheaval. After the celebrated Mortara case of 1858,[76] the Jews were usually the first of a number of co-conspirators against Christendom, a list which included atheists, pantheists, rationalists, Protestants and Saint-Simonians.[77] The association with anti-Christian forces eventually merged with an older plot theory which claimed that the Freemasons were behind the anti-Christian insurrections. By the late 1860s, the potent myth of a Judeo-Masonic theory had coalesced in France, to be developed and propagated steadily over the next two decades.[78] In Quebec, the vision of the Jews not just as Christ-killers but also as contemporary enemies became widespread after Confederation.[79] However, a few hints of the accusation made themselves heard in the 1860s. The earliest appeared in the pro-ultramontane newspaper, La Gazette des Campagnes, one of many such papers in the mid-nineteenth century. Its particular emphasis dealt with the beneficial aspects of rural life, but it was also noted for its extreme positions, especially those of one of its contributors, Alexis Pelletier. This journal castigated the Jews in 1866 for propagating the ideals of progress in partnership with infidels, sectarians and Satan. The Jews were also listed as among those who call for the 'elevation of the flesh', in company with idol-worshippers, Protestants and Catholics (i.e., wayward Catholics).[80] By 1870, the ultramontanists had crystallized a list of ideologies that were anathema to Catholic Quebec, with the place of priority (following Pius IX's directives) reserved for liberalism, secret societies, evil books and evil journals (*mauvais livres, mauvais journaux*).[81] The *Institut canadien*, an institution disseminating liberal ideas, attracted the ire of the ultramontane clerics; one reverted to the religious language of the crucifixion story, calling it a "sanhédrin rouge."[82] "Le juif Crémieux" was among those liberals guilty of plundering France.[83]

Two points, however, must be made in order to understand the social and political impact of these clerical teachings. In the first place, various shades of Catholic thought and practice competed with each other for public acclaim. Several years after Labbé's description of the Holy Land was published in Montreal, a French-Canadian cleric, Léon Gingras, recorded and published his travels in the Middle East. His account of the Jews and Judaism is far less hostile than Labbé's, although the troublesome term *déicide* is used.[84] In the second place, the ultramontane clergy achieved success only in certain fields of activity. Although they asserted the theory of the superiority of Rome over the state, they ultimately had to deal with the realities of politics, and negotiate the precise relationship between church and state. French-Canadian politicians, while appreciative of the clergy's emphasis on civil obedience, especially after 1837, were unwilling to surrender their power to the clerics in all spheres, forcing the ultramontane clergy to be satisfied with a limited influence in public affairs. The area in which the ultramontanists were best able to appropriate a degree of power was education; in other areas, they were essentially circumscribed.[85] Perhaps it is not coincidental that the school question eventually proved explosive in Quebec. For the beginnings of an ideological attack on the Jews are found in the pre-Confederation era — an attack linked to the significant but by no means monopolistic place occupied by ultramontane piety and ideology in the Quebec church.

English Canada

Under English domination, the legal assumptions about Jews changed dramatically. Already in 1749, shortly after the Treaty of Aix-la-Chapelle, a scheme was hatched to settle poor Jews in Nova Scotia, although Jewish settlers did not arrive in Halifax until 1752.[86] Unlike the situation in much of France, and certainly in the French colonies, the Jews had achieved effective civil, if not political, rights in England by the middle of the eighteenth century. These had been acquired by various judicial decisions, as legislation was not forthcoming until the middle of the nineteenth century. With these decisions, British Jews acquired protection for their per-

sons and property in both England and the colonies, although some critics
maintained that they could not hold real property beyond their own
homes, citing restrictive legislation from the Middle Ages.[87] Such objections apparently found their way to British North America, since, when
Levy Solomons petitioned for a land grant in 1797, he was informed in no
uncertain terms by the Upper Canada executive council that "Jews cannot
own land in this province."[88] This verdict, however, proved to be no more
a precedent than in Great Britain, and Jews settling in Toronto certainly
owned property by the mid-nineteenth century. As for political rights,
there was never in English Canada a controversy that excited – either at
the time or later – the passions of *L'Affaire Hart*.[89] One challenge to the
political rights of the Jews (on the west coast) was short-lived. The governor of Vancouver Island, James Douglas, proposed a bill of naturalization
that included the phrase "on the true faith of a Christian" in the relevant
oath, and the press took him to task for prescribing "a form of oath which
it is well known Jews cannot and will not take. . . . After a 12 year struggle,
the British parliament, . . . has admitted Baron Rothschild to a seat in the
House of Commons, and has by a formal resolution allowed Jews to omit
[these] words. . . ."[90] Three days later, Douglas backtracked, and came up
with a wording exempting both Quakers and Jews.[91] In 1860, when Selim
Franklin, a Jew, was elected to the provincial legislature in Victoria, a
debate took place as to whether he could be seated, since it was alleged
that he had not taken the oath with the proper wording. A committee
investigated the matter, and it was found that the proper oath had been
administered, allowing Franklin to retain his seat.[92]

More consistent and significant expressions of anti-Jewish sentiment in
English Canada erupted over business matters. On occasion the hostility
was public. In Victoria, a member of the legislature, Major Foster,
offended the well-integrated Jewish community when he called in doubt
their commitment to the colony, arguing that they were only interested in
their own commercial success. At issue was the exemption of certain types
of agricultural improvements from taxation; Foster believed that everything possible should be done to attract farmers to the colony. But the
attorney general, he argued, was not of that opinion.

> The Attorney General has been conversing with the little Jews on John-
> son Street. Ask them if they want 20 000 Indians brought here; they will
> reply – "By all means, Mr. Attorney General, bring them along; they
> will buy our goods and make business brisk." What does that class of
> people care if the town was burnt up tomorrow; the next day they are
> off for San Francisco.[93]

This allegation was denounced not only by Jews but by non-Jews as well,
who stated that the "Hebrews of Victoria are both [*sic*] numerous, wealthy

and public spirited."[94] In 1878, similar assumptions about Jewish selfishness were challenged by the behaviour of a Jew in Nanaimo. A savage fire threatened this town, which lacked a fire department; somebody issued a call for wet blankets to protect the buildings still untouched by the flames. One Alex Mayer provided rolls of blankets, whereas a certain John Hirst failed to provide any assistance, with the result that "there were loud comments on the generous Jew and the skinflint Englishman."[95]

A scrutiny of the records of the most important credit-rating organization of nineteenth-century America reveals that influential members of society held stereotypes about the Jews, and with serious implications. R. G. Dun and Company utilized a series of agents to assess the worthiness of merchants for loans and other forms of commercial credit, and passed this information on to potential creditors for payment. Because it had agents in locations across North America, the head office was able to cross-list the information and follow the careers of particular merchants, say, from Montreal to Toronto to New York. While valuable to business historians, these company records betray the attitudes of local agents of Protestant background and, occasionally, of the population as a whole.[96] In an important study of the relationship between credit-rating and feelings about Jews in Buffalo, David Gerber has noted that such agents revealed a marked tendency to combine marketplace perceptions with a series of older prejudices; for example, that Jews are secretive and deceptive, practising a dubious morality in their dealings with non-Jews.[97]

The hostility discovered by Gerber applied in English Canada as well. The agents assumed that Jews in general should not be trusted: thus, M. Feintuch, a jeweller in Toronto was labelled in 1863 as a "Jew of the regular type," which the agent goes on to define as "not in good repute and is not sold to here by the trade. Has made some money by peddling but is a risky customer & only pays when he cant help it, should be avoided could pack up and leave at any moment."[98] A decade later, another agent reported that the members of the Trester family have "the reputation of possessing the characteristics of their race, looking after their own interests, but are not likely to incur any debt they cannot correct."[99] Occasionally, a correspondent of R. G. Dun overcame his prejudice for certain individuals, but this did not change his assumptions about Jews in general; speaking of I. G. Joseph, for example, an agent commented as follows in 1853: "should advise caution — is a *Jew*, would rather not speak as to character," and, a year later, "For a Jew his engagements are all O.K. I should say good. I have doubt about Jews generally, but consider him an exception."[100] These attitudes had important socio-economic consequences. While Jews may have compensated with their own credit arrangements, both informal and formal,[101] the prejudices of the agents could prevent easy access to credit as long as these stereotyped views prevailed. On occasion, attitudes of suspicion had other consequences; in November 1860, an agent noted that the Benjamin brothers did little business in the fall of that year "on account of the prejudice felt towards them as Jews."[102] While the matter requires greater exploration, this evidence suggests the presence of a genteel, hidden antisemitism of the marketplace in English Canada that had no counterpart in French Canada of the same era.

The theological anti-Judaism in English Canada also found a different mode of expression than in French Canada. The nineteenth century was a period of great evangelical activity among Protestants, and missions to the Jews were organized early on both sides of the Atlantic. In Britain the London Society for the Promotion of Christianity among the Jews (1809) was the most significant; in the United States, the Society for Meliorating the Condition of the Jews began its missionary work with great gusto in 1820. In Scotland, Andrew Bonar, a central figure of the evangelical revival in Presbyterianism in the 1830s, urged a special mission to the Jews. While these societies often professed love of the Jewish people, and occasionally attempted to improve their social situation, the underlying messages which they propagated among Christians (they did not succeed greatly in converting Jews) ultimately denigrated Judaism.[103] In short, wittingly or unwittingly, they promoted a theological anti-Judaism which merits our attention as the counterpart to the image of Jews and Judaism in the catechisms and popular pietistic practices of the Catholic church.

This missionary impulse arrived on Canadian soil by a variety of routes. Canadian publications such as the evangelical newspaper, the *Montreal Witness*, reported on the activities of missionaries elsewhere.[104] Some clergy had observed missions to the Jews before they settled in Canada: thus, Robert Burns, a leading figure in mid-nineteenth century Presbyterianism in Toronto, heard the founder of the London Society for Promoting Christianity among the Jews preach in Scotland.[105] Burns's contemporary — sometimes adversary and sometimes friend — Michael Willis, participated in 1839 at a conference in Glasgow where he delivered an address seeking to demonstrate that Jesus fulfilled the Old Testament prophecies regarding the messiah.[106] Foreign missionary organizations also sent representatives to various parts of English Canada (along with, incidentally, various charlatans who hoped to pocket the collection money they raised in churches).[107] An auxiliary society of the London Jews' Society supposedly existed in 1847, and a Rev. Buchan Wright came to preach and organize branches in the Canadas and the Maritimes in 1863.[108] The first indication of the arrival of agents of the American Society for Meliorating the Condition of the Jews in Montreal, Kingston and Toronto dates from the early 1850s,[109] although a backwoodsman in Canada West stipulated a donation to the Society in his 1844 will "for helping to Convay coppies of the Scripture and sending Missionaries to the Jews. . . ."[110] This suggests an earlier presence. On one occasion, a mission to the Jews was organized directly by Canadian Christians. In 1858, the members of the Synod of the Presbyterian Church of Canada in Connection with the Church of Scotland decided to take this step; in 1860, after some correspondence with foreign missionaries, they agreed to send a converted Jew, Ephraim Epstein, to Monastir, near Salonica,[111] the first foreign mission arranged by Protestants outside of the Maritimes. Before his departure, Epstein preached in Canada West, Canada East, Nova Scotia and New Brunswick.[112] The mission in Monastir lasted only two years; in 1863, the synod, while still "believing that every Christian Church must of necessity be a missionary Church . . ."[113] decided to invest its resources elsewhere. Although the idea of a mission to the Jews was revived occasionally, the next intense phase of this enterprise had to await the late nineteenth and early twentieth centuries.[114]

Since there were few Jews in Canada in the mid-nineteenth century, missionary speakers were sent to attract support — especially financial — in order to convert Jews elsewhere rather than in their midst; nevertheless, they had an effect on public opinion. How convincing their sermons were, and exactly what view of Jews and Judaism they promoted, is often hard to discern. The abrasive Presbyterian minister, Robert Burns, supported Jewish missions[115] but was not impressed by the emissary to Toronto of the Society for Meliorating the Condition of the Jews. Burns claimed *inter alia*, that the agent delivered "a pernicious paper . . . far better fitted for bringing back Christians to Judaism in its worst form, than for leading on the minds of the children of Abraham to the glories and the grace of the Messiah the Prince. . . . intelligent Jews will say 'that is all very good, and therefore we wait for your joining *us*, instead of our going over to *you*.' "[116] In Toronto, however, others did not appreciate these criticisms,[117] and in Montreal the missionary was praised for his remarks in a public meeting, and the audience was asked for a good collection.[118]

The call issued by these missionary groups for Jewish evangelization lay behind — and possibly provoked — a still extant sermon by a cleric of some stature in Montreal. In July 1851, a Congregationalist minister, the Reverend Henry Wilkes, preached in his church "Jesus, the Divine Messiah: An Address to the Jews," which was published as a pamphlet later that year.[119] At present, this sermon is the best evidence we possess of the manner in which Jews and Judaism were represented to evangelical Christians in the mid-nineteenth century. The thrust was that the Old Testament laid down specific details on how to recognize a messiah, and that these were fulfilled perfectly in Jesus. The evangelist Wilkes had little need of extra-biblical sources, and his sermon consists largely of unadorned prooftexts drawn from Scripture. In fact, he rejected modern approaches, dubbing

them the "perversions of a misguided rationalism," and was irritated that
the Jews had taken to using these arguments to reject Christian readings of
the Hebrew Bible. Wilkes held precise images of the misguided Jew and
the ideal Jew. He proclaimed that he was motivated by love, for "no true
Christian despises the Jew." In fact, however, a suitcase of sentiments and
images hostile to professing Jews and to Judaism accompanied his "love."
Jews who could not accept Jesus as the messiah predicted in the Hebrew
Bible had a "veil upon their heart," implying both a moral and emotional
blindness. Thus, all Jewish strivings outside of conversion were futile:
"You have entertained in many ages since, many hopes of deliverance
apart from faith in Jesus, but their issue has shown them to be a mockery,
as will that of others save faith in the Lord Christ." The ideal Jew for
Wilkes was the converted Jew, who then became an evangelist like himself. He spoke highly, for example, of the convert Neander, the church
historian. Jews were not valued otherwise. How could they be? To be an
adherent of Judaism was to be attached to an outmoded and antiquated
religious system. Wilkes held a markedly Christian supersessionist outlook: "The Mosaic institutions were manifestly preliminary and temporary; Christianity is their designed and adapted end." This outlook was
anti-Judaic; unlike the missionaries of the late nineteenth and early twentieth centuries, however, Wilkes did not attempt to link Christianity with
national identity, nor did he regard Jews as intrinsically a foreign element
in the social and political order, requiring conversion in order to be Canadian. He focused instead on the conversion of the individual through a
recognition of the truth of Scripture. Hence, his message did not move
from theological anti-Judaism to nativist antisemitism.

Not all Christians felt comfortable with missions to the Jews. According
to the rabbi of Montreal Jewry, Abraham De Sola, the Church of England's Bishop Fulford of Montreal resisted such efforts. In part, this was
because the needs of Anglicans were not receiving sufficient attention,
making Jewish missions an unaffordable luxury. However, he also
believed that it was easy to shake the faith of another, but difficult to
replace the lost faith, with the result that the missionized is "left in state of
infidelity."[120] But this did not prevent a certain zeal from taking hold
among other Church of England officials. According to a report in the
London *Jewish Chronicle*, in 1862 the Jews of Victoria "in a body" with-
drew their children from the public school "in consequence of the
attempt made by the teaching staff-members of the Church of England to
seduce them from the religion of their fathers."[121] The available evidence
on the Protestant denominations suggests that Jews and Judaism did not
attract a great deal of attention in this early period. With many other concerns — the struggle to assert their place in new lands, the struggle over the
relationship between church and state, and the need to convert far larger

groups of non-Protestants — it is not surprising that the Jews were hardly an issue. Nonetheless, missionaries and clergy did insert an anti-Judaic element into the religious discourse of the era, with an impact still to be determined.

Conclusion

The legacy of anti-Judaism and antisemitism of the pre-Confederation era reveals a low level of inconsistent hostility toward Jews and Judaism, with different emphases in French and English Canada. French Canada developed in planned isolation from non-Catholic influences and peoples, including the Jews, although this isolation was not always enforced vis-à-vis the Protestants. Yet since the tradition of a purely Catholic Quebec was never idealized by the mainstream nationalist parties in the post-conquest period, the Jewish issue only rarely became politicized. That the nationalists were capable of drawing on anti-Jewish arguments is clear from *L'Affaire Hart*, but these arguments did not become entrenched. In 1832, Lower Canada, with the blessing of the contemporary nationalists, ensured that Jews received full political rights, emancipating them earlier than anywhere else in the British Empire. These rights were never challenged; even with the antisemitic campaign mounted by the supporters of ultramontanism, the rights of the Jews were not assailed, and antisemitism was not yet politicized. While a harsh ideological evaluation of the Jews was emerging in French Canada in the mid-nineteenth century, especially in certain sectors of the clergy, the social consequences were still minimal by the time of Confederation.

In English Canada, in contrast, the British tradition of civil rights toward the Jews prevailed, so that, from the outset of the British era, the latter enjoyed a degree of explicit protection not available in New France, with some early exceptions. Some English Canadians criticized the behaviour of the Jews in the marketplace, and this may have had some negative social consequences. The activities of the missionaries served to promote a negative view of Judaism, but missions to the Jews were not numerous in the pre-Confederation period.

The twin legacies of anti-Judaism and antisemitism, then, were present but weak in both French and English Canada; whether and how they were picked up and joined to more powerful streams in the late nineteenth century is for others to determine.

Notes

Unfortunately, space prevents me from thanking the many individuals who offered assistance and advice in this project, which was completed in late 1989. However, I must acknowledge the kind permission granted by Dun and Bradstreet to cite the records of R. G. Dun and Company.

1 Louis Rosenberg (*Canada's Jews: A Social and Economic Study of the Jews in Canada* [Montreal: Canadian Jewish Congress, 1939], p. 31) gives the figure .03 percent, and as Gerald Tulchinsky has pointed out in "The Jewish Experience in Ontario to 1960" (*Patterns of the Past: Interpreting Ontario's History*, ed. Roger Hall et al. [Toronto and Oxford: Dundurn Press, 1988], p. 305), there is undoubtedly an error in the Ontario returns for that year.

2 M. M. Lazar and Sheva Medjuk, "In the Beginning: A Brief History of Jews in Atlantic Canada," *Jewish Historical Society of Canada Journal* 5 (hereafter *JHSCJ*) (1981): 91-108; *History of the Spanish and Portuguese Jews Shearit Israel* (Montreal: n.p., 1918), pp. 11-17; Tulchinsky, "The Jewish Experience in Ontario," pp. 303-306; Arthur A. Chiel, "Manitoba Jewish History — Early Times," *JHSCJ* 1 (1977): 55-74; David Rome, *The First Two Years: A Record of the Jewish Pioneers on Canada's Pacific Coast* (Montreal: H. M. Caiserman, 1942); and Cyril E. Leonoff, *Pioneers, Pedlars and Prayer Shawls: The Jewish Communities in British Columbia and the Yukon* (Victoria, BC: Sono Nis Press, 1978), pp. 13-28, 54-57.

3 Stephen A. Speisman, *The Jews of Toronto: A History to 1937* (Toronto: McClelland & Stewart, 1979), pp. 21-38; and Tulchinsky, "The Jewish Experience in Ontario," p. 304.

4 Unfortunately, because of the paucity of research and because the unpublished materials are scattered in numerous collections across the country, a thorough investigation of the topic is at present impossible. As a first step, I have limited my investigation to the available secondary and published primary materials, with only limited forays into unpublished materials. I hope that this essay will help delineate areas requiring further research.

5 In this, then, I take polite issue with the thesis presented by Michael Brown in *Jew or Juif? Jews, French Canadians, and Anglo-Canadians, 1759-1914* (Philadelphia, New York, Jerusalem: Jewish Publication Society, 1986). This argument was criticized when Brown presented a preliminary account of his findings to the Canadian Jewish Historical Society by Cornelius J. Jaenen, "Thoughts on French and Catholic Anti-Semitism," *JHSCJ* 1 (1977): 16-23. More recently, Pierre Anctil has taken issue with Brown, especially in the latter's tendency to treat the whole period between 1760 and 1940 as a homogeneous unit, not noting some of the apparent differences between the pre-Confederation era and the period from about 1870 to the outbreak of World War I. Anctil's review of Brown is in *American Jewish History* 78 (1988): 136-43; especially relevant to our discussion are 138-40.

6 For a useful discussion of the varieties of antisemitism, see Ben Halpern, "What is Antisemitism?" *Modern Judaism* 1 (1981): 251-62. I accept Halpern's position, which advocates the utility of a broad understanding of antisemitism.

7 The important distinction between latent antisemitism and the more potent antisemitism which finds a voice in official acts is emphasized by Henry L. Feingold, "Finding a Conceptual Framework for the Study of American Antisemitism," *Jewish Social Studies* 47 (1985): 313-27. See also Earl Raab, "Jews among Others," *Understanding American Jewry*, ed. Marshall Sklare (New Brunswick and London: Transaction Books, 1982), pp. 217-30, who uses a slightly different terminology, contrasting individual attitudes and institutional behaviour.

8 Although anti-Judaism and antisemitism are distinct, it would be unwise to exclude anti-Judaism in a survey of this sort. Religion has had a powerful impact on Canadian society, particularly in the nineteenth century, and anti-Judaism provided a bedrock upon which later antisemites have built.

9 The name Brandeau was, incidentally, not found among the Jews of southwestern France. It is more likely that her name was originally either Brandam or Brandon, common names in the region. See Gérard Nahon, ed., Les "Nations" Juives Portugaises du Sud-Ouest de la France (1684-1791). Documents (Paris: Funação Calouste Gulbenkian, 1981), p. 471.

10 Dictionary of Canadian Biography (hereafter DCB), s.v. Brandeau, Esther, by Gaston Tisdel 2: 95-96.

11 W. J. Eccles, New France in America (Vancouver: Fitzhenry & Whiteside, 1972), pp. 26-27, and Peter N. Moogk, "Reluctant Exiles: Emigrants From France in Canada before, 1760," William and Mary Quarterly 3rd ser. 46 (1989): 467, n. 13.

12 Cornelius J. Jaenen, The Role of the Church in New France (Toronto: McGraw-Hill, 1976), p. 152.

13 Frances, Malino, The Sephardic Jews of Bordeaux: Assimilation and Emancipation in Revolutionary and Napoleonic France (University, AL: University of Alabama Press, 1978), p. 5; the 1723 letters patent defining the Jewish status of the Jews of southwestern France have been published in Nahon, Les "Nations" Juives, pp. 36-39.

14 On the Jewish status in the French Caribbean, see Yvan Debbasch, "Privilège réel ou privilège personnel? Le statut des 'Juifs portugais' aux Iles," Religion, société et politique: Mélanges en hommage à Jacques Ellul (Paris: Presses Universitaires de France, 1983), pp. 215-31, and the literature cited there.

15 On the firm David Gradis et fils and New France, see Guy Frégault, François Bigot, Administrateur, français, 2 vols. (Ottawa: Les Études de l'Institut d'histoire de l'Amérique Française, 1948), 1: 283-38 and 2: 122-27, 280-82; and Richard Menkis, "The Gradis Family of Eighteenth Century Bordeaux: A Social and Economic Study" (Ph.D. diss., Brandeis University, 1988), pp. 178-245. Bertram Wallace in Korn, The Early Jews of New Orleans ([Waltham: American Jewish Historical Society, 1969], p. 5), has suggested that, despite the restrictions of the Code Noir, the true cause of no Jewish settlement was because of the colony's "languishing economic potential." See also Mathé Allain, "Slave Policies in French Louisiana," Louisiana History 21 (1980): 1299-30. A work which analyzes the status of both Jews and Protestants in the various colonies remains a desideratum.

16 J. F. Bosher, "French Protestant Families in Canadian Trade, 1740-1760," Histoire sociale/Social History 7 (1974): 179-81; the quote is on p. 181, from a letter of Bigot to the Minister of the Marine, October 3, 1749. See also Cornelius J. Jaenen, "The Persistence of the Protestant Presence in New France, 1541-1760," Proceedings of the Meeting of the Western Society for French History 2 (1974): 29-40 for a description of the struggle between religious officials keen on preserving the Catholic character of New France and royal officials who, for economic reasons, often favoured a policy of permitting Protestants to reside there.

17 It is possible that there were a few conversos in Louisbourg and Quebec. Whatever the case, there is no evidence of any special treatment of this population either legally or in religious and social attitudes.

18 Joseph Tassé, "Droits politiques des Juifs en Canada," *Revue canadienne* 7 (1870): 406-22; Julius J. Price, "Proceedings Relating to the Expulsion of Ezekiel Hart from the House of Assembly," *Publications of the American Jewish Historical Society* 23 (1915): 43-53 (he reproduces the information in the *Journals* of the Assembly); Benjamin G. Sack, *History of the Jews in Canada: From the Earliest Beginnings to the Present Day* (Montreal: Canadian Jewish Congress, 1945), pp. 80-95; Raymond Douville, "L'Affaire Hart: Historical Circumstances of the Legislation Giving Jews a Status of Political Equality," *Canadian Jewish Year Book* 1 (1939-40): 149-52; Jean-Pierre Wallot, "Les canadiens français et les Juifs (1808-1809); l'Affaire Hart," in *Juifs et Canadiens*, ed. Naïm Kattan (Montréal: Éditions du Jour, 1967), pp. 113-21; Abraham Arnold, "Ezekiel Hart and the Oath Problem in the Assembly of Lower Canada," *JHSCJ* 3 (1979): 10-26; David Rome, comp., *On the Early Harts* (parts 3-4) (Montreal: National Archives, Canadian Jewish Congress, 1980); Brown, *Jew or Juif*, pp. 196-98. The description by John Garner in *The Franchise and Politics in British North America* ([Toronto: University of Toronto Press, 1969], pp. 148-50), while inaccurate in some details, and without an analysis of the ideological context, is probably the best discussion of the legal context of the affair, and certainly the least partisan.

19 As was described in *Journals of the House of Assembly of Lower Canada* (hereafter *JHALC*), February 17, 1808, p. 120.

20 *JHALC*, January 29, 1808 and January 30, 1808, pp. 22 and 28.

21 *JHALC*, February 9, 1808, p. 60.

22 *JHALC*, February 12, 1808, p. 76.

23 *JHALC*, February 20, 1808, p. 144.

24 *JHALC*, May 5, 1809.

25 Brown, *Jew or Juif*, p. 197.

26 *Le Canadien*, April 18, 1807, p. 87: "Si Caligula l'Empereur/Fit son *Cheval* Consul à Rome,/Ici notre peuple Electeur/Surpasse beaucoup ce grand homme;/Il prend par un choix surprenant,/Un *Juif* pour son/représentant. . . ."

27 Ibid.

28 Conveniently ignoring France and the United States; perhaps he did not consider them among the "pays chrétiens."

29 See *Le Canadien*, March 2, 1808, pp. 57-58, reporting on the debates which had taken place in February of that year in the assembly: ". . . leur condition n'étoit pas meilleure dans les autres pays chrétiens, que nulle part on ne leur accordoit le droit de citoyen, et que ce n'étoit pas leur faire une injustice, parcequ'ils ne vouloient être eux-mêmes citoyens d'aucun pays. Qu'ils étoient repandus dans tous les pays où ils faisoient bien leurs affaires, et qu'ils ne lui donnoient point d'autre titre que celui *du pays de leur residence*. Qu'ils étoient liés par leur croyance à en agir ainsi, qu'ils étoient dans l'attente du Messie leur Prince, et qu'en attendant ils ne peuvent engager leur fidelité à aucun autre Prince que celui-là auquel ils reservent."

30 As noted by Wallot, "Les canadiens français et les Juifs," p. 117.

31 Fernand Ouellet, *Lower Canada: Social Change and Adaptation*, trans. Patricia Claxton (Toronto: McClelland & Stewart), p. 104.

32 Philippe Reid, "L'émergence du nationalisme canadien-français: l'idéologie du *Canadien* (1806-1842)," *Recherches sociographiques* 21 (1980): 15-18, and Ouellet, *Lower Canada*, pp. 87-91.

33 See the discussions in Sack, *History of the Jews in Canada*, pp. 96-107; David Rome, comp., *Samuel Becancourt Hart and 1832* (Montreal: National Archives, Canadian Jewish Congress, 1982), pp. 9-33; and Brown, *Jew or Juif*, p. 198.

34 Tassé, "Droits politiques," p. 424.

35 National Archives of Canada (NAC), Provincial and Civil Secretary's Office, Lower Canada, RG 4 A1 vol. 351, Hart to Glegg, February 14, 1931. This letter has gone unnoticed in the various histories of the affair.

36 *JHALC*, 1834, appendix G. G. Kimber, from Trois-Rivières, was himself friendly with Jews there; thus, in 1835, Kimber hosted for the visiting Papineau and Viger, inviting several prominent Jews. As Papineau wrote to his wife: "Kimber was proud that he had several of the Harts and his son-in-law and Mr. Judah the father so drunk that in the morning they could not remember what happened the previous evening." Cited in David Rome, comp., *The Early Harts — Their Contemporaries*, Part 2 (Montreal: National Archives, Canadian Jewish Congress, 1981), p. 212.

37 Tassé, "Droits politiques," p. 425, and Siméon Pagnuelo, *Études historiques et légales sur la liberté religieuse en Canada* (Montréal: Beauchemin & Valois, 1871), especially p.259.

38 Mgr. de Saint-Vallier, *Catéchisme du diocèse de Québec 1702* (Paris: Urbain Coustelier, 1702; repr. with notes by Fernand Porter, Montréal: Éditions Franciscaines, 1958), pp.1-6. On the catechism and Saint-Vallier, see Fernand Porter, *L'Institution catéchistique au Canada français 1633-1833* (Washington: Catholic Press, 1949), pp. 104-11, and Guy Plante, *Le rigorisme au XVIIe siècle: Mgr de Saint-Vallier et le sacrement de pénitence (1685-1727)* (Gembloux: Éditions J. Duculot, 1970), pp. 45-47.

39 Saint-Vallier, *Catéchisme*, pp. 26-27.

40 Ibid., p. 27.

41 Ibid.

42 Ibid., pp. 62-63.

43 Arthur Hertzberg, *The French Enlightenment and the Jews: The Origins of Modern Antisemitism* (New York: Schocken, 1970), pp. 41-42. On the influence of Fleury on Saint-Vallier, see Plante, *Le rigorisme*, p. 46 and the unpublished literature cited there on p. 46, n. 64.

44 Ibid., pp. 151-68.

45 Saint-Vallier, *Catéchisme*, p. 63.

46 Bernhard E. Olson (*Faith and Prejudice: Intergroup Problems in Protestant Curricula* [New Haven and London: Yale University Press, 1963], especially pp. 233-39) has argued that a crucifixion theology in which the Christian identifies with the suffering Christ ("I-with-Christ") is generally associated with a more negative image of the Jews than the "I-against-Christ" (as in the case with Saint-Vallier) portrayal. Although he deals with Protestant theologians, the distinction also holds for Catholicism as well.

47 Saint-Vallier, *Catéchisme*, p. 165.

48 The story is told in some detail by Robert-Louis Séguin, *La sorcellerie au Québec du XVIIe et XIXe siècle* (Montréal: Lemeac, 1971), pp. 149-75; the rumour that he was a Jew is related in Jaenen, *The Role of the Church*, p. 150.

49 Jaenen, *The Role of the Church*, p. 150 suggests this possibility, and Joshua Trachtenberg (*The Devil and the Jews: The Medieval Conception of the Jew and Its Relation to Mod-*

ern Antisemitism [New Haven: Yale University Press, 1943]) provides ample evidence that Jews were associated with witchcraft in the middle ages; see especially pp. 57-75 and 207-16. The association of Jews with witchcraft also found expression in early seventeenth-century France in the writings of Pierre de Lancre; see Israel Lévi, "Le traité sur les Juifs de Pierre de l'Ancre," *Revue des études juives* 19 (1889): 235-45.

50 The accusation that Jews attack the cross was far less common than the suspicion that they profane the host, but it nevertheless did have precedents in the early literature (see Trachtenberg, *Devil and the Jews*, p. 118).

51 Séguin, *La sorcellerie au Québec*, p. 175, and see Marie-Aimée Cliche, *Les pratiques de dévotion en Nouvelle-France: Comportements populaires et encadrement ecclésial dans le gouvernement de Québec* ([Québec: Laval, 1988], p. 73) for a photograph of the "crucifix outragé."

52 Porter, *L'Institution catéchistique au Canada français*, pp. 111-17.

53 Jean-Joseph Languet, *Catéchisme du diocèse du Sens* (Québec: Brown & Gilmore, 1765), p. 55.

54 Ibid., p. 124.

55 Claude Fleury, *Catéchisme historique, contenant en abrégé l'histoire sainte et la doctrine chrétienne* (Québec: La nouvelle imprimerie, 1807).

56 Ibid., p. 90.

57 Ibid., pp. 114-15.

58 *Histoire sainte, par demandes et par répoises, suivie d'un abrégé de la vie de N.S. Jésus-Christ, à l'usage de la Jeunesse* (Québec: T. Cary, 1832), pp. 81-82. This work was reissued several times during the period under discussion.

59 On this legend, which became especially widespread in the early seventeenth century, see the classic analysis by George K. Anderson (*The Legend of the Wandering Jew* [Providence: Brown University Press, 1965]), and more recently, for a variety of descriptions and interpretations, Galit Hasan-Rokem and Alan Dundes, eds., *The Wandering Jew: Essays in the Interpretation of a Christian Legend* (Bloomington: Indiana University Press, 1986).

60 Narcisse Faucher Saint-Maurice, *À la veillée: contes et récits* (Québec: C. Darveau, 1877), pp. 26-29. The emphasis is mine.

61 Nive Voisine, gen. ed., *Histoire du catholicisme québécois* 3 vols. in 5 (Montréal: Boréal, 1989), vol. 2: *Les XVIIIe et XIXe siècles (1760-1890)*. Vol. 1, *Les années difficiles (1760-1839)*, by Lucien Lemieux, pp. 308-11.

62 *Méthode de faire le chemin de la Croix* (Québec: C. LeFrançois, 1823; repr. in 1830 and in Montreal in 1832).

63 *Pèlerinages à Mont Saint-Hilaire, suivi des Stations du Chemin de la Croix, par St. Alphonse de Liguori* (Montréal: Bureau des Mélanges religieux, 1841). This volume was originally a series of articles in the ultramontane newspaper *Mélanges religieux*. The important place of Italy in nineteenth-century Quebec has recently been discussed by Pierre Savard, "L'Italie dans la culture canadienne-français au XIXe siècle," in *Les Ultramontains canadiens-français*, ed. Nive Voisine and Jean Hamelin (Montréal: Boréal Express, 1985), pp. 255-66. On the role of the "morale liguornienne" in ultramontanism, see Guy Laperierre, "Vingt ans de recherches sur l'ultramontanisme," *Recherches sociographiques* 27 (1986): 92-93, and the literature cited for France in Laperierre, "Vingt ans," p. 93, nn. 28-31.

64 *Methode de faire le chemin de la Croix* (Québec: C. LeFrançois, 1823), p. 8.

65 G. Labbé, *La terre sainte, ou lieux célebrés dans l'écriture sainte, suivie d'une nouvelle méthode de faire le chemin de la Croix* (Montréal: Louis Perault, n.d., but opposite 3: "vu et approuvé Montréal 22 septembre 1841).

66 Ibid., p. 75.

67 See above, note 63.

68 René Hardy, "La rébellion de 1837-38 et l'essor du protestantisme canadien-français," *Revue d'histoire de l'Amérique française* 29 (1975): 182-87, and Robert Merrill Black, "Different Visions: The Multiplication of Protestant Missions to French-Canadian Roman Catholics, 1834-1855," *Canadian Protestant and Catholic Missions, 1820-1960s: Historical Essays in Honour of John Webster Grant*, ed. John S. Moir and C. T. McIntire (New York: Peter Lang, 1988), esp. pp. 56-57.

69 This discussion of the early growth and the background factors is based on Nive Voisine, "L'ultramontanisme canadien-français au XIX^c siècle," in *Les Ultramontains canadiens-français*, pp. 68-72, and Nadia F. Eid, *Le clergé et le pouvoir politique au Québec: une analyse de l'idéologie ultramontaine au milieu du XIXe siècle* (Montréal: Hurtubise HMH, 1978), pp. 28-30.

70 Claude Galarneau, "Monseigneur de Forbin-Janson au Québec en 1840-1841" (in *Les Ultramontains canadiens-français*, pp. 121-42), is the most recent study of Forbin-Janson in Quebec. The standard histories of ultramontanism discuss the significance of the French cleric's visit, understanding its success in the context of the Quebec political and social climate after 1837 (Galarneau, "Monseigneur de Forbin-Janson," p.121); Galarneau stresses the French connection and the long history of Catholicism in Quebec. These are not mutually exclusive emphases.

71 *Pèlerinages à Mont Saint-Hilaire*, pp. 9, 24.

72 David Rome, comp., *Antisemitism VI: Early Antisemitism: The Holy Land; Tardivel* (Montreal: National Archives, Canadian Jewish Congress, 1985), p. 5.

73 Labbé, *La terre sainte*, p. 18.

74 Ibid., p. 21.

75 Ibid., pp. 39-40.

76 The Mortara case was a *cause célèbre* of nineteenth-century liberals and Protestants versus Catholics. Edgar Mortara, a Jewish child in Bologna, was abducted from his parents by papal police in 1858, when he was not yet seven years old, because he had been secretly converted by a zealous nurse five years earlier. She arranged for the baptism, she claimed, because he was close to death.

77 Austin Gough, *Paris and Rome: The Gallican Church and the Ultramontane Campaign 1848-1853* (Oxford: Clarendon Press, 1986), p. 70 and n. 21.

78 Jacob Katz has outlined the real and imaginary connections in his *Jews and Freemasons in Europe, 1723-1939* ([Cambridge, MA: Harvard University Press, 1970]); he has summarized his findings with respect to France in his *From Prejudice to Destruction: Anti-Semitism 1700-1933* (Cambridge, MA: Harvard University Press, 1980), pp. 143-44.

79 Most of the evidence of antisemitism in Brown, *Jew or Juif*, and David Rome, comp., *Early Antisemitism IV: Across the Dominion* (Montreal: National Archives, Canadian Jewish Congress, 1983) dates from the late nineteenth and early twentieth centuries.

80 As cited in Pierre Galipeau, "La Gazette des Campagnes," *Recherches sociographiques* 10 (1969): 301; David Rome has discussed it in his *Antisemitism III: Early Antisemitism:*

Threats to Equality, part 1 (Montreal: National Archives, Canadian Jewish Congress, 1983), pp. 64-65.

81 Eid, *Le clergé et le pouvoir politique au Québec*, pp. 126-34.

82 Lucien H. Huot, *Le rougisme en Canada; ses idées religieuses, ses principes sociaux et ses tendances anti-canadiennes* (Québec: A Coté, 1864), p. 55.

83 Huot, *Le rougisme en Canada*, p. 72.

84 On Gingras and his work, see Jean Ouelette, "La Palestine au XIX^c siècle vue par un voyageur du Québec," *Bulletin du Centre de Recherche en civilisation canadienne-française de l'Université d'Ottawa* 19 (1979): 15-22, esp. p. 19, and Rome, *Antisemitism VI*, pp. 5-8.

85 Eid, *Le clergé et le pouvoir politique*, pp. 255-79.

86 Cecil Roth, *A History of the Jews in England*, 3rd ed. (Oxford: Clarendon Press, 1964), p. 203, and Lazar and Medjuk, "In the Beginning," pp. 91-108.

87 In 1738 Tovey discovered the 1721 statute *de iudaismo*, which restricted the Jewish ownership of land to their own residences. After Tovey's "discovery" various individuals of the eighteenth and nineteenth centuries pointed out that, because the 1271 statute had not been repealed, it was in force and therefore limited the rights of contemporary Jews to own property. The statute was formally repealed in England in 1846, but the restrictive argument never took hold, and Jews owned land. H. S. Q. Henriques, *The Jews and English Law* (Oxford: Oxford University Press, 1908; repr. Clifton, NJ: Kelley, 1974), pp. 192-93.

88 Cited in Tulchinsky, "The Jewish Experience in Ontario," p. 301, from *Twentieth Report of the Department of Public Records and Archives of Ontario, 1931* (Toronto: H. Ball, 1932), p. 109; the latter also indicates that in the same year Moses Hart was also "not recommended" in his petition for land.

89 More work remains to be done on the civil and political rights of Jews in Upper Canada. For some tantalizing hints, see Sheldon and Judith Godfrey, *Burn This Gossip: The True Story of George Benjamin of Belleville, Canada: First Jewish Member of Parliament, 1857-1863* (Toronto: The Duke and George Press, 1991), pp. 34-35 and 42-43.

90 Victoria *Colonist*, May 20, 1859, p. 2.

91 Ibid., May 23, 1859, p. 2.

92 In fact the only opposition to the committee's report was from Franklin himself, who felt that he had not been completely exonerated. On this episode, see Rome, *The First Two Years*, pp. 65-67.

93 *British Colonist*, September 11, 1860, p. 2; also Rome, *The First Two Years*, pp. 106-12.

94 *British Colonist*, November 26, 1862, p. 3.

95 Cited in Lynne Bowen, *Three Dollar Dreams* (Lantzville: Oolichan Books, 1987), p. 214.

96 For some comparative information, see David A. Gerber, "Cutting Out Shylock: Elite Antisemitism and the Quest for Moral Order in the Mid-Nineteenth Century Marketplace," in *Anti-Semitism in American History*, ed. David A. Gerber (Urbana and Chicago: Illinois University Press, 1986), pp. 201-25 (originally in *Journal of American History* 69 [1982]), and Stephen G. Mostov, "Dun and Bradstreet Reports as a Source of Jewish Economic History, 1845-1875," *American Jewish History* 72 (1984): 333-39.

97 Gerber, "Cutting Out Shylock," pp. 217-20.

98 R. G. Dun & Co. Collection, Baker Library, Harvard University Graduate School of Business Administration, Canada, vol. 26, n.p.

99 Ibid., vol. 7, p. 117.

100 Ibid., vol. 26, p. 202 (old pagination). Emphasis in the original.

101 See ibid., vol. 5, p. 249, regarding Meyers Ronkaal: "... is a foreign Jew. ... His char for now not the best with his own people, although they do trust him to small amounts." In the later period, Jews organized free loan societies to help new immigrants establish themselves.

102 Ibid., vol. 6, p. 38.

103 Jonathan Sarna ("Jewish-Christian Hostility in the United States: Perceptions from a Jewish Point of View," in *Uncivil Religion: Interreligious Hostility in America*, ed. Robert N. Bellah and Frederick E. Greenspahn [New York: Crossroads, 1987], pp. 11-15) succinctly summarizes some of the negative images of Judaism which emerge in missionary literature in the United States; see also Robert M. Healey, "From Conversion to Dialogue: Protestant American Missions to the Jews in the Nineteenth and Twentieth Centuries," *Journal of Ecumenical Studies* 18 (1981): 379-81.

104 A systematic study of the newspapers such as the *Montreal Witness* should contribute a great deal to the understanding of Jews and Judaism in early Canada; thus far, I have taken a sampling for the years 1849-51. For some examples from these years, see *Montreal Witness* (1849), pp. 307, 411; (1850), pp. 30, 215; (1851), p. 427.

105 Robert Burns, *The Jewish Society of New York, Arraigned at the Bar of Public Opinion* (Toronto: Charles Fletcher, 1853), p. 5.

106 Michael Willis, "The Christology: or Doctrine of the Messiah as unfolded in the Old Testament," *A Course of Lectures on the Jews by Ministers of the Established Church in Scotland* (Philadelphia: Presbyterian Boards of Publication, 1840; repr. New York: Arno Press, 1977), pp. 293-333.

107 According to R. F. Burns (*The Life and Times of the Rev. Robert Burns, D.D., including an unfinished autobiography edited by his son, Rev. R. F. Burns* [Toronto: James Campbell and Son, 1872], pp. 241-42), his father unmasked a certain Lublin "a pretended Hungarian nobleman, Moravian bishop and convert from Judaism" as an imposter and swindler. Friends of Burns awarded him a medal for his role in exposing this and other frauds. The quote is taken from the inscription on the medal, cited in ibid., p. 242, note.

108 David Max Eichorn, "A History of Christian Attempts to Convert the Jews of the United States and Canada" (thesis, Hebrew Union College, 1938), p. 307.

109 *Montreal Witness* (1850), p. 250, and Burns, *The Jewish Society of New York*, passim.

110 Cited in David Max Eichorn, *Evangelizing the American Jew* (Middle Village, NY: Jonathan David, 1978), p. 88.

111 *Acts and Proceedings of the Synod of the Presbyterian Church of Canada in Connection with the Church of Scotland* (hereafter *APSPCC*), *Session 30* (Montreal: Lovell, 1858), p. 50.

112 *APSPCC, Session 31* (Montreal: Lovell, 1859), p. 66, and *APSPCC, Session 32* (Montreal: Lovell, 1860), p. 86.

113 *APSPCC, Session 35* (Montreal: Lovell, 1863), p. 57.

114 On later missions, see, recently, Paul R. Dekar, "From Jewish Mission to Inner City Mission: The Scott Mission and Its Antecedents in Toronto, 1908 to 1964," in *Canadian Protestant and Catholic Missions, 1820s-1960s*, pp. 246-47; R. Gruneir, "The

Hebrew Mission in Toronto," *Canadian Ethnic Studies* 9 (1977): 18-28; and Speisman, *The Jews of Toronto*, pp. 131-44.
115 R. F. Burns, *The Life and Times of the Rev. Robert Burns, D.D.*, pp. 240-41, 430.
116 Burns, *The Jewish Society of New York*, pp. 13-14. Emphasis is in the original.
117 Burns had other complaints about the Society and its agents. His treatment of the
latter evidently led to harsh exchanges between himself and Michael Willis (see *DCB*,
s.v. Burns, Robert, by H. J. Bridgman, 11: 107). The incident, to the best of my
knowledge, has not been investigated in full. I hope to return to mid-nineteenth-
century missions and the Jews and their implications in future study.
118 *Montreal Witness* (1850), p. 250.
119 Henry Wilkes, *Jesus the Divine Messiah: An Address to the Jews* (Montreal, 1851). All
quotes in the chapter are taken from this short pamphlet. I discuss the sermon, its
author and its context in greater detail in a forthcoming article "A Missionary Sermon to the Jews in Mid-Nineteenth Century Montreal: Text and Contexts," to
appear in the Frank Talmage Memorial Volume, edited by Barry Walfish.
120 Fulford's comments were cited in a letter by Abraham De Sola to the *Asmonean*,
February 28, 1851.
121 Cited in Sack, *History of the Jews in Canada*, p. 165, although he has listed the wrong
date; it should be *Jewish Chronicle*, January 31, 1862, not February 7, 1862.

2

From Stereotype to Scapegoat: Anti-Jewish Sentiment in French Canada from Confederation to World War I

Michael Brown

Background

Seldom, in the first quarter-century after Confederation, did Jews rise to the forefront of the French-Canadian consciousness. In 1867 there were only about 1000 Jews in all of Canada. The Jewish community was too small to be considered in the constitutional arrangements. In fact, the British North America Act sowed the seeds of future problems, especially with regard to schooling. The Fathers of Confederation envisioned a binational, bicultural, bilingual, bireligious, biracial state, not a pluralistic melting pot. That meant that Jews, who were neither Catholic nor Protestant, and for the most part, neither British nor French, were constitutional outsiders. In 1867, however, few addressed this difficulty, partly because Canadians were more concerned with communal prerogatives than with individual liberties. For a time, the Jews in Canada managed to fit between the cracks of the two loosely federated major nationalities. Most affiliated with the English and Protestant community, finding French Canada unreceptive to their persons and their religion. Some married French Canadians and converted to Catholicism, virtually the only way to enter the latter society.

Few French Canadians in the 1870s enjoyed first-hand contact with Jews. As a result, their notions were shaped largely by theology and folk-

---

Notes for Chapter 2 are on pp. 60-66.

lore. Some, like R. P. Hyacinthe, a Roman Catholic priest, acknowledged that it had been "from the Jews, [albeit] through Christianity, that the world had received the fullest idea of a living God," and even that "our morality is the morality of the Jews, and their dogma . . . ours."[1] Others, however, maintained the antique, negative stereotypes of medieval Europe, which associated Jews with exorbitant wealth, undue power, the death of Jesus, and nefarious designs on Christendom. Typical was Joseph Tassé's 1870 characterization of Jews as having achieved wealth because they had no aptitude for any worthy endeavour. Tassé claimed that they "prefer the cult of the golden calf and are addicted exclusively to commerce, which has made a number of them the richest capitalists in the world."[2]

The 1860s and early 1870s witnessed a heightened militancy and insularity on the part of the Roman Catholic Church. Papal condemnation of Catholic liberalism in the "Syllabus of Errors" of 1864, the Vatican Council of 1869 (which led to the acceptance of papal infallibility as dogma) and the Programme Catholique of 1871 (which defended Vatican interference in the political affairs of nations with large numbers of Catholic voters), promoted a religious aggressiveness. The intimate association of Catholicism with the French-Canadian sense of national identity added a distinctive Canadian aspect to the militant ecclesiastical tendencies emanating from Europe.[3]

The terms of Confederation gave Quebec a free hand in its own affairs, and thus, ironically, served to encourage local nationalism. Since the mid-century, the Catholic clergy had been active in the colonization movement, which sought to reclaim the Eastern Townships and other regions of Quebec long settled by Anglo-Canadians.[4] In Montreal, Ignace Bourget, who served as bishop and later archbishop from 1840 to 1876, fought "ceaselessly against the liberal and anti-clerical spirit" of the era.[5] Ecclesiastical policies were directed against all who were not French and Catholic; however, Jews felt particularly threatened. Among the English-speaking émigrés from the Townships to Montreal was Dr. David Alexander Hart, a member of Canada's pioneer Jewish family, and one of the country's first Jewish physicians.[6] Another member of the Hart family, politician-historian Adolphus Mordecai Hart, expressed his antipathy to French-Canadian nationalism in a work apparently suppressed by the Government of Canada. In this 1871 tract, he complained that non-Roman Catholics could only be elected to office in French Canada "under such terms . . . that they forfeit their own self-respect . . . [by having to make] concessions on matters of faith humiliating to their consciences." Confederation, he charged, had come about only as a result of the "jesuitry" employed by French Canadians "in making [naive] British statesmen believe, that . . . the Protestant minority in the Province of Quebec would

be guaranteed in the preservation of their rights, liberties, and properties."
What the future really held for non-French residents in Quebec, the angry
author predicted, was quite different. "The tide of intolerance and bigotry,
which has been settling in for some time past . . . ," he asserted, "will eventually lead to the same sufferings and exile . . . endured [over the years by
Jews and Protestants] in . . . France."[7] Hart refrained from mentioning
Jews, either because of the small size of the Jewish community or because it
seemed prudent to maintain a low profile on the Jewish question.

For the most part, anti-Jewish sentiment in French Canada at this time
was subtle and implicit rather than overt. Jews simply were excluded from
society. An instructive example is that of Rabbi Abraham De Sola. The
first ordained rabbi to serve in Canada, De Sola officiated at Montreal's
Spanish and Portuguese Synagogue from 1847 until his death in 1882,
becoming one of the most active and best known intellectual figures in
North America. He taught Spanish and Hebrew at McGill, which
awarded him an honorary degree in 1858, probably the first such degree
bestowed on a Jew in the English-speaking world. His gentile contemporaries saw him as one of Canada's "brightest luminaries," a man who
exhibited "more sound scholarship" than almost anyone else in Montreal.[8] According to the Montreal *Gazette*, the rabbi was associated "with all
the movements tending to promote the moral and intellectual welfare" of
the country.[9] There were few subjects on which he did not write or lecture, appearing before almost every cultural and scholarly group in the
city's Anglophone community: the Mercantile Library Association, the
Mechanics Institute, the Young Men's Christian Association of St.
George's Church, the Literary Club, and the Natural History Society (of
which he was president for some years); he also lectured widely in the
United States and England. These exploits, especially an invocation
delivered at a session of the United States House of Representatives in
1872, received much acclaim.[10] To French Canadians, however, De Sola
was almost a nonentity; no record exists of his ever having addressed any
French group. Montreal's French press ignored him. Admittedly, the
rabbi's attitude was condescending. He claimed that French Canadians
lacked "intellectuality, enterprise, [and the] . . . free spirit of enquiry . . . in
matters spiritual or secular."[11] Such views, to be sure, were hardly excep-
tional in mid-nineteenth-century English society, and perhaps even
expected. Had he been invited to address a French audience, De Sola, who
seldom refused invitations, probably would have accepted. Since there is
no evidence of any special personal animus, one is forced to conclude that
his absence from the academic and scholarly circles of French Montreal
was a result of the general exclusion of Jews in this period.

The prospect of a Jewish return to Palestine supplies further evidence
of the disengagement of French Canadians from Jews and Jewish issues in

the 1870s. The Holy Land and its Jewish connection have preoccupied Christians for ages, although the tempo has varied. The English-speaking world, in particular, often exhibited considerable interest in the subject; and the 1870s witnessed an unusual amount of this fascination. Several books of Palestine pilgrim literature appeared in English Canada during this decade, as well as works of poetry and fiction on the theme of Jewish religion.[12] Religious figures, such as the Reverend Charles Freshman, a convert to Christianity from Judaism, and the Reverend J. W. Beaumont, championed the cause of restoration, while people with scholarly interests became involved with the work of Britain's Palestine Exploration Fund.[13] The most vigorous restoration activities emanated from the British Israel movement, especially its Canadian-born leader, Henry Wentworth Monk.[14] This extraordinary degree of ferment reflected a growing sensitivity to the plight of Jews in eastern Europe, as well as the emergence of Jewish national sentiment. In French Canada, however, there was no ferment. The Jewish question, at least in relation to Palestine, aroused little interest at this time.

The 1880s

Although their implications did not become clear until the turn of the century, a number of seemingly unrelated events in both Europe and in Canada in the 1880s foreshadowed a change for the worse. In central and western Europe, there was an increasing tide of anti-Jewish agitation, sometimes of dramatic proportions. A well-publicized ritual murder trial in Tisza-Eszlar, Hungary, dragged on from 1882 to 1884. Although the charge of ritual murder had been declared a libel by various popes, the belief that Jews required the blood of Christian children for their rites persisted in the popular mind. (Incidentally, one of the few North American publications that supported the accusation was Quebec's radical Catholic journal, La Vérité.[15]) In France, the 1880s witnessed the initial successes of Edouard Drumont, the most popular modern anti-Jewish polemicist before Adolf Hitler, and the author of La France Juive, published in 1886; three years later, he inspired the founding of the Ligue Nationale Anti-sémitique. During the same era, certain events in Canada intensified French Canadian nationalism. The execution of Louis Riel in 1885, and, at the end of the decade, the Jesuits' Estates Bill in Quebec, which compensated the church for expropriated property, assisted the rise of nationalist sentiment. There was also the vexed issue of French language rights in the Manitoba schools. In reaction, French Canadians turned increasingly to their roots in the France of the ancien régime. That epoch inspired considerable nostalgia, and its clerical and monarchical traditions aroused new enthusiasm. Since the rulers of old France had excluded the Jews from public life, indeed, from the nation itself at times, this revived interest in the "good old days" produced renewed ill will toward the Jews. This mood enabled Drumont and other European reactionaries to find an audience in Canada as well as in Europe.

Reverberations from eastern Europe also began to reach Canada. Between 1871 and 1881, Canada's Jewish population almost doubled, although 2443 Jews were still a negligible presence. The outbreak of pogroms in Russia in 1881 and the persistence of violence in Romania fuelled a dramatic increase in the number of European escapees. By early 1882, committees to assist Jewish refugees had been established in London, New York, Paris and elsewhere. All considered Canada a likely place of refuge, and some Canadians, at least, believed their country should open its doors. The organizational meeting of London's Mansion House Committee, an important agency dealing with relief and relocation, was attended by Sir Alexander Tilloch Galt, Canada's High Commissioner to great Britain, a public sign of Canadian concern for the Russian Jews. In March 1882 a mass meeting at the Montreal YMCA established the Jewish Relief Fund. Among the organizers were the Anglican bishop of Montreal and John Redpath Dougall, editor of the militantly Protestant *Daily Witness*. French Canadians, however, did not become involved; only a few made small donations, while the French press, unlike the English press, ignored the relief activities. Most of French society was unmoved by the Russian and Romanian depredations, and part was becoming actively hostile to the newcomers in Quebec. Such attitudes explain why Montreal's Jewish leadership organized the Montefiore Agricultural Aid Association in 1885 "to direct the enterprise and industry of" immigrant Jews to "new fields of labour" on the western prairies far from French Canada. Such a step was deemed "desirable at the present stage of our relations with other races and peoples."[16]

During the 1880s, the Palestine question received new attention in French Canada. No longer was apathy the rule; instead, a growing anti-Jewish sentiment prevailed. Several accounts of travels to the Holy Land appeared, coloured by traditional Roman Catholic notions as well as political developments in Europe and Canada. In general, these works, unlike those by English Canadian pilgrims, had little to say about Jews that was favourable, nor were they sympathetic to the notion of Jewish restoration. Abbé Léon Provancher's *De Québec à Jérusalem* (1884) was the most hostile. True, the travelling priest perceived the beauty of Mary, "the mother of God," in the faces of young Jewish girls praying at the Wailing Wall.[17] Yet he believed in the truth of the ritual murder charge. Having arrived in Alexandria just as the body of a Greek Christian girl, who had been in the care of Jews, was discovered, he proclaimed that, on several occasions, local dissident Jewish sects had committed this "revolting" crime. Only a few years earlier, he added, Alexandrian Jewry had been forced to pay over half a million francs in bribes in order to avoid the consequences of one of its murders. Jews, in his eyes, were nothing but liars and Christ-killers.[18] Four years later, Provancher founded *La Semaine religieuse de Québec*, a widely read and openly antisemitic church journal.

The work of another priest, Abbé J. F. C. Delaplanche, provided a somewhat more charitable survey of the Jews of Jerusalem. In *Le Pèlerin de Terre Sainte* (1887), printed under the imprimatur of Cardinal Taschereau of Quebec, Delaplanche expressed "compassion" for the "unhappy children of Jacob," but, at the same time, deplored "the blindness" of the "Jewish debris" who "still obstinately await the Messiah . . . despite the fulfillment of the prophecies [in Jesus]."[19] Such comments were not calculated to awaken a desire to assist the persecuted Jews of Europe.

The 1890s

In the 1890s, the tenor of the Jewish relationship with French Canada changed considerably. In fact, from this point on, Jews figured prominently in the consciousness of French Canadians, and seldom favourably. While little was said that had not been said earlier, and while antisemitism was more often the symptom than the cause of local discontent, the growing anti-Jewish rhetoric and activity—even violence—in Quebec after 1890 represented a new departure. The two decades prior to the outbreak of World War I constituted an era of ever-increasing tension between the French and English in Canada, with almost every political question an occasion for communal dispute. The new Liberal government of Wilfrid Laurier was determined to open the doors of the country to more immigrants in order to populate the west. French Canadians feared that this policy would diminish their political power, since the size of the English-speaking population would increase. Little attempt (or so they thought) was being made to attract French-speaking Europeans to Canada. Immigrants, moreover, tended to congregate in the cities, a development which portended major alterations in Canadian society, especially in Quebec, hitherto largely rural. Many French Canadians also believed that, except for an anti-French bias, the vast expanses of the west might have been filled with French settlers.[20]

The Anglo-Boer War at the turn of the century caused another major dispute between the two national communities. Even before its outbreak, English Canadians had been swept by a wave of imperial sentiment. The war, which promised to be a romp, generated an outburst of enthusiasm for the empire. Its supporters clamoured for Canada's full participation on the side of the mother country, and eagerly volunteered for service in South Africa with the Canadian contingent.[21] French Canadians, on the other hand, tended to oppose the war, identifying with the Boers, another "small non-English people bullied by British might." Why, it was asked, "should French Canadians fight the Boers, who were [also] struggling for their independence, language, and peculiar customs?"[22] The abuse heaped on Quebec for its lukewarm support of the imperial cause by Anglo-Canadians heightened the tension. The English-language yellow press, led by the Montreal *Star*, figured prominently in the jingoist agitation.

Other seemingly unresolvable problems emerged. No sooner did the South African conflict recede from the public eye than new tensions arose over a proposal to integrate Canada's naval forces into the Royal Navy. Also, the question of French-language rights in Ontario and the west continued to fester. Even issues less obviously calculated to divide the country along ethnic lines, such as Prohibition, seemed to add fuel to the fire. The continuing confrontation meant that each solitude became ever more vigilant regarding what it saw as its rights, and more aggressive in asserting what it believed to be its own unique character. Language, culture, religion and "race" now became highly charged issues. In seeking to define itself against the other nationality, each drew its own boundaries more narrowly than before, becoming less tolerant of outsiders or hangers-on. André Siegfried, the French political economist and acute observer of turn-of-the-century Canada, remarked that, in these years, each of the two national entities was "so strongly attached to that which constitutes its individuality, that it would not sacrifice the smallest particle of it to the cause of unity of the nation." Power shifted increasingly in favour of English Canada because of its growing population, its natural ties with Great Britain, its financial clout and other reasons. In reaction, French Canada grew more and more defensive, clinging tenaciously to the old two-nations idea that had inspired Confederation.[23]

As Montreal contained Canada's largest Jewish community, Jews were located at the geographical hub of the confrontation. In other ways also, they became entangled in Anglo-French battles, invariably finding themselves on the English side of whatever dispute was raging. As a consequence, they became on occasion the target of an animosity really directed at English Canada. Rejected by one community, and not altogether accepted by the other, they turned increasingly to Jewish nationalism (Zionism) as a solace.[24] Immigration — a matter on which Jews and French Canadians could hardly have found common ground — illustrates their dilemma. Since many English Canadians were unhappy about the large numbers of non-British, non-French immigrants who had been arriving prior to World War I, anti-immigrant agitation and antisemitism were by no means absent from Anglo society either. But it was French Canada that felt profoundly threatened by the "horde of strangers," especially Jewish strangers, pouring into the country, even though Prime Minister Laurier was a son of Quebec. The Jewish population of Canada multiplied seven times over between 1881 and 1901. In the subsequent decade, it grew by more than four and a half times again. By World War I, some 40 000 Jews were living in Montreal, forming about 6 percent of the city's population, and they were no longer a negligible presence. Like other immigrants, Jews, even in Montreal, learned English and affiliated with the English community. Probably the most urban of the immigrant groups, they exemplified the urban threat to traditional French-Canadian rural values. To a religiously homogeneous society with a heritage of excluding Jews, and during an era of militant religiosity, Jewish immigrants were particularly unwelcome.

Already, in 1893, a group of young people, "pure of race and imbued with the apostles' sense [of mission]," were moved by "the first Jewish invasions" to found *L'Association Catholique de la Jeunesse Canadienne* (l'ACJC), the organization that would become French Canada's premier youth group and a spearhead of the nationalist battle against the Jewish presence in Quebec.[25] Meetings of L'ACJC were often graced by diatribes against the "immigration laws which give the least desirable elements entry into our [i.e., French-Canadian] large cities."[26] The Association was one of a number of platforms for the expression of strident opposition to Jewish immigration, opposition which often invoked old negative stereotypes. Two other forums for anti-Jewish agitation were the press and the nationalist movement. Not atypical of the former was Montreal's *La Croix*. "Jewish immigration," its editors declared in 1905, "threatened to overrun us. Three or four hundred Jews recently arrived in Montreal. They fled Russia in order to evade military service. These penniless immigrants for the most part have no aptitude for productive labour. In order to stay alive, they will have to exploit us in their usual way. Such immigration is not good for our country and we are astonished that the Canadian government has not seen fit to prevent it. . . ."[27] Only slightly milder were the words of Henri Bourassa, the paramount nationalist voice in the turn-of-the-century era. In 1906 he decried "a system which peopled the West with a mixture of foreigners, neglecting prospective French and Belgian colonists in favour of Jews from Poland and Russia."[28]

On the language issue, Jews and French Canadians were already at loggerheads. Outside of Quebec, Jews were augmenting the population of English Canada; in Quebec, because the insular French Community did not welcome them, they affiliated with the Anglo population. Indeed, even Francophone immigrants to Quebec found it easier at this time to integrate into English society.[29] English, in any case, was the language of the dominant group in the country, and, for that reason, more appealing to newcomers, generally speaking. Quebec Jews had family bonds, business connections and institutional ties with their co-religionists in the United States, Great Britain and elsewhere in Canada, making English a more useful language than French. French Canadians, moreover, regarded their language as a kind of holy tongue. "The French language as guardian of the faith is one of the classic themes of French Canadian rhetoric."[30] As André Siegfried noted in 1906, French constituted the "outworks protecting Catholicism in Canada."[31] As a result, French Canadians were often reluctant to have their children learn English well. Many, such as the nationalist politician and journalist Oliver Asselin, thought that, when a French Canadian politician had to "groom his whiskers in Semitic style [or] learn Yiddish and make speeches in the synagogue" his honour had been besmirched.[32] On the other hand, non-French Canadians, and especially Jews as non-Christians, regarded French as a vehicle for the transmission of an alien religion as well as an alien culture.

The Jews also became enmeshed in the Boer War issue. At first, many, like the majority of French Canadians, favoured the Boers, a kindred, small and downtrodden nation. In general, however, Canadian Jews felt a deeper kinship with Great Britain, which had offered them freedom and self-respect, while protecting their interests in Palestine and elsewhere. As the war developed, the pro-Boer Jews grew increasingly uncomfortable as Canadian antisemites began to appropriate the Boer cause. Anti-war polemicists, such as Toronto's Professor Goldwin Smith, tried to smear the British war effort by pointing to the Jewish origins of some of British South Africa's mine owners. Smith claimed that the war was being fought for the benefit of Jewish financiers, who sat sipping wine in Capetown hotels while Canadians died to enrich them.[33] French Canadians unsympathetic to both the British cause and Jewry were readily persuaded by such arguments. Henri Bourassa and other nationalist leaders opposed the war with vigour. In 1900, the *Jewish Times* of Montreal asserted that "all anti-Semites are pro-Boers,"[34] referring mainly to French Canadians. Rabbi Meldola De Sola of Montreal, son and successor of Rabbi Abraham De Sola, was acquainted with "some people who profess to admire the Boers."[35] The rabbi, an ardent British patriot, also had in mind fellow Montrealers of French-Canadian origin.

The Dreyfus and Nathan Affairs

The South African war was a European affair into which Canada was drawn because of her political ties to Great Britain. Other European issues became part of the domestic Canadian political scene in these years because of the historical and emotional bond of French Canada to France, and her religious ties to the Vatican. Foremost were the Dreyfus affair in France and the affair of Mayor Ernesto Nathan of Rome. Both aroused controversy in Canada, and both followed the familiar pattern of causing a face-off of French and English Canadians. These issues, however, were different from the South African question. In the Boer War, Canadians enlisted as participants; in the Dreyfus and Nathan affairs, they were only spectators. The Boer War raised the Jewish question only peripherally; the Dreyfus and Nathan affairs placed it at the centre.

As is well known, the Dreyfus episode revolved around Captain Alfred Dreyfus, a Jewish officer on the general staff of the French army accused of spying for Germany. The case began with his arrest in 1894, and dragged on for 12 years through a trial, a retrial, imprisonment on Devil's Island, until his final vindication. Such was the public agitation that France itself was nearly brought to its knees. Eventually, it was discovered that certain senior army officers and others had sacrificed Dreyfus in order to salvage their own reputations and those of the forces of political reaction. *L'Affaire* was a play-within-a-play involving the major political conflicts of late nineteenth-century France: modernity and the revolutionary tradition versus the medieval tradition, republicanism versus monarchy, civilian control versus militarism, the secular state versus clericalism, the civic equality of Jews (and all other citizens) versus their exclusion from the body politic. In the end, republicanism, the secular state, and Jewish emancipation triumphed, although the forces of reaction were far from finally vanquished, as became evident during the later Vichy regime.

In Canada, the Dreyfus affair was appropriated by both English and French Canadians as emblematic of their respective values. As such, it prompted French Canadians to reaffirm their long-severed historic roots. English Canadians, like most of the English-speaking world, tended to sympathize with Dreyfus, believing in his innocence, while scorning the French military justice system. While not republicans themselves, they were committed to popular government (as opposed to dictatorship) and to the idea of a modern society. They regarded French-Canadian anti-Dreyfusard sentiments as illustrative of Quebec's benighted, reactionary political tastes. The English-language press of Montreal unequivocally demonstrated these sympathies, especially as the movement for a retrial gathered momentum in France. The *Star*, the *Gazette* and the *Daily Witness* gave extensive coverage to *l'Affaire*, and consistently supported the Dreyfusards in editorials. All three papers seized the opportunity to emphasize the differences between France and England, the two "mother countries" of Canada, and thus also between French Canada and English Canada.[36]

The Francophone press was a study in contrasts, reflecting the strong emotional attachment of many French Canadians to *ancien régime* France, with its conservative religious and political ideas, including the exclusion of Jews. The very presence of a Jew in the seat of the French military establishment was evidence of the decline of a cherished world. His guilt became a canon of belief. Special attention was paid to the scandal by fringe journals espousing a radical Catholic nationalist line, and by priests in close touch with Europe, such as Abbé Henri Cimon, professor at the Seminaire de Chicoutimi.[37] Many of these journals reprinted the tracts of

Edouard Drumont, France's foremost anti-Dreyfusard publicist. In fact, the influence of Drumont had made itself felt in Canada even before the arrest of Dreyfus, with the establishment in Montreal in 1893 of a publication named, like Drumont's Paris daily, *La Libre Parole*. The Canadian *Parole* lasted only a few months. Three years later, however, when the affair was raging, W. A. Grenier founded *La Libre Parole Illustrée*. The first issue of the revived journal featured "a satire against the Jews in the style of the celebrated daily of Drumont."[38] Although Canada's second *Parole* lasted no longer than the first, its demise did not reflect public apathy. Grenier launched an attack on J. Israel Tarte, minister of public works in the Laurier government, which earned him a jail term for libel. During his incarceration, the journal expired; it was never renewed. In 1905, a third Canadian *La Libre Parole* was launched in Quebec. Edited by Jacques-Edouard Plamondon, it was more successful than its predecessors and lasted a number of years.[39] Other fringe publications which exposed Drumont to Canadian audiences in these years, helping to whip up anti-Dreyfus and antisemitic sentiment, were *La Croix* of Quebec and *La Croix* of Montreal, *Le Pionnier*, *Le Feuille d'Érable*, *La Semaine religieuse de Québec* and *La Vérité*. The last was the most extreme, declaiming against the "Christ-killer race," accusing Émile Zola, the novelist defender of Dreyfus, of pornography, and recommending that Jews everywhere be returned to the ghetto.[40]

Montreal's major French-language dailies, although somewhat less inflammatory in tone, reflected the prevailing political and religious attitudes of the province. *Le Cultivateur* was the most neutral.[41] *La Presse*, the largest paper, was edited during these years by Jules Heilbronner, who was of Jewish origin; for that reason, perhaps, it almost never editorialized about *l'Affaire*, giving it scantier coverage than the other papers. Still, until quite late in the matter, *La Presse* maintained that the two Dreyfus trials had been fair, and that the French military must be just, even when the opposite seemed to be the case.[42] *La Patrie*, although even-handed at first, moved close to *La Vérité* in its treatment of Dreyfus, and of Jews in general. This paper printed articles by Alphonse Daudet, Henri Rochefort and other well-known French advocates of antisemitism and the anti-Dreyfusard cause. In one of its most vitriolic attacks on Dreyfus, *La Patrie* drew upon the old stereotype of the Jew as a wealthy, satanic agent of disintegration seeking to undermine Christendom, in addition to lending credence to the more recent notion of a Jewish syndicate seeking world domination. In the eyes of *La Patrie*, Jews were a menace, not only to French Canadians, but to the entire human race.[43] Both *La Presse* and *La Patrie* lent their support to *La Libre Parole Illustrée*.[44]

In the military, the Roman Catholic Church and other quarters, French Canadians sympathetic to anti-Dreyfusard, anti-Jewish sentiments also made their voices heard in these years.[45] The suppression of the religious orders in France in the wake of the affair brought to Canada a number of *émigré* ecclesiastics who continued to propagate their political and religious ideas.[46] Canadian Jews viewed the arrival of "the black-gowned traitors that were justly driven out of France" for their hatred of "constitutional government and republicanism" with apprehension.[47] Not surprisingly, they felt increasingly threatened by local anti-Dreyfusard polemics, which came to serve as a code for a French-Canadian political program. The Canadian *Jewish Times* editorialized frequently on the issue. Outspoken but typical was a piece which appeared in January 1902. It was "passing strange," the weekly asserted, that

> men who profess a religion which holds its mission everywhere as that of "peace on earth to men of good will" should cherish the blackest, most unreasoning malice against their fellowmen, and urge a cruel, lying murderous propaganda of social incendiarism, for which no language of denunciation could be too strong.[48]

Long after its conclusion in France, reverberations of the Dreyfus affair could still be heard in Canada. Drumont's voice, now largely discredited in his own country, lingered as well. The ACJC continued to provide a forum for antisemitic ideas. In a 1908 address to the youth group, L.-C. Farly proposed, among other measures, the establishment of an antisemitic league in Canada after the French model. This suggestion met with opposition from Jews and gentiles alike, both English and French. In 1913, however, the *Ligue des Droits du Français* was founded in imitation of the French organization with the same name established by anti-Dreyfusards during the Dreyfus agitation.[49] In 1914, Abbé Antonio Huot delivered one of the strongest anti-Jewish statements ever heard by the ACJC. Although he felt the book was not "entirely" convincing, the priest opened his remarks by citing "the praiseworthy *France Juive* of Drumont."[50] This French propagandist also maintained his standing in the nationalist press. In 1912, *L'Étudiant*, the student newspaper of Laval University, described him as "the only person in all of Judaized Europe, who had the courage to speak out against the evil being done to the Christian nations by the deicide race." According to the students, the "venerable polemicist" had predicted 20 years earlier that "Canada would [one day] be the promised land of the Hebrews."[51] *Le Devoir*, the organ of the Quebec nationalist intelligentsia founded by Henri Bourassa in 1910, also retained a fondness for Drumont, reprinting his articles and those of other columnists of *La Libre Parole*.[52]

If the Dreyfus affair was a foreign graft on the tree of Canadian politics, the Nathan affair was even more so. It concerned a remote event in Italy which acquired significance as an illustration of the alleged threat posed by

Jews to the power of the church and traditional Christian society. Ernesto Nathan, a British-born Jew and a Freemason, was elected mayor of Rome in 1907. Rome's Jewish population at the time was modest in size and means. Not Jewish, but Catholic votes had elected the popular Nathan. Still, the notion that the office of mayor of the "Eternal City" should be occupied by a Jew disturbed conservative Catholics, especially outside of Italy. When, in September 1910, Nathan spoke out against Catholic ultramontanism, the pent-up resentments of traditionalists against Jews, and against the ills of modernity, were released. In Montreal a censure motion was passed by the city council. Although city councils usually limit their purview to local affairs, Mayor James Guerin, an Irish Catholic, railroaded the motion through a meeting before the arrival of the Protestant councillors.[53] The pope was pleased and sent thanks to the "illustrious" council which had spoken out in defence of Catholic interests.[54] However, the matter did not end there. One of the Protestant councillors protested that a body representing several nationalities and religions had no right to approve such a notion. Montreal's Yiddish-language daily, the *Keneder Adler*, noted that over the years there had been "many famous Christian speeches against the Vatican that have been met with silence. But when a Jewish speaker attacks their principles, the event is blown out of proportion."[55] In a similar vein, the *Daily Witness* remarked that Catholic "orators . . . are allowed to say whatever of insult they please about the 'Protestants' and Freemasons, [and Jews. But] . . . what is sauce for the goose, does not appear to be sauce for the gander. . . ."[56] The Protestant Ministerial Association and the city's most prominent rabbi also deplored the council's action, as pressure for rescinding the censure began to mount.[57]

Partly to head off revocation, and partly to demonstrate where the real power lay, Archbishop Bruchési and his advisers planned a mass meeting to display support for the council and disapproval of Mayor Nathan. To ensure that the point would not be lost on the Jewish populace, and to demonstrate the new centrality of the Jewish question for French Canadians, the rally was scheduled for the Monument Nationale, a theatre located in the heart of the Jewish quarter and used by Yiddish-language troupes. Perhaps to placate angry Protestants, perhaps to isolate the Jews, Bruchési invited Protestant attendance, claiming that Nathan's "insult" to the pope had been an insult to all Christians.[58] The French press carried prominent advertisements urging a large turnout, and lurid articles designed to guarantee one. The desire to be inflammatory was palpable; little effort was made to be true to the facts. Typical was an account in *La Presse*, which claimed that Nathan had called "the papacy nothing but a mummy and the Christian religion a disappearing force whose light no longer shines, or some such thing."[59] Another article in the same paper was entitled, "L'Anti-pape du Rome." In *Le Devoir*, Omer Héroux, the nationalist leader, described Nathan as "hereditary hatred of the Church incarnate."[60] Local Jews, most of whom were recent refugees from the violence of eastern Europe, found the rhetoric frightening, even though they enjoyed the support of most of the city's Anglo-Protestants.

When the day of the protest dawned, it was clear that the agitation had been successful. Over 25 000 people gathered, quickly overflowing the Monument National and moving on to the Champ de Mars. Students and young people, prompted by their teachers and priests, were out in force, as well as the leaders of l'ACJC "protest[ing] energetically the injurious words of the Jew Nathan."[61] There was official representation in the persons of Provincial Secretary Jérémie Décarie and Mayor Guerin, who prudently focused his remarks on Nathan's Masonic affiliations. In an ultramontane speech bordering on sedition, Archbishop Bruchési told the crowd, that "no faithful subject could allow an insult to his king" (i.e., the pope) to pass, and urged them "to avenge the outrage." Henri Bourrassa asserted that the "attack of the Jew Nathan against the Pope and Christianity is not something new. This is just a further variation of the attack on Jesus Christ of 2000 years ago by the enemies of the Christian religion. . . . These enemies," he told the protesters, who could have had no doubts about whom he meant, "still live; and they are trying with all their might to bury Christianity."[62]

Some days later, "a much worse and blacker demonstration" was held in the Church of St. Roch, in Quebec City, at which "the Jew and Freemason, Nathan, . . . the cowardly insulter of the Pope and vile blasphemer of Christ," as *La Vérité* described the Roman mayor, "was spat upon" and burned in effigy to the tune of "O Canada!"[63] In Montreal, Protestants held a counter-demonstration "to show that we have given too much power to the Catholics in our city."[64] Although media interest finally waned, these spectacles were not easily forgotten in a country tense with partisan conflict. Jews remained fearful. When the *Keneder Adler* received an anonymous letter threatening open warfare against Quebec Jews should they get out of line again, the paper took the warning seriously.[65] The Jewish community was understandably sensitive to religious bigotry, worried about violent passions and "Russian pogrom tactics," and mindful of current disabilities in conservative European societies in which there was no separation of church and state.[66] The anti-Nathan demonstration and the anti-Dreyfus polemics seemed sufficient proof that Montreal was becoming "the Rome of America," the chief city of "a land where fanatic zealotry was gathering force."[67]

Other Factors

Besides the Dreyfus and Nathan affairs, other contemporary European events affected relations between Jews and French Canadians. The Russian pogroms of 1905 sparked a worldwide wave of anger against Russian barbarity, leading to the revocation of the Russian-American trade treaty by the United States Congress. In Montreal, a protest meeting in November was attended by a number of the city's most prominent English Canadians. French Canadians, however, did not show up. Senator Laurent Olivier David sent his regrets; Mayor Préfontaine sent greetings; Archbishop Bruchési "greatly deplore[d] the massacres," which, he acknowledged, "were contrary to the Christian spirit." Still, he thought it "inopportune to take part in the assembly."[68] The next year, during a debate in the House of Commons over a resolution condemning the Russians, Henri Bourassa distinguished himself by speaking out, not against the perpetrators of the pogroms, but against its victims. "For centuries," Bourassa averred, "Russian peasants have been the prey of Jewish usurers." More recently, he added, "Jews have been the instigators of most of the disorders which have taken place in Russia," financing their acts of disintegration "from the pennies subscribed" for Russian Jewish relief "in foreign countries."[69] The Canadian *Jewish Times* noted that Bourassa presumed to speak for his "French Canadian fellow countrymen." The weekly hoped that Sir Wilfrid Laurier, who supported the resolution, was "a better and truer exponent of French Canadian feeling."[70] In fact, Bourassa was probably closer to public opinion. It is possible that the French-Canadian responses to the pogroms were coloured by immigration anxieties. Many English Canadians, Americans and Britons were no more enthusiastic about large-scale Jewish immigration to their countries than were their French counterparts. Yet the English-speaking peoples did not hesitate to express genuine sympathy for the Russian Jews, and horror at the behaviour of the Russian government. In French Canada, however, a feeling a kinship with backward, Christian Russia had developed over the years. With their rural, anti-urban, anti-industrial Christian ethos, French-Canadian nationalists sometimes idealized Russia as a country unspoiled by modernity, and Russian peasants as the embodiment of their own disappearing, idyllic way of life. Conversely, they tended to demonize Jews.[71] In those attitudes lay the source of Bourassa's hard-hearted remarks, and the reluctance of others to speak out.[72]

The trial of Mendel Beiliss in Russia for ritual murder was in some ways as shocking to world opinion as were the pogroms. That this medieval accusation, frequently declared false by popes and scholars, and disproved in trials such as that as Tisza-Eszlar, still found credence in the twentieth century seemed unbelievable to Western liberals. That it took almost two years (from 1911 to 1913) to vindicate Beiliss seemed even more incredible. Outside of Russia, public opinion perceived that the trial was a travesty. The pope himself intervened by sending evidence to counteract the testimony of a Roman Catholic priest who had testified against the accused.[73] In French Canada, however, where the Jews had become a compelling symbol of a feared loss of local control over Quebec's destiny, there were many people prepared to regard them as capable of almost any evil. That Abbé Huot should have supported the libel in his 1913 speech to l'ACJC was not surprising. The Association, after all, often entertained and promoted extreme anti-Jewish views,[74] and other French Canadian clergy and church officials had accepted the charge as true.[75] Perhaps it was also not surprising that La Patrie supported Beiliss's accusers.[76] But it was highly disturbing that Armand Lavergne, once an intimate associate of Laurier, and now a close co-worker of Bourassa and editor of Le Nationaliste, believed in the accusation.[77]

The belief in ritual murder may have been simply a natural extension of other long-held beliefs about Jews imported into French Canada from Europe. In contrast to Calvinist Protestants, with their affinity for the Hebrew Bible and language, many pious Catholics were accustomed to thinking of Jews in medieval terms as members of "the deicide race." Palestine pilgrims assured their readers that Jews harboured an "implacable hatred for Jesus Christ and his Church."[78] Christ-killing Jews were said to be "like Cain," and to have a deservedly "guilty heart." Their suffering "affirmed" Christian faith. Jesus, himself, most Catholics believed, had declared their "anguish ... incurable."[79] If they were killers, and killers of God at that, Jews would, of course, have other dangerous characteristics. They were widely regarded as "pretentious, devotees of cunning [and] cowards,"[80] and often depicted in French-Canadian literature as physically repulsive, their ugly bodies reflecting their twisted souls. Joseph A. l'Archévêque, an Acadian from New Brunswick and a Recollet friar, was yet another of the French-Canadian pilgrims to the Holy Land who wrote a book about his travels. He described the Jews of Jerusalem as "having hooked noses, hunched backs, ghastly faces. They are," he stated, people of "frightening debilitation, displaying the degeneracy [typical] of their race."[81]

These notions were not new in themselves; most had enjoyed some currency in French Canada from the beginning. What was new was the presence in Quebec of a significant Jewish population. Earlier, anti-Jewish tales had been little more than the stuff of religion and folklore, unrelated to real people; they had been told less often, and in generally more moderate language. Now, these strident beliefs pertained to neighbours and fellow citizens, making them much more dangerous. In these years of intercommunal tension, being English in French Canada or French in English

Canada, was difficult enough. Being an outsider, especially a Jewish outsider, in French Canada was especially difficult. Jews had to bear the burden of medieval superstition in a state of rejuvenation, as French Canadians waxed nostalgic about their past, a past without Jews. This was the
fin de siècle. An old, quiet, pastoral Christian world was waning, giving way
to a new one—commercial, industrial, urban and secular in character.
Jews in French Canada were part of this new world, in fact, its more
potent symbol, since they had been absent from the old. As such, they
became the target of considerable animosity, indeed, the scapegoats for
people who viewed the present with distaste and the future with anxiety.

Hard-core Antisemitism

While many French Canadians in the early years of the twentieth century
perceived Jews as emblems of unwelcome change, a small hard core of
committed antisemites regarded them as its actual catalysts. Such individuals saw their presence, not as one of several novelties ushered in by the
modern era, but rather, as the paramount feature of modernity. This
mindset was manifested in a number of exaggerated, even fantastic, images
and dogmas. The fanatics usually recognized no broad social or intellectual context for their ideas; rather, antisemitism provided the framework
for their understanding of world affairs. In normal times, they would
probably not have gained a wide hearing. In the stressful decades before
World War I, however, the ideas of Jules-Paul Tardivel, the long-time editor of Quebec's *La Vérité*, and of Friar Pierre Zacharie Lacasse, missionary
to the Inuit and publicist-collaborator of Tardivel, and of others as well,
struck some responsive chords. On occasion, they even prompted overt
antisemitic behaviour. Their beliefs became part of a reservoir of ideas and
slogans upon which the later anti-Jewish polemicists of the 1920s and
1930s would draw.[82]

Probably the most frequently reiterated obsession of the antisemitic
hard core was Jewish financial power. The association of Jews with undue
wealth was, of course, an ancient myth, the origins of which cannot be
discussed here. It was reasonable for French Canadians to be concerned
about financial power in the turn-of-the-century years. Quebec developed
less rapidly than Ontario, gradually losing its place at the centre of Canadian manufacturing and industry. French Canadians, including Laurier,
conscious of their inferiority in commerce and manufacturing, knew that
this decline served to weaken their political clout in the country at large.[83]
While it was not, for the most part, Jews who were buying up Quebec, but
rather, large companies based in the United States and Great Britain, it
was more prudent to attack the Jews than the British or the Americans.[84]
Although no hard evidence for the charge was ever produced, it became
common "knowledge" in nationalist circles at this time that European

Jewish financiers, such as the Rothschilds and the Bleichröders, were interested in Canada, and that the "great international money handlers" stood behind "Simon Pawnshopvitch from Odessa" and "Abraham Oldragsky of Warsaw," as Oliver Asselin referred to the eastern European Jews.[85] Once, in fact, a representative of the Rothschilds did investigate the possibility of establishing steel mills in Quebec, but there is no indication of his having had any contact with local Jews; and in any case, the project was stillborn.[86] That the Jewish petty traders of Quebec would some day be "dominating everything with their capital" was little more than a nightmarish fantasy of hard-core antisemitism.[87] Yet it retained its currency for many years.[88]

Hand in hand with the notion of wanton Jewish economic power went a belief that Jews sought to undermine the moral fibre of Christians in general, and of French-Canadian Catholics in particular. Clerics frequently pontificated on the degeneracy of Judaism, and the ACJC provided a forum for their preachments. In his 1908 address to the Association, L.-C. Farly informed his audience of young people that "the Jew" had "rejected the Bible and adopted the Talmud, which excuses all crimes [and] gives him the right to do anything [he wants], while dispensing with every [law] that might restrain his caprices."[89] Some years later at Trois-Rivières, Bishop Cloutier told Association members that Jews were a detriment to religion and morals, while *La Vérité* proclaimed "the morality of the Talmud" so "injurious to people" that any means of fighting it is "justified."[90] C. Edmond Chartier, an early observer of l'ACJC, asserted that that organization represented a "counter-poison" to a "new disease, which was attacking the vital forces of our race and undermining the very bases of our national existence." The germs were being spread, Chartier claimed, by "underhanded men," who were "attempting to shake . . . our faith . . . with revolutionary doctrines."[91]

The purpose of Jewish immorality and economic power was said to be domination. In French Canada, as in Europe, in the turn-of-the-century years, there emerged the notion of a well-organized cabal of "underhanded" Jews. *La Vérité* and other publications professed belief in the existence of a Jewish — in some versions, a consortium of Jews, Freemasons and socialists (Ernesto Nathan was both a Jew and a Freemason) — syndicate, working "for the abrogation of laws made by the goïms [the non-Jews, in order to] . . . dictate to the world, what it should believe, what it should honour."[92] Jews were said to believe that "domination over other peoples was the[ir] lot . . . alone," and that the Messiah would "confer upon Jews the royal sceptre of the world."[93] France, the beloved motherland, had already become "the prey of the Jewish vulture."[94] In New York, perhaps in the entire United States, "it was Jews who were the masters."[95] Soon French Canada, too, would fall under the sway of the "Hebrew peril," if the syndicate were not exposed and halted.[96] Quebec's *La Croix* predicted in 1897 that within 50 years the Jews would "devour" Canada, and that the country would cease to exist. Other nationalist organs, such as *Le Nationaliste, L'Action Sociale* and *Le Pionnier* (whose editor L.-G. Robillard, fled Canada after being charged with libel by Jules Heilbronner, and after being exposed as an embezzler of the Union Franco-Canadienne insurance scheme), were no less hysterical than *La Croix*.[97]

Jews could achieve domination over others, the antisemites suggested, only by insidious, unscrupulous means. They were an inferior race, and extremely dangerous. At the same time, many French Canadians came to regard themselves as members of a superior race. Such notions were a reflection, in part, of the "scientific" racial theories increasingly popular in Europe and the United States. The goal of the ACJC was said to be "to create a superior type of humanity" which would assume the "apostolic vocation of our race" and ensure "the salvation of the fatherland."[98] It was believed by many that the task of Quebec was to be the standard bearer of French civilization, since France had fallen to the Jews. To achieve that goal, "the unity" of the French-Canadian race had to be protected from possible defilement.[99] Racist doctrines led some French Canadians in the direction of European fascism, then in its genesis. In 1910, *Le Devoir* wrote in praise of both Karl Lüger, the antisemitic mayor of Vienna and role model of the young Adolf Hitler, and Maurice Barrès, the founder of French fascism.[100] Two decades later, a more intimate connection between the antisemitism of French Canada and that of central Europe would emerge.[101]

All of these ideas found their way into sermons, lectures and print, and at times inspired action. At the local level, sporadic attempts were made to enact legislation which would harass Jews, and thus discourage them from remaining in Quebec. These measures included special taxes on peddlers in Quebec and Montreal, and early closing by-laws. The latter were particularly onerous for observant Jews, who already kept their stores closed on Saturday because of the Jewish sabbath and on Sunday because of the Sunday blue laws. When they could not make up for the extra day lost by remaining open longer hours on other days, they found themselves unable to compete with gentile merchants.[102] The expropriation of the old Jewish cemetery in Trois-Rivières in 1901 was another legislative measure apparently intended to arouse resentment. The cemetery, which had been bequeathed to the Jewish community by the pioneer Hart family as a communal burial ground, was relinquished by the last remaining descendant in Trois-Rivières, who was no longer a Jew. Worse yet, the bodies were removed without concern for Jewish religious laws. Some years later, the alternative burial ground in Trois-Rivières was also expropriated, because the religious order of the Christian Brothers wanted the land.

Although the Montreal Jewish community was allowed on the latter occasion to remove the bodies in accord with Jewish practice, and to reinter them in Montreal, they had to do so at their own expense.[103]

Social pressure was also employed to make French Canada an uncomfortable place for Jews to settle. Parish priests in Montreal and Quebec sometimes urged their congregants from the pulpit not to sell property to Jews, thereby protecting the integrity of their neighbourhoods. In 1908, Curé Joseph-Avila Bélanger of Montreal warned his parishioners that the "Jews are our greatest enemy." He implored the faithful to resist the temptation to profit by selling to them. It is, he said, "incumbent upon us to make it harder for them to come here."[104] At times, even physical violence erupted. In 1905, the famous actress, Sarah Bernhardt, who was of French-Jewish origin, appeared in Quebec. After the publication of an apparently fabricated interview, in which the star allegedly called French Canadians "priest-ridden Iroquois," referred to Sir Wilfrid Laurier disdainfully and likened the province of Quebec to Turkey, she was charged by a mob shouting, "Down with the Jewess!" Bernhardt fled the town in fear.[105] More serious were the increasingly frequent attacks on Jews by hooligans in the streets of Montreal and Quebec, and the smashing of windows in Jewish-owned shops in the decade before World War I. In May 1910, Jacques-Edouard Plamondon, editor of Quebec's La Libre Parole, delivered a fiercely anti-Jewish address to the ACJC chapter in his home town. Afterwards, the inflamed audience went on a rampage of window-breaking and other acts of violence in the tiny Jewish quarter of the city. Two of the victims sued Plamondon for inciting a riot and for group libel. Plamondon called on priests to back up his allegations, and his opponents called on Rabbi Herman Abramowitz of Montreal to refute them. Some three years of litigation resulted in the victory of the Jewish plaintiffs, but only on appeal. In fact, the wishy-washy verdict seemed almost to vindicate Plamondon.[106]

Conclusion

A superficial observer might assume that the position of the Jews in French Canada before World War I was not much different from what it had been half a century earlier. In 1914, no less than in 1867, Jews lived outside the mainstream of French-Canadian life. In fact, however, much had changed. Until the last decade of the nineteenth century, Quebec Jews had been a tiny group which seemed destined to survive on the periphery of society, if at all. By 1914, the Montreal Jewish community was the second-largest in the British Empire, exceeded only by that of London, and there were a few small communities elsewhere in the province. Most Jews in Canada in 1914 were immigrants of recent, eastern European origin, not yet ready to participate fully in the life of the country. In Quebec, however, it was already clear that they would one day become part of the Anglo community. This decision was only partly a Jewish decision. In reality, there was no choice. English Canada, like Great Britain and the United States, had come to accept a measure of pluralism and individual rights. As a result, Jewish life was more congenial in the English-speaking nations, generally speaking, than elsewhere in the world at this time.

French Canada, on the other hand, was concerned largely with preserving what it regarded as its communal prerogatives. These included "racial" and religious homogeneity, now even more zealously asserted than in the past. In 1910, just before the demonstration against Mayor Nathan, Abbé Garrequet, the superior general of the Sulpician order, was received by the Montreal city council. He told the municipal politicians, that "his predecessors [had] aimed to make Canada what it is, prosperous and Catholic."[107] That he was received at all was a sign of the councillors' conception of their role; his words expressed their views and hopes. The survival of their unique society was more of a concern than ever to French Canadians in the years before World War I. In a 1912 Saint-Jean Baptiste Week speech, Archbishop L. P. A. Langevin of St. Boniface in Manitoba reminded the faithful that French Canada had remained French, "because we have remained Catholic," and that only "by guarding our religion, [do] . . . we guard our race."[108] The French Language Congress of the same year was an eloquent public demonstration of commitment to church and race.

Since the 1880s, French Canadians had perceived their power in the Canadian Confederation to be steadily waning. They had struggled with English Canada over almost every major issue affecting the country; Jews had become an integral part of a number of those issues. The French Canadians remained steadfastly loyal to the two-nations, two-cultures, two-races, two-religions conception of Canada that underlay Confederation. They allowed themselves little sympathy for Jewish immigrants or pogrom victims who might threaten that duality. During the pre-World War I period, they witnessed the relentless encroachment of the modern world on their ancestral ways. A "large number" came to "regard . . . Jews . . . as a grave threat to the longstanding norms of the[ir] . . . community."[109] By the end of this era, Jews had moved from the periphery of French Canadian concern to the centre, even geographically in Montreal. They became a living reality, rather than a literary or theological stereotype. To many — at times, most — French Canadians, they became a convenient symbol of unwanted change and even decay. Because they inclined toward English Canada, but, even more, because traditional French-Catholic society had always excluded them, they were unwelcome in the French community. Their presence was associated with the undesired process of modernization and disintegration in Quebec, and their political and social interests clashed with the majority. Increasingly squeezed between French and English because of the binational "political composition" of the country, Quebec Jews found themselves in a twilight zone.[110] Most, however, felt that their "French [neighbours] in Quebec" were more likely to "impugn their national honour than Anglo-Canadians."[111]

To a small number of French Canadians in the turn-of-the-century years, the Jews became a consuming obsession. This hard-core antisemitism depicted them as a dangerous, destructive force to be opposed at all costs and by all means for the sake of racial purity and religious tradition. To such individuals, "the Jew [had become] ... a convenient scapegoat" for all the ills of Canadian society.[112] While extreme antisemitism was still a fringe phenomenon, it was already finding a place in the mainstream before World War I. After the war, it would gain a wider hearing. A change for the worse was under way.

Notes

1 "L'église des Juifs dans son rapport avec l'église des Chrétiens," *L'Echo de la France* (April 1869): 346-47. All translations unless otherwise noted are the author's.

2 Joseph Tassé, "Droits politiques des Juifs en Canada," *Revue canadienne* (June 1870): 425.

3 See Oscar Douglas Skelton, *Life and Letters of Sir Wilfrid Laurier*, vol. 1 (Toronto: Carleton Library, McClelland & Stewart, 1965), pp. 30-34, and William David Kenneth Kernaghan, "Freedom of Religion in the Province of Quebec with Particular Reference to the Jews, Jehovah's Witnesses and Church-State Relations, 1930-1960" (Ph.D. diss., Department of Political Science, Duke University, 1966).

4 André Siegfried, *The Race Question in Canada*, trans. Eveleigh Nash (New York: D. Appleton, 1907), p. 3. See also *Canadian Annual Review* (1912): 425, and Ramsay Cook, *Canada and the French Canadian Question* (Toronto: Macmillan, 1966), p. 13.

5 Jean-C. Falardeau, "Role et importance de l'Église au Canada français," in *La Société canadienne-française*, ed. Marcel Rioux (Montreal: Éditions Hurtubise HMH, 1971), p. 354. See also Elizabeth H. Armstrong, *The Crisis of Quebec, 1914-18* (New York: Columbia University Press, 1937), pp. 19-20, and Kernaghan, "Freedom of Religion," p. 2.

6 "Dr. D. A. Hart," in *The Jew in Canada*, ed. Arthur Daniel Hart (Toronto and Montreal: Jewish Publications, 1928), p. 411.

7 Hampden [Adolphus Mordecai Hart], *The Political State and Condition of Her Majesty's Protestant Subjects in the Province of Quebec (Since Confederation)* (Toronto: Canadian News and Publishing, 1871), pp. 2, 5-6, 38. The entire printing of the book was apparently bought up by the government at the time of publication and destroyed. Only six copies survived the purge, according to Gerald E. Hart, in a handwritten note dated March 15, 1898, in the flyleaf of one of the surviving copies.

8 George Maclean Rose, ed., *A Cyclopaedia of Canadian Biography* (Toronto: Rose Publishing, 1886), p. 100.

9 Montreal *Gazette*, June 7, 1882.

10 Among other sources, see Minutes of the Spanish and Portuguese Synagogue, Montreal, 1847-82; Henry J. Morgan, *Bibliotheca Canadensis* (Ottawa: G. E. Desbarats, 1867), p. 104; Henry Samuel Morais, *Eminent Israelites of the Nineteenth Century* (Philadelphia: Edward Stern, 1880), pp. 53-57; and Michael Brown, *Jew or Juif? Jews, French Canadians, and Anglo-Canadians, 1759-1914* (Philadelphia: Jewish Publication Society, 1986), passim.

11 Abraham De Sola, *The Sanatory Institutions of the Jews* (Montreal: [n.p.], 1861), p. 34n.

12 Pilgrim literature included Alexander William Kinglake, *Eöthen, or Traces of Travel* (Toronto: Adams, Stevenson, 1871), and Thomas Stirson Jarvis, *Letters from East Longitudes* (Toronto: James Campbell, 1875). Novels included two Canadian editions of George Eliot's *Daniel Deronda* in 1876, as well as Montreal novelist Mary Ellen (Mrs. Alexander) Ross's *The Wreck of the White Bear, East Indiaman* 2 vols. (Montreal: John Lovell, 1870), and *The Legend of the Holy Stone* (Montreal: A. A. Stevenson, 1878). An anthology of poems largely concerned with the Holy Land was the Reverend John Douglas Borthwick's *The Harp of Canaan (or, Selections from the Best Poets on Biblical Subjects)*, 2nd ed. (Montreal: Geo. B. Desbarats, 1871).

13 See Freshman's *The Jews and the Israelites* (Toronto: A. Dredge and Co., 1870), and Beaumont's *Judaea for the Jews* (London, ON and Toronto: Hart and Rawlinson, 1876). On Canadians and the Palestine Exploration Fund, see Michael Brown, "Canada and the Holy Land," in *With Eyes Toward Zion*, vol. 3, ed. Moshe Davis (New York, forthcoming).

14 On Monk, see Richard S. Lambert, *For the Time Is at Hand* (London: Andrew Melrose, [1947]).

15 *La Vérité*, August 1883.

16 Invitation letter from Mark Samuels, president, and Lewis A. Hart, secretary, Montefiore Agricultural Aid Association, Montreal, January 8, 1885, in Jewish Public Library, Montreal, Bronfman Collection of Jewish Canadiana, Scrapbook on Jewish Farming. See also, Montreal *Gazette* March 16, 1882; Montreal *Daily Witness*, May 23, 1882; and New York *Jewish Messenger*, March 24, 1882.

17 Léon Provancher, *De Québec à Jérusalem* (Quebec: Typ. de C. Darveaux, 1884), pp. 114-15, 341.

18 Provancher, *De Québec à Jérusalem*, pp. 244-45.

19 [J. F. C.] Delaplanche, *Le Pèlerin de Terre Sainte* (Quebec: N. S. Hardy, 1887), p. 106. Compare also, J. M. Emard, *Souvenirs d'un voyage en Terre Sainte* (Montreal: J. Chapleau, 1884), and Léon Provancher and Frédéric de Ghyvelde, *Le Chemin de la Croix à Jérusalem* (Quebec, 1882).

20 Joseph Schull, *Laurier* (Toronto: Macmillan, 1966), p. 529. See also William Petersen, "The Ideological Background to Canada's Immigration," in *Canadian Society*, ed. Bernard Blishen et al. (Toronto: Macmillan, 1961), p. 73.

21 Norman Penlington, *Canada and Imperialism* (Toronto and Buffalo: University of Toronto Press, 1965), pp. 251, 259-60.

22 Joseph Levitt, *Henri Bourassa and the Golden Calf* (Ottawa: Les Éditions de l'Université d'Ottawa, 1969), p. 6.

23 Siegfried, *The Race Question*, p. 61. See also Pierre Anctil, *Le Devoir, les Juifs et l'immigration* (Quebec: Institut Québécois de Recherche sur la Culture, 1988), passim;

Cook, *Canada*, pp. 51, 147; and John Barlet Brebner, *North Atlantic Triangle* (Toronto: Carleton Library, McClelland & Stewart, 1970), p. 270.

24 See Michael Brown, "Divergent Paths: Early Zionism in Canada and the United States," *Jewish Social Studies* 44 (Spring 1982): 149-68.

25 Lionel Groulx, "La Jeunesse canadienne-française," *Revue canadienne* (October 1911): 297.

26 "Les Centres ouvriers," address of M. Arthur Sainte-Pierre, Le Congrès de la Jeunesse à Québec — *Rapport officiel*, 1910, p. 78. See also, "Young Catholics Against Jews" [Yiddish], *Keneder Adler*, July 6, 1909.

27 "Encore des Juifs," Montreal, *La Croix*, January 7, 1905.

28 Quoted in Mason Wade, *The French Canadians, 1760-1967*, vol. 1, rev. ed. (Toronto: Macmillan, 1968), p. 546.

29 See *Le Canada et la France* (Montreal: Chambre de Commerce française de Montréal, 1911), p. 26, and John Murray Gibbon, *Canadian Mosaic* (Toronto: McClelland & Stewart, 1938), pp. 205-206.

30 Falardeau, "Role et importance de l'Église," p. 356.

31 Siegfried, *The Race Question*, p. 22. See also Levitt, *Henri Bourassa*, pp. 21-25.

32 Oliver Asselin, "The Jews in Montreal," *The Canadian Century* 16 (September 1911): 14.

33 Carl Berger, *The Sense of Power* (Toronto and Buffalo: University of Toronto Press, 1970), p. 7.

34 April 13, 1900. For a short description of Jewish war interests, see Miriam Rothschild, *Dear Lord Rothschild* (Philadelphia and London: Hutchinson, 1983), pp. 80-85.

35 Quoted in Montreal *Daily Herald*, December 9, 1901.

36 See, for example, "The Jewish Question in France," editorial, Montreal *Gazette*, January 25, 1898, and numerous other articles and editorials in all three Montreal papers.

37 Henri Cimon, *Aux Vieux Pays*, 3rd ed. (Montreal: Librairie Beauchemin, 1917), p. 295. This very popular work of pilgrim literature was first published in 1895. For an indication of the role of Montreal's *La Croix* in importing radical French Catholic antisemitism into Canada during the 1890s, see Phyllis M. Senese, "*La Croix de Montreal* (1893-1895): A Link to the French Radical Right," *Canadian Catholic Historical Studies* (1896): 81-95.

38 *La Libre Parole Illustrée*, September 5, 1896.

39 See "Grenier Is Free," Montreal *Star*, November 18, 1897, and Pierre Anctil, *Le Rendez-vous manqué* (Quebec: Institut Québécois de Recherche sur la Culture, 1988), pp.269-70.

40 See "L'Église et les Juifs" and "Zola-Dreyfus," *La Vérité*, February 5, and March 5, 1898. See also David Rome, *Clouds in the Thirties*, vol. 3 (Montreal: Canadian Jewish Congress, 1977), p. 74.

41 See, for example, "L'Exil du capitaine Dreyfus" and "Le Scandale Dreyfus," Montreal *Le Cultivateur*, November 27, 1897.

42 See, for example, "L'Affaire Dreyfus," January 31, 1898.

43 See, for example, "L'Affaire Dreyfus," December 3, 1897.

44 See the testimonials in *La Libre Parole Illustrée*, September 5, 1896.

45 See untitled editorial, *Canadian Jewish Times*, August 12, 1904, for an account of the fulminations of one of the French-Canadian officers at the Royal Military College in Kingston.

46 Siegfried, *The Race Question*, p. 17, and Kernaghan, "Freedom of Religion," pp. 51-52.

47 Untitled editorial, *The American Israelite*, February 20, 1902, and Carroll Ryan, "Jewish Immigration to Canada," Baltimore *Jewish Comment*, May 20, 1904.

48 "Imported Mischief Makers," January 3, 1902.

49 Farly, "La Question Juive," in Le Congrès de la Jeunesse à Québec — *Rapport officiel*, 1908, pp. 118-33; "The Press on the Subject of the Antisemitic League" [Yiddish], and "Antisemitic League in Canada" [Yiddish], *Keneder Adler*, June 28 and July 6, 1908; and Kernaghan, "Freedom of Religion," p. 45.

50 Antonio Huot, *La Question Juive* (Quebec: Éditions de l'Action Sociale Catholique, 1914), p. 4.

51 "À l'oeuvre," February 22, 1912, and "Dans la Youpinstrass," November 8, 1912. See also, "Nos Cousins de France," January 10, 1913.

52 Edouard Drumont, "Les élections françaises," April 13, 1910, and Oscar Havard, "L'inondation," February 23, 1910. See also, Omer Héroux, "Les élections françaises," April 16, 1910.

53 Untitled editorial, Montreal *Daily Witness*, October 11, 1910; "Catholic Protest Meeting Against Mayor Nathan" [Yiddish], *Keneder Adler*, October 12, 1910; and "Le Conseil censure le maire Ernesto Nathan," Montreal *La Presse*, October 12, 1910.

54 "Le Conseil censure," and "The Pope Sends Thanks," Montreal *Daily Witness*, October 19, 1910.

55 "Catholic Mass Meeting Sunday" [Yiddish], *Keneder Adler*, October 14, 1910.

56 "A Protest and a Quarrel," editorial, October 17, 1910. See also, "Monster Meeting to Protest Attack Aimed at Pope Pius," Montreal *Daily Herald*, October 15, 1910.

57 "Catholics to Make Protest," *Daily Witness*, October 11, 1910.

58 "Catholics to Make Protest"; "Catholic Mass Meeting Sunday"; and "Protestation monstre contre Ernesto Nathan," *La Presse*, October 11, 1910.

59 "Les Insultes du maire de Rome contre le pape," October 12, 1910.

60 "L'Anti-pape du Rome," *La Presse*, October 13, 1910, and "Une Protestation nécessaire," *Le Devoir*, October 12, 1910.

61 "La Protestation des Catholiques de Montréal," *La Presse*, October 17, 1910.

62 "Protestations contre les insultes du maire de Rome à la Chrétienté," *La Patrie*, October 17, 1910; "La Protestation des Catholiques de Montréal," *La Presse*, October 17, 1910; and "City Council Approves the Protest Resolution against Mayor Nathan" [Yiddish], *Keneder Adler*, October 20, 1910. See also, "Montréal contre les insultes de Nathan," *Le Devoir*, October 17, 1910; "Great Crowd on Champ de Mars," Montreal *Gazette*, October 17, 1910; "A Catholic Gathering Makes Protest," Montreal *Star*, October 17, 1910; and "Censured Mayor Nathan," *Daily Witness*, October 17, 1910.

63 "L'insulteur du pape est couspuer," Quebec *La Vérité*, October 29, 1910, and "Antisemitic Demonstration Also in Quebec" [Yiddish], *Keneder Adler*, October 24, 1910.

64 "Protest Meeting of Protestants" [Yiddish], *Keneder Adler*, October 23, 1910.

65 "Frenchman Warns the Jews" [Yiddish], *Keneder Adler*, November 1, 1910.

66 "To a Black," editorial [Yiddish], *Keneder Adler*, November 1, 1910.

67 Ben Zakkai (pseud.), "Letters from Abroad" [Hebrew], Warsaw *Hazefirah*, 24 Teveth 1911.

68 Letter of L. O. David, November 17, 1905, mentioned in Rabbi H. Abramowitz and Lawrence Cohen, *Schedule of Material in the Ansell Collection*, typescript, Canadian Jewish Congress Archives, Montreal, no. 646. Letter of Bruchési, November 15, 1905, in *Letterbook* of the Baron de Hirsch Institute – Young Men's Hebrew Benevolent Society, Jewish Public Library, Montreal. See also, "Help for the Jews," *Daily Witness*, November 21, 1905; and "Christians Join with Hebrews," Montreal *Star*, November 21, 1905.

69 Quoted in Anctil, *Le Devoir*, p. 39.

70 "Mr. Henri Bourassa, M.P., and the Russian Atrocities," editorial, March 23, 1906.

71 Compare "A Roman Catholic View of Russia," editorial, and "A Barbaric Yowl from an Anti-Semite," editorial, Canadian *Jewish Times*, October 21, 1904, and December 29, 1905; 1943 speech of Henri Bourassa, quoted in Anctil, *Le Devoir*, p. 39; and Levitt, *Henri Bourassa*, p. 60.

72 Pierre Anctil argues convincingly in *Le Devoir* (passim), that, in his later years, Bourassa overcame his initial animus toward Jewish immigration and in the 1920s even supported it. Before World War I, however, Bourassa maintained a hard line.

73 "Pope Sends Information Against the Priest Franiatis" [Yiddish], and "The History of the Blood Libel and the Great Blood Libel Trial" [Yiddish], *Keneder Adler*, October 27, 1913, and October 19, 1913. For a full account of the trial, see Maurice Samuel, *Blood Accusation* (New York: Alfred A. Knopf and the Jewish Publication Society, 1966).

74 Huot, *La Question*, passim.

75 See the discussion of Abbé Léon Provancher above, pp. 43-44.

76 "La Fin du procès de Beiliss," *La Patrie*, November 10, 1913.

77 "French Canadian Nationalist Attacks the Jews" [Yiddish], *Keneder Adler*, October 27, 1913.

78 See, for example, Cimon, *Aux Vieux Pays*, p. 165; Frédéric de Ghyvelde, *Album de Terre Sainte* (Quebec: [n.p.], 1905), p. 17; and Jos.-A. L'Archévêque, *Vers la Terre Sainte* (Montreal: La "Croix", 1911), p. 175. See also Pierre-Georges Roy, "L'émancipation politique des Juifs au Canada," *Le Bulletin des recherches historiques* (March 1905): 89, and "Le Fléau de Dieu," Quebec *La Croix*, August 1897, p. 51.

79 *La Vérité*, March 19, 1910; Cimon, *Aux Vieux Pays*, pp. 184-85; and J.-F. Dupuis, *Rome et Jérusalem* (Quebec: Léger Brousseau, 1894), pp. 400-401.

80 L'Archévêque, *Vers la Terre*, p. 175.

81 Ibid., pp. 175-76.

82 Compare Michael Marrus, "The Theory and Practice of Anti-Semitism," *Commentary* (August 1982): 28-42. On Tardivel, see Pierre Savard, *Jules-Paul Tardivel, la France et les États-Unis, 1851-1905* (Quebec: Publications de l'Université de Laval, 1967). On Lacasse, see his *Une quatrième mine dans le camp ennemi* (Montreal: Cadieux et Derome, 1893); and Jacques Langlais and David Rome, *Juifs et Québécois français – 200 ans d'histoire commune* (Montreal: Fides, 1986), pp. 107-108.

83 Compare Albert Faucher and Maurice Lamontagne, "L'histoire du développement industriel au Québec," in Rioux, *La Société*, pp. 265-77.

84 For a discussion of such economic scapegoating in a somewhat later period, see Everett Cherrington Hughes, *French Canada in Transition* (Chicago: University of Chicago Press, 1943), p. 217.

85 Farly, "La Question Juive," p. 124, and Asselin, "The Jews in Montreal," p. 14. See also, "Les Finances d'Israël," *La Libre Parole Illustrée*, September 19, 1896.

86 See "Le Capital français et le Canada," *Le Devoir*, February 2, 1910.

87 "Le Fléau de Dieu," *supra*, n. 78. See also, Pathelin Cade, "Les Canadiens français et les entreprises commerciales et industrielles," *L'Étudiant*, April 18, 1912.

88 See, for example, Robert Rumilly, *Histoire de la province de Québec*, vol. 12 (Montreal: Fides, 1942), p. 133.

89 Farly, "La Question juive," p. 120.

90 Cloutier, quoted in *American Jewish Yearbook* (1914-15), p. 179, and *La Vérité*, May 7, 1910.

91 C. Edmond Chartier, "L'A.C.J.C. à Sherbrooke," *Revue canadienne* (October 1912): 313.

92 "Le Programme Juif," *La Vérité*, March 5, 1898. On the notion of a Jewish syndicate seeking to control the world, see Norman Cohn, *Warrant for Genocide* (New York and Evanston: Harper & Row, 1967), passim. For accusations against Freemasons, see "Sur Quoi Compter?" Montreal, *La Croix* January 7, 1905; and Quebec, *La Croix*, August 1897.

93 Huot, "La Question juive," p. 19, and Farly "La Question juive," p. 121.

94 "Le Fléau de Dieu," *supra*, n. 78. See also, Farly, "La Question juive," p. 118; "Les éléctions françaises," *Le Devoir*, April 13, 1910.

95 "À travers le monde," *L'Étudiant*, March 21, 1912.

96 Marc (pseud.), "Que doit être notre patriotisme?" *L'Étudiant*, March 28, 1912.

97 "Le Fléau de Dieu," *supra*, n. 78; "An Open Attack," *Canadian Jewish Times*, November 3, 1908; "The Black Choir" [Yiddish], "The Jewish Question in Canada" [Yiddish], *Keneder Adler*, November 13, 1910, and November 27, 1910. See also Quebec *La Croix*, February 15, 1908; "L. G. Robillard, the Anti-Jew and Swindler," *Canadian Jewish Times*, February 28, 1902; and Carroll Ryan, "Letter from Canada," Baltimore *Jewish Comment*, May 16, 1902.

98 Lionel Groulx, "Le vingt ans de L'A.C.J.C.," *L'Action française*, June 1924, p. 364.

99 Siegfried, *The Race Question*, pp. 20, 232-34.

100 O.[mer] H.[éroux], "Carl Lueger," March 12, 1910, and "Pour la défense des églises," same date.

101 See Lita-Rose Betcherman, *The Swastika and the Maple Leaf* (Toronto: Fitzhenry & Whiteside, 1975), passim; Anctil, *Rendez-vous*, pp. 223-31; and Rome, *Clouds*, 13 vols., 1977-81.

102 See Baron de Hirsch Institute, *Annual Report*, 1892, p. 4; "The Early Closing Law," editorial [Yiddish], *Keneder Adler*, August 18, 1909; and Quebec *Le Soleil*, April 5, 1910.

103 "The Jewish Cemetery at Three Rivers," editorial, *Canadian Jewish Times*, August 16, 1901; "Desecrator of Graves," *Daily Witness*, November 5, 1901; Ben Sirach [Isaac Landman], "Canadian Jews and Judaism," *The American Israelite*, November 21,

1901; Carroll Ryan, "Letter from Canada," Baltimore *Jewish Comment*, February 14, 1902; "Jewish Cemetery at Trois Rivières," in Arthur Daniel Hart, *The Jew in Canada*, pp. 499-500; and Bernard Figler, *Sam Jacobs, Member of Parliament*, 2nd ed. (Ottawa: By the author, 1970), pp. 21-22.

104 Bélanger, quoted in "The Black Choir," *supra*, n. 97. See also, "An Open Attack," *supra*, n. 97; "Important Meeting of Legislative Committee," *Canadian Jewish Times*, February 18, 1910; and Anctil, *Rendez-vous*, pp. 267-68.

105 "The Attack on Mme. Bernhardt," editorial, *Canadian Jewish Times*, December 15, 1905; Gilles Marcotte, "Le Romancier canadien français et son Juifs," in *Juifs et Canadiens*, ed. Naim Kattan (Montreal: Éditions du Jour, 1967), p. 63.

106 See *Canadian Jewish Times*, August 10, 1906; "Stones Thrown in Jewish Windows" [Yiddish], *Keneder Adler*, June 22, 1908; "Frenchman Stabs a Jewish Boy" [Yiddish] *Keneder Adler*, July 1, 1908; "A Deplorable Incident," *Canadian Jewish Times*, August 27, 1909; "Antisemitism in Canada" [Hebrew], Warsaw *Hasman*, November 5, 1909; "Jews Demand Police Protection" [Yiddish], *Keneder Adler*, November 5, 1910; "The Kiev Trial," Montreal *Gazette*, November 11, 1913; "Anti-Semitic Trial to Begin in Quebec Court" [Yiddish], *Keneder Adler*, November 7, 1913; "The Trial of the Talmud" [Hebrew], Warsaw *HaZefirah*, 27 Tishrei 1913; "The Quebec Trial" [Yiddish], *Keneder Adler*, October 26, 1913; "Jugement dans la cour supérieure en appel: Benjamin Ortenberg vs. Joseph Edouard Plamondon et René Leduc, défendeurs," typescript, December 28, 1914, in Bronfman Collection of Jewish Canadiana, Jewish Public Library, Montreal, Plamondon File; Hirsch Wolofsky, *Journey of My Life* (Montreal: Eagle Publishing, 1945), pp. 57-60; W. E. Greening, "Guilty as Charged," *The ADL Bulletin* (April 1964); and Anctil, *Rendez-vous*, pp. 265-70.

107 Quoted in *Daily Witness*, November 10, 1910.

108 Quoted in Schull, *Laurier*, p. 540.

109 Kernaghan, "Freedom of Religion," p. 319.

110 A. Segal, "From Canada" [Hebrew], Jerusalem, *He-Ahdut*, 24 Teveth 5673 [1913].

111 David Rubin, "Letters from Canada" [Hebrew], New York *Haibri*, March 30, 1917.

112 Louis Rosenberg, *Canada's Jews* (Montreal: Bureau of Social and Economic Research, Canadian Jewish Congress, 1939), p. 301.

3

Goldwin Smith: Victorian Canadian Antisemite

Gerald Tulchinsky

Most of those who read the works of Goldwin Smith are impressed by the brilliance of his intellect and the enormous range of his interest in and knowledge of the political and intellectual world of Britain, the United States and Canada during the last half of the nineteenth century. A reformer and a liberal of the Manchester school, he fought throughout his life for the separation of church and state, the liberalization of trade and the termination of British imperialism, as well as for the union of Canada with the United States. Above all, Goldwin Smith pursued the liberalization of the intellect from the shackles of the past. In his voluminous writings of nearly 70 years, he championed these causes with remarkable tenacity and single-mindedness in three countries: England, where he was born (in 1823) and educated, and where he became Oxford's Regius Professor of History; the United States, where he was one of the founders of Cornell University; and Canada, where he settled in 1871 (Toronto), becoming one of the nation's leading intellectuals until his death in 1910. An assessment of Smith by the Canadian historian Frank Underhill stresses these liberal views as well as Smith's "enlightening . . . criticism of the nature of Canadian nationality, and . . . far-reaching conception of the place of Canada in the English-speaking world."[1] Placing him in the wider sphere of Victorian liberalism, Elizabeth Wallace writes as follows: "As the champion of a liberal creed [Smith] tried to shape opinion and thus the course of events."[2] One of a small group engaged in a vigorous debate over the Canadian identity, as well as a leading writer and reformer, he enjoyed enormous prestige among the city's intelligentsia: a prestige enhanced by his marriage to Harriet Boulton, a wealthy widow who

---

Notes for Chapter 3 are on pp. 85-91.

owned "the Grange," one of Toronto's great houses. Professors Maurice Hutton and James Mavor of the University of Toronto were regular members of the Round Table circle that met at the Grange for dinner and conversation.[3] As an undergraduate at the University of Toronto in 1906, Vincent Massey, the son of one of the city's wealthiest families, was in transports of awe when he walked through its gates to be ushered into the presence of the great man.[4] When leaving the University of Toronto for Harvard in 1897, William Lyon Mackenzie King carried a letter of introduction from Smith, a family friend.[5]

While Smith always has been regarded as a leading liberal spirit of his era, Ramsay Cook points out that his liberalism was highly selective, even by nineteenth-century standards.[6] Although he advocated colonial emancipation, free trade, an extended franchise and reform on numerous other imperial and economic questions,[7] he harboured a "faith in the superiority of Anglo-Saxon civilization that is his most striking trait."[8] Smith was also an outspoken Jew-hater, one of the most prominent of his day in the English-speaking world. Many of the "Professor's" antisemitic tirades are recounted in the memoirs of his secretary, Arnold Haultain; for example, his claims that the cause of the Boer War was Britain's demand that the franchise be extended to "the Jews and gamblers of Johannesburg"; that Jews were gaining greater control over the world's press and influencing public opinion; that "the Jews have one code of ethics for themselves, another for the Gentile"; that Disraeli was a "contemptible trickster and adventurer. He couldn't help it because he was a Jew. Jews are no good anyhow"; and that "the Jew is a Russophobe," etc.[9]

These were not merely the ruminations of an elderly and bitter social critic; Smith had embraced antisemitic views at least since the late 1870s, expressing them often in print with force, conviction, persuasiveness and skill. His anti-Jewish articles were published in some of the most prestigious journals of the English-speaking world, such as the *Nineteenth Century*, the *Contemporary Review* and the *Independent*, as well as in his own Canadian papers, *The Bystander, The Week* and the *Weekly Sun*. While he had an astonishingly wide range of interests, and several other long-standing hatreds, antisemitism was a major preoccupation.[10] In Smith's mind, the very presence of Jews in society posed serious problems that required urgent resolution. Their removal from Europe, he asserted ominously in 1878, would remove a "danger from western civilization."[11] Four years later, he prophesied that unless Jews turned to "the grand remedy" of assimilation, "there is further trouble in store . . . collisions which no philanthropic lecturing will avert . . . Coheleth's [the Jews'] end will come."[12]

The Historians

It is remarkable that such a prominent aspect of Smith's thought has received practically no attention from Canadian historians concerned with his contribution to the intellectual life of the English-speaking world, particularly that of Canada during the post-Confederation debate over nationhood. Neither Underhill nor Wallace even mentions Smith's antisemitism. In his doctoral thesis, written in 1934, Ronald McEachern notices that Smith drew heavily on the "research" of a paid agent in London, and concludes that his antisemitism was essentially social and economic, not religious: Smith was only opposed to "Jewish tribalism . . . [the Jews'] refusal to coalesce with the rest of the population, their business habits and the type of employment to which they usually devoted themselves." Moreover, since his antipathy was directed "only against the Jewish nation, parasitical, separatist, and . . . un-English," his anti-Jewish views are dismissed as xenophobia or nativism, essentially harmless and in their context understandable — after all, he was opposed to the influx of almost any foreign group.[13] In his study of Canadian imperialism, Carl Berger briefly mentions Smith's antisemitism when dealing with the latter's opposition to the Boer War, which, the 'sage of the Grange' had alleged, was "instigated on behalf of Jewish financiers."[14] Malcolm Ross's otherwise insightful and sensitive essay on Smith says only that he "looked a-squint at Jews," and that it is "disturbing to find the Oxford apostle of the Christian brotherhood of man brought finally to such a view as this: 'Two greater calamities have never befallen mankind than the transportation of the negro to this hemisphere and the dispersion of the Jews'."[15] In his extended discussion of Smith's contribution to the late nineteenth-century debate in Canada on the role of religion in modern society, Ramsay Cook makes no mention of Smith's antisemitism.[16] The only real examination of the latter is provided by non-Canadian histories.[17] Steven G. Bayme, an American who studied the reaction of Jewish leadership to antisemitism in Britain from 1898 to 1918, places Smith among those English liberals to whom Jews as universal citizens were acceptable, but Jews as Jews were not.[18] Why Anglo-Canadian historians have neglected to discuss Smith's antisemitism is puzzling, since it was well known to some of his Canadian contemporaries.[19]

Wallace's omission of this subject from her intellectual biography was not an oversight. In a letter to the Canadian Jewish historian Benjamin Sack, who had expressed surprise, she admitted that she had done so deliberately: while "it must be admitted that among the groups against which he was prejudiced were the Jews. . . . It seems to me to be going a bit far to say that he used any of his journals as a forum for anti-Semitic propaganda. . . . He certainly did not descend to anything approaching our modern 'hate literature'."[20] However, these conclusions are in need of revision. At least in part, his ideas were derived from the epicentre of antisemitic propaganda in western Europe, chiefly Germany and France, making him a major disseminator of Jew-hatred at the end of the nineteenth century.

Nativism and Antisemitism

The special nature of antisemitism, as distinct from the opprobrium generally felt for immigrants, is not always easy to detect. In the popular views of journalists, members of the House of Commons and many other Canadians preceding World War I, Jews usually were seen as undesirable settlers, but Ukrainians (known then as Ruthenians or Galicians) also frequently received unfavourable mention on grounds of their racial "inferiority," their dress or other habits.[21] James Shaver Woodsworth, whose book about immigrants, *Strangers Within Our Gates*, was suffused by the racism characteristic of some turn-of-the-century Social Gospellers, preferred Jews to Ukrainians, Italians, Chinese or blacks because, in his opinion, they were more adaptable, assimilable and culturally suitable.[22] The Winnipeg general strike of 1919 witnessed more anti-Ukrainian than anti-Jewish sentiment even though the strike probably had as much support among the Jewish working class as among Ukrainians, and even though Abraham Heaps — an English Jew — was among its major leaders.[23]

Moreover, notwithstanding popular prejudices, Jewish immigrants found entry into the country comparatively easy before 1914, whereas only a trickle of East Asians, Japanese and Chinese immigrants managed to enter during the same period. Riots and bloodshed against Orientals occurred on the west coast, but nothing comparable happened to Jews.[24] The latter, in fact, may have enjoyed certain advantages over other immigrants during the early 1900s. After all, the Jewish community was an old one, having been a feature of the Montreal scene since 1768, Toronto since the 1840s, and Victoria since the 1860s; by the early twentieth century, it had established an economic, social and political presence in Canada. Whereas the nation's Jewish population was only 6501 in 1891, 10 years later it was 16 401 and by 1911 numbered 74 564.[25] Also, the Canadian response to Jewish sufferings at various times during the late nineteenth century had been empathetic and generous;[26] for example, on the part of Protestant laymen and church leaders in Montreal and Winnipeg during the Russian pogroms of the early 1880s.[27] Subsequently, Jewish organizations in western Europe, the United States and Canada had collected funds, and, with varying success, interceded with political authorities to facilitate immigration and settlement.[28] The scholarly investigations of Jaroslav Petryshyn, John Zucchi and Anthony Rasporich suggest that Ukrainian, Italian and Croatian immigrants before World War I had fewer political and social mechanisms of support than Canada's Jews possessed.[29] By 1917, Canadian Jewry also had a representative in the House of Commons as well as aldermen on the Montreal and Toronto municipal councils.[30] A small number with sufficient wealth and political connections succeeded in exerting some influence in federal and provincial affairs on issues directly affecting the Jewish community; most other ethnic communities had no such power. During the late nineteenth- and early twentieth-century period, Jews probably suffered less from serious discrimination than most ethnic groups in Canada. Antisemitism, therefore, cannot be abstracted entirely from the fairly generalized distrust of and dislike for foreigners prevalent at this time.

Yet, in certain respects, it remains significantly different from xenophobic nativism. Unlike other minorities, even those regarded with contempt or fear on other grounds, Canada's Jews were the only sizeable immigrant community before 1914 outside the Christian communion. Furthermore, they continued to suffer the disadvantages of that self-imposed exclusion even after the secularization of the state during the nineteenth century. There is no better proof of this liability and of the perpetuation of ancient prejudices in the modern world than that provided by Goldwin Smith.

Smith and Disraeli

The origins of Goldwin Smith's antisemitism are not entirely clear. Some of his writings indicate that he shared popular medieval notions about Jews that persisted in early nineteenth-century England.[31] The controversy in the 1840s and 1850s over the civil emancipation of the Jews in Britain may have inflamed deep-seated resentments even among political liberals, although Smith was willing to accept Jews as members of the House of Commons.[32] In 1848, as a young correspondent for London's *Morning Chronicle*, he wrote a series of articles attacking Benjamin Disraeli. A critic of the Tories, Smith did not make an issue of Disraeli's Jewish origins immediately, but "there was an acrimonious feud between them which led each to seize every opportunity for personal attacks on the other"; at one point, Smith referred to Disraeli as an "adventurer."[33] Their mutual antipathy simmered in the 1860s over various foreign policy issues, such as the cession of the Ionian Islands and Smith's advocacy of domestic legal reforms.[34] Disraeli described Smith contemptuously in 1863 as a "rhetorician," "prig" and "pedant" — rebukes which Smith apparently never forgave. During the debates over the second Reform Bill, he attacked Disraeli again, provoking the bemused and disdainful reply that Smith must have spent his life "in a cloister."[35] In 1870, Disraeli referred to his enemy in his novel *Lothair* as a "social parasite," causing Smith to call him a "coward" in return.[36] While it caused a stir for a few months, the contretemps seems to have fizzled out.[37] Smith not only disliked Disraeli's political style but detested him personally, confiding to a friend in 1880 that "Dizzy's life had been one vast conspiracy, the first object of which was the gratification of his own devouring vanity, the second the subversion of Parliamentary government."[38] To another friend, he wrote of his antagonist in 1896: "It is surprising that his [Disraeli's] Hebrew flashiness should have so dazzled a practical nation."[39] Smith's antisemitism may have begun with his hatred of Disraeli. But by the end of the 1870s, it began to develop into a broad belief that Judaism posed a "danger" to the kind of "civilization" that Smith aspired to achieve.

Early in 1878, while visiting England, Smith published an article attacking Disraeli for risking war with Russia by supporting Turkey over the Bulgarian uprising.[40] Not only did Smith castigate the Turks for their cruelties, but he also condemned Islam, which he described contemptuously as "not a religion of humanity." Then he turned his attention to Judaism and the Jews, whom he described as "another element originally Eastern [which] has, in the course of these events, made us sensible of its presence in the West." He contended further that, during the debate over the Bulgarian issue, "for the first time perhaps Europe has had occasion to note the political position and tendencies of Judaism. . . . In fact, had England been drawn into this conflict it would have been in some measure a Jewish war, a war waged with British blood to uphold the objects of Jewish sympathy, or to avenge Jewish wrongs."[41] Providing no evidence to support this assertion, which, however, was believed widely by opponents of Disraeli's pro-Turkish policies,[42] Smith went on to say that Judaism was not "like any other form of religious belief." The nations of Europe "have acted on the supposition that by extending the principle of religious liberty they could make a Jew a citizen, as by the same policy citizens have been made of ordinary Nonconformists," but they are in error. Jewish monotheism is "unreal" because the Jewish God "is not the Father of all, but the deity of His chosen race." After

> the nobler part of the Jewish nation, the real heirs of David and the Prophets, heard the Gospel, and became the founders of a human religion: the less nobler part . . . rejected Humanity, and . . . fell back into a narrower and harder tribalism than before . . . bereft of the softening, elevating, and hallowing influences which . . . link patriotism with the service of mankind.

"Wanderers," "plutopolitans" and "partners of royal and feudal extortion" for 18 centuries, Jews "have now been everywhere made voters," he continued, "[but] to make them patriots, while they remain genuine Jews, is beyond the legislator's power . . . patriots they cannot be; their only country is their race, which is one with their religion."

Jewish Tribalism

Smith's position became clearer a few months later when he also attacked Herman Adler, Britain's Chief Rabbi, who had responded to Smith's allegations by asserting that Jews can be and, in fact, are patriots in their countries of residence. On the contrary, Smith insisted, Jews are like Catholics, whose primary allegiance was to another country, i.e., Rome. They cannot yield undivided political allegiance to Britain because their highest loyalty is to their race or religion:

> Judaism is not, like Unitarianism or Methodism, merely a religious belief in no way affecting the secular relations of the citizen; it is a distinction of race, the religion being identified with the race, as is the case in the whole group of primaeval and tribal religions, of which Judaism is a survival. A Jew is not an Englishman or Frenchman holding particular tenets: He is a Jew, with a special deity for his own race. The rest of mankind are to him not merely people holding a different creed, but aliens in blood.[43]

While recognizing that the spirit of Judaism is universal in character, Smith maintained that in reality the Jewish religion is "confined to the tribe."[44] Why else do Jews pray only to the God of Israel ("Jehovah"), fail to proselytize, practice the "primaeval rite" of male circumcision (in order to separate themselves from other peoples), shun intermarriage with non-Jews (whom they call gentiles) and regard themselves as the chosen people? Furthermore, they crucified Christ and persecuted his followers. As a liberal, Smith professed to tolerate as full members of society those Jews willing to integrate into "the full element of European civilization . . . by putting off their Judaism." But the "hard-shell Jew," the strictly-observant, religious, orthodox or "genuine" Jew, was anathema because of his "primaeval and tribal" resistance to "the sun of modern civilization."[45] Such a Jew's public morality is tribalistic in the worst sense; if he possesses patriotism, the "object is not England, France or Germany, but the Jewish race."[46] To Smith, Jews were also guilty of "wealth worship, stock-jobbing, or any acts by which wealth is appropriated without honest labour."[47] This trait was explained as follows:

> Among the great calamities of history must be numbered the expatriation of the Jews and their dispersion through the world as a race without a country, under circumstances which intensified their antagonism to mankind and forced them more and more as objects of aversion and proscription to live by arts such as were sure at once to sharpen the commercial instinct and to blunt the conscience, the more so as they were placed beyond the healthy pale of public opinion and could look to no moral judgment but that of their tribe.[48]

In uttering these accusations, Smith was echoing the latest wave of anti-semitism in central and western Europe. From distant Canada, where there was no public perception of a "Jewish problem," Goldwin Smith began his entry into the international brotherhood of antisemitic propagandists. Heralded in Germany in 1879 by the publication of Wilhelm Marr's *Der Sieg des Judenthums über das Germanenthum*, a series of articles by University of Berlin history professor Heinrich von Treitschke, and the establishment of Pastor Adolf Stöcker's antisemitic *Christlichsoziale Arbeitspartie*, this movement alleged that the German economy, judiciary, legislature and press were controlled by Jews.[49] Its proponents called on "non-Jewish Germans of all confessions, all parties, all positions in life to one common and close union, that will strive towards one goal . . . to save our German fatherland from complete Judaization."[50] In this way, all evil in society was ascribed to Jewish influence; hence, if the cause were removed, the consequences would disappear as well. Marr, a political radical who espoused democracy, emancipation and anticlericalism, reviled Jews — he actually coined the term 'antisemitism' — for their "innate tribal peculiarity."[51] Stöcker claimed that the emancipation of the Jews in Germany had induced them to think that they were the equals of Germans; therefore they must be put in their place and reminded that they were no better than tolerated strangers. Treitschke declared that the Jews were Germany's "misfortune."[52] In spite of its occasional religious overtones, this recent antisemitism was secular in mood, repudiating Jews not for traditional Christian reasons but because they were politically, socially and culturally alien. While reviving old images of the foes of Christendom, it also possessed a new and radical nationalistic dimension.[53] The German economist, Eugen Dühring, went a significant step further by arguing that the Jews were a unique human species with distinctive physical and moral qualities, all of them negative.

In his views on Jews and Judaism, Smith was especially indebted to Ernest Renan, a leading French intellectual tainted with racism, who disparaged what he regarded as the "fanatical spirit of prophetic Judaism" and its negative influence on Christianity. This must be combatted, Renan believed, "in order that the spirit of the Indo-European race predominate in its bosom"[54] — an idea that originated with Count Arthur de Gobineau, whose *Essai sur l'inégalité des races humaines* (1853-55) enjoyed considerable, if delayed, influence among European intellectuals. By 1870, Renan had despaired of liberalism and democracy, while attributing Germany's recent victory to the preservation of its virility as founded upon its blood, notably the blood of its aristocracy.[55] Smith referred often to Renan's critique of the modern Jew, particularly his notion that "He who overturned the worldly by his faith in the Kingdom of God believes now in wealth only."[56] Smith also drew from contemporary German and Russian antisemitism, and actively solicited fashionable new European anti-Jewish ideas.[57] He absorbed these notions, and propagated them throughout Britain, the United States and Canada in some of the most potent antisemitic compositions in the English language. He issued periodic warnings of "dangers," "troubles" and "collisions." He was not simply a critic of Jewish "tribalism"; he challenged the legitimacy of Judaism and the right of the Jewish people to survive as a distinct cultural group in the modern world. This was antisemitism of the most fundamental and dangerous kind.

Joseph Laister

Aside from his abiding suspicion and dislike of Disraeli—in his mind a Jew who used England as a "gaming table" for Jewish interests—Smith nurtured his anti-Jewish passions during the late 1870s and the 1880s by means of a long personal association with a publicist in London, Joseph Laister. A minor government employee, Laister was obsessed with hatred for Jews and Judaism—he referred to them as "'the enemy"—and wrote blatant antisemitic articles with titles such as "The Imperishable Jew" that argued that Jews "deserved what they had suffered."[58] From at least as early as December 1881, Laister wrote regularly to Smith, informing him about Jewish religious beliefs, the differences between Talmud Jews and Bible Jews, the "real" reasons for the outbreak of anti-Jewish rioting in Russia during the early 1880s, the "barbaric rites" of the Jews, various aspects of Jewish sexuality and a number of other Jewish-related matters. He was probably Smith's most important source of antisemitic material, sending him countless pamphlets and articles from all over Europe, as well as his chief avenue of contact with the leading European antisemites of the day. Smith's replies have not been preserved in his papers at Cornell University, but it can be inferred that the Canadian pundit wrote frequently to offer advice, ask questions and remit cheques (sometimes referred to by Laister as "encouragement") in payment for the services rendered.[59] Clearly, Smith regarded Laister as an indispensable supplier of information that he could not obtain easily by himself. He incorporated much of this material into his own articles.

One of Laister's most laboured themes was that Jewish religious works, chiefly the Hebrew Bible and the Talmud, as well as the oral traditions based on these texts, allow, even encourage, Jews to treat their non-Jewish neighbours "immorally."[60] Allegedly, Jewish hostility toward non-Jews in the ancient world was so deeply ingrained that usury and slaveholding became widespread and normative. The Old Testament, according to him, is so replete with "immorality" that it "is responsible for the low tone of morals prevailing among Bible reading Christians."[61] Smith enlarged this claim by recommending in Marcionite terms the elimination of the Old Testament from the Christian canon. "There was a Judaism of the Prophets, and a Judaism of the Law, ... the first broadened into Christianity, while the second was narrowed into Pharisaism and the Talmud," he solemnly informed the readers of *The Bystander* in 1882.[62]

Laister combed the *Jewish World* and the *Jewish Chronicle* for reports and editorials on interesting Jewish matters and was in touch with continental antisemitic publications, such as the Paris newspaper *L'anti-Juif*, and the pronouncements of Treitschke and Stöcker, copies of which he began sending to Smith in 1882.[63] He also attempted to help Smith by writing replies to London newspapers that published letters critical of the latter's antisemitism.[64] Laister's most important contact was probably Stöcker in Berlin, with whom he regularly corresponded. One of the leading demagogues of the day, the Kaiser's court preacher popularized anti-Jewish ideas tirelessly during the 1880s.[65]

An important feature of Laister's Judeophobia was his conviction that the Jews secretly exercised control or, at least, undue influence over much of the English press.[66] Pressing further, he reached other disturbing conclusions, such as the belief that the Jews had "got at" various Church papers.[67] Fully as worrisome was Jewish control over the news elsewhere as well. As pogroms raged in Russia, Laister reminded Smith that "the great News Agent Baron Reuter is himself a Jew," thereby raising doubts about the veracity of reports concerning the outrages.[68] Also sensitive to possible Jewish interference in the book industry, he informed Smith that "Green's history is often quoted in favour of the Jews. Green is a name commonly assumed by Jews." "Is he one?" he asked.[69] He objected even to the existence of the Yiddish press in London. "Why is this," he complained to Smith in 1891, "and why is the national [Jewish] language [such at least as it has degenerated to be] kept up if not for a *nation*?"[70]

Obviously tutored by Laister, Smith, in almost every article he composed on Jewish matters, alleged Jewish control over the press to explain why the real truth could not reach the public. "What organs can they not command," he asked rhetorically in July 1883, when dealing with Jewish claims of persecution in Europe.[71] In July 1897, he informed the readers of the *Weekly Sun* that "the Jews control the European press. They are sometimes found behind even Christian religious journals."[72] Like Laister, Smith was always on the *qui vive* for Jews in journalism and was quick to report his findings. In April 1897, for example, he informed the readers of Toronto's *Weekly Sun* that "the originator of this style" (the "yellow press") of journalism was "not a native American but a Hungarian Jew, reckless, as men of that tribe often are."[73] Whenever the London papers were less than favourable to Jewish complaints of persecution in Russia, or whenever "Jewish domination" of the fourth estate was being resisted, Laister passed the news to Smith who passed it on. "Evidently here is strong anti-Jewish feeling on the staff of the Spectator. Probably elsewhere as well, only they dare not speak their minds — at present."[74] "Is there such a thing as a paper or periodical which is not controlled by Jews or afraid to print the truth, . . . about them?" he lamented to a friend in May 1906. "They seem to be behind the press everywhere, or at least be able to muzzle it."[75]

The Jewish Character

The Talmud, the great storehouse of Jewish law and commentary, held for Smith, as for many antisemites, an enormous fascination. Laister seems to have devoted considerable time gleaning 'insights' on the subject from Dr. Alexander McCaul's book, *Old Paths*, as well as the hostile writings of Jacob Brafman, a Russian Jewish apostate, and P. I. Hershon, another Jewish apostate and a compiler of Talmudic miscellany.[76] The Talmud, he explained to Smith, "is really translated according to taste," meaning that Jews are not obliged to treat gentiles in the same way as other Jews, and that robbery and possibly even murder are condoned, as well as a host of other horrible depravities.[77] The Talmud and "Talmud Jews" were frequent objects of Smith's derision as well, and he repeated the same myths about biblical Judaism, which he regarded as legitimate, and Talmudic Judaism, which he excoriated as evil.[78] In a lengthy article for the *Nineteenth Century* (November 1882) Smith wrote that

> Talmudism is the matter from which the spirit has soared away, the lees from which the wine has been drawn off. It is a recoil from the Universal Brotherhood of the Gospel in a Tribalism . . . which . . . built up ramparts of hatred. . . . It is a recoil from the moral liberty of the Gospel in a legalism which buries conscience under a mountain of formality, ceremony and casuistry. . . . It is a recoil from the spirituality of the Gospel . . . to a religious philosophy which . . . makes the chief end of man consist in the pursuit of wealth, as the means of worldly enjoyment.[79]

The Talmud, he informed the readers of *The Bystander* in 1883, is "a code of casuistical legalism [and] . . . of all reactionary productions the most debased, arid, and wretched."[80] Non-Talmudic Jews were better than Talmudic Jews. Smith, less of a racist than Laister, regarded the religion as the source of the offence, arguing that Jews would be acceptable if they assimilated into the surrounding cultures.[81] Yet, in demanding the eradication of all their religious and cultural traces, he was really demanding the eradication of the Jewish people as a distinctive entity. This, in effect, was tantamount to an anti-Jewish crusade, and it is difficult to see much difference between the two men at this point.

Laister also evinced considerable interest in Jewish sexuality, and wrote to Smith on this subject. While Smith seems to have avoided explicit sex-

ual allusions, he poured contempt on Jewish claims that Jewish women
were raped during the 1881-82 pogroms. Using reports from British consular officials in southern Russia in a selective and polemical manner, he
stated that these complaints were ridiculous, and repeated canards current
among Russian antisemites that Jews lacked "civic honesty," exploited
their female servants sexually, corrupted the Russian peasants with drink,
abused Christian burgesses, raised prices of food unjustly, mixed vodka
with impure substances, traded on the Christian sabbath and holidays and
put peasants into debt.[82] While never sinking to quite the poisonous levels
of some contemporary antisemites, Smith made frequent oblique references to "facts," such as "the fact that the Oriental character, in its leading
features, is inferior to the European . . . race."[83] It was his view that assimilation was essential in order to avert "danger to western civilization";
Jews who wished to remain fully Jewish should emigrate to Palestine.
However, "those who refuse to mingle with humanity must take the consequences of their refusal. They cannot expect to enjoy at once the pride
of exclusiveness, and the sympathies of brotherhood."[84] He believed that
the Jews and their religion would disappear in the course of time—the
sooner the better. In a viciously humorous piece for the *Weekly Sun*, July
1897, he wrote:

> The discovery of the Ten Lost Tribes is another religious fancy of
> which we ought to have heard the last. "I am very much out of funds,"
> was the reply of one who had been asked to subscribe for that object,
> "and I really cannot afford at present to give any thing to your associa-
> tion for finding the Ten Tribes, but if you have an association for losing
> the Two Tribes, poor as I am, I will try to contribute."[85]

The major threat was Jewish financial power. Smith alluded frequently
to Jews as exploiters and extortionists. It was probably his favourite allegation, and he waxed eloquent on the theme. "Their usurious oppression of
the people" would have to be given up before they could be absorbed into
their host societies.[86] Smith feared the effects of public sympathy in light
of the Russian atrocities. Many of Laister's reports concerned the reaction
in Britain to these events, including sermons by leading clergy.[87] Thus in
February 1882, he argued that the early information from Russia was
unreliable, and that vigorous British protests were unnecessary.[88] More
than a year later, he wrote to Smith to complain that "the news agencies
have never ceased to let the world know how the Jews were being persecuted."[89] Smith gave the consular findings large play in Britain and Canada, claiming that Jewish losses "were in most cases exaggerated, and in
some to an extravagant extent."[90] In any case, he claimed, the troubles
started over "bitterness produced by the exactions of the Jew, envy of his
wealth, jealousy of his ascendancy, combined in the lowest of the mob

with the love of plunder."[91] He repeated these allegations over 20 years
later after anti-Jewish pogroms broke out in Romania in 1907. "Any race,"
he avowed, "let its religion and its historical record be what they might,
which did what the Jews have done would have provoked the same
antipathies with the same deplorable results.[92]

Laister and Smith

The relationship between Laister and Smith was reciprocal; although
Smith paid for Laister's research, he regarded him as a friend and a valuable source of information about Jews.[93] Laister, of course, was a visceral
antisemite — he regarded Jews as disgusting — with his own special agenda.
He agreed with Smith's observation that the newspapers were not reprov-
ing the Jews for their "immoral doings."[94] On occasion, Laister wrote
simply to raise a technical question: in January 1882, he asked whether it
was true — as Jews often asserted — that throughout European history they
had always been prevented from owning land. "These [historical ques-
tions] are peculiarly your province and I wished to put the matter for your
consideration. . . . Please think it over. It seems to me very important to
get this point cleared up authoritatively."[95] Smith took Laister's suggestion
and incorporated some discussion of this subject in the article he was
preparing for the *Nineteenth Century*.[96]

Laister's major aim was the fostering of antisemitism through willing
associates. Sometimes, he suggested that Smith adopt a certain line of
attack: "a telling retort to the . . . boasted superiority of the Jewish race by
reason of its hygienic and other regulation . . . wd. be why don't the Jews
ask us to participate why don't they condescend to teach us something if
they have something good to teach?"[97] On one occasion, he recommended that Smith buttress his arguments with biblical references.[98] He
not only advised the latter on what points to cover, but also on what subjects to focus. For example, Smith's reply to Rabbi Adler's counter-attack
to the former's first major antisemitic foray drew advice concerning
"points that seem to still want answering, omitting those of course which
you are quite sure to have dealt with. . . ."[99] He rushed fresh material to
Smith to "read . . . *before* the opportunity passes for incorporating something in the Jewish article."[100] He also offered suggestions on the drafts of
articles that Smith sent him for comment,[101] asking his correspondent to
help him track down information in turn.[102] When Smith requested the
name of a certain antisemitic German writer, Laister replied that it was
Richard Andree, whose book *Zur Volkskunde der Juden* was "creating much
attention in Germany."[103] Although he welcomed his collaboration with
the famous Canadian, and made use of his ideas, Laister was nevertheless
anxious to establish himself as his own man.

> I regret to find that both the Jewish *Chron* and *World* have fixed me as a
> disciple of yours; I thought that I had struck out all references to you,
> but they have fastened on one quotation apparently to justify their con-
> jecture. I will take the next opportunity of disclaiming this connection.
> Meanwhile I hope it may not have caused you any annoyance.[104]

Their correspondence reveals that Smith reciprocated by confiding his
own dark thoughts, such as his view on the link between Jewish money
and nihilism.[105] Smith, too, was a regular reader of the London *Jewish
World*, as well as the antisemitic literature published in the United States
during the 1880s, such as the pamphlet *Conquest of the World* (St. Louis).[106]
Hence, he was able to contribute material of his own. "Pray let me know
where I can get particulars," Laister wrote to Smith in November 1882
concerning the latter's statement that certain Italian newspapers belonged
to Jews.[107] Like Laister, Smith was interested in circumcision, and wrote
about it.[108] Despite this reciprocity, however, the evidence suggests that
Laister was mostly the tutor and the "Professor" mostly the pupil. As a
pupil, moreover, Smith was particularly valuable, because of the fame of
his articles on religion and the Irish question.[109] Laister also regarded
Smith's social and political connections in Britain as useful, urging him,
on the eve of his departure from London in May 1882, to "make me
acquainted with any sympathisers here in England so that I may not be
entirely isolated when you go."[110] So anxious was Laister for Smith's continued collaboration that he implored him to accept "anything I think
worth your while to see, and to write when needful — for which, please, I
shall take no remuneration whatever."[111] In fact, he sent drafts of his
antisemitic essays.[112] Moreover, the two men shared their feelings as well
as their ideas.[113]

Stöcker's London visit brought Laister directly into contact with other
potentially useful Germans.[114] He described the visitor's address on Jews
in Germany as a "parting shot for the trouble they [the Jews] have given
him." By this time also, he was in touch with Canon August Rohling, a
German Catholic priest whose antisemitic tract *Der Talmudjude* (1871) had
aroused considerable public controversy in Germany.[115] He sent the pamphlet, which purported to show the depravity of the Jews on the basis of
extracts from the Talmud, to Smith for his edification.[116]

Smith's Goals

While Smith's writings on the Jewish question did not reflect all of Laister's beliefs in the essential immorality of Judaism, he saw the Jews as a
most serious social menace nonetheless. Between 1878, when he charged
that Jewish influence was "strong both in the money-world and in the
press," and 1906, when he wrote his last essay on the subject, he remained
consistent.[117] Because Jews could not be loyal to the countries in which

they lived, this influence created a political danger.[118] "The political tend-encies should be watched with solicitude, not only with reference to spe-cial questions like the present where the separate objects or sentiments of their race seem likely to conflict with the interests of the nation or of mankind, but with reference to the general progress of civilisation" because "... they now seem disposed as plutopolitans, to cast into the scale of reaction a weight which would be that of mere wealth untem-pered by any larger consideration either national or European."[119] Later, he elaborated this thesis: "Few greater calamities perhaps have ever befall-en mankind than the transportation of the negro and the dispersion of the Jew."[120] Following Renan, Smith had no doubt that the Jews were fully responsible for their own troubles:

> Take any race you please, but with an intensely tribal spirit; let it wan-der in pursuit of gain over the countries of other nations, still remaining a people apart, shunning intermarriage, shrinking from social commu-nion, assuming the attitude assumed by the strict and Talmudic Jews toward the Gentiles, plying unpopular, perhaps oppressive, trades and gleaning the wealth of the country without much adding to it by pro-ductive industry; you will surely have trouble.[121]

If there was persecution, Jews had invited it by persecuting others. "To pronounce the antipathy to the Jews utterly groundless is in fact to frame an indictment against humanity."[122] Had not Tacitus and Juvenal written about Jew-hatred in the ancient world, and did not Gibbon find evidence of it in his research? In medieval times, Jews "provoked the hatred of the people by acting as the regular and recognized instrument of royal extor-tion";[123] Jews avoided military service; they bought land and thereby undermined the feudal system; they attacked Christian religious proces-sions; they loaned money at high interest; they sympathized with and sup-ported the forces of Islam, notably in medieval Spain; they showed them-selves to be intolerant of religious dissenters like Spinoza and Acosta within Judaism. Jews like Disraeli and the merchants of Johannesburg fos-ter war for their own financial gain. In Russia, Jews are "eating into the core of her Muscovite nationality," while in Germany they "lie in wait for the failing Bauer" and in the southern United States "a swarm of Jews" have engaged in "an unlawful trade with the simple negroes ... [thus] driving out of business many of the old retailers."[124] In short, Smith pro-claimed in 1874, "the cruel maltreatment which they often received was caused less by hatred of their misbelief than by their rapacity."[125] To prove this claim, he pointed to the situation in Germany in the late 1870s. "His-tory in fact shows, that, of all the European nations, the Germans have been the most free from the vice of persecution." It was merely the struggle of the people against

the progress of an intrusive race, which is believed by its patient Oriental craft, to be getting into its hands not only the money of the nation
but the newspaper press and other organs of influence, while it is said
to avoid manual labour, seldom to produce or even to organize production, to decline as much as possible public burdens, to retain its exclusive nationality, and to be little more attached to the particular country
in which it happens to sojourn than is the caterpillar to the particular
leaf on which it feeds.[126]

For Smith, there were only two possible solutions to the Jewish problem: repatriation and assimilation. Until the end of his life, he favoured
returning their own land to the Jews once the Turkish empire was dissolved. He even suggested that Britain surrender Cyprus to Turkey in
payment for Turkey's granting Palestine to the Jews.[127] If this occurred,
the most "exclusive" Jews might return to Palestine, and "their with-
drawal might facilitate the fusion of the more liberal element into European society."[128] Consequently, either assimilation or, "what the Zionists
desire, repatriation, is the cure."[129] He was doubtful, however, that more
than "a few of the race" would desert the stock exchanges for the "courts
of Zion."[130] "To propose to him (the Jew) to change New York, London
or Amsterdam for Zion is little better than mockery."[131] The second
option included the acceptance of Christian and patriotic values. Jews
should be invited to

cease to cling to this miserable idolatry of race . . . [and] accept Humanity, and in its service find again a nobler exercise for those ancestral gifts
which, since they rejected that service, have been employed mainly in
money-getting by means often low, and sometimes inhuman.[132]

Only by eliminating all aspects of Jewish exclusiveness, such as the concept that the Jewish God is the "deity of his chosen race," and only by
abandoning barbaric "tribal" practices such as circumcision and economic
pursuits such as money-lending, could Jews become full, equal and truly
patriotic members of any of the European civil societies in which they had
been granted equal rights. In short, Jews had to reject their Jewishness,
their social and economic habits, and adopt "the softening, elevating, and
hallowing influences which, in such a patriot as Mazzini, link patriotism
with the service of mankind" in order to merit this status.[133] They must be
willing to "melt into the general population of the West" — in effect, to
disappear. Clearly, Smith never wavered from his primal conviction of
Judaism as a danger to Western civilization.

The exact nature of this danger was pointed out in 1878, and in a series
of subsequent articles. First was the possibility that Disraeli, a Jew
masquerading as an Englishman while secretly representing Jewish interests, would involve Britain in a war with Russia over the Balkans. "Let the

electioneering agents, who are Lord Beaconsfield's chief counsellors and the real framers of his policy, tell him what they will," he thundered, "the nation has declared for peace.... England must have sunk low indeed before she can allow herself to be tricked by a political intriguer, to whom she is a gambling table, not a country, for the purposes of his game, into a needless, iniquitous, dishonourable, and ruinous war."[134] Smith raised the same allegation in 1882 when, during the controversy over the pogroms, he asserted that "an attempt is being made to drag us into a Russian war."[135] Jews, in Smith's view, were the enemies of the state. In an article for the *North American Review* in 1891 he stated that "the Jew is detested not only because he absorbs the national wealth, but because, when present in numbers, he eats out the core of the nationality."[136] To the readers of the *Weekly Sun*, he declared that the Jews were "a cosmopolitan tribe of money-dealers whose influence threatens to be baleful to our civilization."[137]

Conclusion

These were most serious charges and, coming from a person of Smith's stature in the intellectual life of the English-speaking world, they must have inflicted considerable damage. It is impossible to estimate the true effect of his antisemitic declarations on public opinion or public policy in Canada. There appears to have been little reaction. One prominent Canadian did react strongly, however. In a review of Smith's *Essays on Questions of the Day*, George Munro Grant, Principal of Queen's College, pointed out that Smith's explanation for the rise of antisemitism amounted to blaming the victims: "The fault is thrown wholly upon the Jews and not upon those who treat them with brutal violence."[138] While his antisemitic views do not appear to have had any discernible influence on Canadian immigration policy during his life, his disparagement of Jews (and other Europeans) in some of the articles he wrote for the *Weekly Sun* during the 1890s and 1900s possibly contributed to general tensions over immigrant issues during those decades.[139] Smith received many letters from readers of his articles in support of his antisemitic writings. However, he wrote only sporadically and without much fervour in criticism of reigning practices. "What is the use of excluding the Chinaman when we freely admit the Russian Jew?" he asked despondently in July 1897. Ten years later, he lamented: "We have been welcoming a crowd of ... Russian and Polish Jews, the least desirable of all possible elements of population."[140] Nor did Smith, a prolific writer of letters to prime ministers Sir John A. Macdonald and Sir Wilfrid Laurier, even raise this question with them, though he did protest against proposals to establish Jewish farm colonies in western Canada.[141] The major manifestations of antisemitism in that era were either related to French-English political conflicts, or bound up with the nativism current during the great wave of immigration into Canada after 1900. This was insufficient for a successful antisemitic movement in Canada, and, unlike some of his European counterparts, Smith never attempted to form one.

Still, he was a confirmed antisemite, reviling Jews with an animus that far surpassed mere dislike. He mounted nothing less than an outright assault on the right of the Jewish people to live as Jews in European civil society. He sought out and paid for professional assistance on this subject, and pursued a vigorous literary campaign across the English-speaking world for over 30 years, serving as a leading conduit for some of the worst forms of European antisemitism to the New World and providing those prejudices with his imprimatur.[142] In his correspondence with some of the English-speaking world's leading intellectuals, Smith frequently injected his views of the "Jewish question." Therefore, he merits special attention in the history of modern antisemitism, even if he lacked the political ardour and ambition of his continental mentors. Most likely, Smith would not have wished to lead an overt antisemitic political party or movement in any of the English-speaking countries, even if this had been possible. He was ultimately too much of a mid-Victorian believer in the existing British party system to advocate such measures, and he might have sensed the revolutionary dangers of single-interest parties. Yet he made no secret of his views to all who would listen, and his influence on at least one young student was profound. Writing in his diary in February of 1946 about the threat of communism, Prime Minister King confided these thoughts:

> I recall Goldwin Smith feeling so strongly about the Jews. He expressed
> it at one time as follows: that they were poison in the veins of a com-
> munity . . . the evidence is very strong, not against all Jews . . . that in a
> large percentage of the race there are tendencies and trends which are
> dangerous indeed.[143]

Contempt for Jews, therefore, was intrinsic to a most illiberal Goldwin Smith, whose antisemitism filled only one compartment in a valiseful of hatreds. He also reviled the Irish, the Roman Catholics and the French Canadians and held distinctly reactionary views on the question of female suffrage.[144] These passions in themselves raise serious reservations about his reputation as a liberal. Yet, paradoxically, his liberalism was genuine and pervasive. Smith's antisemitism was not personal only, as his hatred for Disraeli—ironically, the personification of the assimilated Jew that Smith idealized—demonstrates, since Disraeli died in 1881, and Smith continued to publish anti-Jewish articles almost until his own death in 1910. It was general and theoretical, arising from the very nature of the philosophy he so keenly espoused. The liberal deity of the nineteenth

century was a most jealous god. His creed, and that of continental radicalism, brooked no dissenters and no deviation, especially from those who,
like the Jews after their emancipation, were expected to leap joyfully into
the brave new world of freedom and toleration, with its opportunities for
total assimilation into a higher culture. That most Jews declined this invitation astonished, dismayed and disgusted his liberal mind, just as it had
enraged Marr and Renan. Antisemitism was integral to this part of the liberal worldview. Interestingly, Smith did not pursue his other enemies
with nearly the zeal he invested in the Jewish question, nor did he challenge other minorities as fundamentally as he did the Jews. For the latter
alone, a special detestation was nurtured, based on such strong personal
feelings and imported revulsion that their very right to exist was in effect
annulled. That antisemitism was inherent to his liberalism was confirmed
by Smith himself: "Our Liberalism," he wrote in the *Nineteenth Century* in
November 1882,

> is at present in a flaccid state, fancying that because it has thrown off the
> tyranny of kings, its principles bind it to a Quaker-like quietism, and
> forbid it to guard the Commonwealth against conspiracy and encroach
> ment: as though it were lawful to defend oneself against a tiger, but not
> against a tape-worm . . . the forces in favour of Hebrew ascendancy.[145]

For Smith, Jews and Judaism were more than just a modern-day anachronism that liberals would find alien; they were a "conspiracy" and an
"encroachment" posing fearsome dangers to be understood and then
eliminated. Smith's antisemitism was also more than just a manifestation
of his growing pessimism, or what Ramsay Cook described as "a severe
case of 'cultural despair'."[146] It was, it seems, a much deeper matter of visceral feeling rather than of cool reason, about the Jewish "danger." To
avert this danger, Smith issued to the entire English-speaking world a clarion call to awareness and action.

Notes

I acknowledge with thanks the helpful comments of Ramsay Cook, Paul Christianson, Jack Granatstein, Klaus Hansen, Phyllis Senese, Marguerite Van Die,
Barry Mack and Brian Young on an earlier draft of this paper.

1 Frank Underhill, "Goldwin Smith," *University of Toronto Quarterly* (1933): 285-309,
   esp. 286.

2 Elizabeth Wallace, *Goldwin Smith: Victorian Liberal* (Toronto: University of Toronto
   Press, 1957), p. vi.

3 Samuel E. D. Shortt, *The Search for an Ideal: Six Canadian Intellectuals and Their Convictions in an Age of Transition, 1890-1930* (Toronto: University of Toronto Press,
   1976), pp. 80, 1223.

4 Claude T. Bissell, *The Young Vincent Massey* (Toronto: University of Toronto Press, 1981), p. 32.

5 R. MacGregor Dawson, *William Lyon MacKenzie King: A Political Biography, 1874-1923* (Toronto: University of Toronto Press, 1958), p. 70.

6 G. Ramsay Cook, "Goldwin Smith," *Dictionary of Canadian Biography*, vol. 13 (forthcoming).

7 See Ian Bradley, *The Optimists: Themes and Personalities in Victorian Liberalism* (London: Faber, 1980), passim.

8 Cook, "Goldwin Smith."

9 Arnold Haultain, *Goldwin Smith, His Life and Opinions* (Toronto: McClelland & Goodchild, 1910), pp. 68, 125, 146, 189, 206.

10 See Goldwin Smith, *Essays on the Questions of the Day: Political and Social* (New York: Macmillan, 1893), pp. 183-220, 263-308.

11 Goldwin Smith, *Contemporary Review* 31 (February 1878): 619.

12 Goldwin Smith, "The Jews. A Deferred Rejoinder," *Nineteenth Century* (November 1882): 708-709.

13 Ronald Alexander McEachern, "Goldwin Smith" (Ph.D. thesis, University of Toronto, 1934), pp. 304, 343.

14 Carl Berger, *The Sense of Power: Studies in the Ideas of Canadian Imperialism, 1867-1914* (Toronto: University of Toronto Press, 1970), p. 7.

15 Malcolm Ross, "Goldwin Smith," in Claude T. Bissell, ed., *Our Living Tradition, Seven Canadians* (Toronto: University of Toronto Press, 1957), pp. 29-47, esp. 32, 45.

16 Ramsay Cook, *The Regenerators: Social Criticism in Late Victorian English Canada* (Toronto: University of Toronto Press, 1985), pp. 26-40.

17 Thus Colin Holmes in Britain has noted the incongruity of Smith's "liberalism" and "antisemitism" (Colin Holmes, "Goldwin Smith: A 'Liberal' Antisemite," *Patterns of Prejudice* 6 [September-October 1972]: 25-30), while the American Jewish historian, Naomi Cohen, focuses on the sharp reaction of US Jewish communal leaders to Smith's virulent attacks (Naomi Cohen, *Encounter with Emancipation: The German Jews in the United States, 1830-1914* [Philadelphia: Jewish Publication Society, 1984], pp. 278-81).

18 Steven G. Bayme, "Jewish Leadership and Anti-Semitism in Britain, 1898-1918" (Ph.D. thesis, Columbia University, 1977), University Microfilms, no. 48108, pp. 126-27. See also Michael N. Dobkowski, *The Tarnished Dream: The Basis of American Anti-Semitism* (New York: Greenwood Press, 1979), p. 32.

19 See Hector Charlesworth, *Candid Chronicles: Leaves from the Note Book of a Canadian Journalist* (Toronto: Macmillan, 1925), p. 119. I am grateful to Ian McKay for this reference.

20 Benjamin G. Sack, *History of the Jews in Canada* (Montreal: Harvest House, 1965), p. 236.

21 See Jaroslav Petryshyn, *Peasants in the Promised Land: Canada and the Ukrainians, 1891-1914* (Toronto: James Lorimer, 1985), chap. 7.

22 See James S. Woodsworth, *Strangers Within Our Gates: Coming Canadians* (Toronto: F. C. Stephenson, 1909), pp. 111-59.

23 David J. Bercuson, *Confrontation at Winnipeg: Labour, Industrial Relations and the General Strike* (Montreal: McGill-Queen's University Press, 1974), pp. 126-27; Kenneth

McNaught, *A Prophet in Politics: A Biography of J. S. Woodsworth* (Toronto: University of Toronto Press, 1959), pp. 119, 135-36; and Henry Trachtenberg, "The Winnipeg Jewish Community and Politics: The Interwar Years, 1919-1939," *Historical and Scientific Society of Manitoba*, Transactions, Series 3, nos. 34 and 35 (1977-78; 1978-79), pp. 115-53, esp. 119-20.

24 See Peter Ward, *White Canada Forever* (Montreal: McGill-Queen's University Press, 1978), p. 197, passim.

25 Louis Rosenberg, *Canada's Jews: A Social and Economic Study of the Jews in Canada* (Montreal: Bureau of Social and Economic Research, Canadian Jewish Congress, 1939), p. 10.

26 See Stephen A. Speisman, *The Jews in Toronto: A History to 1937* (Toronto: McClelland & Stewart, 1979), p. 67.

27 Gerald Tulchinsky, "Immigration and Charity in the Montreal Jewish Community to 1890," *Histoire Sociale-Social History* 16, 33 (November): 370-71.

28 See Simon Belkin, *Through Narrow Gates: A Review of Jewish Immigration, Colonization and Immigrant Aid Work in Canada 1840-1940* (Montreal: Eagle Publishing, n.d.), passim.

29 Petryshyn, *Peasants*, passim; John Zucchi, *The Italians in Toronto* (Montreal: McGill-Queen's University Press, 1989), passim; and Anthony W. Rasporich, *For a Better Life: A History of the Croatians in Canada* (Toronto: McClelland & Stewart, 1982), passim.

30 Bernard Figler, *Biography of Sam Jacobs, Member of Parliament* (Ottawa: Published by the author, 1959), and Speisman, *Jews in Toronto*, p. 251.

31 Todd M. Endelman, *The Jews of Georgian England, 1714-1830: Tradition and Change in a Liberal Society* (Philadelphia: Jewish Publications Society, 1979), pp. 86-87.

32 Arnold Haultain, *A Selection from Goldwin Smith's Correspondence* (Toronto: McClelland & Goodchild, n.d.), pp. 2-3.

33 Wallace, *Goldwin Smith*, p. 11.

34 Goldwin Smith, *The Empire: A Series of Letters Published in "The Daily News," 1862, 1863* (Oxford: J. Henry and J. Parker, 1863), pp. 255-56.

35 *The Times*, February 27, 1867.

36 Wallace, *Goldwin Smith*, p. 184.

37 See *Appleton's Journal of Popular Literature, Science, and Art* (June 1870): 51-52, and *New York Tribune*, May 16, 1870.

38 Haultain, *Correspondence*, p. 85.

39 Ibid., p. 296.

40 Goldwin Smith, *Reminiscences*, ed. Arnold Haultain (New York: Macmillan, 1910), p. 380, and "England's Abandonment of the Protectorate of Turkey," *Contemporary Review* 31 (February 1878): 603-21.

41 Ibid., p. 619.

42 Colin Holmes, *Anti-Semitism in British Society, 1876-1939* (New York: Holmes & Meier, 1979), p. 11.

43 Goldwin Smith, "Can Jews Be Patriots?" *Nineteenth Century* (May 1878): 877.

44 Ibid., p. 878.

45 Ibid., p. 876.

46 Ibid., p. 882.

47 Ibid., p. 884.

48 Ibid.

49 Jacob Katz, *From Prejudice to Destruction: Anti-Semitism 1870-1933* (Cambridge: Harvard University Press, 1980), pp. 260-72.

50 Ibid. (quoted), p. 261.

51 Moshe Zimmerman, "From Radicalism to Antisemitism," in Shmuel Almog, ed., *Antisemitism Through the Ages*, Vidal Sassoon International Centre for the Study of Antisemitism, The Hebrew University of Jerusalem (Oxford: Pergamon Press, 1989), pp. 251-54.

52 Cf. Fritz Stern, *Gold and Iron: Bismark, Bleichröder and the Building of the German Empire* (New York: Knopf, 1977), p. 512.

53 Ibid., p. 264.

54 Ernest Nolte, *Three Faces of Fascism*, trans. Leila Vennewitz (New York: Mentor Books, 1969), p. 68.

55 Ibid. See also Shmuel Almog, "The Racial Motif in Renan's Attitude to Jews and Judaism," in *Antisemitism Through the Ages*, pp. 255-78.

56 Smith, "The Jews. A Deferred Rejoinder," p. 707.

57 *The Bystander* 3, 1883, pp. 250-52.

58 Queen's University Archives, Goldwin Smith papers, microfilm, Laister to Smith, April 12, 1882; November 17, 1883; January 3, 1884.

59 Laister to Smith, February 12, 1882; "Many thanks for the cheque . . . the money is welcome and will help to get me a holiday this year . . ."; Laister to Smith, May 19, 1882.

60 Laister to Smith, December 6, 1881; February 27, 1882.

61 Ibid., December 6, 1881.

62 *The Bystander* 3, July 1883, p. 251.

63 Laister to Smith, January 17, February 6, 1882; see also Peter Pulzer, *The Rise of Political Anti-Semitism in Germany and Austria* (New York: John Wiley, 1964), pp. 249-50.

64 Laister to Smith, January 6, 1882.

65 Pulzer, *Rise of Political Anti-Semitism*, p. 94, and *Encyclopedia Judaica (EJ)*, vol. 15, pp. 408-409.

66 Laister to Smith, February 12, 1882.

67 Ibid., January 6, 1882.

68 Ibid., January 22, 1882.

69 Ibid.

70 Ibid., October 15, 1891.

71 *The Bystander* 3, July 1883, p. 251.

72 *Weekly Sun*, July 28, 1897.

73 Ibid., April 29, 1897.

74 Laister to Smith, November 17, 1883.

75 Haultain, *Correspondence*, p. 462.

76 Norman Cohn, *Warrant for Genocide: The Myth of the Jewish World-Conspiracy and the Protocols of the Elders of Zion* (London: Eyre & Spottiswoode, 1967), pp. 53-55; *EJ*, vol. 4, pp. 1287-88; and Smith Papers, Laister to Smith, May 17, 1882.

77 Laister to Smith, January 6, 1882.

78 See *The Bystander* 3, 1883, pp. 250-52.

79 Smith, "The Jews. A Deferred Rejoinder," p. 706.

80 *The Bystander* 3, July 1883, p. 251.

81 See *The Bystander* 3, July 1883, pp. 251-52.

82 See Kenneth Bourne and D. Cameron Watt, gen. eds., *British Documents on Foreign Affairs: Reports and Papers from the Reports of the Foreign Office, Confidential Print, Part I, From the Mid-Nineteenth Century to the First World War, Series A, Russia, 1859-1914*, ed. Dominic Lieven, *Russia, 1881-1905* (Washington: University Publications of America, 1983), pp. 1-65, and Smith, "The Jews. A Deferred Rejoinder," p. 692.

83 *The Bystander* 1, August 1880, pp. 445-46.

84 Ibid., March 1880, p. 156.

85 *Weekly Sun*, July 15, 1897.

86 *The Bystander* 3, July 1883, p. 251.

87 Ibid., February 6, 1882.

88 Ibid., February 17, 20, 1882.

89 Ibid., November 17, 1883.

90 Smith, "The Jews. A Deferred Rejoinder," pp. 688-94, and Goldwin Smith, "New Light on the Jewish Question," part 2, *North American Review* 153 (August 1891): 129-43, esp. 131.

91 Ibid., p. 133.

92 *Weekly Sun*, March 27, 1907.

93 McEachern, "Goldwin Smith," p. 343; Smith Papers, Laister to Smith, January 17, 1882; and Haultain, *Goldwin Smith*, p. 125.

94 Laister to Smith, March 2, 1882.

95 Ibid., January 6, 1882.

96 Smith, "The Jews. A Deferred Rejoinder," passim.

97 Laister to Smith, February 12, 1882.

98 Ibid.

99 Ibid., February 27, 1882.

100 Ibid., May 21, 1882.

101 Ibid., April 12, 24, 30, 1882.

102 Ibid., February 20, 1882.

103 Ibid., January 22, 1882.

104 Ibid., February 12, 1882.

105 Ibid.

106 Ibid., November 6, 1882.

107 Ibid.

108 Ibid., November 17, 1883.

109 "Altogether they tend to reconcile parties of *all* shades to you, — to disabuse them of wrong impressions about you, consequently give what you have to say about Judaism more weight than it had two or three years ago. . . . If there is a God, He is on our side in this matter, and will rule us aright." (Ibid., April 30, 1882.)

110 Ibid., May 14, 1882.

111 Ibid., May 19, 1882.

112 Ibid., November 17, 1883.

113 "What you tell me about the suppression of your proffered article on the Anti-Semitic movement is most exasperating," Laister wrote in early June 1890. "How long are we to submit to this invidious foe! The worst of it is that so very few people seem to realize the danger. However if the Jews have rope enough they will hang themselves by & by." (Ibid., June 6, 1890.)

114 Ibid., November 17, 1883. See C. C. Aronsfeld, "A German Antisemite in England: Adolph Stöcker's London Visit in 1883," *Jewish Social Studies* 49, 1 (Winter 1987): 43-52.

115 Smith Papers, Laister to Smith, November 17, 1883; see Pulzer, *Rise of Political Anti-Semitism*, p. 163.

116 "I like this blood accusation business as little as you; but if they [defenders of Jews?] will have it they must; and I am always glad to give the thoughtless Gentile defenders of the tribe a rap on the knuckles." (Laister to Smith, November 17, 1883.)

117 Goldwin Smith, "Is It Religious Persecution," *The Independent* [New York] 60 (1906): 1474-78.

118 Smith, "Can Jews Be Patriots?" pp. 875-87, esp. 875.

119 Ibid., p. 885.

120 Ibid.

121 Smith, "Is It Religious Persecution," p. 1474.

122 Ibid.

123 Ibid.

124 Ibid., pp. 1476-77.

125 *The Bystander* 1, March 1880, p. 156, and 3, July 1883, pp. 251-52.

126 Ibid., 1, August 1880, pp. 444-45.

127 Smith, "The Jews. A Deferred Rejoinder," p. 709.

128 Smith, "Can Jews Be Patriots?" p. 884.

129 *Weekly Sun*, March 27, 1907.

130 *The Bystander* 3, March 1880, p. 155.

131 *Weekly Sun*, July 15, 1897.

132 Smith, "Can Jews Be Patriots?" p. 886.

133 Smith, "England's Abandonment," p. 619.

134 Ibid., p. 620.

135 Smith, "The Jews. A Deferred Rejoinder," p. 687.

136 *North American Review* 153, 2 (August 1891): 129-43.

137 *Weekly Sun*, July 15, 1897.

138 *The Week*, February 24, 1894. If, as Smith suggested, the state should forbid the Jewish rite of circumcision because "it has nothing to do with religious opinion, nor in repressing it would religious liberty be infringed," then, Grant argued, the state would have the right to forbid the Christian rite of baptism on the same grounds." However, "the law against it [circumcision] would be a dead letter. Their [the Jews] respect for us would be gone forever, and our self-respect would go at the same time." As for Smith's demand that the Jew forget his allegiance to Zion and Jerusalem, Grant observed: "Why should he be obliged to forget the city that is bound up in his mind with everything that he esteems glorious in the past as well as eternally sacred? The Jew that forgets Jerusalem is not likely to be a better citizen of the country in which he lives." I am grateful to Barry Mack for this reference.

139 *The Week*, February 18, 1897; *Farmer's Sun*, May 1, June 1, September 28, 1904. See John Higham, *Strangers in the Land: Patterns of American Nativism, 1869-1925* (New York: Atheneum, 1975), chap. 4, "The Nationalist Nineties."

140 *Weekly Sun*, July 29, 1897; August 28, 1907.

141 Arthur A. Chiel, *The Jews in Manitoba: A Social History* (Toronto: University of Toronto Press, 1961), pp. 49-50.

142 Cohen, *Encounter with Emancipation*, p. 278.

143 NAC, MacKenzie King Diary, February 20, 1946. I am indebted to Jack Granatstein for this reference.

144 See Smith, *Essays on Questions of the Day*.

145 Smith, "The Jews. A Deferred Rejoinder," p. 708.

146 Cook, *The Regenerators*, p. 36.

4

Antisemitic Dreyfusards: The Confused Western-Canadian Press[1]

Phyllis M. Senese

L'Affaire Dreyfus and Canada

In the late summer of 1899, worldwide attention was riveted on the French provincial city of Rennes, the scene of the second court-martial of Captain Alfred Dreyfus. At the time of his arrest in 1894, it was generally only the scurrilous antisemitic press, following the lead of Edouard Drumont's *La Libre Parole*, that had been interested to any great extent in the apparent treason of a Jewish artillery officer. By 1899, however, a great deal had changed. The novelist Émile Zola had ignited a public outcry on Dreyfus's behalf through the publication of *J'Accuse*. This celebrated article was the centrepiece of Zola's sensational libel trial in 1898, which forced a re-opening of the case. Brought back to France from the appalling conditions of Devil's Island that he had endured for five years, Dreyfus found himself at the centre of the most bitter public controversy that was to afflict the Third Republic.

The *Affaire*, as the Dreyfus controversy came to be known, proved in painful detail that the antisemitic passions of the 1880s had been embraced by powerful segments of French society. However, beyond the borders of France itself, public opinion was more sympathetic, and international support for the beleaguered captain was at its height by the time the Rennes court-martial rendered its verdict of guilty. International opinion was so offended by this travesty of justice, and so convinced that the verdict had flowed from the antisemitic prejudices of his accusers that, in many countries, a boycott of the upcoming Paris International Exposition was mooted. Yet despite this worldwide condemnation of French antisemi-

Notes for Chapter 4 are on pp. 108-11.

tism, the non-French reaction to the *Affaire* often revealed the presence of antisemitism in other nations as well.[2]

An antisemitic odour pervaded the entire story wherever it was told, even in remote western Canada. Through their coverage of and comment on the case, the western-Canadian newspapers brought to light a disturbing truth: anti-Jewish feelings not only existed in the western part of the continent, but actually had preceded significant Jewish immigration to the region. Significantly, this social malady does not require the presence of Jews themselves in order to thrive. For this reason, the small number of Jews in western Canada in the 1890s had no direct bearing on how the Dreyfus scandal was received and reported locally. The newspapers denounced vehemently the outrages in France, not because they *really* wished to defend Jews, but because the persecution of Dreyfus supplied them with an easy means of condemning a Catholic and French society. Defending Dreyfus the *man*, instead of Dreyfus the *Jew*, allowed them to denounce an alien religious and social system that they disliked in any case. As they embraced Dreyfus as the innocent victim of French-Catholic hatred, the western editors repeated routinely the antisemitic canards that were circulating widely in Europe and America. Thus they demonstrated an inability to recognize in their own attitudes the same prejudice that they condemned in the anti-Dreyfusard French. Western Canadians committed no outrages against Jews in the 1890s. However, the reporting of the local press of the day proves that a habitual, unthinking, vaguely articulated, but real antisemitism was sinking deep roots into the Canadian west. As immigration to the prairies accelerated at the turn of the twentieth century, many western Canadians, influenced in part by the regional newspapers, were predisposed to regard all "foreigners" and "outsiders" with hostility.[3] The public coverage of the Dreyfus case exemplified an Anglo-Canadian ethnocentrism that, for all its seemingly benign character, inflicted untold damage on many immigrants, among them Jews.

In late 1894, when Alfred Dreyfus first came to public attention, Canada west of the Great Lakes was an immense, thinly settled area of some 400 000 people, over half of whom were under the age of 16.[4] Major centres of population had already developed in Winnipeg, Victoria and Vancouver; Brandon, Nanaimo, New Westminster, Calgary, Edmonton and Regina were soon to follow. Across the prairies, and throughout British Columbia, villages and hamlets dotted the countryside. Wherever towns appeared, Jews were found, struggling to establish synagogues, schools and communal organizations. In the villages and rural areas, individual Jewish families, agricultural colonies and itinerant peddlers became familiar features of western-Canadian life. The Jews had been a small part of each stream of migration: with the fur trade companies, among the eager hordes attracted to the Pacific coast by the Fraser gold rush, and among

the homesteaders who began to filter across the plains after Confederation. A small and scattered Jewish presence was well established in the
west when Dreyfus's alleged treason first made the headlines.[5]

Western Canadians followed the vicissitudes of the Jewish officer in
much the same manner as the rest of the world — through the daily press.[6]
Newspapers had sprung up almost as quickly as the towns and villages of
the newly populated territories, and their fortunes rose and fell with the
local economy. Until 1900, most western newspapers were published in
English, although a few were published in French. Some very small Ice-
landic, Swedish and German papers began appearing in Manitoba in the
1880s, a sign of the ethnic diversity that would later characterize the vast
expanses of the western segment of the new nation. The Dreyfus story
was carried in the Canadian press primarily through the printing of wire
service copy. For this reason, it is not surprising to find exactly identical
reports about the case from one end of the country to the other. In 1894,
the Canadian Pacific Telegraph Company, a subsidiary of the Canadian
Pacific Railway, had a virtual monopoly on supplying wire service copy.
Wherever its lines reached, it collected, edited and transmitted news for a
fee to its subscribers. Its international exposure was supplemented by an
exclusive contract with the New York-based Associated Press, which had
its own connections with major European wire services. For western
Canadians, the wires provided a rapid link to events in France; within a
day of a new development in the *Affaire*, reports were found in the regional
newspapers. Occasionally, a newspaper might offer articles from a "special
correspondent," as did *The Herald* (Calgary); others reprinted items from
London or New York papers. These reports reflected the capacity of the
wire service to deliver a large volume, but narrow range, of material concerning Dreyfus.[7]

Constituting less than 1 percent of the total population of western Canada, the Jewish pioneers by all accounts rarely encountered antisemitism.
Their numbers were too small before the 1890s to attract much attention.
The earliest large Jewish community in the west was that of Victoria,
when the gold rush boom of 1858 attracted Jewish entrepreneurs from
San Francisco. Many of them became prominent in local business, enjoying considerable success in local, provincial and federal politics.[8] The prejudices that arrived in Victoria and British Columbia with the gold rush
were directed more often at the significant black community that had also
migrated from San Francisco, or at the local native peoples.[9] Like their
counterparts in Winnipeg, the Jews in Victoria in the 1860s and 1870s
were of British or German origin. Mostly educated and assimilated, they
were difficult to distinguish from their Christian neighbours. The
antisemitic rhetoric of Victorian British North America was rarely
directed at this type of Jew; an attitude of sympathetic, if occasionally

patronizing, goodwill was far more common. In Victoria, for example, when the dedication ceremonies were held on June 2, 1863, for the new synagogue, the entire town turned out to participate.[10] However, various tensions simmered below the surface. Only the previous winter, the *Jewish Chronicle* of London had published a report that Jewish parents in Victoria had removed their children from the local schools because of attempts by Church of England teachers to "seduce them from the religion of their fathers."[11]

Antisemitism enjoyed an international resurgence in the 1880s, with currents of violence swirling across Europe. The latter received ample exposure in the western-Canadian press. Local feelings were shifting as well. In the spring of 1880, for example, the *Manitoba Free Press* carried detailed dispatches on the systematic pogroms unleashed in the Ukraine by Tsarist authorities.[12] Two years later, destitute refugees from Russia began arriving in Winnipeg, which counted only 23 Jews among its 8000 residents. The pages of the *Free Press* chronicled the relief effort mounted by the entire city; it reported and enthusiastically endorsed the call of the mayor and council for the population to rally around the newcomers with material and moral support.[13] When the *Winnipeg Daily Times* denounced the arrival of such undesirable immigrants, it was denounced in turn by the *Free Press*.[14] As the numbers of impoverished eastern European Jewish refugees arriving in Manitoba grew, the two papers frequently engaged in bitter exchanges on the new turn of events. It is difficult now to determine with much precision the degree to which their opposing views represented a division of opinion in Winnipeg itself. By the end of the nineteenth century, the question of Jewish immigration was incorporated into the larger debate that was erupting about all 'foreigners'.

The Press

In early November 1894, when reports began to circulate that Captain Dreyfus had been arrested for passing French military secrets to German agents, most newspapers in western Canada simply reprinted the wire service copy they had received, sometimes as a small item tucked away in a column of news from around the world, and sometimes in prominent display with a sensational headline. The *Victoria Daily Colonist* announced the arrest as evidence of a "Traitorous Conspiracy," while Dreyfus's conviction by a secret military tribunal on December 24 produced the Christmas Day headline: "Dreyfus the Traitor Knave."[15] The Vancouver *Daily News-Advertiser* was not certain as to who or what to believe; on December 27 it ran a lengthy article composed of excerpts from various French and American newspapers repeating *all* of the conflicting rumours that surrounded the case.[16] In this vein, the *Regina Leader* contributed "Skirted Court Spies," which recounted the accusation that Dreyfus had passed military secrets via his Italian mistress; this, in turn, introduced a detailed story about women agents in recent times who had duped gullible men for sensitive information.[17] Newspapers throughout the west carried extensive accounts of Dreyfus's degradation in the courtyard of the École Militaire on January 7, 1895.[18] His transfer to prison in French Guiana later that month received more restrained coverage, as interest in the case was beginning to wane.[19]

As the first act of the drama ended, the Vancouver *Province* reprinted an editorial from the *Times* of London assuring its readers that secret trials of the sort inflicted on Dreyfus could never have occurred in England; while the "susceptibility" of the French people to such barbarity was not singled out, their justice system obviously left much to be desired.[20] The French had managed the trial badly, but the case was closed. The Nanaimo *Free Press* was one of the few newspapers to warn that antisemitism figured in the business. On January 12, 1895, under the headline "Anti-Jewish Crusade," it advised its readers that a number of French-Canadian papers, led by *La Vérité*, had taken up the same kind of campaign against Jews that was so evident in Paris during Dreyfus's humiliation.[21] However, the story began to fade by the spring of 1895, not receiving much attention until September 1896, when Lucie Dreyfus petitioned the Chamber of Deputies demanding justice for her husband. The day before she presented her petition, *The Progress* (Qu'Appelle) carried a report that she had helped Dreyfus escape from his Devil's Island prison, and that the couple were now safe in the United States.[22] The report was part of the campaign of planting rumours conducted by Dreyfus's brother Mathieu to keep his brother's plight before the public.[23] Occasionally, these rumours surfaced in the western-Canadian press. Despite such efforts, however, general interest was fading, at least until events in France suddenly changed everything.

During the summer of 1896, the case against Dreyfus, which was a total fabrication, began to unravel. As the forgeries used to convict him were exposed, as the responsibility of certain officers for the subversion of justice was discovered, and as the growing scandal renewed international interest in the entire affair, western Canadians were once again riveted to the controversy surrounding the artillery captain whose guilt few, at least initially, had doubted. Relying, as they did, on wire service copy, the western-Canadian press was slow at first to step beyond the mere reproduction of foreign material. The journalists seemed to find it difficult to appreciate the gravity of the situation. As late as November 1897, when the scandal was engulfing rapidly the French army and government, the *Semi-Weekly World* of Vancouver continued to insist that Dreyfus was "convicted on the clearest evidence," and "caught at his infamous work" — since his family was German to the core, he must have been a German spy.[24] Six weeks later, when Émile Zola's publication of *J'Accuse* assured his trial for libel, the *Semi-Weekly World* finally took notice of the "frenzied prejudices" sweeping France, pushing that nation into a state of crisis.[25] Many newspapers acknowledged in January 1898 that the anti-Dreyfus demonstrators roaming Paris daily were in fact antisemitic mobs.[26] The belief that Dreyfus was the victim of a "villainous conspiracy" was growing.[27] More and more reports began to warn of a mounting "anti-Jewish crusade" in France.[28] Even French socialists helped to whip public passions to a frenzy by demanding that the country rise up against the "Hebrew and Catholic capitalist."[29] From January 1898, until after the Rennes trial, the wire copy reported regularly that the "feeling against Jews is increasing in France."[30] The turmoil that *J'Accuse* had produced — anti-Jewish riots in Paris and other cities, growing fears among French Jews for their personal safety, and the escalation of inflammatory rhetoric in French newspapers — was well chronicled in the western-Canadian press. All the more striking, therefore, was what was missing: a clear denunciation of antisemitism. Public disorder was condemned, but its antisemitic roots, even when they were acknowledged, were not censured.

There were other blind spots. Shortly before Zola's trial began, the *Victoria Daily Times* insisted that it was unwise to pay too much attention to the troubles in France, since, aside from the Dreyfus business, Madagascar and the Panama scandal, that nation was at peace and in a state of prosperity. Admittedly, Paris was a problem — a "cancer spot" — but not France as a whole. As for Zola, he would be "execrated by people today . . . [and] idolized tomorrow." This paper had no doubt that the "real enemies of France should be looked for inside the city limits of Paris."[31] The Vancouver *Province* carried columns by "Candide," who identified anarchists — "the advanced guard of the communists" — as the most dangerous elements in the disturbances rocking Paris.[32] The *Winnipeg Daily Tribune* gave front page coverage to the New York *Herald*'s speculation that the rioting might be the result of police provocation.[33] Many western-Canadian papers accepted eagerly and uncritically every scrap of information or misinformation that came their way.

Zola's conviction and sentence generated worldwide outrage; the western-Canadian press joined the clamour, but the papers still did not seem to have a clear sense of why they should be outraged. The *Winnipeg Daily Tribune* denounced Zola' conviction as "Savage and Brutal," and reported that the Winnipeg Jews were proposing to send him a telegram "conveying the sympathies of the Jews of Western Canada in his fight."[34] However, the true significance of such a gesture on the part of Canadian Jewry was not grasped. In an editorial, the Vancouver *Semi-Weekly World* condemned the "farcical system of justice in France," and insisted that the conviction in no way detracted from Zola's reputation.[35] This type of denunication was fairly standard, but the deeper issues of the scandal were not probed. The Vancouver *Province* hoped that the so-called "criminals," Zola and his publisher Georges Clemenceau, would take "consolation that they are supported in their action by the better opinion of the civilized world."[36] Such a pious hope scarcely penetrated beneath the surface of contemporary events.

More than anything else, Zola's trial and conviction effectively resuscitated public interest in the Dreyfus affair. Immediately, his name returned to the front pages. *The Herald* (Calgary) made its sympathies clear by finding the precedent for his conviction in the trial in *Alice in Wonderland*.[37] The *Province* reported approvingly a month later that a play about Dreyfus was playing to packed houses in Amsterdam.[38] Western Canada was *engagé* in the *Affaire*, but more in the fashion of a spectator sport than in recognition of some disturbing questions with implications for Canadian society. During the months that the drama was unfolding, the threads of an explanation—one that missed the central issue completely—wove their way through the pages of the western-Canadian press. The fundamental deficiencies of the French as a people were blamed. It was not only French law that was defective; the French temperament and character were hopelessly flawed. A suspect judicial system and a corrupt army suggested a decadent race, which, when wedded to Catholicism, naturally spawned a virulent antisemitism.

Anglo-Saxon Superiority

Without exception, the British and American wire service reports from Paris praised the inherent superiority of Anglo-Saxon legal traditions and practices, while deploring those current in France. The *Winnipeg Daily Tribune* sneered at French "secret trials" and lamented the "wretched plight" of French society that Zola's trial revealed.[39] The Vancouver *Daily News Advertiser* insisted that it was impossible for the British peoples to comprehend "French ideas and habits of thought."[40] Throughout 1898 and 1899, the western-Canadian press frequently returned to these alleged French failings, and consequently those of their judicial system. No paper offered any positive assessment. When, in the late summer of 1898, it became evident that forged documents had been used to convict Dreyfus, and that this criminal act had been covered up by the military and civilian authorities, the *Saskatchewan Herald* expressed its indignation without much thought given to its choice of words: "tried in secret by a tribunal worthy of the days of the inquisition, and punished with a cruelty that would make an Apache blush through his paint, it turns out that Capt. Dreyfus is innocent."[41] A month before the Rennes trial, the Qu'Appelle *Progress* echoed this sentiment by concluding that it was impossible for Dreyfus to get a fair trial "in the country that boasts of liberty and equality." Fortunately, the paper continued, this scandal could not have occurred in Canada "because there is British government."[42] *The Herald* (Calgary) described the trial as mixed "farce, comedy, burlesque and tragedy," adding that it ought "to inspire a movement for an act of national thanksgiving... for this country being free from the judicial system that sullies the honour of France."[43] That nation, the editor concluded, "is rotten both politically and socially."[44]

The conviction of inherent Anglo-Saxon superiority was so firmly rooted in the western-Canadian mind that many western papers predicted that Dreyfus would choose to live anywhere but in France after his pardon. In September 1899, *The Herald* (Calgary) published a dispatch from London which had him moving to the Edmonton area;[45] three weeks later, he was heading to San Antonio, Texas.[46] Most papers had him relocating in England. The *Victoria Daily Colonist* practically gloated that " 'le perfide Albion' perpetually puts France in an unpleasant light before the world."[47] The *Regina Standard* expected Dreyfus to recover his broken health in England: "if he chooses to reject France, he will be welcome for he is honest and true as is England."[48] Only occasionally did a more reflective note creep into a British bulletin. In June 1899, the *Victoria Daily Times* carried a piece from the *Pall Mall Magazine* by Mrs. Belloc-Lowndes in which she suggested that the dominant view of the *Affaire* might be too simple. She believed that "English observers did not pay sufficient attention to the remarkable variety of the elements which went to make up anti-Dreyfus feelings in France."[49] However, most papers preferred the simple explanations offered via the wire, rather than contemplate complexities that might have unwelcome implications.

In addition to a hopeless judicial system, the French character and temperament were deemed responsible for an officer corps that had corrupted the army and placed the Third Republic in peril. The *Victoria Daily Times* and *The Herald* (Calgary) produced some of the most blistering editorial condemnations of the French army to be found anywhere. In November 1898, *The Herald* explained that "the officers of the French army are drawn to a great extent from what in France may almost be called the dangerous classes.... Their whole habit of mind is disloyal and nothing but opportunity is needed to make them active enemies of the government their country has chosen for itself."[50] During the Rennes trial, the *Victoria Daily Times* argued that each day's testimony supported no other conclusion except that Dreyfus had been the "victim of an infamous conspiracy hatched in high military circles."[51] The *Saskatchewan Herald* condemned officers who "overreached themselves,"[52] a view shared by many other papers. The *Victoria Daily Times* went further: "Every turn in the Dreyfus case reveals a lower depth of infamy in French officialdom."[53] Editors across western Canada not only blamed the army for the turmoil in

France, but many concluded that revolution and civil war might well await that nation now "at the mercy of an army of hypocrites and scoundrels."[54] Many believed that Dreyfus was simply "chosen as a sacrifice for the honor of the French Army."[55] Their perspective on this aspect of the *Affaire* was best summarized by the Vancouver *Province*:

> Were it not that the peculiar temperament of the French people is so well known it might almost be thought that the crises which daily arrive exist only in the imagination of correspondents.... The French cannot or will not see that their army in which they place their complete confidence is absolutely untrustworthy... The bureaucracy which has ruled the army for years has been rotten to the core ... but the French in their blind faith refuse to recognize it.... In fact France is almost in a state of civil war. The time is opportune for the arrival of a new Napoleon for a strong man could beyond question establish himself as an autocrat in France now.[56]

The senior officers of the army—royalist, Catholic and conservative— were loyal to the traditional past; hence, their oath of loyalty to the Third Republic was worthless. Such royalist and Catholic inclinations might tempt them to stage a *coup d'état*.

Even casual observers of the *Affaire* recognized that powerful Catholic voices and organizations were prominent among the anti-Dreyfusards. The Catholic religious orders, especially the Assumptionists, were highly antisemitic. Throughout the tumult in 1898 and 1899, Leo XIII had not commented on the situation. In the fall of 1898, he had urged respect for constituted authority, but had done nothing to curb Catholic antisemitism. Not surprisingly, therefore, few French Catholics spoke out against the victimization of Dreyfus, and those who did soon became targets of abuse themselves.[57] From the time of the Zola trial, the religious question began to filter into the western-Canadian press. In February 1898, the *Victoria Daily Times* reported Max Nordau's insistence on Catholic complicity in the scandal, as well as warnings from the French minister of justice in September that the Jesuits and the pope were seeking to stir up antisemitic passions in the army in order to establish a military dictatorship in France under their direction.[58] The paper also carried F. C. Conybeare's attack on Catholicism in 1899.[59] The Nanaimo *Free Press* reported anti-Jesuit riots.[60] Such criticisms of French Catholicism, and everything else French, were easily accepted by Anglo-Saxon Protestants in a decade of Protestant Protective Association propaganda in North America. In fact, they were typical of the times. The new Anglo-Saxon hegemony of the United States and Britain, and the manifest destiny of Anglo-Saxondom to lead the rest of the world to 'civilization', was a constant theme in the British and American press and among politicians in the late 1890s.[61] At the time of the *Affaire*, the majority of western Canadians were primarily of Anglo-

American origin; thus it was perfectly natural, and in accord with the Darwinist determinism of the age, to regard any non-Anglo-Saxon people or polity as deficient. Anglo-Saxondom was revered and glorified. In the absence of French and Catholic influences, such a monstrous crime as that committed against Dreyfus would have been inconceivable. Besides its consequences for the fragmented and widely scattered French-speaking and Catholic minority of western Canada in the 1890s and afterwards, this constant denigration of the French caused the central issue of the *Affaire* — antisemitism — to disappear from sight.

Antisemitism

The realization that antisemitism was the essential ingredient in the persecution never quite materialized in the western-Canadian press. In October 1898, before international support for Dreyfus began to form, an editorial in the *Victoria Daily Times* simply proclaimed his guilt, although Russia, and not Germany, was identified as the beneficiary of his treason.[62] However, not all western Canadians were so easily deceived. Three days later, in a long and tightly reasoned letter to the editor, a Victorian lawyer, S. D. Schultz, insisted that antisemitism was the heart of the matter. He warned that "when the Drumonts and Rocheforts attempt to deduce from the isolated case of Dreyfus's alleged treason the generalization that all Jews are constitutionally traitors, then something more is involved than a mere academical discussion." His letter continued:

> What guarantee has the Jew in any country of being accorded the ordinary safeguards of justice, when the liberty-loving Frenchman at the close of the nineteenth century visits upon the Jew the vilest charges, tracing to him their social and economical troubles, and when enlightened Frenchmen, or "cultural criminals," like Drumont and Rochefort account it the loftiest patriotism to stir the masses to riot and rage against the "alien Jew." . . . The world will apparently never forget that twenty centuries ago the Jew produced a Judas. It pretends to remember, but really forgets, that the Jew also produced a Jesus.[63]

No newspaper editor grasped the central issue as thoroughly or forcefully.

Only at the time of Zola's trial did the western-Canadian press begin to attempt to explain the antisemitic outrages in France. Its readers were informed about current events and, on occasion, about who was instrumental in fomenting public passions. The *Victoria Daily Colonist* reported that, according to accounts from most of the large French towns, "the anti-Jewish crusade is assuming most menacing proportions."[64] To its credit, the *Victoria Daily Times* gave considerable attention to antisemitism during the Rennes trial, proffering the opinion that "the sympathy of Christendom is with the Jew."[65] The *Saskatchewan Herald* concluded that the verdict at Rennes was a deliberate judgment against Jews, not just Dreyfus.[66] The Nanaimo *Free Press* was one of many newspapers to report that European Jews were planning an international association to defend themselves against the anti-Jewish crusade that was expected to follow the Rennes trial.[67] It was one thing to recognize the presence of antisemitism; it was another thing to explain the demonstrations, riots and physical threats against French Jews. The simplest explanation was to resort to a circular argument. "Candide," whose column from Paris appeared on occasion in the Vancouver *Province*, informed his readers that, in the minds of most French citizens, the prevailing unrest was the result of "a vast Jewish conspiracy." Only his British readers "and an educated minority [in France] correctly understood its origins to lie in a miscarriage of justice."[68] The *Victoria Daily Times* noted that "Dreyfus is a Jew, and on the continent that is the bar sinister in politics."[69] The inference to be drawn was that only the French, and only the Catholics, were predisposed to antisemitism because of a profoundly corrupted character, temperament and religious sensibility. Antisemitism could not exist in any truly civilized country; it existed in France, therefore France was not truly civilized.

Such a smug, myopic view raises the obvious question as to how the western-Canadian newspapers usually portrayed Jews, and how western Canadians treated their own Jewish neighbours. Interestingly, the former usually had little to say about the Jews in their own communities. When they did deal with the subject, their reports and opinions were often flavoured with an antisemitic taste of their own. This glaring contradiction — castigating French antisemites while printing antisemitic material themselves — for the most part escaped editorial notice. Nor did any situation arise in Canada to force the journalists to examine this contradiction. This point is vital. The manner in which the western-Canadian newspapers treated Dreyfus, Jews and Judaism in their pages uncovers some blind spots in Canadian society during this period. Canada itself, in spite of popular opinion to the contrary, was not devoid of antisemitism.

In September 1898, several papers carried informative pieces about Rosh Hashanah and Yom Kippur. The Qu'Appelle *Progress* reported celebrations in Winnipeg, while the *Province* and the *Semi-Weekly World* described those in Vancouver.[70] The *Province* published a respectful recounting of the local rabbi's explanation of the new year, giving special place to his theme of "peace and goodwill."[71] The *Semi-Weekly World* described Yom Kippur in moving detail, proclaiming that "our Jewish fellow-citizens — and they are classed amongst our most enterprising and progressive people — will celebrate the Day of Atonement... this day which is so dear to the hearts of an ancient people who have done so much good in the world."[72] The *Victoria Daily Times* reprinted a short article extolling "A Remarkable Jewish Woman,"[73] and another praising Jews, especially British Jews, for living longer than their Christian neighbours because, as a rule, their lives were exemplary.[74] Many papers did not hesitate to laud Jewish abilities, ambitions or achievements. Yet, paradoxically, those same newspapers often seemed unable to recognize antisemitic undercurrents in other material that they published concurrently.

In the midst of the Rennes trial, the *Victoria Daily Colonist* agreed with Joseph Jacobs, president of the Jewish Historical Society, on the question of Jewish identity, declaring that the Jews "constitute a race of marvellous vitality." The editors were moved by the Jewish capacity to survive centuries of persecution. To elaborate this marvel, however, the *Colonist* developed at length a fundamentally racist hypothesis about head size and type as a scientific means of identifying Jews, a theory that was popular among European antisemites. Employing dubious mathematical calculations, the paper concluded:

> If in six generations the Jews have increased 900 per cent., they are in a fair way to become the dominant race in the whole world. . . . No other race is keeping pace with progress such as this. Indeed, it is unfortunately too true that some of the most advanced races of peoples are scarcely increasing at all. This is true of the French, and to a very large extent holds good of the New Englanders and the inhabitants of Ontario.[75]

In such speculations, antisemitic lies about impending Jewish domination and its nefarious consequences slip in easily.

Sometimes antisemitic rhetoric appeared in the guise of news from somewhere else. In early 1898, the *Winnipeg Daily Tribune* carried a report from Saginaw, Michigan, about a Jew who had feigned conversion to Christianity as a ruse to obtain money from the local churches. "Let me tell you one thing," he confessed, "there is no such thing as a converted Jew. Any Jew who pretends to be one is as big a swindler as I am."[76] Later in the same year, the Vancouver *Province* ran a sneering item entitled "Trouble in Jewry"[77] about a scuffle involving some Jews, following it a few weeks later with another piece about a "Dishonest Jew" in New York's garment district.[78] A year later, the *Victoria Daily Times* reprinted an article on "Jews and the Sweatshop," which accused Jewish clothing factory owners of operating sweatshops, "a condemnation . . . visited upon [them] with good cause."[79] This kind of generalization and innuendo turned up in most western-Canadian papers at some point in the late 1890s. The strangest example appeared in *The Regina Standard* in January 1899.[80] Rev. Clifton Harby Levy composed a three-column history of European antisemitism, detailing in a lurid fashion the central medieval accusations against Jews: poisoning wells, spreading the bubonic plague

and murdering Christian children for blood rituals at Passover. Two grue-
some illustrations accompanied his piece. Levy apparently hoped that this
detailed description of hoary myths and false charges would serve to ridicule contemporary Austrian antisemites, who were busily engaged in
reviving the plague accusation. However, no editorial comment accompanied his submission, leaving a certain ambiguity, if not a mixed message,
for the public to decipher. The article posed a critical dilemma. On the
one hand, the attempt to ridicule antisemitic ideas was apparently
intended to enable the *Standard*'s readers to recognize and reject them. On
the other hand, reprinting in this fashion the historic libels against Jews
ran the risk of resurrecting their visceral appeal as far as the credulous and
the superstitious were concerned. As the Dreyfus case demonstrated
unequivocally, it is not difficult to convert lies into truth.

A final example of the confusion evident in the western-Canadian press
is found in the response of *The Herald* (Calgary) and the *Victoria Daily
Times* to the American novelist Mark Twain's article "Concerning the
Jews," which was published in *Harper's New Monthly Magazine* in September 1899.[81] Intermingled with some philosemitic compliments, a little
sarcasm, and even a brief reference to the Dreyfus case, are found the
essential elements of antisemitism. For him, the word "Jew" signified
"both religion and race"; the "Jew" became all Jews everywhere, and in
every age.[82] Twain explained the persecution of the Jews as the consequence of their inherent greed for wealth and the power wealth conveys.
At least since the days of Joseph in Egypt, this grasping instinct has made
their neighbours jealous, causing them to feel hatred;[83] thus the victims
are to blame for their misfortunes, since financial success breeds justifiable
resentment and hatred. A standard antisemitic canard holds that all Jews
are financially successful; therefore, by Twain's reasoning, they invite and
should expect persecution. The American specifically excluded the crucifixion as the origin of antisemitism. Insisting instead on a Jewish predilec-
tion for deception, he offered many examples of the different kinds of
deceit. He was convinced, for instance, that Jews hide their true identities, causing him to conclude that their numbers are far greater than the
non-Jewish world realizes. Since Jews have a certain "reputation," and
since their true numbers are probably seriously underestimated, it is not
hard to exaggerate their influence. Twain attempted to excuse the
antisemitic tone of his article by couching it in terms of "what people
say"; however, he made no effort to refute the accusations that he
recounted. He insisted that the Jew will always be the "foreigner," the
"stranger" and the "outsider." As long as there are Jews in the world, they
will be pursued by the scourge: 'Jewish persecution is not a religious passion, it is a business passion."[84] Persecution is not personal; it is merely a
natural reaction to success. Significantly, Twain identified *no* other groups

whose financial acumen merited such resentment or justified persecution. The famous author's intentions in writing this article are not entirely clear, but its character is clear enough. It is a vindication of antisemitism.

The *Victoria Daily Times* printed three excerpts from the article immediately following its publication. The first excerpt, "Mark Twain on the Jews," was taken from a sympathetic section describing the ways in which "the Jew is not a disturber of the peace in any country," or a financial burden on society.[85] The other two excerpts are different. "Why Jews Have German Names" is Twain's recounting of the allegation that Jews do not always reveal their identities, thereby making it impossible to estimate accurately their numbers in any given country. It concludes with these words: "I am strongly of the opinion that we have an immense Jewish population in America."[86] Did the *Daily Times* intend to imply that the same might be true of Canada? Twain's opinion was in no way qualified or challenged by the editor. "Why Germans Persecute Jews" is an extract from a section of the *Harper's* article which sneers at German anxieties of the day that Jews control too much of the German economy, despite their supposedly small numbers. Twain was convinced that politicians adopted such postures in order to gain votes.[87] There the excerpt ends; however, the original article continues to explain why the Germans might be correct, in spite of the excessive shrillness of their declarations. This third extract, moreover, by citing a German lawyer and an Austrian agitator, contains an explicit expression of anti-Jewish hatred, including the view that Germany and Austria can be saved only by expelling and banishing their Jewish populations. Neither Twain nor the *Victoria Daily Times* condemned the obvious antisemitism of these men. The net effect was to imply that they were right.

The *Herald* (Calgary) took a somewhat different approach. In an editorial lauding Twain's article as having been written "in a spirit of absolute fairness and clearly without prejudice,"[88] the paper printed two extracts from Twain's explanation of the origins of the persecution of Jews: the story of Joseph in Egypt, and an account of so-called Roman anti-Judaism in the Christian era in order to demonstrate that hatred of Jews pre-dated Christianity. Immediately following the Twain excerpts, the editorial printed the reply to Twain by Cyrus L. Sulzberger in the *American Hebrew*, which attributed the Roman persecutions to the crucifixion of Jesus. Sulzberger noted that Twain was correct in recognizing that Jews made good citizens, but completely wrong on the question of greed: "that while superficially he [the Jew] may seem to have no purpose but material success, history attests again and again his willingness to forego this, rather than his world-purposes . . . his ideal of the brotherhood and unity of man and the fatherhood and unity of God." The *Herald's* editor took no stand on these matters, but did attempt to provide a forum for discussion.

Conclusion

The way in which the *Victoria Daily Times* and *The Herald* (Calgary) handled the Twain material underlines the basic problem. Unlike many parts
of Europe, antisemitism was not an evident social disorder in western
Canada. Jews were few in number, widely scattered and, for the most part,
invisible in the larger community. The legacy of the *Affaire* did not lie in
its immediate impact, but rather in the fact that the Canadian public was
conditioned by the press to accept the rise of a manifest antisemitism at a
later period. The western newspapers tended to explain the latter as a foreign phenomenon. While they printed frequent items on situations
involving Jews in Russia, Austria and Germany as well as France, their
appreciation was restricted geographically, first to these European countries, then to Europe itself. There was a pronounced inability to comprehend the pervasive influence of evil ideas and rhetoric *across* national lines.
To a large extent, this problem of perception was intensified by the habit
of glorifying Anglo-Saxon civilization, which, by definition, was free from
unseemly passions. Difficulties faced by Jews in Britain could be explained
in other ways; antisemitism was not seen as part of the British national character. Thus the papers never noticed that some of their material was riddled
with negative language and images. Editorials denouncing antisemitism per
se did not appear. While stories praising Jews were not absent, an understanding of the connection between the individual Jew and Jews in general
was missing. No one saw that antisemites assailed Jews in general in order
to provoke action against Jews as individuals. No one saw that antisemitism
was socially dangerous in Canada as well as elsewhere. Instead, the manner
in which the Dreyfus case was reported encouraged the acceptance of
antisemitic arguments more or less at face value. When attacks on Jews were
condemned, it was the violence that was castigated, not the ideology from
which it arose. This failure tacitly implied that the accusations might have
some validity after all, although certain standards of decorum were sacred,
and should always be observed in a British society.

By not attacking antisemitic ideas as such, the western papers revealed a
willingness to tolerate a vague and unreflective antisemitism in their own
society. This kind of amorphous prejudice went hand in hand with the
prevalent contempt for all 'foreigners', and 'outsiders' that dominated
western-Canadian thinking at the turn of this century. Such an attitude
was fraught with far-reaching consequences. It should surprise no one
that, in the 1920s, the Ku Klux Klan found western-Canadian sympathizers, or that the antisemitic undercurrents of early Social Credit rhetoric
were so easily accepted in Alberta, or that the University of Manitoba
established quotas to restrict the number of Jewish students admitted.[89]
Indeed, the very vagueness of the prejudice has ensured its survival in the

Canadian west to this day. Moreover, the entire approach of the western press to the Dreyfus affair casts light on the evolution of a popular twentieth-century Canadian habit of mind: terrible things happen in other places, but they do not happen at home. Consequently, racism and antisemitism do not exist in Canada. Canadians have taken comfort in the fact that Canadian history has been *relatively* free of these social evils. By assuming that Canada was *entirely* free of them, however, great harm has been done to countless minorities — the Jews and all other "outsiders." Worst of all, by virtue of this habit, such harm continues to be inflicted in our time.

Notes

1 This is a preliminary report of findings from a major research project in progress, examining the reaction across Canada to the Dreyfus case as a means of assessing the extent and nature of antisemitism in Canada during the 1890s.

2 The bibliography on the Dreyfus case is extremely large. The best, and now standard, work is Jean-Denis Bredin, *The Affair: The Case of Alfred Dreyfus*, trans. Jeffrey Mehlman (New York: George Braziller, 1983). As an example of how reaction to the Dreyfus case reveals something about antisemitism and attitudes toward Jews see: Egal Feldman, *The Dreyfus Affair and the American Conscience, 1895-1906* (Detroit: Wayne State University Press, 1981).

3 J. S. Woodsworth, *Strangers Within Our Gates* (reprinted [Toronto: University of Toronto Press, 1972]) is often regarded as representative of the attitudes of western Anglo-Canadians at the beginning of the twentieth century. A full-scale historical study of the question has yet to be undertaken.

4 F. H. Leacy, ed., *Historical Statistics of Canada*, 2nd ed. (Ottawa: Statistics Canada, 1983), series A2-14 and A78-93.

5 Leacy, *Historical Statistics*, series A125-63 and A164-84, and Louis Rosenberg, *A Gazeteer of Jewish Communities in Canada: 1851-1951* (Montreal: Canadian Jewish Congress, 1957).

6 An excellent general study of the press in late Victorian Canada is Paul Rutherford, *A Victorian Authority: The Daily Press in Late Nineteenth-Century Canada* (Toronto: University of Toronto Press, 1982).

7 For the history of the development of wire services in Canada, see M. E. Nichols, *(CP): The Story of the Canadian Press* (Toronto: Ryerson Press, 1948).

8 Harry Gutkin, *Journey into Our Heritage: The Story of the Jewish People in the Canadian West* (Toronto: Lester & Orpen Dennys, 1980), pp. 68-73, and Stuart E. Rosenberg, *The Jewish Community in Canada*, vol. 1 (Toronto: McClelland & Stewart, 1970), pp. 114-25.

9 Crawford Kilian, *Go Do Some Great Thing: The Black Pioneers of British Columbia* (Vancouver: Douglas & McIntyre, 1978), pp. 41-84, and Colin A. Thomson, *Blacks in Deep Snow: Black Pioneers in Canada* (Don Mills, ON: J. M. Dent, 1979), pp. 19-20.

10 Gutkin, *Journey*, pp. 73-75, and Rosenberg, *Gazeteer*, p. 74.

11 Cited in B. G. Sack, *History of the Jews in Canada*, trans. Ralph Novek (Montreal: Harvest House, 1965), p. 174.

12 *Manitoba Free Press*, May 8, 1880.

13 Ibid., May 27-30, 1882.

14 *Winnipeg Daily Times*, June 3, 1882, and *Manitoba Free Press*, June 5, 1882.

15 "Traitorous Conspiracy," *Victoria Daily Colonist*, November 16, 1894, and "Dreyfus the Traitor Knave," December 25, 1894.

16 "The Sentence of Capt. Dreyfus," *Daily News-Advertiser* (Vancouver), December 27, 1894.

17 "Skirted Court Spies,"*Regina Leader*, January 24, 1895.

18 E.g., "Dreyfus Degradation," *Free Press* (Nanaimo), January 5, 1895, and "A Soldier's Disgrace," January 7, 1895.

19 E.g., "Prison of a Traitor," *Victoria Daily Times*, May 9, 1895, a reprint from the *Herald* (New York).

20 *The Province* (Vancouver), January 26, 1895, untitled.

21 "Anti-Jewish Crusade," *Free Press* (Nanaimo), January 12, 1895.

22 "His Wife Gave Him Freedom," *The Progress* (Qu'Appelle), September 17, 1896.

23 See Bredin, *The Affair*, pp. 163-65.

24 "The Case of Dreyfus," *Semi-Weekly World* (Vancouver), November 23, 1897.

25 "Zola to Be Prosecuted," *Semi-Weekly World* (Vancouver), January 18, 1898.

26 E.g., "Anti-Jewish Riots," *Winnipeg Daily Tribune*, January 24, 1898; untitled, *Bulletin* (Edmonton), January 17, 20, 1898; and "The Anti-Semitic Disturbances," *Daily News-Advertiser* (Vancouver), January 21, 1898.

27 "The Dreyfus Case," *Daily News-Advertiser* (Vancouver), January 16, 1898.

28 E.g., "Anti-Hebrew Riot [St-Malo]," *Semi-Weekly World* (Vancouver), January 25, 1898; "The Antisemitic Demonstrations," *Daily News-Advertiser* (Vancouver), January 20, 1898; "A Jew Attacked," *The Vedette* (Fort Qu'Appelle), November 3, 1898; "The Hated Jews," *Daily News-Advertiser* (Vancouver), December 15, 1898.

29 "Jewish Circles Feel Panic," *Victoria Daily Colonist*, January 19, 1898.

30 Untitled, *Bulletin* (Edmonton), February 14, 1898.

31 "La Belle France," *Victoria Daily Times*, January 22, 1898.

32 "From Paris," *The Province* (Vancouver), February 12, 1898.

33 *Winnipeg Daily Tribune*, February 15, 1898, from the *Herald* (New York).

34 "Savage and Brutal Sentence of Zola," *Winnipeg Daily Tribune*, February 24, 1898.

35 "The Case of Zola," *Semi-Weekly World* (Vancouver), February 25, 1898.

36 Untitled, *The Province* (Vancouver), February 26, 1898.

37 "Two Famous Trials," *The Herald* (Calgary), March 8, 1898. A number of biting satires appeared in various newspapers: e.g., "Dooley on Dreyfus," *The Province* (Vancouver), September 12, 1898; "Mr. Dooley" was the Irish-American pundit on everything under the sun created by American humorist Finley Peter Dunne. *The Herald* (Calgary) ran "Mr. Dooley" on February 23, 1899 and a satire on "French Justice" on August 30, 1899; *The Regina Standard* reprinted a parody "Dreyfus and the Judge" from the Memphis *Commercial Appeal* on September 20, 1899.

38 "Dreyfus on the Stage," *The Province* (Vancouver), April 9, 1898. The *Regina Leader* reported on June 8, 1899 that a salesman for the Manitoba Assurance Company had detected strong similarities between the Dreyfus case and Charles Reade's novel *A Terrible Temptation*; on September 13, 1899 it carried Sir Edward Russell's observation that the *Affaire* resembled *Mathilda* by Eugène Sue.

39 "Zola's Trial," *Winnipeg Daily Tribune*, February 14, 1898, and "Zola Trial," February 25, 1898.

40 "The Situation in France," *Daily News-Advertiser* (Vancouver), September 21, 1898.

41 "Capt. Dreyfus Innocent," *Saskatchewan Herald* (Battleford), October 15, 1898.

42 "Notes," *The Progress* (Qu'Appelle), July 13, 1899.

43 "The Dreyfus Farce," *The Herald* (Calgary), August 29, 1899.

44 "Notes," *The Progress* (Qu'Appelle), August 31, 1899.

45 "Dreyfus in Alberta," *The Herald* (Calgary), September 1, 1899.

46 "Dreyfus Arrives at Nantes," *The Herald* (Calgary), September 21, 1899; "Dreyfus Going to Texas," *Victoria Daily Times*, September 23, 1899; and "Dreyfus Coming to Texas," *Semi-Weekly World* (Vancouver), September 26, 1899.

47 Untitled, *Victoria Daily Colonist*, September 19, 1899.

48 "Our London Letter," *The Regina Standard*, October 11, 1899.

49 "The Dreyfus Case," *Victoria Daily Times*, June 1, 1899.

50 "French Army Officers," *The Herald* (Calgary), November 23, 1898.

51 "The French Tragedy," *Victoria Daily Times*, August 17, 1899.

52 "The Dreyfus Case," *Saskatchewan Herald* (Battleford), June 2, 1899.

53 "Justice for Dreyfus," *Victoria Daily Times*, July 1, 1899.

54 "The Dreyfus Farce," *The Herald* (Calgary), September 11, 1899.

55 "Honor of the Army," *Victoria Daily Times*, September 20, 1899, and "The Rennes Verdict," *The Province* (Vancouver), September 9, 1899.

56 "Troubles in France," *The Province* (Vancouver), June 13, 1899.

57 Bredin, *The Affair*, pp. 288-92, 346-53; Maurice Larkin, *Church and State after the Dreyfus Affair: The Separation Issue in France* (London: Macmillan, 1974), pp. 63-79; John McManners, *Church and State in France 1870-1914* (London: SPCK, 1972), pp. 74-80, 118-28; Edouard Lecannuet, *Les Signes avant-coureurs de la séparation* (Paris: Librairie Félix Alcan, 1930), pp. 132-97; and C. S. Phillips, *The Church in France 1848-1907* (New York: Russell & Russell, 1936) [1937], pp. 237-58.

58 "Massacre of Jews," *Victoria Daily Times*, February 4, 1898. Max Nordau was a Jewish Hungarian expatriate living in Paris famous for his commentaries on European matters which were reprinted widely via the wire services. See also "Taking a Religious Turn — The Jesuits & the Pope Fighting in France's Turmoil," *Victoria Daily Times*, September 29, 1898.

59 "The Dreyfus Affair," *Victoria Daily Times*, June 30, 1899. Frederick Cornwallis Conybeare was a British journalist who reported extensively on the Dreyfus case with a pronounced anti-Catholic bias, often signing his articles "Huguenot."

60 "Anti-Jesuit Riot," *Free Press* (Nanaimo), July 12, 1899.

61 See Feldman, *The Dreyfus Affair*, chaps. 3 and 4, for a particularly fine discussion of this point.

62 "The Dreyfus Case," *Victoria Daily Times*, October 5, 1898.

63 "The Dreyfus Case," *Victoria Daily Times*, October 8, 1898. Samuel D. Schultz, son of a leading pioneer Jewish family in Victoria, was appointed a Judge of the County Court at Vancouver in 1914.

64 "France Boiling Over," *Victoria Daily Colonist*, January 19, 1899.

65 "The Dreyfus Case," *Victoria Daily Times*, June 24, 1899; see also "Rennes, Trial City," July 12, 1899, which described it as a place "fanatic in its hatred of Jews."

66 "The Dreyfus Case," *Saskatchewan Herald* (Battleford), September 13, 1899.

67 "Declared Outlaws," *Free Press* (Nanaimo), August 15, 1899.

68 "From Paris," *The Province* (Vancouver), March 12, 1898.

69 'Justice to Dreyfus," *Victoria Daily Times*, September 14, 1898.

70 "General News," *The Progress* (Qu'Appelle), September 22, 1898.

71 "Jewish New Year," *The Province* (Vancouver), September 19, 1898.

72 "The Tenth Day of Tishri," *Semi-Weekly World* (Vancouver), September 27, 1898.

73 "A Remarkable Jewish Woman" (Mrs. Solomon Sassoon of Delhi), *Victoria Daily Times*, October 21, 1898.

74 "Jewish Tenacity of Life," *Victoria Daily Times*, June 30, 1899.

75 "Are Jews Jews?" *Victoria Daily Colonist*, August 13, 1899.

76 "A Converted Jew — A Confession," *Winnipeg Daily Tribune*, January 11, 1898; see also "Converted Jew's Trouble," *Victoria Daily Colonist*, May 27, 1898.

77 "Trouble in Jewry," *The Province* (Vancouver), September 4, 1898.

78 "Dishonest Jew," *The Province* (Vancouver), September 30, 1898. The same item ran again the next day.

79 "Jews & the Sweatshop," *Victoria Daily Times*, August 29, 1899.

80 "Anti-Semitic Outrages Again Threatened," *The Regina Standard*, January 19, 1899.

81 Mark Twain, "Concerning the Jews," *Harper's New Monthly Magazine* (September 1899): 527-35.

82 Ibid., p. 528.

83 Ibid., p. 530.

84 Ibid., p. 535.

85 "Mark Twain on the Jews," *Victoria Daily Times*, September 27, 1899.

86 "Why Jews Have German Names," *Victoria Daily Times*, September 23, 1899.

87 "Why Germans Persecute Jews," *Victoria Daily Times*, October 11, 1899.

88 "Mark Twain and the Jews," *The Herald* (Calgary), September 30, 1899.

89 Julian Sher, *White Hoods: Canada's Ku Klux Klan* (Vancouver: New Star Books, 1983), pp. 31-59; William Calderwood, "Religious Reactions to the Ku Klux Klan in Saskatchewan," *Saskatchewan History* (Autumn 1973): 103-14; Henry Trachtenberg, "The Winnipeg Jewish Community in the Inter-War Period, 1919-1939: Anti-Semitism and Politics," *Canadian Jewish Historical Society Journal* (Spring 1980): 44-70; David R. Elliott, "Anti-Semitism and the Social Credit Movement: The Intellectual Roots of the Keegstra Affair," *Canadian Ethnic Studies* (1985): 78-89; and Percy Barsky, "How 'Numerus Clausus' Was Ended in the Manitoba Medical School," *Canadian Jewish Historical Society Journal* (October 1977): 75-81.

5

Antisemitism in Ontario: The Twentieth Century

Stephen Speisman

Prelude

Mid-nineteenth-century Ontario was a society that prized what it perceived to be the best characteristics of British civilization: religion, monarchy, respectability, industry and charity. Those few Jews who had settled
in the province during this period fitted the mould precisely. The English
Jews of Toronto, for the most part affiliated with the Toronto Hebrew
Congregation (Holy Blossom, founded 1856), and the central Europeans
of Anshe Sholom in Hamilton (established 1863), were middle-class merchants, sharing the social values of the general population as well as its
loyalty to the Crown. The opening of the Richmond St. synagogue of
Holy Blossom in 1876 was considered a joyous event for the entire community; a significant number of Christians had contributed to the building fund, with many attending the dedication in January of that year.[1]
Local non-Jews responded generously during the following decade to
financial appeals by the Anglo-Jewish Association, which was striving to
locate European Jewish immigrants in the Canadian west. In the late
1890s, when the Toronto congregation erected its new Bond St. building,
financial support was again forthcoming, and, at the opening ceremonies,
its president, Alfred Benjamin, praised the "courtesy, sympathy and liber-
ality" exhibited by gentiles toward Toronto Jews. The dedication was
attended by Mayor Shaw, some members of Parliament and even by the
well-known author and journalist Goldwin Smith, who held pronounced
anti-Jewish views.[2]

Notes for Chapter 5 are on pp. 129-33.

By this time, the Jews of Holy Blossom were sufficiently confident of their relationship with their Christian neighbours to be vocal in matters of civic policy, even when it involved the church. A proposal to introduce Christian instruction into public schools of Toronto elicited a statement of protest from the leaders of the established Jewish community—the Reverend Abraham Lazarus, Alfred Benjamin and Edmund Scheuer— calling upon the church to follow the example of the synagogue in confining religious instruction to congregational schools.[3] In the late 1890s, moreover, Christians frequently attended Mr. Lazarus's Friday evening lectures at Holy Blossom. In addition, the Toronto Jewish Literary and Social Union met occasionally with a club from Bond St. Congregational Church, and English Jews involved themselves socially with non-Jews. This fraternization was illustrated by the large number of Christians who attended the confirmation ceremonies at Holy Blossom in 1899.[4] There were other signs of progress as well. By 1898, Etta Birkenthal, the daughter of the rabbi of Anshe Sholom in Hamilton, had been appointed the assistant principal of a Toronto public school; a few members of Holy Blossom belonged to fashionable social clubs and participated in the St. George Society, the Masonic Order, the Albany Club and the Municipal Reform Association; Rabbi Solomon Jacobs, who served Holy Blossom from 1900 until his death in 1920, was active in civic life, addressing Christian congregations and holding an executive position in the Associated Charities of Toronto.[5] There were even instances of prominent gentile families accepting dinner invitations at Jewish homes.[6]

However, despite the public cordiality, there was a significant social exclusion of even the most acculturated Jewish families. The majority did not belong to the social clubs, and few appear to have been invited to non-Jewish homes. This was accepted as more or less natural, leaving Jews to satisfy their social needs within their own communities. Nevertheless, whatever antisemitism existed in late nineteenth- and early twentieth-century Ontario remained latent as long as the projected image of the Jews was derived from the middle-class Anglo-Jewish members of Holy Blossom.

The Winds of Change

North American Jewry was transformed by events in Europe during the three decades following 1880. The introduction of the May Laws in the Russian Empire, pogroms, conscription and the late arrival of the Industrial Revolution both there and in Austria-Hungary prompted many thousands of Jews across the Atlantic to search for a better life elsewhere.[7] By 1901, there were over 3000 Jews in Ontario, as compared to 534 in 1881; by 1911, the Jews in Toronto had increased by 401 percent, five times the rate of the general population; between 1911 and 1913 alone, the number of Jews in the city increased from just over 18 000 to about 32 000. By the early 1920s, the figure would stand at almost 35 000.[8]

East European Jews arriving in Ontario, as elsewhere in North America, had few choices. They had to live where employment and accommodation were available quickly and cheaply—factors which, coupled with their desire to be together for religious reasons as well as a feeling of security, created easily identifiable settlement areas in the larger cities.[9] Moreover, seeking employment in occupations which required little capital while supplying some degree of independence, the immigrants either gravitated to rag-picking, bottle-washing and trading in used furniture or became peddlers in the cities and in the countryside. In all cases, these were jobs with low prestige, the very success of which often demanded an intrusion into the life and neighbourhood of the prospective customer. By 1916, there were 600 Jewish rag peddlers in Toronto alone.[10] The new Jews were different from the old: Yiddish-speaking, often bearded, poorly dressed slum-dwellers who emerged to hawk their wares or otherwise make their living from the discards of 'respectable' citizens.

The cultural heritage of the non-Jewish Ontarians included considerably more than those British values that they held in common with the Jews of Holy Blossom and Anshe Sholom. Ultimately, it included the hoary Christian belief that, having rejected Jesus as their messiah, the Jews were a people condemned to suffer throughout history. For centuries, church-influenced legislation reflected this attitude, limiting Jewish citizenship and social and economic participation in society with the aim of preventing Jews from ever exercising authority over Christians. As a result of the restrictions imposed upon them, and the manner in which they were forced to earn a livelihood, they came to be branded as social exploiters, devoid of business ethics, yet with a special aptitude for commerce which made them dangerous competitors.[11] Incapable of assimilation into the gentile world, according to conventional wisdom, they were capable nevertheless of positing a constant economic threat. This economic aspect of European antisemitism, more than its explicit religious roots, remained dominant (even if latent) in the minds of many Ontario Christians, especially Protestants. It required only a fear of social and economic upheaval to bring it to the surface.

For the most part, the English and German Jews who had arrived in the province during the nineteenth century did not conform to the traditional image. On the contrary, they exhibited a degree of culture and respectability—even in their religious practices—that supported the social order; therefore they escaped the fate of the pariah in the Christian world and achieved a measure of acceptance. This was not the case with the newcomers. It was not difficult to see in the urban rag picker or the aggressive country peddler the embodiment of the stereotypical Jew. Could such a bizarre creature with such strange manners possibly be absorbed into Canadian society? With such aggressive business traits, would he become a threatening competitor? Or, on the other hand, would his poverty make him a social burden? Having murdered the Russian Tsar (as some accused the new immigrant) would he not import political radicalism into Ontario? Having fled Russian conscription (notwithstanding 25 years of forced service while subject to forced conversion), could the Jew be trusted to become a loyal citizen?[12] In Europe, these sentiments asserted themselves in discriminatory legislation or acts that affected the whole of Jewry. In North America in general, and in Ontario in particular, they affected individuals rather than the entire Jewish community.

Antisemitism

As east European Jews became more visible in Ontario society with the onset of the twentieth century, so too did the evidence of antisemitism. Prior to 1900, only the *Telegram* among the Toronto press seized every opportunity to point out the Jewishness of any Jew unfortunate enough to appear in court, whether as plaintiff or defendant; after 1900, this practice became widespread. Now fearful of an increasing Jewish population, newspapers suggested that Jewish votes could be bought.[13] Jewish visitors to Ontario cities in the years immediately before World War I were struck by this growth in hostility. For the most part, however, this hostility was still directed at Jews not of English parentage, although many of the latter had been born in Toronto, and were prominent, educated and affluent Canadian citizens. If, as late as 1907, the *Jewish Times* could take pride in the fact that Jews were not excluded wholesale from Canadian hotels, as was the case in some localities in the United States, by 1911 this claim could no longer be made. So many Jews in the vicinity of Toronto were being denied admission to swimming facilities that a group of prosperous individuals had to purchase a farm outside the city for the purpose of establishing their own resort.[14]

This decade and the next saw anti-Jewish sentiments appear whenever Jews attempted to find employment outside the factory. Major retail establishments seldom hired them as sales staff, nor did banks as clerks and tellers. Teaching positions in the public schools, as a rule, were unavailable to Jewish applicants, as were internships at hospitals. Those entering law and engineering discovered that gentile firms would not employ them; physicians and other professionals setting up practice for themselves had difficulty renting office space in fashionable districts, and had to disguise the fact that they were Jews in order to acquire suitable facilities. Although two Jewish practitioners held posts at the Toronto Western Hospital during the 1920s, no Jewish doctor was to obtain a clinical appointment at the University of Toronto or, with one possible exception, an indoor staff position at a teaching hospital in Toronto until after World War II.[15]

At the turn of the century, it was not uncommon for bearded Jewish peddlers who ventured outside the immigrant ghetto to be attacked physically in the streets. Hence, in some areas of Toronto, east European Jewish parents had to instruct their children to make themselves inconspicuous in order to avoid being assaulted. While other non-Anglo-Saxon immigrants, notably the Italians, experienced difficulties as well, in few cases was discrimination as widespread or as vehement as that levelled against the Jews.[16] Moreover, the post-World War I era saw Ontario Jewry the object of that widespread paranoia and xenophobia which swept the whole of North America following the Bolshevik Revolution in Russia. Because Jews had been active in European movements for social change, and because Yiddish was so closely related to German, the language which Canadian newspapers associated with anarchism and Bolshevism, it was not difficult to see every Jew as a revolutionary, and Yiddish as the vehicle for the overthrow of Canadian society.[17] Consequently, the 1920s abounded with unfavourable newspaper comments stereotyping Jews as dangerous aliens flooding Canadian cities and gaining positions of influence, while refusing to assimilate. In 1921, the *Globe* complained of a Jewish invasion of the public schools, and in 1923 it published an editorial describing the Jews as possessing an inherent instinct for commerce. In the same year, another *Globe* editorial attributed antisemitism to the Jews' resistance to assimilation, maintaining that they were "the brains of the Communist movement in Germany as in Russia and elsewhere."[18]

Dire Warnings and Ominous Portents

This attribution of radicalism was coupled with and reinforced by the traditional old-world view of the Jew as a threat to Christian society. When Jewish parents in the mid-1920s objected to the practice of compelling Jewish public school pupils in Toronto to sing Christian hymns and memorize passages from the New Testament, Trustee Wanless replied by accusing them of attempting to dominate the educational system. Canada, he declared, was a Christian country, and Jews "are not and cannot be citizens of any country except their own — and that is Palestine."[19] In a similar vein, the Anglican Good Friday message for the Diocese of Toronto in 1926 echoed the popular belief in an insidious invasion of Canada by Jews, warning of the menace to the established order as these unbelievers took over sections of cities, attended the universities, and dominated the press, high finance, drama and politics. In the same period, the *Telegram* observed that "The rate of increase compared with that of Hebrews, does not put the Gentiles in a winning place. The Jews are not creeping in. They are coming by leaps and bounds. . . ."[20] The paper asserted,

An influx of Jews puts a worm next (to) the kernel of every fair city where they get a hold. These people have no national tradition. . . . They engage in the wars of no country, but flit from one to another under passports changed with chameleon swiftness, following up the wind the smell of lucre. They are not the material out of which to shape a people holding a national spirit. They remain cosmopolitan while war drains the blood of the solid citizens of a nation. Not on the frontiers among the pioneers of plough and axe are they found, but in the cities where the low standards of life cheapen all about them.

. . . Jews of all countries should be discriminated against as a race by a poll tax so high that friends in Montreal and Toronto and Winnipeg would have their resources strained to the utmost to lend their tribes-men through foreign post more than enough to bring a baker's dozen per annum. . . .[21]

Blatant declarations such as the above elicited protest from some Jews, but the typical Jewish reaction was to attempt to remain as inconspicuous as possible, ingratiating themselves to the non-Jewish population. For example, *Canadian Jewish Review*, the English-language Jewish periodical most widely read in Ontario in the 1920s, urged its readers to behave in a circumspect manner at summer resorts, while Jewish organizations were careful to eschew dancing and other frivolous behaviour on Sundays.[22] This was in marked contrast to other immigrant groups. Comparing Jews and Italians, the *Canadian Jewish Review* noted sadly in 1924 that, when the great tenor Giovanni Martinelli sang in Toronto, the Italians immediately claimed him as their own. But when the great violinist Jascha Heifetz appeared, he was advertised as a Russian! "Jews though much stronger in numbers are afraid to be that natural. . . ."[23] The community at large was not devoid of support for its Jewish residents. The *Star* maintained that the *Telegram*'s stance "should be repudiated by all decent people. . . . It does not represent Toronto opinion."[24] However, while explicit attacks on the Jewish character were not favoured as a rule by most people in the province, an irrational fear nevertheless prevailed. The Jewish presence in certain neighbourhoods was seen as certain to depreciate property values, and there appears to have been considerable hesitation to deal with Jews in business. Less than a week after its objection to the *Telegram* article in 1921, the *Star* accepted an advertisement from a Toronto retail clothier advising the public that the firm was "strictly Gentile, owned and man-aged by Canadians in Canadian interests."[25]

By the early 1930s, the stereotype of the Jew as undesirable was firmly entrenched, at least among those who had little personal contact with indi-vidual Jews, a fact demonstrated unequivocally in a body of research undertaken during 1933-34 by Esther Einbinder, a graduate student at the University of Toronto. In spite of being perceived as intelligent and hard-working, with a good family life, appreciative of the arts, sometimes a loyal friend and honest businessman (even though he drove a hard bargain), the Jew was characterized primarily as being vulgar, dishonest in business and a ruthless and unfair competitor. Businessmen tended to think that employing Jews would affect their prestige adversely with customers or cause friction with other employees.[26] Their undesirable image was reinforced by the occupations in which many were engaged. One respondent in Einbinder's report described a personal reaction:

> The very appearances of Jews as they went about the streets with their rags or appeared slouching about the doorways of their dirty second-hand stores filled me with dislike and as a small child I always ran for home if I saw one coming. They always struck me as disagreeable. This attitude has lasted.[27]

Einbinder concluded that anti-Jewish hostility was evident least among teachers and the clergy, somewhat greater among physicians and lawyers (who perhaps had to compete with Jews on a professional level) and greatest among businessmen, almost 70 percent of whom preferred not to deal with Jewish firms. She found that attitudes toward Jews ranged from total dislike to total acceptance, with the most favourable opinions coming from those with the most personal contact.

Few of the persons interviewed by Einbinder had experienced actual antisemitism themselves, but Jews then (and now) characteristically avoided situations in which they were likely to encounter discrimination. Those who applied for jobs or moved out of the Jewish neighbourhoods confronted very real prejudice. "Last year I was refused a position on a playground," one Jewish university student replied in response to Einbinder's inquiry, "being definitely told that many Gentiles were waiting for the position so I would not even need to make out an application." Another recounted his experience when his family moved into a predominantly gentile neighbourhood in 1918: the family and their guests alike were pelted with stones by non-Jewish boys! "Complaints to parents met with no success as they were too strongly antagonistic. We lived on the street for fifteen years and yet were always outriders [outsiders]. The greatest compliment offered was 'you are different than other Jews.' "[28]

The onset of the Great Depression, producing, as it did, extremist movements on both the right and the left, affected attitudes toward Jews in Ontario as elsewhere. Canadian fascism was especially significant, since it "drew its basic strength from a prevalent if largely latent anti-semitism," playing on nativist and racist feelings in Canadian public opinion.[29] The movement found its most fertile ground in Quebec, where nationalism, encouraged by the Roman Catholic establishment and intensified by economic decline, made the Jew a convenient scapegoat. Patriotic societies such as the Goglus, founded by Adrien Arcand and Joseph Ménard in 1929, emphasized the purification of society and politics, as well as an *Achat chez nous* policy. From 1930 onward, the three weekly newspapers edited by Arcand spewed forth antisemitic articles playing upon both religious and nationalistic sentiments in the province. Arcand even republished the *Protocols of the Elders of Zion*, which promulgated the theory of a Jewish conspiracy to dominate the world. Ontario was not immune to his propaganda. Arcand's National Social Christian Party, led by an Ottawa policeman, Jean Tissot, urged a boycott of Jewish stores in the capital, particularly the store owned by Archie Freiman, a prominent Jewish layman and the president of the Zionist Council of Canada. During the federal election of 1935, in which Tissot was a candidate, Arcand's *Le Patriote* appeared in an English edition in Ottawa, vilifying Freiman and Jews in general in the most explicit stereotypical terms. Tissot even attempted to organize an association of Christian merchants to drive Jewish competitors out of the city.[30] However, these efforts were largely unsuccessful. The *Ottawa Journal* declared, not altogether with justification, that "racial prejudice is foreign to Canadian tradition and abhorrent to all instincts of fairness and decency,"[31] and, in 1935, Freiman was able to conduct a successful slander suit against *Le Patriote* in the Supreme Court of Ontario. Thus Tissot's attempt to rally Christian storekeepers came to nothing.

Social Exclusion

Elsewhere in Ontario, anti-Jewish feeling was usually expressed in a less overt fashion; nonetheless, it was both profound and widespread, and grew more intense as the Depression deepened. Its foundation lay in the belief, held by many if not most Anglo-Saxon Ontarians, that the essential nature of Ontario, as defined by British traditions of liberty, parliamentary government and Protestantism, was threatened by alien elements incapable of being assimilated into Anglo-Saxon society. Presumably, only those of British stock could understand the institutions which were the pride and soul of the province. These sentiments came to the fore increasingly in urban areas, with their visible concentrations of Jews. In Toronto, for example, there were 45 000 Jews by the early 1930s. Some of the more prosperous sought to purchase homes in the better residential areas, as well as to join social and sporting clubs and even, in a few cases, to enrol their children in private schools. The Anglo-Saxon upper-middle-class especially was revolted by the prospect. Its social atmosphere, as one of its number recalled, "while genteel in tone, was thoroughly anti-semitic. . . ."[32] Not surprisingly, the gentile elite reacted by seeking to minimize contact with Jews, excluding them from positions of authority in major businesses and banks, limiting their participation in the professions and keeping them out of the teaching positions. "We can't get these positions because we are Jews," announced Sam Factor, the Jewish MP from Toronto Centre West in 1933. Jews who entered the professions tended to concentrate in those where they could be self-employed: law and medicine as opposed to architecture, accountancy and engineering.[33]

An effective device in the social exclusion of Jews was the restrictive covenant, a condition written into the property deed preventing its sale to Jews or to others whom the vendor might find objectionable. Such covenants were often found in desirable residential areas (sometimes simply in the form of unwritten "gentlemen's agreements" among neighbours), and in resort districts such as those adjacent to Lake Simcoe.[34] Until after World War II, they were invariably upheld by the courts. Another prevalent manifestation of this antisemitic backlash was the mushrooming of signs in recreation areas indicating that Jews were not welcome. Examples abound throughout the 1930s and into the early 1940s: in May 1937, Clapperson's Camps, Port Loring, advertised as follows in the Cleveland *Plain Dealer*: "excellent fishing, low rates, gentiles only"; signs reading "Christians Only Need Apply," "Gentiles Only" and "No Jews Wanted" appeared on the Toronto Islands and elsewhere in resorts along Lake Ontario; at Musselman's Lake and Mossington Park, Jackson's Point north of Toronto; at Long Branch Dance Hall west of the city; at Lakeside Point, Scarborough; at Highland Park in Rouge Hill; and at resorts as disparately located as Grand Bend near London, Peterborough, Bronte and Gravenhurst. One Oshawa resort, Pleasant Valley Ranch, advertised its restrictive policy by means of a sound truck![35]

There were some interesting configurations. In Toronto, late in the 1930s, the Cawthra Mansions Tea Room blatantly exhibited a sign indicating that the establishment catered only to gentiles. When an atheistic British civil servant visited Ottawa and expressed concern about the number of restaurants and hotels that were restricted to Christians, he was advised that the restrictions applied only to Jews.[36] Atheists were welcome! In Hamilton, when four Jews were refused admission to a tennis club which rented property from the city, provoking a request from the Canadian Jewish Congress that Hamilton Parks revise their agreement to prevent exclusion on social or religious grounds, no reply was received. In Toronto, the Jewish Hudson Tennis Club was refused admission to the local tennis association because of the objection of the Parkdale and Humber clubs.[37] Although liberals such as the Reverend Salem Bland registered their objection to such practices, even they took it for granted that landlords and resort owners had a right to discriminate by race and religion; they simply ought not to advertise so blatantly.[38] Discrimination, therefore, continued unabated and was considered acceptable and natural by the general population. Jews continued to encounter difficulty in finding employment in non-Jewish firms. Insurance companies routinely refused to insure them or charged higher rates, maintaining that they were bad risks. When a certain Dr. Ginsberg of London, Ontario, applied to change his name to "Kingsley," the judge refused his request on the grounds that his only purpose was to conceal the fact that he was Jewish from those not wishing to use a Jewish physician. In 1939, when a Jewish group in Buffalo received a hockey franchise, Conn Smythe, the managing director of Maple Leaf Gardens, expressed his public displeasure. When confronted with the issue by the Canadian Jewish Congress, he declared himself unable to understand its concern.[39]

Political Vicissitudes

Progress in producing provincial legislation to minimize discrimination on the basis of race or creed was slow. In 1932, E. F. Singer, the first Jewish member of the Ontario legislature, was able to secure an amendment to the Insurance Act prohibiting insurance companies from engaging in discriminatory practices, but it was difficult to police the motives behind the "bad risk" designation, and insurers were reticent about their procedures. When, in February of the following year, Hamilton MPP Argue Martin introduced a bill to outlaw signs and advertisements that discriminated on the basis of race, the Legal Bills Committee refused even to send it to the legislature on the ground that it represented a restriction on freedom of speech and was probably unenforceable. Nonetheless, such legislation might have acted as a deterrent. Even before the introduction of Martin's bill, the Toronto City Council had forced the removal of an offensive sign. After the bill was set aside, however, the sign reappeared; the defeat of the bill was rightly seen by local Jews as a licence to discriminate.[40]

Ontario Jews had reason to hope for change when Premier George Henry's Conservative government was replaced by that of Liberal Mitchell Hepburn. John J. Glass, a Jewish lawyer and former Toronto alderman, now sat on the Government side. Glass had long been an advocate of anti-discrimination laws and, in the summer of 1932, as chairman of the City of Toronto Parks Commission, had attempted to eliminate "Gentiles Only" signs on the island by forbidding the erection of any signs on city property without the approval of the Commission.[41] His indignation had been intensified by his experience in the recent provincial campaign. The fascist candidate opposing him had based his campaign on antisemitism, advocating a boycott of Jewish stores. Glass had resolved to secure legislation which would prevent the slandering of groups in the same manner as the law protected individuals. But his proposal met with a less than enthusiastic public response. *The Globe and Mail* called it "mischievous, undemocratic and anti-British" and maintained that, though it might protect the Jews, it would give communists and fascists a right to the same protection. The paper urged Jews to ignore antisemitic advertisements and fascist propaganda; these would disappear for lack of attention.[42] Labour, fearing suppression itself, also expressed concern, while the usually sympathetic liberal clergy saw danger in such legislation as well. Consequently, Premier Hepburn and MPP David Croll decided that, in light of this negative reaction, the time was not ripe for the introduction of such a bill; if thrown out, it would have greater difficult winning acceptance at a later date.[43] Since, moreover, this kind of legislation really belonged constitutionally in the federal sphere, Glass was persuaded not to introduce it. Once again, the Jews saw the antisemites being given *carte blanche*. Even if violent incidents such as those at Balmy Beach and Christie Pits in Toronto in 1933 had not been repeated, they were still fresh in the mind of the community, and, as the decade progressed, fascist propaganda and anti-Jewish discrimination continued unabated.

New Dangers

The Balmy Beach affair, which involved the harassment of Jewish bathers in a lakefront park in eastern Toronto by bands of Anglo-Saxon youths sporting the swastika, almost culminated in a physical clash. Later in the summer, violence broke out in Christie Pits in west-end Toronto following a baseball game in which a largely Jewish team was matched against an Anglo-Saxon team. Here, again, the swastika appeared. Although, in each incident, it was apparent that the motivation for most of the anti-Jewish participants had more to do with local unemployment and general xenophobia than with Nazi-style or fascist-instigated antisemitism, the use of the Nazi symbol and taunts were traumatic for Toronto Jews.[44] Genuine attempts at fascist recruitment in Ontario, such as that led by a German immigrant, Otto Becker, in Kitchener in 1933 — attempts that involved a few members of the Toronto Swastika Club associated with the Balmy Beach incident — did nothing to assuage their fears. Neither did the formation of a Swastika Association of Canada dedicated to supporting the gentile business interests across the country.[45]

As time advanced, economic problems, traditional hostility to Jews and foreigners and, indeed, the effects of Nazi propaganda from overseas disseminated through local fascists produced a deterioration in local relations between Jews and the rest of the population. It became increasingly acceptable in the gentile community not only to discriminate, but to voice open disdain. In the autumn of 1937, for instance, Mayor R. K. Serviss of Galt called a local alderman, S. Lunenfeld, "a bloody Jew" during a council meeting, elaborating his insult with these words: "I have no more respect for a Jew than Hitler has. It is time he was told he was a Hebrew, and what a Gentile thinks of a Hebrew."[46] Another significant factor in the deteriorating position of the Jew in the late 1930s was his association in the public mind with the political left, and Anglo-Ontario feared communists more than it feared fascists. There was a real dread of revolution in Canada at this time. The Winnipeg General Strike of 1919 had been seen by the Ontario middle-class as nothing less than the herald of Bolshevism, a threat not only to property but also to Christianity, morality and everything treasured in Anglo-Saxon civilization. The patriotism and monarchism of veterans returning from World War I had intensified the conservative atmosphere of the province.

Jews had not been the founders of the Canadian communist movement; yet, because so many Jewish immigrants had arrived from eastern Europe following the Russian Revolution, it was easy to believe that they were infected with Bolshevism. To make matters worse, a few Jews did become prominent in the Ontario section of the Communist party in the 1920s. These included Maurice Spector, intellectual and lieutenant to leader Jack MacDonald; Becky and Michael Buhay; Annie Butler, business manager of *The Worker*; and Harvey Murphy (né Chernikovski). Hence, although much of the financial support for the party came from Finnish and Ukrainian ethnic associations, the public associated it primarily with Jews, an attitude reinforced in Toronto by its habit of holding conventions and rallies in the Standard Yiddish Theatre on Spadina Avenue. The public attitude was personified in Brigadier General Denis Draper, who assumed the position of Chief Constable in the city in 1928. Draper's efforts to disperse or restrict left-wing assemblies in Toronto and his ban on foreign-language (i.e., primarily Yiddish) speeches at such meetings — a ban frequently violated — further reinforced the image of the Jew as a political radical. In 1937, *The Globe and Mail*'s editorial dictum that, while most Jews were not communists, many communists were Jews, was not questioned by its readership.[47] Nor were the innuendoes.

A movement to the right in provincial politics was evident in the re-elected Liberal government of that year. Hepburn purged his cabinet of progressives such as David Croll (a Jew) and Arthur Roebuck. John Glass, in response to a letter expressing the hope that a Jew would be appointed to the cabinet, wrote sadly:

> I did not expect nor did I see a Cabinet post. I believe that in these troublesome days a Jewish Cabinet Member is in a very precarious position, both as regards himself and as regards the Jewish people, and perhaps it is just as well that the Premier did not include one of the Jewish Members in his Cabinet this time.[48]

The recent provincial election had brought into further relief fascist and antisemitic activity in the province. The Ontario wing of the National Social Christian Party, which Adrien Arcand had established in the summer of 1937, initially pitted its leader, John Ross Taylor, against Glass in the "Jewish" riding of St. Andrews. Taylor's campaign literature urged the Jews to move to Madagascar, promoted a boycott of Jewish stores and included a cartoon showing a Jewish octopus spreading its tentacles over commerce and finance.[49] On Hallowe'en, Rabbi Maurice Eisendrath of Holy Blossom, the senior and most prominent synagogue in Toronto, found a black crepe nailed to his door — a message from Canadian Nazi groups; the *Deutsche Bund* was distributing German Nazi anti-Jewish propaganda in Toronto, Hamilton and Windsor by means of a fascist publication called *The Thunderbolt*. This literature characteristically described a conspiracy of Jewish bankers, while blaming Jews for the Depression and urging their deportation.[50]

The Nadir

Not surprisingly, in light of these developments, the Canadian Jewish Congress noted in a 1937 report the gradual intensification of antisemitism in Ontario since 1933. Having expected that economic difficulties would exacerbate acts of discrimination that had been rampant since the previous decade, its leaders were not disappointed. However, one thing was surprising: as the Depression waned, antisemitism increased. This the Congress attributed to the growth of Canadian fascism. "The truth is that during the past four years . . . there has been a transition from the sporadic and unorganized type of anti-Jewishness to national organizations directed by professional agents," the report declared, drawing a parallel with developments in Germany in the early years of Nazism.[51] Once again, John Glass attempted to introduce group libel legislation into the Ontario legislature and once again it met with public opposition.[52] Undoubtedly, 1938 represented the nadir in Jewish fortunes in Ontario, with public condemnation and stereotyping now commonplace. A magazine entitled *The Sphinx*, published in Toronto and distributed by news agents, said of the Jews: "Their class was acquisitive and still is," possessing "no notion of enduring the hardships of a pioneer . . ." and having a "strangling effect" on economic life; the Italian paper, *Il Bolletino Italo Canadese*, reprinted antisemitic articles from *The Thunderbolt*. The purchase of Adams Furniture in Toronto by Jewish interests led the *Week-Ender* to claim that the "Joosh-moneyboys" had "purged" gentile employees and created a "semitic" atmosphere in the office. "Mr Hitler" the paper continued,

> also may wish to investigate the rumoured change at Fairweathers. The social dowagers who wrap Fairweather furs about their double chins . . . would probably change their trade if they should discover that the new owners of Fairweathers are of the Tribe of Israel and that the Gentile employees are getting, or are due to get, the gate.

Service establishments advertised "We are Not Jewish," while incidents in which Jews were called "parasites" and other epithets were common. Goel

Tzedec Synagogue on University Avenue was vandalized, as was the Jewish cemetery in Kitchener.[53]

At this time, John Ross Taylor's Canadian Union of Fascists was superseded in Ontario by the Nationalist Party, whose origins can be traced to the Swastika Club of the eastern Beaches in Toronto. Their leader, Joseph C. Farr, who was supported by Arcand, had participated in the Balmy Beach incident earlier in the decade. Canadian fascism now presented itself as a national movement. Their demonstrations in Toronto were broken up half-heartedly by the police; since communists and other radicals were leaders of the anti-fascist movement, and since Draper feared communists and radicals above all, he did not devote his energies to combatting the extreme right.[54]

Further Winds of Change

Nevertheless, Hitler's absorption of Austria in March 1938 marked the beginning of a change in the public attitude to fascists in Ontario. Farr's drilling of his brown-shirted "troops," with their swastika arm-bands, did not sit well in Anglo-Canada. The municipal authorities in Kingston barred a proposed national fascist convention in that city in June, and, when the venue was changed to Toronto, hall operators were urged not to rent space to its organizers.[55] While Farr held public meetings in Jewish districts with impunity, a *Star* photograph depicting a number of uniformed militiamen saluting Arcand met with consternation and the fear that fascists were infiltrating the armed forces. In fact, the Nationalist Party in Ontario did attempt to appeal to the military and to the veterans' sense of law and order as well as their fear of communism. By July of 1938, when the fascists finally did stage their convention in Toronto, the Canadian Legion had come out against them, perceiving them as much a threat to the Canadian way of life as the communists.[56] This turning of the tide became visible when the fascist National Unity Party assembled at Massey Hall in Toronto on July 4. It was apparent that antisemitism would be a major feature of the rally, causing the Reverend Gordon Domm of Bathurst St. United Church to denounce the fascists in a letter to *The Globe and Mail*. "There is probably enough anti-semitism dormant among Canadians of all ranks, which if the stage is properly set, can threaten our whole land. . . ."[57] Despite this prognosis, however, a rival anti-fascist rally sponsored by the League for Peace and Democracy at Maple Leaf Gardens drew a bigger crowd than the fascist convention. Indeed, support for fascism in Ontario dissipated. Betcherman aptly sums up the matter:

Basically . . . , fascism in Ontario in the year leading up to the war was dead because it had no issues to appeal to. It could not appeal to the isolationist sentiment as in Quebec, nor was the large German population as susceptible to Nazi propaganda as that of the West. Only its stand on Jewish immigration was apt to stir a popular response, but even those who agreed with the fascists, such as the Canadian Corps, were too anti-fascist to have anything to do with them.[58]

Discrediting local fascism, however, did not necessarily entail casting into disrepute the antisemitism preached by the fascists. Moreover, a new fear of a massive wave of Jewish immigration following *Kristallnacht* in Germany (1938) aggravated traditional anti-Jewish sentiments, and antisemitic literature continued to be distributed throughout the province by the remnants of the fascist organizations and by groups such as the British-Israel Federation (which resurrected the *Protocols*).[59] Even into the war years, Jewish businesses continued to experience difficulties, and public contempt for Jews continued in some quarters.[60]

Allies and Actions

Throughout the 1930s, Jews had not been without supporters in the non-Jewish community, especially among labour elements and religious liberals such as the Reverend C. E. Silcox of the United Church of Canada and the Reverend W. W. Judd of the Church of England in Canada.[61] However, they were in the minority; the majority remained hostile. Individuals reacted to the hostility by the time-honoured method of avoiding situations in which they were likely to encounter discrimination. On a community level, the major Jewish response was the formation of the Joint Public Relations Committee (JPRC) in 1938 for the express purpose of combatting antisemitism. It had important antecedents. B'nai B'rith, a fraternal order founded in the United States in the 1840s, had been devoted to this struggle since 1913 through its Anti-Defamation League. By the 1930s, a number of anti-defamation committees existed in Canada. The Canadian Jewish Congress, established in 1919 and revitalized in 1934 also as a reaction to the growing antisemitism of the day, was dedicated to the same end. In order to avoid duplication of effort, and after much negotiation, the two organizations established the JPRC as a co-operative body. However, by mutual agreement, all public statements were to be issued by the Canadian Jewish Congress.[62]

The JPRC set about its task on several fronts. To begin with, in the belief that ignorance was the basis of most anti-Jewish sentiments, the committee distributed suitable publications to public libraries, Christian clergy and various public figures as a means of combatting antisemitic propaganda.[63] It attempted also to revise standard texts such as *The Encyclopedia of Canada*, in which the article on Jews perpetuated some of the familiar sterotypes: "Possessing keen business instincts, the Jews have displayed a marvellous power of acquiring wealth, since their arrival in the country. . . . The majority are disinclined to hard manual labour; yet they are the most industrious and make a living where others would starve."[64]

Secondly, the committee attempted to persuade Jews to keep a low profile; for example, by settling disputes among themselves as quickly as possible, and outside of the public courts. It also sought to promote ethical practices among Jewish merchants and proper behaviour at summer resorts.[65] These goals were pursued through its own literature and through editorials in the Yiddish press. In addition, the committee made a point of bringing incidents of discriminatory signs on public property to the attention of both the provincial and municipal governments, while working with human rights activists within the Roman Catholic Church as well as with anti-fascists in the German, Italian and Ukrainian communities to combat the production of antisemitic tracts. It also organized a speaking tour for Dr. Silcox in the northern part of the province, arranged radio time for speeches promoting tolerance, primarily by non-Jews, and initiated a campaign to introduce such topics into the social studies curricula of public schools. In these efforts, the JPRC was not alone. Since 1934 another committee comprising representatives of the Canadian Jewish Congress as well as a few sympathetic Christian clergy and academics had been distributing literature encouraging a better understanding of Jews. The latter consisted mostly of works by Silcox and by the renowned British Anglican historian and theologian James Parkes. The JPRC expanded the work of this older committee, financing a wider distribution of these publications. By the end of the decade, it had reached the Canadian Legion, Baptist, United Church and Presbyterian synods, assemblies and conferences, the Interdenominational Christian Youth Conference and the Canadian Institute of Economics. In February 1940, the Joint Public Relations Committee brought Parkes to Canada for a cross-country tour.[66]

Either because of these efforts or because Ontarians perceived an enemy far greater than the Jews in the struggle with Nazi Germany, the time was auspicious in 1943 for the introduction of a new provincial bill by John Glass. The Racial Discrimination Act passed the following year through Glass's efforts and with the support of a movement led by a Labour-Progressive member of the provincial house, J. B. Salsberg. At last, the posting of signs excluding a particular social or religious group was outlawed. Restrictive covenants would become illegal shortly after the war; fair employment and fair accommodation legislation would pass in the province in 1954, largely through the efforts of the Joint Public Relations Committee. As a result, by the conclusion of World War II, perceptible decline occurred in overt anti-Jewish discrimination. Antisemitism had certainly not disappeared, but at least its public expression was no longer socially acceptable. That, in itself, represented considerable progress from previous decades.

The work of the JPRC and the Christian allies of the Jewish community had doubtless contributed to the new situation, but of overriding importance in this regard was the general transformation of Canadian society by war. The long-awaited victory and unprecedented prosperity that followed in its wake engendered a sense of collective confidence that hitherto Ontario had never experienced. Although the struggle for a province devoid of prejudice was by no means complete — indeed, it continues to this day — the post-war atmosphere enabled Ontarians to believe, perhaps for the first time in their history, that it was possible for the best qualities in a society with Anglo-Saxon foundations to survive in a more cosmopolitan and pluralistic milieu.

Notes

1 *Mail* (Toronto), January 21, 1866.

2 *Evening Star* (Toronto), September 15, 1897; *World* (Toronto), September 16, 1897; and *Mail & Empire* (Toronto), September 16, 1897. For examples of Smith's views see *Jewish Times*, February 4, 1898, p. 69 and *Weekly Sun*, September 20, 1899, as well as Gerald Tulchinsky's essay, this volume.

3 Quoted in *Mail & Empire*, June 12, 1897. The title "Reverend" for Mr. Lazarus reflects the nineteenth-century Reform practice in England of training Jewish preachers as distinct from rabbis.

4 *World* (Toronto), September 15, 1897, and *Jewish Times*, September 15, 1899, p. 321.

5 Personal interviews: Arthur Cohen, December 20, 1971; Mrs. M. Goodman, January 12, 1972; and Bertha Draimin, January 10, 1972.

6 *Jewish Times*, March 31, 1899, p. 134; April 14, 1899, p. 151; June 9, 1899, p. 222; March 15, 1901, p. 119; and November 17, 1904, p. 413.

7 See Mark Wischnitzer, *To Dwell in Safety* (Philadelphia: Jewish Publication Society of America, 1948), and Maldwyn A. Jones, *American Immigration* (Chicago: University of Chicago Press, 1960).

8 Canada, Department of Agriculture, *Census of Canada 1880-81*, vol. 1 (Ottawa: 1883), p. 174; ibid., 1890-91, vol. 1, p. 283; Canada, Census and Statistics Office, *Fourth Census of Canada, 1901*, vol. 1 (Ottawa: 1902), p. 219; Louis Rosenberg, "Jewish Mutual Benefit and Friendly Societies in Toronto: The First Fifty Years 1896-1945" (typescript 63 pp., *ca.* 1947: Toronto Jewish Congress Archives), p. 18.

9 See David Ward, "The Emergence of Central Immigrant Ghettoes in American Cities: 1840-1920," in Association of American Geographers, *Annals* 63 (June 1968): 343-59; Stephen Speisman, "St. John's Shtetl," in *Gathering Place: Peoples and Neighbourhoods of Toronto, 1834-1945*, ed. R. F. Harney (Toronto: The Multicultural History Society of Ontario, 1985), pp. 107-20; and Stephen Speisman, *The Jews of Toronto: A History to 1937* (Toronto: McClelland & Stewart, 1979), pp. 81-90.

10 *Toronto Daily Star*, May 30, 1916.

11 James W. Parkes, *The Jew as Usurer* (Toronto: Committee on Jewish-Gentile Relationships, 1938), passim.

12 See James W. Parkes, *How Russian Jews Came to the West* (Toronto: Committee on Jewish-Gentile Relationships, 1938), p. 7. Even the established Jews were concerned that east European Jewish immigrants be absorbed into Canadian society and were confident that they could be. Holy Blossom Sabbath (Sunday) School at the turn of the century encouraged the minimizing of specifically Jewish behaviour, while the Council of Jewish Women established a Working Girls' Club in the 1890s to enable the young people "to come into touch with the best [of] Canadian life. . . ." The motivations for these activities were several: a genuine desire to help the immigrants and to make them Canadian, but also a fear that they might otherwise prove an embarrassment to the established community and generate antisemitism. National Council of Jewish Women, *Proceedings of the First Convention of the National Council of Jewish Women* (Philadelphia: Jewish Publication Society of America, 1897); Ida Siegel, personal interview, August 12, 1971; and *Jewish Times*, January 6, 1899, p. 38. See also Abraham I. Willinsky, *A Doctor's Memoirs* (Toronto: Macmillan, 1960), p. 13.

13 See, e.g., "Seven Hebrews and Crown Bank Are Being Sued for $10,000 Damages," *Mail & Empire*, March 11, 1909; "Jew Has Disappeared," *Mail & Empire*, February 15, 1909; *Evening Telegram*, June 10, 1907, June 13, 1907; *Jewish Times*, March 1, 1912, p. 1, August 15, 1913, p. 1, February 7, 1913; *Toronto Daily Star* and *Evening Telegram*, February 1912, passim.

14 Dr. Maurice Pollock, personal interview, March 15, 1973; *Jewish Times*, April 19, 1907, p. 167.

15 A. B. Bennett, personal interview, October 3, 1972; David Eisen, "My Life in Toronto" (unpublished typescript, 1973), p. 4; personal interviews: Arthur Cohen, December 20, 1971; Benzion Hyman, October 8, 1972; Dr. Maurice Pollock, March 5, 1973; Ida Siegel, September 2, 1971; D. Eisen, *Toronto Jewish Doctors* (Toronto: Maimonides Medical Society and Canadian Jewish Congress, 1960), p. 14.

16 William Leibel, personal interview, January 28, 1972; *Toronto Daily Star*, July 22, 1913; Ida Siegel, personal interviews, August 5, September 2, 1971.

17 In 1919, for example, when there was an attempt to translate Red Cross circulars and other material into Yiddish by the Mother's Club at Elizabeth St. School in Toronto, the Chief Inspector of the Board of Education forbade the practice (*Toronto Daily Star*, January 15, 1919). For other instances of the association of Jews with radicalism see, e.g., *Evening Telegram*, May 30, 1919, and *Saturday Night*, 1919, passim.

18 *Canadian Jewish Review*, October 12, 1923, p. 7; August 31, 1923, p. 6; *Globe*, November 8, 1923. In 1922 the *Globe*'s survey of Jewish students in Toronto schools reported that principals were reluctant to release exact figures because non-Jewish parents would resent the presence of Jewish students in large numbers (*Globe*, March 21, 1922). See also *Evening Telegram*, July 24, 1923 for further accusations of Jewish disloyalty.

19 Quoted in *Toronto Daily Star*, February 26, 1926. See also *Toronto Daily Star*, November 13, 1924.

20 *Toronto Daily Star*, March 29, 1926, and *Evening Telegram*, August 18, 1922.

21 *Evening Telegram*, September 22, 1924.

22 *Canadian Jewish Review*, August 27, 1926; *Toronto Daily Star*, May 27, 1924; and Holy Blossom Temple, Toronto, *Minutes*, March 22, 1927.

23 *Canadian Jewish Review*, February 8, 1924.

24 *Toronto Daily Star*, September 25, 1924.

25 *Toronto Daily Star*, October 3, 1924.

26 Esther Einbinder, "An Exploratory Study of Attitudes toward Jews in the City of Toronto" (M.A. thesis, Department of Psychology, University of Toronto, 1934), pp. 19-24.

27 Quoted in ibid., p. 30.

28 Both quoted in ibid., p. 34.

29 Lita-Rose Betcherman, *The Swastika and the Maple Leaf* (Toronto: Fitzhenry & Whiteside, 1975), p. 3.

30 Ibid., p. 44.

31 *Ottawa Journal*, March 21, 1935, quoted in Betcherman, *Swastika*, p. 42.

32 D. H. Wrong, "Ontario's Jews in the Larger Community," in *A People and Its Faith*, ed. Albert Rose (Toronto: University of Toronto Press, 1959), p. 53.

33 Factor quoted in *Toronto Daily Star*, April 24, 1933. See also Louis Rosenberg, *Canada's Jews* (Montreal: Canadian Jewish Congress, 1939).

34 See, for example, "Indenture between Ernest Macaulay Dillon, Ethel Zurbrigg and Madeleine Dillon, Part of Lot 22, Township of North Gwillimbury, 1931" (Toronto Jewish Congress/Canadian Jewish Congress Ontario Region Archives [hereafter JCRC], Accession #80-6/4). Jews wishing to purchase property were sometimes able to do so by engaging a gentile intermediary. See, e.g., Ben Dunkelman, *Dual Allegiance* (Toronto: Macmillan, 1976), p. 12. For an example from Hamilton, see I. Namerow to Saul Hayes, March 24, 1943 and C. Davis Goodman to Hon. J. L. Ilsley, February 26, 1943 (Joint Community Relations Committee Papers, JCRC Archives MG8-S File #PR 131.5.95).

35 JCRC File #PR 131.5.15; Betcherman, *Swastika*, pp. 50-51; Wrong, "Ontario's Jews," p. 53; Egmont L. Frankel to Oscar Cohen, July 4, 1939 (JCRC File #PR 131.5.40); JCRC memo July 19, 1939 (JCRC File #PR 131.5.42); and JCRC Files #PR 131.5.43, 131.5.44. See also Oscar Cohen to J. I. Oelbaum, July 3, 1940 (JCRC File #PR 131.5.6); John J. Glass to Hon. Mitchell F. Hepburn, July 21, 1941; S. H. Abrahamson to John J. Glass, August 5, 1941 (John J. Glass Papers, MG6-B JCRC Archives); and Louis S. Hyman to Oscar Cohen, August 1, 1939 (JCRC File #PR 131.5.39).

36 Oscar Cohen to Rabbi M. N. Eisendrath, April 1, 1938 (JCRC File #PR 129). The incident of the British official is cited by Irving Abella, "Anti-Semitism in Canada in the Interwar Years," in *The Jews of North America*, ed. Moses Rischin (Detroit: Wayne State University Press, 1987), p. 243.

37 Oscar Cohen to Rabbi M. N. Eisendrath, June 14, 1937 (JCRC File #PR 122), and Cohen to Eisendrath, June 14, 1937 (JCRC File #PR 121).

38 See, e.g., Bland's column in the *Toronto Daily Star*, March 1, 1933.

39 E.g., Sarah Rhinewine to Oscar Cohen, March 20, 1939; Sherman Ghan to Sarah Rhinewine, March 27, 1939 (JCRC File #PR 131.7.1); David Rome, *Clouds in the Thirties: On Anti-Semitism in Canada 1929-1939*, Section 2 (Montreal: Canadian Jewish Congress, 1977), pp. 52-53; *Toronto Daily Star*, November 15, 1939; Oscar Cohen to Connie Smythe, December 9, 1939; and Smythe to Cohen, December 14, 1939 (JCRC File #PR 198).

40 *Yiddisher Zhurnal* (Toronto) editorial, April 11, 1933.

41 Betcherman, *Swastika*, pp. 50-51.

42 Quoted in Rome, *Clouds*, p. 56.

43 Alexander Brown (Ontario Secretary of Canadian Jewish Congress) to H. M. Caiserman (National Secretary of Canadian Jewish Congress), April 19, 1935 (Canadian Jewish Congress Archives, Montreal).

44 The Balmy Beach and Christie Pits incidents are too well known to require detailed description in these pages. The reader wishing a full account may consult Speisman, *The Jews of Toronto*, pp. 332ff.; Betcherman, *Swastika*, pp. 55ff.; and Cyril H. Levitt and William Shaffir, *The Riot at Christie Pits* (Toronto: Lester & Orpen Dennys, 1987).

45 The fact that Kitchener city council condemned it and that it had little support was small comfort (*Toronto Daily Star*, August 13-19, 1933, and Betcherman, *Swastika*, pp. 57ff.).

46 Quoted in *The Globe and Mail*, September 8, 1937.

47 See, e.g., editorial, *The Globe and Mail*, February 23, 1929; *Toronto Daily Star*, January 23, 1929; and *The Globe and Mail*, November 15, 1937. A full account of the Communist movement in Canada in this period may be found in Lita-Rose Betcherman, *The Little Band* (Toronto: Deneau, n.d.).

48 John J. Glass to Benjamin Goldfield, October 13 (John J. Glass Papers MG6-B, JCRC Archives).

49 Taylor's campaign actually collapsed because of internal divisions.

50 Gordon Menzel to John J. Glass, November 9, 1937 (Glass Papers); *The Globe and Mail*, November 8, 1937; and *The Globe and Mail*, November 26-December 8, 1937, passim.

51 Canadian Jewish Congress, *Report of the Central Division*, 1937, quoted in Rome, *Clouds*, vol. 2, pp. 19-20.

52 See, e.g., *The Globe and Mail*, November 9, 1937.

53 JCRC Memorandum, November 4, 1938 (JCRC File #PR 131.5.14); JCRC File #142; *Week-Ender*, November 10, 1938, p. 11; *The Herald* (North Toronto), May 26, June 2, 1938; French Dry Cleaners, Toronto, advertising card, in JCRC File #JP 147; Hebrew Retail Fishers Association to F. T. James Co. Ltd., November 21, 1938 (JCRC File #PR 131.5.8); and H. M. Caiserman to Toronto office of Canadian Jewish Congress, June 28, 1938 (JCRC File #PR 153).

54 *The Globe and Mail*, June 4, 7, 1938. See also Betcherman, *Swastika*, p. 114.

55 *The Globe and Mail*, May 26, June 6, ff., July 14, ff., 1938.

56 Betcherman, *Swastika*, pp. 118-20.

57 *The Globe and Mail*, June 20, 1938, cited in Betcherman, *Swastika*, p. 120.

58 Ibid., p. 136.

59 Canadian Jewish Congress, "Report of the Executive Secretary, Central Division [Oscar Cohen], 1939," Canadian Jewish Congress Archives, Montreal; Rabbi M. N. Eisendrath and Dr. C. E. Silcox to the editor, *The Globe and Mail*, May 18, 1940 (JCRC File #PR 210).

One group, Gibraltar House on Markham St. in Toronto, distributed antisemitic pamphlets asking: "Do we Nordic-Britishers require/'Jew Guidance,' In Business,/Politics, or Religion? Most/Positively NO!/So – JEWS – MIND YOUR OWN BUSINESS!" (JCRC File #PR 131.5, "Amelia Rees, 1939").

60 In 1940, for example, Central Wholesale Grocers in Toronto felt it necessary to advertise that, while they had nothing against Jews, "we want it clearly understood that there is no one in our entire organization that is not 100% Gentile" (JCRC File #PR 131.5.45). Even during the war, public speakers could be sympathetic to Hitler's statements that Jews were unproductive and did not contribute to society (Eisendrath to National Council of Education, February 28, 1940, JCRC File #PR 205). As late as 1943, when a tenant involved in a dispute with a Jewish landlord called him a "dirty Jew" and the two appeared before magistrate Kelso at City Hall in Toronto, the latter, upon hearing the cause of the disturbance, was reported to have remarked to the landlord, "Well then, don't be a Dirty Jew" (I. Bergson to Canadian Jewish Congress, May 4, 1943, JCRC File #PR 131.5.93).

61 Between 1934 and 1940 Silcox was General Secretary of the Christian Social Council of Canada, a Protestant co-operative body dealing with social work, and served as editor of their publication, *Social Welfare*. Canon Judd was (like Silcox) a member of the Canadian National Committee on Refugees and Victims of Political Persecution.

62 B. G. Kayfetz, introduction to the "Finding-Aid to the Joint Community Relations Committee Papers 1938-78" (Toronto: JCRC Archives, 1988). In 1961, the name of the committee was changed to Joint Community Relations Committee.

63 Rev. J. A. Wilson, Stoney Creek, Ontario to Rabbi M. Eisendrath, May 16, 1936 (JCRC File #160.4).

64 *Encyclopedia of Canada*, published in 1935 and reprinted in 1940, excerpts quoted in JPRC memorandum (JCRC File #131.5.103). See also, Louis Rosenberg to Ben Lappin, March 2, 1944; Ben Lappin to Saul Hayes, January 27, 1944; and Lappin to H. M. Caiserman, March 21, 1944 (all ibid.).

65 Ald. J. B. Salsberg to S. M. Shapiro, June 24, 1943 (JCRC File #PR 131.5.96); Oscar Cohen to Rabbi S. Sachs, August 15, 1939 (File #PR 131.7); Oscar Cohen to Rabbi S. Sachs, March 8, 1940 (File #PR 131.7.7.1); JCRC records File #PR 131.7.7; and Gurston Allen to Rabbi M. N. Eisendrath, March 6, 1939 (JCRC File #PR 131.7.2).

66 JPRC Memo, probably 1939, in JCRC File #PR 131.7.4.

6

Interlude of Hostility: Judeo-Christian Relations in Quebec in the Interwar Period, 1919-39

Pierre Anctil

Any study of antisemitism in Quebec in the interwar period has to take into account a number of factors that have little to do with either Jews or Judaism. A small minority in the total population, and a community that, for the most part, was formed late in the nineteenth century, the Quebec Jews were affected by historical and cultural forces that long predated their arrival, and over which they had little control. When Jewish immigrants started to arrive en masse in Montreal at the turn of the century, Canada was already (at least in French-Canadian eyes), a bicultural and binational country, with Québécois culture as a coherent entity with specific characteristics. A society with its own chosen boundaries, French Quebec could not be ignored, bypassed or reduced to a local manifestation of little significance. Already Quebec had created for itself a culture complex with three salient vectors, each intersecting with the others, and each indispensable to the construction of a national identity. In certain circles, political autonomy was its logical goal.

First and foremost, Francophones in the early twentieth century felt that an important part of their identity was derived from the Catholic spiritual tradition, which had enjoyed a virtual monopoly even since New France. Consolidated by the defeat of the 1837-38 rebellions, and encouraged by the British as a surrogate for a more radical political class, the Quebec church had acquired a central role in the formation of almost every one of Quebec's institutions, whether in the field of superior education, health and social services, voluntary associations or economic and

---

Notes for Chapter 6 are on pp. 161-65.

financial endeavours. Instead of a source of doctrinal domination, ecclesiastical power was regarded as a legitimate element in society, allowing members of the clergy to become involved at all levels of life as chaplains, counsellors, spiritual guides and even at times as politicians, activists and ideologues.[1] No domain in Quebec culture remained untouched by Catholicism. The influence of the church probably reached its peak during the interwar period, when the so-called provincial state was a relatively minor institution in comparison with what was to appear in the following decades.[2] Language, as well as religion, offered a bedrock for Quebec identity; in fact, the two were intertwined in such an intimate fashion that it was understood that the weakening of the one heralded the disappearance of the other. Only the French language could sustain a strong Catholic presence in North America, and only through their Roman faith could the Québécois protect themselves from English-speaking Protestant society: a society that loomed so large on the continent that it threatened to engulf them.

The cause of Catholic Christianity and the survival of the French language were also linked to a predominantly rural and agricultural lifestyle. This triad — language, religion and rural society — had profound social implications. When, in the mid-nineteenth century, French Canadians began to populate the island of Montreal in large numbers, becoming urban workers in what hitherto had been mostly an English commercial centre, they promoted French Catholic institutions, as distinct from English Protestant ones. Only thus, they felt, could their social progress and material betterment be assured. In fact, this process was well on its way in the 1870s, exactly when French Canadians were becoming the predominant cultural community in the city.[3] Nonetheless, urbanization and industrialization remained novel for the Québécois, 70 percent of whom still depended on agriculture as a means of livelihood.[4] Consequently, a conservative social ideology persisted well into the twentieth century. Many Québécois felt ill at ease with modernity, urban life and social innovation, and their discomfort often had political, intellectual and religious repercussions: for example, ultramontanism.[5]

When Jews from eastern Europe began arriving in Montreal at the turn of the century, i.e., immigrants who, unlike the first Jewish settlers in Canada, could not be considered British subjects of Judaic origin, they immediately encountered a society rigidly divided along ethnic lines, both religious and linguistic. No amount of goodwill in the name of the larger Canadian interest had been able to reconcile the two major and virtually separate entities that co-existed in the city: a Franco-Catholic population in the eastern part of the island and an Anglo-Protestant one in the western.[6] However, a consensus between the two groups had emerged, whereby each, albeit grudgingly, accepted the existence of the other.

Although French Canada regarded the British conquest as a profoundly traumatic event and disliked English domination of the local economy, by and large, with the passage of time, it had accepted a *modus vivendi* with its old enemy. This allowed the Dominion to harbour two major autonomous cultural communities.[7]

Such a historical equilibrium, especially as far as the French Canadians were concerned, was too important to be upset by external factors such as the arrival of a few thousand Jews. To a society that was already defensive by virtue of its minority status as well as its lack of real power in the economic and political system, the Jews became alien symbols: a group that stood outside of the Canadian tradition altogether, and one which could not easily be brought into it. To French Quebec, strongly coloured by Catholic values and practices, they were simply an aberration (the Anglo-Protestants, at least, were also Christians). They disturbed Canada's religious character. In all innocence, of course, the newcomers really did constitute a radically divergent spiritual, cultural and linguistic entity. This situation must not be underestimated in the study of Quebec antisemitism, especially during the period between the two world wars, when the subdued French nationalist emotions of the previous decades erupted during the Great Depression. The timing of the *Ashkenazic* emigration from Russia and Poland had placed the newcomers on a collision course with Francophone aspirations in a dualistic Canadian society. Such was the fate of the first non-Christian community to come into direct contact with French Canada and its deeply instilled identity. The encounter proved difficult for both parties.

A Community of Recent Immigrants

The Jewish community in Quebec during the 1920s and 1930s was located mainly in Montreal, the home of 96.5 percent of all Québécois Jews in 1931. Not only were these Jews almost entirely urban,[8] but most of them lived in a specific neighbourhood as well: a narrow strip of land wedged between the predominantly French-speaking east end and the predominantly English-speaking west end known as the "immigrant corridor." Here, north from Sherbrooke St. to Jean-Talon St., Jewish households were clustered along such arteries as rue Saint-Urbain, boulevard Saint-Laurent and avenue du Parc. In 1938, Jews represented slightly over 50 percent of the population of quartier Saint-Louis, quartier Laurier and quartier Saint-Michel, while they accounted for about one-third of quartier Saint-Jean-Baptiste. Elsewhere in Montreal, they formed less than 7 percent of the population and, in most cases, less than 1 percent.[9] Not only were they concentrated residentially, but they also suffered from the effects of immigration, so that, at best, their adaptation to Canadian society was incomplete. In 1931, only 44.7 percent of the Quebec Jews had been born in Canada, and another 33.1 percent naturalized, leaving almost one fifth of the community with the somewhat uneasy status of aliens.[10]

The fragility of this situation is illustrated by the fact that, in 1931, 99.02 percent of all Jewish residents in the province above the age of 10 considered Yiddish to be their mother tongue. To be sure, most Jewish adults in Montreal at that time had learned one of the two predominant languages of the city (usually English), but, for most of the community, Yiddish was still the *lingua franca*, with the exception of a few dozen families established before the great east European *Ashkenazic* wave of immigration. The predominance of the Yiddish-speaking *Ashkenazim* in Montreal in the interwar period is demonstrated by a few simple statistics (Table 1). In 1931, almost 85 percent of the first-generation Jews were of Russian, Polish, Romanian and Hungarian origin, the rest having either American or western European backgrounds — hardly enough to influence the mass of the city's Jewish inhabitants. The influx was both recent and sudden, taking place almost entirely between 1904 and 1914, and again between 1920 and 1929, with its peak years in 1912, 1913 and 1921. Most Montreal Jews had arrived at the beginning of the century, causing the Jewish population to quadruple between 1901 and 1911, and to double again between 1911 and 1931, at which date demographic progression levelled off, never to grow again at such a pace (Table 2). Because of the sharp surge, the proportion of Jews in the general Canadian and Quebec population reached an all-time high in 1931 of 1.5 percent and 2.09 percent respectively, not enough to offset the demographic balance of the country.

In 1931, the 48 000 Jews of Montreal accounted only for 5.9 percent of the city's population, but their urban concentration in a few blocks on the Plateau Mont-Royal, their relatively divergent customs, and their discomfort with the majority languages made them highly visible. Moreover, except for a handful of established merchants in Westmount and Outremont, most of the Jewish community during the interwar period subsisted near the poverty level, in occupations traditionally reserved for immigrants. This made them vulnerable as well as visible. Montreal was no different from the other major centres of Jewish influx in North America, with their sweatshops and factories, low pay, deplorable health conditions and frequent work stoppages. A full 35 percent of the Jewish work force in the city found employment in the manufacturing industries, especially in the textile and garment factories. Commercial activities accounted for another 31 percent of Jewish employment at this time, most of which (24.7%) was confined to small family retail businesses with one or two employees.[11] All in all, the Jewish economic profile in Montreal (and Canada) was clearly different from that of the rest of the Canadian population during the 1930s, a fact aggravated by the Depression and an almost total absence of social mobility.

Table 1
Country of Birth of the Jewish Population
of Canada and Quebec, 1931

Country	Canada %	Quebec %
Canada	43.85	44.67
Russia	26.05	27.24
Poland[a]	15.94	10.64
Romania	4.87	7.64
United States	2.77	2.34
Great Britain	2.49	2.10
Austria	1.71	2.45
Hungary	0.26	0.32
Germany	0.25	0.33
Czechoslovakia	0.09	0.08
France	0.07	0.10
Other countries	1.65	2.09
Total of those born abroad	56.15	55.33

a Poland as created in 1918. Before that date, most
   Polish Jews were Russian subjects, with a minority
   as Austrian subjects.
   Source: Rosenberg, *Canada's Jews* (1939), Table 55,
           p. 78.

Table 2
Demographic Profession of the Jewish Population
of Canada and Quebec, 1901-41

	Canada		Quebec	
Year	Total Jewish population	% of Jews in the total population	Total Jewish population	% of Jews in the total population
1901	16 131	0.31	7 607	0.46
1911	75 681	1.05	30 648	1.52
1921	126 196	1.44	47 977	2.03
1931	156 606	1.50	60 087	2.09
1941	179 241	1.47	66 277	1.99

Sources: Rosenberg, *Canada's Jews* (1939), Table 27, p. 41; and federal census of 1941.

The sectors in which Jews could succeed in improving their lot — the liberal professions — remained under conditions of economic hardship. To become a lawyer, a doctor, a dentist or a professor did not require large amounts of capital, nor was it necessary to go beyond basic professional training. Already, in the 1930s, many second-generation Jews who had developed linguistic skills sought to obtain access to institutions of higher education and hence entry to the bar or medicine. By 1931, there were 97 doctors, 73 lawyers and 47 dentists of Jewish origin in Montreal, with nursing, accounting and engineering also under siege. Sooner or later, Jewish professionals were bound to seek admission to institutions not controlled by the Jewish community, and with a non-Jewish clientele. This movement into sectors previously occupied, with rare exceptions, only by gentiles, became one of the catalysts of the Jewish crisis in Quebec, especially as Francophones from the same social background sought to enter the professional middle-class themselves. In a period of economic slowdown, this Jewish social mobility, however restricted, produced an ethnocentric reaction in French nationalist circles that often took the guise of antisemitism. Nor did only the French Canadians feel a need to protect their social status; Anglo-Canadians in Montreal also opposed the influx of Jewish professionals and white-collar workers in sectors that hitherto had been reserved almost exclusively for persons of British origin.

McGill University

With the great migratory surge of the second decade of the twentieth century, Jews became the dominant immigrant group in the Montreal region, surpassing the Italian, Greek and German-speaking communities. This fact in itself had important consequences with respect to antisemitism in the interwar period. The Jew was no longer, as in the previous century, a symbolic creature against whom Judeophobes could rave almost *in absentia*, without directly impinging on the Jewish community itself. A crisis was in the making, because Jews were now perceived as a demographic threat in Quebec, with a generation of Canadian-born *Ashkenazim* demanding access to all aspects of its social and cultural life. Although no political impediments had stood in their way since the 1832 law granting them full rights under the British regime as citizens of the Judaic faith, the Jewish population of Quebec had been too small until the end of the nineteenth century to attract much attention on the part of the two Christian majorities. It had also been extremely close to the Anglo-British cultural model in all respects except the confessional.[12] But this older relative invisibility was swept away by the east European migrations, with lasting repercussions on Quebec society.

The "Jewish crisis" of the 1920s and 1930s first erupted in the English-speaking community, where signs of resistance to Jewish advancement appeared shortly after the end of World War I. This was hardly surprising. Indeed, matters could not have been otherwise for several reasons, notably the greater attraction of Anglo-Canadian society to non-French immi-

Table 3
Percentage Distribution of Jews Gainfully Occupied Among the Various Occupation Groups, as Compared with the Total Population of All Origins in Canada, 1931

Occupational groups	Canada		Quebec		Montreal	
	Jews	All origins	Jews	All origins	Jews	All origins
Merchandising	35.93	7.99	33.16	8.14	31.03	11.81
Manufacturing	29.62	11.27	32.27	13.81	34.98	18.95
Clerical	10.16	6.14	11.41	6.33	10.82	10.73
Professional	5.06	6.08	4.78	7.04	4.25	7.06
Professional Service	3.44	8.52	3.67	9.45	3.47	11.32
Building Construction	3.20	5.17	3.00	6.15	3.30	8.86
Transportation and Communication	2.83	6.77	3.03	6.46	3.37	9.24
Labourers and Unskilled Workers	2.67	11.12	2.41	13.70	2.72	15.12
Laundering, Dyeing and Pressing	2.48	0.57	2.69	0.69	3.10	1.27
Primary Industries	1.37	32.62	0.38	25.00	0.06	0.60
Warehousing and Storage	1.21	0.89	1.32	0.73	1.38	1.42
Insurance and Real Estate	1.17	0.66	1.30	0.66	1.02	0.96
Entertainment and Sport	0.48	0.25	0.25	0.16	0.22	0.28
Finance	0.21	0.28	0.19	0.25	0.14	0.35
Public Administration	0.10	0.80	0.07	0.76	0.05	1.25
Electric light and Power	0.04	0.83	0.06	0.63	0.05	0.72
Unspecified Occupations	0.03	0.04	0.01	0.04	0.04	0.06

Source: Rosenberg, *Canada's Jews* (1939), Table 108, p. 160.

grants in Montreal, with the sole exception of the Italian Catholics.[13] Anglo-Saxon domination of the economy, and the fact that, until World War I, Montreal had been Canada's major port and manufacturing centre near the Atlantic Ocean, drew most Jewish newcomers to the English milieu. Of course, the presence of some well-established British Jews in Lower Canada assisted this process. Already in the 1880s the vast majority of Jewish school children in Montreal were attending classes administered by the Protestant school board, where rapid anglicization (including the instillation of British political and cultural values) was soon begun. Like most immigrants to North America, Montreal Jews were attracted to the language and culture that seemed to promise greater economic benefits. As long as the number of families seeking assimilation was small, few voices were raised in protest. Matters were different, however, when 50 000 Yiddish-speaking immigrants suddenly knocked on the doors of the Anglo elite, seeking rapid integration into English Canada.

When all these factors — linguistic, socio-economic and historical — converged, McGill University immediately assumed great importance in the eyes of ambitious young Jewish men and women. As unheralded as the influx of their parents into Canada, the Jewish influx into McGill in the early 1920s acquired the proportions of a tidal wave. Only 6.8 percent of McGill students were Jews in 1913 (112 persons) on the Sherbrooke St. campus; by 1924-25, a quarter of the first-year class belonged to the Jewish confession.[14] The proportion was even higher in certain faculties such as arts (32%), the beginning point for most of the liberal professions, law (41%), dentistry (27%) and medicine (25%) (see Table 4). Never before had so many Jewish candidates been admitted to McGill, an institution founded by the British community of Montreal and closely identified with its social elite. According to Stanley Frost, "At the commencement of World War I the student body was still a compact and homogeneous group of young men and women, mostly from the middle economic strata of society and of British, or at least anglophone, Protestant stock."[15] These young, first-generation Canadian Jews intended to enter the portals of a sub-economy already occupied by lawyers, doctors and businessmen of Anglo-Christian origins. Although stemming from different ethnic roots, the former clearly planned to make English their working language, if not their maternal tongue.

McGill administrators were quick to realize the likely impact of hundreds of Jewish graduates on the Anglo-Saxon-dominated economy of Montreal. Although the fact was never stated explicitly, McGill had always served the ethnocentric interests of the British merchant class, while French Catholic institutions of higher learning had played a similar role for the Québécois petty bourgeoisie. Facing the "Jewish problem" for the first time in its history, McGill decided in 1926 to respond by not admitting "Hebrews" from outside of the Province of Quebec.[16] As this was insufficient to stop the flow of Jewish candidates, in 1928-29 the Dean of Arts was forced to conceive of a more effective scheme. Higher marks at high school matriculation would be required of Jewish applicants than those required of Christians:

> I am now leaving for Métis, until September 10th. From now on therefore, and until my return, kindly admit all Hebrews with an aggregate over 700 (in matriculation marks), and all non-Hebrews with an aggregate of over 630, unless you think their marks in Latin, English and Mathematics are not credible.[17]

Table 4
Percentage of Jewish Students at McGill University,
for Certain Faculties and Schools,
1924-27, 1930-31, 1935-36

	1924-25	1925-26	1926-27	1930-31	1935-36
Faculty of Arts	32	34	31	24	13
Department of Sciences	—	—	—	15	19
Department of Commerce	19	21	18	19	9
Faculty of Law	41	39	44	40	5
Faculty of Dental Science	27	19	23	47	27
Faculty of Medicine	25	24	24	15	11
Faculty of Applied Science	3	4	4	—	—
Department of Pharmacy	—	88	77	—	—
School of Social Work	—	16	27	3	—
Nursing School	—	—	—	—	5
School of Physical Education	—	—	3	5	11
Faculty of Engineering (Eng. Div.)	—	—	—	7	7
School of Architecture	—	—	—	25	28
Total	—	25	24	17	12

Source: Registrar's Archives, McGill University Archives and "McGill University.
Distribution of Jewish Students, 1930-31," undated document, Archives of the
Canadian Jewish Congress, Montreal.

The impact was devastating. Jewish enrollment fell by half in ten years, reaching a 12 percent low in 1935-36, while in most target faculties the reduction was even more drastic. In arts, the Jewish percentage was cut by two thirds, and by half in commerce, while in law the figures went from a full 40 percent to a meagre 5 percent (see Table 4). In medicine, a different system was devised whereby a specific *numerus clausus* was established, putting a 10 percent ceiling on Jewish candidates, after they had already been weeded out by the faculty of arts' unequal points requirement at the matriculation examination.[18]

McGill's motive in these actions was largely economic. Any increase in students seriously taxed the institution's fragile financial position, and Jewish applicants, for the most part sons and daughters of impoverished east European immigrants, were unlikely to contribute much in terms of endowments and donations. However, the university had other motives as well. Dean Ira Mackay of the Faculty of Arts wrote the following to Principal Arthur Currie: "I must confess that I never see a new Jew crossing this threshold [the Dean's doorway] without muttering *inaudibly*, 'There goes another clean, wholesome, upstanding Canadian boy across the frontier to practice [*sic*] his profession in the United States of America.'"[19] Furthermore, Jews were perceived as willing to enter only urban occupations. Did not Canada need men and women of vision to develop and exploit its vast unoccupied spaces? What gifts could these parvenus bring to a country sinking into economic ruin? They simply did not have the proper pedigrees.

Despite the legacy of classic Western antisemitism, McGill had little against Jews in cultural terms. Certainly, social discrimination was often justified by cultural stereotypes, as in *Earth and High Heaven*, a novel published in 1944 by Gwethalyn Graham. But Montreal Jews in the 1930s were so intent on assimilating to British models that little of their original *Ashkenazic* traits survived on campus.[20] The university's attitude toward its Jewish clientele was hardly unusual: most Ivy League institutions in the United States had shut their gates to recent Jewish immigrants prior to World War I.[21] McGill's reaction can be regarded as typical of Quebec's Anglo-Saxon milieu in the two decades between the world wars. What was deemed appropriate by the Anglophone university was not considered inappropriate by St. James Street, the large transportation companies or the leading professional and commercial associations of British tradition. Ultimately, despite itself, McGill could not avoid assisting the Jewish determination to penetrate an English marketplace virtually monopolized by professionals of British stock. Hence, the degree to which its Jewish students wished to anglicize themselves while retaining some part of their original Judaic heritage was of minor importance.

The McGill case was merely a variation on North American Anglo-Saxon nativism aggravated by the economic climate of the 1930s. Among Anglo-Montrealers, the main fear was the rise of an upstart class, ready to emulate British ways and to compete directly with the older Anglo-British establishment. Were not Jews about to create a new ethnic force in Montreal that might dislodge the city's founding elite from its place of pre-eminence? Thus, according to John Higham:

> As we have already noticed, ideological anti-Semitism in America concentrated on economic rather than religious themes, on Shylock rather than Judas. In an intense form, it conjured up secret intrigues to gain control of the money supply and wreck the financial system. A milder version depicted the Jews as parasites, living by their wits on the hard work of others.[22]

The conspiracy theory was further substantiated by the decline of British Montreal, although it was due to totally different reasons than those suggested by the antisemites. American investments in Canada were on the rise; so was the influence of a continental mass culture that was gradually undermining Montreal, a seaport that faced the Atlantic, in favour of a city previously considered of secondary significance: Toronto. Not Jews, but French Catholics were resurgent, with the emergence of a middle-class destined to gain enough political momentum in the 1950s and 1960s to force major institutional and linguistic changes on Quebec.

L'Université de Montréal

As McGill University was emblematic of Anglo-Protestant attitudes in the interwar period, l'Université de Montréal and its "Jewish problem" was representative of French Quebec. Whereas Jewish enrollment at McGill had risen to 25 percent of the student body in the early 1920s, the Jewish constituency at its French counterpart never rose above 5 percent for the entire era. Clearly, Jews in Montreal much preferred a British environment, and only when the latter was denied them at the university level did they contemplate the possibility of studying in a Franco-Catholic milieu (see Table 5). Even the faculties most likely to attract Jews at l'Université de Montréal fared poorly compared to McGill, with only 15 percent in law in 1933-34, 6 percent in medicine and 22 percent in pharmacy (see Table 6). It is true that Jews on the other side of the mountain were bound to experience obstacles not found at McGill, but these limitations were not primarily the result of antisemitic policies. Rather, l'Université de Montréal was officially and canonically a Catholic university that, according to strict Vatican doctrine, required its students to engage in the daily practice of their faith.[23] Besides the normal linguistic problems, Jewish students could hardly be comfortable in an institution where most of the teachers and administrators were priests, where crucifixes were common in the classrooms, and where prayers before instruction were a daily habit in certain faculties.

A major difference between the two dominant ethnic communities in Montreal regarding Jews can be seen in how the "Jewish crisis" was handled by their respective universities. At McGill, no public statement was issued concerning Jewish enrollment, and no internal regulations were drafted with a specific policy in mind. The *numerus clausus* in medicine and the more general system of varying matriculation requirements in the faculty of arts were never written in any official document; instead, they were part and parcel of a general consensus among senior administrators in the form of a gentlemen's agreement.[24] At l'Université de Montréal, on the other hand, as soon as the signs of trouble were noticed, agitators and ideologues in the French population at large seized the occasion to air their own ideas. The result was a public debate as to how much religious plurality should be tolerated in Catholic institutions. While the Anglo-Saxons stood silent, the Francophones literally assailed their university to obtain information on the number of Jews in its midst. At the same time, opposing factions within the nationalist movement did not miss the

Table 5
Distribution by Faculty of the Total Number of Students,
and the Number of Students of Jewish Origins,
Université de Montréal, 1920-36

Faculties	Total number of students			Students of Jewish origin		
	1920-21	1930-31	1935-36	1920-21	1930-31	1935-36
Arts	645	723	726	8	36	36
Commerce	29	222	125	–	11	10
Applied Sciences	396	467	478	5	2	3
Medicine	240	303	318	3	16	20
Total	1310	1715	1647	16	65	69
Graduate students	11	28	21	–	–	–
Total	1321	1743	1668	16 (1.2%)	65 (4.1%)	69 (4.4%)

Source: "Distribution of Total Students and Jewish Students at University of
Montreal," Canadian Jewish Congress Archives, Montréal.

Table 6
Distribution of Jewish Students at l'Université de Montréal,
for Certain Faculties and Schools, 1932-34

Faculties and and schools	No. of Jewish Students		Total no. of students	Percentage of Jewish students
	1932-33	1933-34	1933-34	1933-34
Law	34	32	218	15
Medicine	15	15	246	6
Sciences	1	5	124	4
Dental Surgery	2	2	84	2
Pharmacy	29	22	102	22
Total	82	76	774	10

Sources: "Les Juifs à l'Université de Montreal, 1932-33, 1933-34," Archives de
l'Université de Montréal, fonds du secrétariat général (1876-1950) et Mgr.
A. V. J. Pietter: Lettre au frère Hilaire, C. S. C., Montréal, March 2, 1934, in
Bulletin des études 7 (April): 138-40.

opportunity to settle accounts with each other. The desire to intervene in
university affairs reached endemic proportions in 1934 with the Gobeil
incident, when a Conservative backbencher from Compton, in an attempt
to sting the provincial Liberals, declared in the House of Commons: "Si

vous l'aimez tant que cela, notre race, allez donc épurer l'Université de Montréal de son élément rouge qui la domine, de la juiverie qui y contamine notre jeunesse, des professeurs athées qui y forment nos jeunes gens."[25]

The public exposure of the university's policy toward its Jewish clientele was a source of extreme embarrassment for its senior administrators, the majority of whom were high officials of the church, accustomed to clerical discretion and religious authoritarianism. In fact, from the date of its foundation as an independent institution of 1920, l'Université de Montréal had conceived a policy of *laissez-faire* toward Jewish admissions, generally accepting without condition the handful of candidates who cared to study in the particular climate that prevailed within its walls. However, the discriminatory policies of McGill University changed this relative indifference, so that, by the early 1930s, Jewish attendance had entered a phase of modest increase in certain schools and faculties. Still, it was the pressure of nationalist elements that compelled the university to spell out a coherent policy by the mid-1930s, when a mounting campaign in certain radical circles seized on the issue as an excuse for increased anti-Jewish agitation. In a private memoir written in October 1933 by Mgr. Piette, the rector of l'Université de Montréal, for the chancellor,[26] Mgr. Gauthier, in order to justify to the diocesan authorities the institution's liberal policy toward its Jewish students, it was declared: "Les Juifs sont astreints à toute notre discipline à l'Université de Montréal. Nous sommes intransigeants avec eux et ils se soumettent docilement à nos règlements. En certaines facultés, ils sont les plus appliqués."[27] Two years later, in what appeared as an official statement, a Dominican member of the University's Commission des études published these significant lines in a Catholic journal:

> Un seul motif pourrait faire écarter les Juifs de l'Université [de Montréal]: ce serait le danger que cette fréquentation ferait courir à nos étudiants. Or ce danger est nul. Les Juifs n'ont guère donné jusqu'ici que des exemples de travail et de bonne tenue. Ceux qui ont la charge de la discipline universitaire n'hésitent pas à en témoigner.[28]

The main objections to Jewish admissions did not stem from the rector's cabinet or from high officials, as had been the case at McGill, but from the student body itself. On March 13, l'Association générale des étudiants de l'Université de Montréal (AGEUM) submitted to the rector a petition that requested the expulsion of all persons of Jewish origin: "Qu'il soit résolu que l'exécutif de l'AGEUM attire respectueusement l'attention des autorités universitaires sur ce problème d'exceptionnelle gravité [. . .] cela en vue d'obtenir l'exclusion d'un élément [les Juifs] que les étudiants proclament publiquement non désirable."[29] The most dra-

matic incident occurred in the summer of 1934, when a dozen interns at
l'Hôpital Notre-Dame, an institution affiliated with l'Université de Montréal, called a general strike in response to the admission of a Jew to their
group: Samuel Rabinovitch. Although fluent in French and dedicated to
his profession,[30] the Jewish intern was forced to resign after three days as
the strike spread to other hospitals, much to the dismay of the university
authorities. The spontaneous movement of the Francophone interns took
the latter completely by surprise.[31]

The Notre-Dame Hospital incident probably represented a peak in the
antisemitic agitation that erupted in Quebec during the interwar period.
In itself, it could scarcely be compared with *Kristallnacht* or with other
violent acts soon to be perpetrated against Jews in Europe, but it brought
sinister portents to the threshold of the Montreal Jewish community and
was perceived by many as a sign of the times. Nearly every French newspaper in Quebec reacted to the strike, and, as the news reached the rest of
Canada, the recently reactivated Canadian Jewish Congress was shaken to
its foundations. The roots of this student opposition to Jews in a Catholic
institution of higher learning, as exemplified by the Notre-Dame Hospital
boycott, lay in the fear of economic competition as well as professional
overcrowding (similar to McGill). Although sometimes draped in terms
more pertinent to Catholic religiosity than ethnic friction on the marketplace, French resentment arose from the prospect of well-educated Jews,
cognizant of the French language and Québécois social customs, taking up
positions that had hitherto been the preserve of French Canadians. In this
respect, the 1929 petition of the AGEUM leaders had been quite clear, even
if it had called for the disfranchisement of Jews on religious grounds:
"Attendu qu'en les acceptant comme étudiants réguliers [les Juifs],
l'Université de Montreal leur fournit l'occasion et les moyens de lutter sur
le même terrain professionnel que les autres étudiants et les met en état de
leur nuire plus tard dans la vie."[32] Whereas McGill administrators had
employed a covert strategy to cope with Jewish admissions, playing their
cards behind closed doors, Francophone opponents of the admission policies de l'Université de Montréal paraded their anger in public, initiating a
bitter controversy of unprecedented proportions in Quebec. Despite this
difference, however, the grievances were similar on both sides of the
linguistic fence. Only the style and social basis of these ethnocentric
claims differed, a fact that could hardly be disguised, in light of the many
socio-economic factors separating French and English society.

It is important to stress that not all Catholics supported the antisemitic
agitators of French-speaking Montreal. Unlike the Anglo-Saxon community, which seemed to present a united front on the Jewish question,
refusing to discuss the issue in the media, Francophones often used the
Jewish issue in order to define broader problems, e.g., outside domination

of the provincial economy, foreign cultural influence and even indifference to Catholic teachings and dogmas. Thus the Jews served as a catalyzing impulse during an era of social crisis in the face of which French Canadians felt impotent because of their minority status. Was it not more convenient to point the finger at a minority than to examine the real problem and its possible solutions? Even worse, various factions in the nationalist movement often used the Jewish issue as a means of attacking ideological rivals in their own political family. Was Jewish admission to l'Université de Montréal not proof that Catholics were being undermined in their own institutions?

> En feuilletant le "Manuel des Étudiants" de l'Université, il est pénible de constater que les nouveaux règlements adoptés au printemps de 1931 portent l'empreinte de l'influence juive, au point d'affecter visiblement le caractère de cette institution. Partout perce le souci constant de ne pas blesser l'arrogance toujours croissante des non-chrétiens juifs qui ont pris d'assaut les différentes facultés universitaires.[33]

Nonsense, argued Edmond Turcotte, editor of *Le Canada*, the organ of the provincial Liberal party. If Jews are allowed to pass through the gates of l'Université de Montréal, it means that the French intelligentsia is now recognized outside of a purely Catholic milieu:

> En s'inscrivant à l'Université de Montréal, plutôt qu'à McGill, l'Israélite rend un hommage indirect à l'université, à la valeur de son enseignement, à la science de ses maîtres. Cela vaut mieux que si tous les Israélites [. . .] fuyaient l'Université de Montréal comme un cénacle d'ignorance et un foyer d'obscurantisme.[34]

The School Question

Nothing exemplifies more than the Jewish school question the complex and ambiguous character of the position of the Jewish community in Montreal, where specific legal provisions had created a situation virtually unique in Canada. The signing of the Canadian Confederation in 1867 occurred when few Jews resided in the country, and when those who did were willing to adapt to Protestant notions of individualism and religious liberalism because of their British origins. Few Quebec Jews, if any, protested when the public school system was established on a confessional basis.[35] This meant that Protestants and Catholics (a distinction that corresponded roughly at the time to the linguistic division between English and French) would administer separate denominational school commissions with public funds, free from state interference.[36] In a society without significant non-Christian minorities, and in which religious affiliation was seen as an integral part of the ethnic identity of the two dominant communities, it stood to reason that church involvement in the educational affairs of the province was entirely legitimate. No one foresaw the day when new ethnic communities would be formed, claiming their share of the public funds allotted to primary education. In Quebec, under the *British North America Act*, only Christians of Catholic and various Protestant persuasions were granted the right to declare themselves dissidents from the majority rule for educational purposes.

When *Ashkenazic* Yiddish-speaking Jews began arriving in Quebec en masse at the turn of the century, they immediately found themselves in a legal void with respect to education, since every conceivable right had been granted to the Catholic and Protestant establishments alone. The latter administered together the all-powerful *Conseil de l'Instruction publique*. Thus, school taxes were collected exclusively for Catholic or Protestant purposes, with individual taxpayers declaring their denominational affiliation, while "neutral" combinations, such as those levied from corporations, were divided between the two school boards. For reasons already given, wealthy Jews had chosen in the second half of the nineteenth century to be registered on the Protestant lists for taxation purposes, and most had elected to send their children to English-language institutions. What was reasonably acceptable when only a handful of non-Christian families resided in Montreal became far more problematic a generation or two later, when neutral enrollment in the Protestant schools skyrocketed. The informal entente that had tolerated a Jewish presence in the Protestant sector was applicable only to class attendance, with no Jewish participation allowed on school committees or Jews hired as teachers. In 1903, with mounting demographic pressure on the part of Jewish immigrants, a provincial law was passed stipulating that, for administrative purposes, Jews would be considered as persons of Protestant origin, whose aspirations in every sphere but the religious could be satisfied by the Protestant school commission.[37] That year in Montreal, 23 percent of the children registered in English-language Protestant schools were Jewish, or a little over 2000 pupils, a figure that represented a dramatic increase over the previous decade.[38]

By the end of World War I, the Jewish percentage in the Protestant schools had nearly doubled from the time of the 1903 law, reaching 40 percent in 1919. Almost 14 000 Jewish children, an all-time high in absolute numbers, were enrolled in 1923, so abrupt had been the Jewish demographic surge in the early twentieth century. The tensions between Jews and Protestants had been acute enough in 1903, but a state of permanent crisis ensued during the interwar period. Not only were Jews being massively introduced into the heart of the Protestant educational domain, as defined by the constitutional law of 1867, but by sheer weight of numbers, they began to agitate for just representation in the Protestant school administration of the city. Several campaigns were mounted to insure the election of a school commissioner of Jewish origin, but they all failed.[39] The situation deteriorated further when it became clear that the Anglophone community would not abandon its legal prerogatives, demanding the strict application of the confessional principle as stated in the 1867 pact in order to exclude all non-Protestants from school affairs.[40] Financial tensions appeared as well, as the cost of educating Jewish children was falling entirely on Protestant heads, since few Jewish households were wealthy enough to be placed on the Protestant taxpayers' list. The matter came to a critical juncture in 1922, when negotiations were being conducted in the *Conseil de l'Instruction publique* to obtain additional sources of revenue for the education of Jewish children. The Protestant authorities, no longer amicable to the notion of Jews on Montreal's only Protestant school commission, succeeded in rescinding the privileges granted to the Jewish population by the 1903 law. To the Jewish community, this news came as a crushing blow, annihilating 60 years of patient lobbying in favour of a progressive Jewish integration into the Protestant sector.

The impending expulsion of Jewish pupils could only be halted by government intervention, and, in 1924, Quebec premier Louis-Alexandre Taschereau created a special commission to inquire, among other subjects, into the Jewish school question.[41] Twelve thousand pupils of Jewish origin awaited the verdict of the Gouin commission, whose only contribution was to suggest that the provisions of the 1903 provincial law should be tested before a superior court. On this occasion, both Protestant and Catholic members were quick to reiterate the strict application in the school system of the confessional exclusiveness devised by the Fathers of Confederation; no legal breakthroughs or alternate solutions could have been expected from them. Moreover, the three-member Jewish delegation in the Gouin commission revealed that the Jewish community was now profoundly divided on the issue, with opposing factions contemplating different avenues for obtaining a settlement. On the one hand, Michael Hirsch and Samuel W. Cohen proposed a prolongation of the current agreement with the Protestant authorities, with certain rights of representation begin awarded to Jewish taxpayers — a reassertion of the traditional community position. On the other hand, Joseph Schubert demanded the creation of a new Jewish educational structure, based on confessional lines and endowed with the same prerogatives as the two existing school commissions. The reasoning behind Schubert's statement was that the legal rights granted to the two so-called founding denominations could be extended to include other religious traditions on an equal basis, regardless of historical prerogatives.[42] While the status quo was defended by established "uptown" Jews, Orthodox *Ashkenazic* Jewry and "downtown" immigrant secularists and nationalists, as represented by the newly founded Montreal *Va'ad Ha'ir*, pushed for the creation of a separate Jewish school commission. Regardless of the precise alignment of Jewish opinion, a new moment in history had arrived: Jews, finding no place for themselves in a bipartite, Christian, Canadian society, proposed the institution of a parallel structure, financially and legally autonomous, and modelled on the already existing principle of confessional exclusivism.

Perhaps, more than any other contemporary event, the school question illustrates the nature of the obstacles that prevented a satisfactory integration of citizens of Jewish origin into Quebec society. The educational provisions of 1867 had not been drafted in an anti-Jewish light per se, but they could certainly be used as formidable barriers to Jewish social mobility. Much of the antisemitism of the interwar period, once the economic factors have been taken into account, derived from this incapacity of Quebec society, both Protestant and Catholic, to entertain the view that other traditions than the Christian could occupy a position of responsibility in the legal sphere. No matter how the Jewish community defined its social aspirations, it was bound to be marginalized by virtue of its spiritual deviation, or at best held hostage by one of the two dominant confessions to which it was forced to submit for educational reasons. To many Christians, Jews appeared as a force bent on destroying a political status quo achieved with great difficulty, a fragile yet viable social consensus in a country where military conquest and the subjugation of one European colonial tradition by another had left deep cleavages. In tandem with this abhorrence of religious compromise, there appeared in the 1920s the first signs of a resurgence of a classic antisemitic discourse among both Catholics and Protestants exactly when the foundations of Canadian society were being tested by the school question. Among French Canadians in particular, a constant feeling of vulnerability added extra weight to the fear that their national identity would be weakened, once its religious and institutional safeguards had been removed. Were not French Canadians first and foremost Catholics, and was not Catholicism the protector of the French language? Surely the Roman church, dominated by a conservative clerical elite, was of the utmost importance in the struggle for cultural survival.

The Jewish school question in Quebec was ultimately resolved to the satisfaction of the assimilationist "uptown" Jewish party. After several years of litigation, it was decided in 1928 by the Privy Council in London that the only legal right that Jewish children in Montreal could claim was to attend the classes of one of the two legally established school commissions. It was also determined that the provincial government had the constitutional power to create separate school commissions, based on confessional exclusivism, if it so wished. Immediately, the "downtowners" began lobbying for the establishment of a Jewish school commission in Montreal, endowed with an entirely autonomous body of administrators and a budget tailored to its needs. Negotiations were begun, and a law to that effect was drafted by the Taschereau government, called the David Bill of 1930. Meanwhile, Jewish uptowners were conducting intense secret negotiations with the Protestant school authorities, convinced that the only viable alternative for the community rested in an administrative compromise with the commission under which Jewish children were already receiving an education. The threat of a separate Jewish entity served only as a lever to gain advantages within the already existing system as far as the assimilationists were concerned. Campaigning against the David project throughout 1930, the uptowners finally announced the ratification of a 15-year contract between the Jewish community and the Protestant school commission. When the final version of the David Bill was finally passed in the Quebec legislature in April 1931,[43] no provisions other than those already contained in the 1903 law were added, leaving Jewish children exactly where they were before. Another generation would have to pass before Jews were to gain fair representation in the Protestant school commission of Montreal, this time on a purely voluntary basis.

Francophone Nationalism

The Quebec Catholic hierarchy had been quite adamant in its opposition to the creation of a separate school commission for Jewish children in the late 1920s.[44] The church feared that such a legal act might trigger a chain reaction leading to the establishment of a purely neutral school system alongside the confessional structures, entirely supported and run by a Quebec secular bureaucracy. It was simply inconceivable to the clergy that infrastructures and social entities in the province, and in Canada in general, could be founded on principles other than those supplied by the Christian faith. Ultimately, this prospect remained in the realm of pure ideas, since the Catholics were not called to the negotiating table when final arrangements were worked out to reintegrate the Jews in the Protestant school commission. Nonetheless, the agitation around the Jewish school question signalled the beginning of a new wave of antisemitic rhetoric in the French Catholic population, which reached its climax around 1934-35, probably the peak moment of anti-Jewish sentiment in twentieth-century Quebec. These years also constituted the most difficult period of economic hardship in the interwar period, when fears of foreign domination were pronounced in the province. It is not surprising, therefore, that the ideology of nationalism flourished at this time.

The Catholic church possessed an Augustinian understanding of Judaism and Jews that remained basically unchanged, except for minor variations depending on the political climate of the times.[45] Jews were regarded as enemies of the Roman faith in the midst of Christendom, sometimes in an active and aggressive fashion, but most often as blind and stubborn disbelievers in the truth of salvation through Christ.[46] They could not be admitted as active members of the *urbs*.[47] Furthermore, Jews appeared as expatriates par excellence, in a constant state of residential instability, unwilling to strike roots or pay homage to a king or a country and abide by the laws of a given society. This rootlessness, instead of being recognized as a result of civil marginalization inflicted by Christian majorities, was deemed a punishment for the deicide perpetrated against the Son of God by their ancestors. Such rationalizations led to their being perceived as unproductive, usurious creatures, parasites on the isolated and underdeveloped local peasantries. Despite all the accusations of immorality and corruption, however, the church never denied that the Jews were also part of the divine plan revealed in Scripture and consequently sought them as potential converts. In the modern era, especially in countries and cultures deeply influenced by Catholicism such as French Canada, nationalists often drew on these traditional teachings. Ideas and perceptions endlessly repeated in Catholic literature, theology and sermons affected the secular mind in spite of itself. This fact is corroborated amply in Quebec by the Plamondon trial of 1913-14.[48] However, Quebec nationalism developed along less religious lines as well, finding in the early twentieth century new sources of friction with the Jewish community of Montreal. Unlike older Catholic doctrine, nationalism in Quebec was never a coherent school of thought, but a multiplicity of currents, some with quite precise goals, and others more broadly conceived. Often they have collided with each other. Hence, there has never been a single nationalist party, only a collection of movements emerging from different segments of society, whose sole common ground is the desire to secure the survival and health of the French presence in North America.[49]

In the interwar period, three major planks in the nationalist platform were likely to raise hostility against Montreal Jews. First and foremost was the openly avowed goal of francization, or the desire to make French the predominant language in daily business and the affairs of the provincial and local governments. With the rise of a French merchant class in the mid-nineteenth century, the public use of French became a vital symbol of Québécois nationalism. This movement steadily gained momentum in Quebec society, especially after the passing of the Lavergne law of 1910 in the provincial legislature, which required that French be given priority in public administration. Its turning point was reached in September 1910, when, at an international eucharistic congress in Montreal, Henri Bourassa reaffirmed publicly[50] the desire of the nationalists to preserve as one indivisible unit both the Catholic faith and the French language of the founding colonists.[51] After that date, the drive to make Quebec a Francophone society intensified to the point of providing the various nationalist factions with their single most important goal, thereby supplying a measure of unity to a wide ideological family that otherwise tended to splinter in all possible directions. No stone was left unturned during the interwar period to ensure that French would emerge as the dominant language,[52] and church-oriented institutions as well as purely secular organizations joined in the effort. It was a movement that had noticeable effects in urban centres, notably in Montreal—a city where business had been conducted almost entirely in the English language until the late nineteenth century.

Quebec nationalism also sought to expand the economic basis of French Québécois society. From the decades immediately following the conquest, when the economy rested almost entirely on agriculture and the exploitation of natural resources, Quebec emerged rapidly in the early twentieth century as an urbanized and industrialized province, especially in the Montreal region.[53] This change produced a defensive attitude, since most of the social innovations had been initiated by English or even by foreign influences.[54] Soon, nationalist movements agitated for the upper hand in certain sectors of the economy, notably in areas that required little capital and could benefit from the patronage of a vast French-speaking clientele, such as in the retail trades and light manufacturing. One specific issue temporarily fused the various forms of nationalism in the 1920s and 1930s: a staunch opposition to mass migration and the admission of immigrants from distant and radically divergent cultures, especially ones with different political mores. The period from 1910 to 1914 had seen many people of alien extraction come to Canada, assimilating, for the most part, into English society. As the percentage of Francophones in the nation diminished slowly, immigration was regarded as a threat to the reasonable equilibrium between the two founding peoples (see Table 7). Despite the decline in the number of individuals received as immigrants following the beginning of the Great Depression, French opposition to an open door policy remained unflagging until well after the end of World War II.

Table 7
Percentage of French Mother-tongue
Population in Canada, 1871-1931

	%
1871	31.1
1881	30.0
1891	–
1901	30.7
1911	28.6
1921	27.9
1931	28.2

Source: Federal Census of Canada, 1921, 1931.

On all these counts—refrancization, economic aspiration and anti-immigration agitation—the Jews appeared as an obstacle to the nationalist agenda. The Jewish community, moreover, was in a phase of rapid anglicization. This does not mean that some Jews, especially those engaged in petty trade, did not learn some French, but simply that the Jewish community had adopted English as a lingua franca, and was moving increasingly into the Anglo-Saxon orbit. In fact, Jewish social mobility resembled that of the French petty bourgeoisie, causing Jewish merchants to be seen as competitors in a society severely affected by the Depression. In the business world especially, where key positions were reserved for Anglo-Canadians, Jews and French Canadians often collided as they scrambled for new markets. Thus, in the 1930s, when the *Achat chez nous* movement reached its peak in an effort to encourage local French merchants, Jewish store-owners and peddlers were singled out as convenient examples of economic exploitation on the part of foreign entrepreneurs.[55] Moreover, although Jews accounted for only a small fraction of the total immigration to Canada in the first third of the twentieth century,[56] they were seen as one of the most vocal lobby groups in favour of an open door policy, further intensifying the suspicion with which the nationalists regarded them.[57]

This complex of nationalist causes did much to stir the hostility of the masses, giving the antisemitic mood of the interwar period its special colour and intensity. Most Quebec nationalists denounced the Jewish intrusion into the affairs of the province or used the Jewish case as a prime example of conduct that could only be detrimental in the long run to Quebec interests. Yet, for the most part, Jews did not rank very high in their preoccupations. Except for a brief interval in 1934-35, the Jewish question took a back seat to more urgent issues, such as the American and Anglo-Saxon domination of the Quebec economy, the education and moral improvement of the population, and ordinary political partisanship. In *Le Devoir*,[58] for instance, the leading nationalist daily of the period, while frequent anti-Jewish quips and gibes appeared in minor articles, full editorials devoted to the "Jewish problem" appeared only a dozen times in 1934-35, and even they were written in a mild and reasonable manner. The same can be said of *L'Action nationale*, a monthly publication published by the *Ligue d'action nationale*, an interest group without political affiliation under the influence of l'Abbé Lionel Groulx. One more case is that of the *Jeune-Canada* movement, made up of a handful of young activists, whose denunciation of the Montreal Jewish community in April 1933 seemed to herald a new climate of mutual suspicion.[59] In the two or three years during which *Jeune-Canada* caught the public eye, the Jewish question was raised only once (although admittedly at a sensitive moment). Mostly, the group embroiled itself in issues limited exclusively to the Francophone political realm. Studies by Richard Jones on *L'Action catholique*, a Quebec City daily, confirm these conclusions.[60]

The only exception to this rule of moderation was the movement launched in the late 1920s by Adrien Arcand, a journalist by trade and a proponent of the fascist ideologies of Mussolini and Hitler.[61] With his associate, Joseph Ménard, Arcand founded a number of vicious antisemitic publications, such as *Le Chameau, Le Patriote* and *Le Goglu*. In a pseudo-humorous vein, he attempted to disseminate in Quebec the classic accusations of blood-libel, world conspiracy and economic domination, similar to Julius Streicher's demagogic *Der Stürmer*.[62] Arcand's themes, however, apart from his obsession with Jews, were consistent with the predominant nationalist and agrarian spirit of the day, and he co-operated for some years with the federal Conservatives for reasons of political expediency. This Judeophobia was further stimulated by Hitler's rise to power, and, in 1934, the "Canadian Führer," as he was sometimes called, created a political party to advance his ideas: *Le parti national social chrétien*. While it is difficult to assess the exact influence and importance of the fascist movement in Quebec,[63] the longevity of its publications are suggestive. None of the half-dozen or so newspapers initiated by Arcand and his sympathizers received wide attention throughout the province, and most disappeared after only a few months. Furthermore, the better established and more professional nationalist press totally ignored his existence and his repeated attempts to vilify the Jews, leaving him in a void. *Le Devoir* does not seem to have mentioned his name once in its column throughout the 1930s nor were his party's activities on ideas reported in its pages.

The Jewish community of Montreal saw matters quite differently when it came to fascism. While most French intellectuals contemptuously rejected Arcand, Jews were seriously alarmed by his propaganda. In the summer of 1932, a Jewish merchant residing in Lachine, A. Abugov, decided to take Arcand to court on the basis of the false accusations levelled against Jews by *Le Goglu* and *Le Miroir*. The crux of Abugov's argument was that the fascists had committed libel against the entire Jewish population, and, by their verbal attacks and slanders, had actually threatened its physical security. Much to the dismay of the Jewish community, however, Abugov's cause was rejected in September of the same year on the ground that current provincial laws addressed themselves only to individual cases, and did not cover collectivities.[64] Despite several efforts in 1932 on the part of Peter Bercovitch and Joseph Cohen to introduce a bill in the provincial legislature specifically designed to cover cases of group libel, the Jewish community finally had to resort to other means to silence Arcand.[65] The reactivation of the Canadian Jewish Congress in 1933-34 and the incessant anti-defamation campaigns orchestrated by H. M. Caiserman from his Bleury Street office succeeded somewhat in restricting fascist influence among the general population. Meanwhile, because of Arcand's radical and racist form of nationalism, Canadian Jews became obsessed with local manifestations of antisemitism. Although Montreal Jews were suffering at Anglophone hands as well, the Catholic brand of Judeophobia seemed far more malignant than the Protestant, and French Canadians more willing to damage Jewish interests than their English counterparts.

Continuity and Rupture

Antisemitism in Quebec in the interwar period did not differ much from its antecedents around 1870. It only became more intense because of the social crisis of the Depression era and because of the ideological radicalization that followed. After the end of World War I, the appearance in Italy and Germany of fascist governments with full-fledged racist programs only aggravated the lure of supremacist ideas and the impact of Judeophobic propaganda on this side of the Atlantic.[66] The 1930s brought little that was not already known and well circulated in the realm of antisemitic ideas; however, the legal implementation of antisemitic agendas in Europe that had been confined previously to defamation pamphlets and marginal organizations was unique to the decade. Naturally, the Jewish reaction to antisemitism in the Nazi era was affected profoundly by the fate of European Jewry, and Jews in Canada were tempted to judge the reactions of their Christian neighbours in light of events in Hitler's Germany or in Pilsudski's Poland. Such a climate of mutual suspicion greatly reduced any chance for understanding between Jews and Christians in Montreal and served to isolate the minority further.

In Quebec, because of the existence of two solitudes, each served by its own educational and social institutions, and each with its own niche in the economy, Jews had to contend with two varieties of anti-Jewish feeling. It is false to imagine that the blame for antisemitic agitation rested only or mostly at the door of the French Catholics. As is illustrated in the case of the two universities, hostility to Jews could take different forms in these different milieux, and, at least in the realm of higher education, Anglophones were in a position to do the most harm to an emerging Jewish professional class. Both French and English in Quebec conceived of their societies along confessional as well as linguistic lines, and, for this reason, Jews could not easily penetrate the fabric of Quebec's social life. In the eyes of both Catholics and Protestants, with their 1867 constitutional safeguards, especially in the field of primary and secondary education, Quebec remained an entity founded on Christian principles. Within its borders, the two founding nations had achieved a reasonable measure of political equilibrium and mutual tolerance. This view of Québécois society was reflected in the Jewish school crisis of the 1920s, when Jews were denied access to Christian institutions.

In the 1930s, Montreal Jewry, because of its massive attraction to Anglo-Canadian society, became quite perplexed by French-Canadian politics. When antisemitic incidents began to occur, and the feeling of estrangement between the two Canadian minorities began to deepen for economic reasons, Quebec nationalism and activism grew increasingly ominous.

> The Jewish community developed a suspicion of the Quebec movement. It became more nearly unanimous in its association with federalism and consequently with the major Anglophone element. Decades were to pass before some Jews came to see the value of French Canada and its tradition. In the meantime very few were able to summon much sympathy for the distinct aspirations of French Canada.[67]

Thus, Montreal Jews came to fear French and Catholic extremism, even when the latter contained no elements of Judeophobia, or only its marginal traces. Yet, for all the anxiety it generated, antisemitism in French Quebec generally remained rhetorical and metaphorical in character, as well as confined to specific publications connected with ideological movements whose impact on society as a whole was minimal. Certainly, antisemitic acts were committed in the province, as the archives of the Canadian Jewish Congress reveal, but, except for the Notre-Dame Hospital strike of 1934 and the Arcand-led rallies later in the decade, most were individual in nature, consisting of verbal insults, street-corner brawls and placard-waving.[68] By and large, in the interwar period, Quebec Jews, as in the last decades of the nineteenth century, basically were not endangered by French antisemitic agitation:

> We have always had traces of antisemitism in French Canada. When I was a boy, there were intrusions into French-Canadian journalism of the propaganda led in France by Drumont, and made smart and fashionable by "l'Affaire Dreyfus." The ultramontane organs — "La Vérité," "La Croix" — were just as continuously bitter as Adrien Arcand's though perhaps a little more delicate in expression. . . .
> Both papers died of arrested circulation. The strong common sense of the French-Canadian gagged at and refused to swallow such stuff. While these newspapers lived and agitated, there was not a village in Quebec where a Jew could not set up his store, with absolute security for his person, his family and his stock.[69]

This is not to imply that the Jewish community did not feel the sting of prejudice, or that antisemitism was not a force to be reckoned with. But, for the most part, Quebec Jews suffered more from public indifference, although a few activists selected them as targets in a much wider national agenda. If a difference existed between French and English antisemitism, it was a difference in style. As French nationalist publications quarrelled publicly among themselves about how many Jews were acceptable in the country, Anglo-Canadians quietly implemented discriminatory policies in their institutions without broadcasting their prejudices. Understandably, the sound and fury of some of the Québécois literary and ideological circles became a source of great concern to Quebec Jews, particularly when racist regimes were being established in Europe. However, their alarm was deepened by their unfamiliarity with the nuances of the French language and the intricacies of Quebec politics. Despite the apparent hostility in some quarters, French Canadians harboured a highly ambivalent attitude toward Jews and Judaism, even during this troubled era. As John Higham has pointed out, racial or ethnic stereotypes need not produce direct behavioural consequences; they may even be accompanied by sympathy for the aggrieved minority.[70] Because the French Canadians themselves recognized their own minority status in Canada, and sometimes even exaggerated it, French nationalists actually proposed on occasion an emulation of Jewish financial and commercial success as a prime example of what could be achieved by an underdog competitor. One Jewish attribute especially appealed to the Québécois: group solidarity in the face of difficult odds! Many articles and texts otherwise hostile to Jews nevertheless stressed and admired their sense of collective unity:[71] "Ce sont les Juifs qui se chargent de nous rappeler nos devoirs. Ils se permettent bien, eux aussi, des querelles de famille, des rivalités. Devant l'étranger, ils savent serrer les rangs, présenter un front uni. Nous leur devons cet hommage."[72]

This fundamental ambivalence should be taken into account in any consideration of Quebec antisemitism. Perhaps it serves to explain the moderation with which the vast majority of French Canadians dealt with the Jewish question in practical terms. Novelist Roch Carrier, portraying a young man's first experience in an ethnically diverse Montreal, captured in a few sentences the mood of much of the Judeo-Catholic relationship in Quebec before the Quiet Revolution. In *Il est par là, le soleil*, Philibert, the son of a farmer from a distant parish, roams the downtown streets in utter desperation, finally entering one of the Jewish pawnshops on Craig Street in order to steal some object for resale later:

> S'il peut voler un Juif, il peut ne pas désespérer. Peut-être deviendra-t-il riche?
> [...] La police protège les Juifs parce que les Juifs contrôlent la police, les gouvernements et le commerce; tout le monde sait que les Juifs contrôlent même les Anglais. *Ah! pourquoi n'est-il pas Juif?*
> — *Ce serait moins difficile que d'être une bête puante de Canadien français.* Les Juifs, ils sont riches, puis, comme on a pas de fours crématoires au Québec, ils ont la sécurité complète. Si on avait des fours crématoires, c'est eux qui les auraient vendus. Ah les maudits Juifs![73]

Although the interwar period was continuous with earlier forms of anti-semitism in Quebec, the end of World War II signalled a complete break with established patterns. In retrospect, 1945 was a major turning point in the relations between Jews and Christians in Montreal, when most, if not all, of the visible manifestations of hostility and suspicion disappeared almost as suddenly as they had emerged in the 1870s.[74] In *Le Devoir*, despite its staunch opposition to mass migration that persisted well into the 1950s,[75] Jews were not mentioned once in the editorials as potential enemies of French Canada. Even Adrien Arcand and Joseph Ménard, who recovered their freedom in 1945, could not muster enough interest in their usual anti-Jewish demagogy to reappear in the public eye.[76] Other preoccupations had arisen, notably the urge to modernize and desecularize the province's education and social infrastructures. Under the aegis of a new intelligentsia led by André Laurendeau, the state acquired the primacy previously held by the church. With the passing of clerical domination and conservative nationalist ideologies, and with the increasing integration of Quebec into the North American liberal economy, Jews were no longer perceived as harbingers of new and dangerous forms of modernity dominated by materialism and immorality. Thus, the last major obstacle to the quiet integration of the Jewish community in Montreal was removed; a conclusion verified by the vigorous social mobility which Jews have enjoyed in Quebec after World War II. No parallel exists in any other recent immigrant community. The only recent moment de vérité occurred in 1976, when René Lévesque was elected on a neo-nationalist agenda with the promise of a referendum on sovereignty-association.

Notes

1 Jean Hamelin, *Histoire du catholicisme québécois* (Montreal: Boréal Express, 1984). See vol. 1, pp. 175-291.

2 Paul-André Linteau, et al., *Histoire du Québec contemporain: de la Confédération à la crise* (Sillery, PQ: Boréal Express, 1979), pp. 517-44, and Bernard L. Vigod, *Quebec before Duplessis: The Political Career of Louis-Alexandre Taschereau* (Montreal: McGill-Queen's University Press, 1986), pp. 156-61.

3 Paul-André Linteau, "La montée du cosmopolitisme montréalais," *Questions de culture* 2 (1982): 23-53 (Quebec).

4 Jean Hamelin, *Histoire économique du Québec, 1851-1896* (Montreal: Fides, 1971), pp. 161-84.

5 A doctrine within the Catholic Church that supported the absolute authority of the pope in matters of religious doctrine as well as social and political philosophy. Ultramontanism sought to submit the state to the moral teachings and spiritual direction of the church.

6 Jean-Claude Marsan, *Montréal in Evolution: Historical Analysis of the Development of Montreal's Architecture and Urban Environment* (Montreal: McGill-Queen's University Press, 1981), pp. 173-78.

7 Susan Mann-Trokimenkoff, *The Dream of Nation: A Social and Intellectual History of Quebec* (Toronto: Gage, 1982), pp. 100-14.

8 Whereas 99.23 percent of the Jewish population of Quebec was urbanized in 1931, only 59.5 percent of the Francophones lived in an urban environment. See Louis Rosenberg, *Canada's Jews: A Social and Economic Study of the Jews in Canada* (Montreal: Canadian Jewish Congress, 1939).

9 According to a study (p. 18) conducted by the Commission métropolitaine de Montréal and published in *La Presse*, March 11, 1938.

10 Unless otherwise noted, all the figures cited in this section are taken from Louis Rosenberg's excellent study, *Canada's Jews*.

11 Ibid.

12 Benjamin Gutelius Sack, *History of the Jews in Canada* (Montreal: Harvest House [1945], 1965).

13 Ronald Rudin, *The Forgotten Quebecers: A History of English-Speaking Quebec, 1759-1980* (Quebec: Institut québécois de recherche sur la culture, 1985), pp. 151-73.

14 Stanley B. Frost, *McGill University: For the Advancement of Learning* (Montreal: McGill-Queen's University Press, 1984). See vol. 2 (1895-1971), pp. 124-29.

15 Ibid., p. 125.

16 Letter from Ira Mackay, Dean of the Faculty of Arts, to J. A. Nicholson, Registrar, June 15, 1926, archives of McGill University, Montreal.

17 Letter from Ira Mackay to J. W. Jenkins, assistant registrar, August 27, 1928, archives of McGill University, Montreal.

18 Letter from L. Simpson, Assistant Dean in the Faculty of Medicine, to Principal L. W. Douglas, January 14, 1938, archives of McGill University, Montreal.

19 Letter, April 23, 1926, archives of McGill University, Montreal.

20 For an interesting and probably representative description of what life was like for Jewish students on the McGill campus during the 1920s, consult Usher Caplan's biography of A. M. Klein, *Like One that Dreamed* (Toronto: McGraw-Hill Ryerson, 1982).

21 Dan A. Oren, *Joining the Club: A History of the Jews and Yale* (New Haven: Yale University Press, 1985), and Harold S. Wechsler, *The Qualified Student: A History of Selective College Admission in America* (New York: John Wiley and Sons, 1977).

22 John Higham, *Send These to Me: Jews and Other Immigrants in Urban America* (New York: Atheneum, 1975), p. 181.

23 See *L'annuaire général 1934-35* (Montreal: Université de Montréal, 1934), pp. 10-13.

24 In the university archives, passages pertaining to Montreal Jews are to be found in the private internal correspondence of a handful of administrators such as the Principal, the Dean of Arts and the Registrar.

25 Cited in a pamphlet published shortly after the incident and entitled; *La Griffe rouge sur l'Université de Montréal* (p. 9). It was printed by Adrien Arcand's *Le Patriote*, and a swastika adorned its front cover.

26 According to its charter, the highest position within the university's administrative structure was held by the Bishop of Montreal, who personally had a final say in all matters affecting the institution's internal policy.

27 Document entitled: "Juifs à l'Université de Montréal, 1933-34," archives of l'Université de Montréal, Montreal.

28 M.-Ceslas Forest, "La Question juive chez nous," *Revue dominicaine* 61 (December 1935): 329-49.

29 Document entitled: "Extrait du procès-verbal de la réunion de l'AGEUM," March 1, 1929, archives of l'Université de Montréal, Montreal.

30 Rabinovitch had obtained the highest marks in his class when graduating from the faculty of medicine.

31 For a published account of the strike, although written from the point of view of the strikers, see "Echo de la grève de Notre-Dame," *L'Action médicale* 10, 7 (July 1934): 351-53.

32 "Extrait du procès-verbal."

33 See "Les Juifs contaminent l'Université de Montréal," *Le Miroir*, Montreal, October 22, 1932, p. 3.

34 Edmond Turcotte, "Les Juifs à l'Université de Montréal," *Le Canada*, Montreal, October 7, 1933, p. 2.

35 According to the *British North America Act*, education was entirely a matter of provincial jurisdiction.

36 Antonin Dupont, *Les Relations entre l'Église et l'État sous Louis-Alexandre Taschereau, 1920-36* (Montreal: Guérin, 1973), pp. 253-73.

37 "Loi amendant les lois concernant l'instruction publique relativement aux personnes professant la religion judaïque," *Statuts du Québec*, chap. 16, April 25, 1903. See Harold Ross, "The Jew in the Educational System of the Province of Quebec" (M.A. thesis, McGill University, Montreal, 1947).

38 Before World War II, la Commission des écoles catholiques de Montréal had virtually no English-language sector, save for schools attended by the Irish Catholics. It was only with the important Italian influx of the 1950s that English classes became more commonplace on the Catholic side. See Hyman Neamtan, "The Rise and Fall of the Jewish Attendance in the Protestant Schools of Greater Montreal," *The Canadian-Jewish Year Book, 1940-41*, vol. 2 (Montreal: Woodward Press, 1940), pp. 180-96.

39 Ross, "The Jew in the Educational System."

40 Elson I. Rexford, *The Jewish Population and the Protestant Schools: Our Educational Problem* (Montreal: Renouf, 1924).

41 Vigod, *Quebec before Duplessis*.

42 David Rome, "On the Jewish School Question in Montreal, 1903-1931," in *Canadian Jewish Archives*, new series, no. 3 (Montreal: Canadian Jewish Congress, 1945), p. 136. See also Pierre Anctil, *Le Rendez-vous manqué: Les Juifs de Montréal face au Québec de l'entre-deux-guerres* (Quebec: Institut québécois de recherche sur la culture, 1988), chap. 4.

43 "Loi concernant l'éducation de certains enfants dans Montréal et Outremont," *Statuts du Québec*, chap. 63, April 4, 1931.

44 Antonio Huot, abbé, "La Question juive chez nous," *L'Action catholique* (Québec), May 17, 1926, p. 3; May 18, 1926, p. 3; and May 19, 1926, p. 3.

45 Léon Poliakov, trans., *The History of Anti-Semitism*, vol. 4 (New York: Vanguard Press, 1985),

46 Jules Isaac, *L'Enseignement du mépris: Vérité historique et mythes théologiques* (Paris: Fasquelle éditeur, 1962).

47 Jacob Katz, *Out of the Ghetto: The Social Background of Jewish Emancipation, 1770-1870* (New York: Schocken Books, 1973).

48 David Rome, "The Plamondon Case and S. W. Jacobs," in *Canadian Jewish Archives*, vol. 2, new series, no. 26-27 (Montreal: Canadian Jewish Congress, 1982).

49 In Quebec, a politically oriented nationalism appeared only after the Quiet Revolution of the 1960s and was largely a product of it.

50 The event and the speech itself became known as "le discours de Notre-Dame," in reference to the name of the church in which it was pronounced.

51 Henri Bourassa, *Religion, langue, nationalité* (Montreal: Imprimerie du "Devoir," 1910).

52 In that sense, the successive language laws of the 1960s and 1970s in Quebec appeared at the end of a long maturation process extending back almost a century.

53 Jean Hamelin, *Histoire économique du Québec, 1851-1896* (Montreal: Fides, 1971), pp. 261-303.

54 Yves Roby, *Les Québécois et les investissements américains, 1918-1929*, Cahiers d'histoire de l'Université Laval, no. 20 (Quebec: Presses de l'Université Laval, 1976), pp. 81-118.

55 The *Achat chez nous* campaigns were often conducted quite independently by specific interest groups. In English their slogan would translate as: "Buy from your own."

56 From 1911-20 Jews represented only 1.72 percent of the total immigration to Canada, 4.02 percent in 1921-30 and 5.19 percent in 1931-40. For further statistical information, consult Morin and Rosaire, *L'Immigration au Canada* (Montreal: L'Action nationale, 1966), p. 172.

57 Irving M. Abella and Harold Troper, *None Is Too Many: Canada and the Jews of Europe, 1933-1948* (Toronto: Lester & Orpen Dennys, 1982).

58 The editorials most directly concerned with the Jewish presence in Montreal appeared in *Le Devoir* on January 18 and 22, on February 3 and 8 and on March 3, 1934. See Pierre Anctil, *"Le Devoir," Les Juifs et l'immigration. De Bourassa à Laurendeau* (Quebec: Institut québécois de recherche sur la culture, 1988), p. 161.

59 The *Jeune-Canada* had reacted to the presence of French-Canadian politicians at a rally held by the Jewish community of Montreal on April 6, 1933, to protest against Jewish persecutions in Nazi Germany. For a complete transcript of the speeches pronounced on April 20, 1933, at a meeting of the *Jeune-Canada*, consult *Politiciens et Juifs*, no. 1 (Montreal: Les Cahiers des Jeune-Canada, 1933). See also Denis Chouinard, "Des contestataires pragmatiques: les Jeune-Canada, 1932-1938," *Revue d'histoire de l'Amérique française* 40, 1 (1986): 5-28 (Montreal).

60 Richard Jones, *L'Idéologie de l'Action catholique, 1917-1939*, Collection histoire et sociologie de la culture, no. 9 (Quebec: Presses de l'Université Laval, 1974), pp. 69-92, 269-81.

61 Réal Caux, "Le Parti national social chrétien. Adrien Arcand, ses idées, son oeuvre et son influence" (M.A. thesis in political science, Université Laval, Quebec, 1958).

62 Lita-Rose Betcherman, *The Swastika and the Maple Leaf: Fascist Movements in Canada in the Thirties* (Toronto: Fitzhenry & Whiteside, 1975).

63 The federal authorities seized all the documentation pertaining to Arcand's political activities in June 1940, when most sympathizers of the Axis powers were arrested in Canada and interned for the duration of the war.

In 1938, H. M. Caiserman, Secretary-General of the Canadian Jewish Congress, estimated the membership of Arcand's fascistic party at 5000, while admitting that:

"The Mounted Police of Montreal, who claim to know the situation well, know of only 450 members of the Nazi party in the district of Montreal." See letter by H. M. Caiserman to A. G. Brotman, Secretary of the Board of Deputies of British Jews, London, England, March 15, 1938, Archives of the Canadian Jewish Congress, Montreal.

64 See "L'honorable juge Désaulniers refuse d'accorder une injonction en faveur d'un marchand Israélite," *La Presse*, September 13, 1932, p. 3.

65 Betcherman, *Swastika and the Maple Leaf.*

66 Michel Winock, *Edouard Drumont et Cie: Antisémitisme et fascisme en France* (Paris: Seuil, 1982).

67 David Rome, *Clouds in the Thirties: On Antisemitism in Canada, 1929-1939* (Montreal: Canadian Jewish Congress, 1977-81), p. 32.

68 A few Jews perceived early that such was the nature of French-Canadian antisemitism but, for reasons of political strategy, chose not to stress the point publicly. In an undated and probably unpublished article written during the first Duplessis term of the late 1930s, H. M. Caiserman expanded on the moderate character of Francophone reaction, noting for instance: "This simple truth (the necessity of co-operation between ethnics) is probably understood by the French Canadian masses, which explains the small success attained by "l'Achat chez nous" movement, in spite of the wide propaganda spread throughout the province during the last 4 or 5 years." Quoted from "Antisemitism in Canada," undated document in the Caiserman papers, Canadian Jewish Congress Archives, Montreal.

A study conducted in 1986 by Quebec's Justice minister, Herbert Marx, concluded that no laws based on racial or ethnic discrimination had ever been implemented by the Quebec legislature. See "Marx vante l'absence de discrimination dans la législation du Québec," *Le Devoir* June 13, 1986, p. 2. It might be useful to add as well that none of the fascist-oriented activists of the interwar period were ever elected to public office in Quebec, Adrien Arcand included.

69 R. L. Calder, "Is the French Canadian a Jew-Baiter," *The Canadian Jewish Year Book, 1940-41*, vol. 2 (Montreal: Woodward Press, 1940), pp. 153-55.

70 Higham, *Send These to Me.*

71 One of the most remarkable pieces in this vein was published anonymously under the title "Trois Israélites," in *Le Devoir*, September 8, 1934, p. 1.

72 Roger Duhamel, "Chroniques dans la cité," *L'Action nationale* 12, 4 (December 1938): 326 (Montreal).

73 Roch Carrier, *Il est par là, le soleil* (Montreal: Éditions du Jour, 1970), pp. 118-19.

74 The Jewish community was keen on noticing this *retournement*, as is evident in an editorial published anonymously in the official organ of the Canadian Jewish Congress, "The State of Anti-Semitism in French Canada," *Congress Bulletin* 4, 4 (May 1947): 24-25. See Pierre Anctil, "A. M. Klein: The Poet and His Relations with French Quebec," in *The Jews of North America*, ed. Moses Rischin (Detroit: Wayne State University Press, 1987), pp. 247-64.

75 Consult, for instance, the editorials in *Le Devoir* of September 13, 1946; March 26, May 8, October 7 and 15, 1947.

76 W. E. Greening, "Adrien Arcand Rides Again," *The Chicago Jewish Forum* 13, 4 (1955): 207-12.

7

Politics, Religion and Antisemitism in Alberta, 1880-1950

Howard Palmer

Introduction

Although the Keegstra affair has drawn attention to antisemitism in rural Alberta, its provincial roots have never been fully explored. Because of the complexity of public attitudes toward Jews, the absence of documentary evidence and its covert and diffuse nature, the exact degree of its presence at various times in the history of the province is difficult to determine. Antisemitism found organized expression during the 1930s and 1940s primarily in one wing of the Social Credit movement. Since Protestant fundamentalism acted as midwife in the birth of Social Credit, the religious ethos requires examination. Despite dispensationalist support for Zionism as a fulfillment of biblical prophecy — a harbinger of the second coming — North American fundamentalism frequently has taken an anti-Jewish twist: some sociologists have even found a connection between conservative religiosity itself and antisemitism.[1] Yet the fundamentalist Social Credit leaders, William Aberhart and Ernest Manning, both denounced antisemitism as unChristian. If it did not stem from these important figures, what were its true origins in Alberta? Did Social Credit antisemitism come from south of the border? After all, the movement was populist in character, and some American historians have detected an anti-Jewish cast in American populism. These questions will be addressed.

Jews and the Pioneer Period

Perhaps the most important factor affecting Jews in the pioneer period from the 1880s to the 1920s was their small numbers. Although Jewish

---

Notes for Chapter 7 are on pp. 190-95.

immigrants in flight from persecution in eastern Europe began arriving in Alberta in the 1880s, they were largely ignored in the broader settlement of the west. By 1901, there were only 17 Jews in the territories destined to become Alberta; by 1911, in the midst of a massive influx of newcomers, the number had only increased to 1505 – 0.4 percent of the total population of 375 000. Early attempts were made to establish Jewish farming settlements, but these projects were small, isolated and dispersed, attracting little public attention. Most Alberta Jews, largely from Russia and Poland, settled in the cities and successfully adjusted to urban life, predominantly in small business.[2] By 1921, two thirds of Alberta's 3200 Jews lived in Calgary and Edmonton, where they developed a wide variety of religious, cultural and educational institutions.

The first public controversy over Jews in Alberta occurred in 1893, with the arrival in the central part of the province of 17 Jewish families (about 70 people). Having gone first to Chicago from eastern Europe, they had been recruited by an Alberta colonization agent to take up farmland near Red Deer after the opening of the Calgary-Edmonton railway in 1891. Both major papers in southern Alberta, the *Macleod Gazette* and *The Herald* (Calgary), looked askance at the newcomers, evoking the image of Shylock and questioning whether they were suited for farming. *The Herald* compared them unfavourably with other immigrants.

> If these people are the only settlers that can be obtained for the Northwest, there would even then be no reason to spend money in bringing them here to let them loose on the public, while practical men who can turn the prairies into fruitful fields are being forced away by the petty annoyances to which they are subjected. . . .[3]

Local dominion land officials were also unimpressed, feeling that the newcomers were unsuited to rural life; they also found their requests for financial help annoying. One official reported in 1894:

> They say they have no money at present. Altogether they are most undesirable immigrants, being miserably poor and knowing absolutely nothing about farming. Then again the white settlers in the locality object strongly to them as neighbors and are dreading a further incursion.[4]

Although assistance was received from a Jewish relief agency in England, the group was not able to adjust to pioneer conditions, and most returned to the United States within a couple of years. Later Jewish farming settlements established at Trochu, Rumsey and Sibbald between 1904 and 1911 with the help of the European-based Jewish Colonization Association were more successful, and did not arouse adverse publicity.[5]

For the Anglo-Saxon Protestants, mostly from Ontario and Britain, who had established almost exclusive control over the political, legal, cultural and educational institutions in Alberta during the formative era, the desirability of other immigrant groups was almost directly proportionate to their physical and cultural distance from London, England. In the local ethnic pecking order, Jews were near the bottom. British and American immigrants were regarded as the most desirable, followed by northern Europeans. There was considerable debate over central and eastern Europeans, since it was feared that they could not be assimilated. The bases of prejudice were many, including at times an alleged connection between eastern European immigration and slums, intemperance, criminality and radicalism.[6] Jews were seen as culturally and racially distinctive. Yet racial antisemitism, based on notions of Jewish racial inferiority, was limited. Those Jews who settled in Alberta encountered relatively little overt prejudice, despite being non-Christians in a society that defined itself as Christian; in the large influx of thousands of settlers of many different nationalities, they were simply ignored. On the other hand, because of their much larger numbers, controversial Christian religious sects, such as the Mormons, and eastern European immigrants, such as the Ukrainians, stirred far more public debate.[7] Urban Jews were mostly small entrepreneurs who did not belong to elite social groupings. However, they had a higher social status than most other central and eastern Europeans due to their higher degree of education and economic success. By the early 1900s, the urban press carried occasional features describing Jewish holidays and rituals.[8] When leading Jewish businessmen in Calgary appealed for funds in December 1905 to assist Jewish widows and orphans in Russia, much of the Calgary business and social elite responded favourably.[9]

The stereotype of the Jew as Shylock—greedy and deceitful—occasionally surfaced. The *Banff Crag and Canyon* reported in 1919 that two Jews had been arrested for carrying home brew. The trunk of their car was reported to have "camouflaged frankincense to be poured upon the altar of the Hebrew God—money—in the guise of a ten gallon jug of home brew."[10] Such comments, however, were rare in the press. While antisemitism existed in the province, it was relatively weak, lacking in ideology, organization and public expression. Jewish merchants who lived in the 1920s and 1930s in predominantly German, Ukrainian and Scandinavian small towns in northern and central Alberta enjoyed generally good relations with their neighbors.[11]

The Populist Revolt of the 1920s and Antisemitism

The 1920s witnessed the appearance of the United Farmers of Alberta and the Ku Klux Klan. Both, particularly the latter, were associated with antisemitism in the United States. Economic and political discontent in western Canada during World War I had led to a farmers' revolt, culminating in a sweep to power of the United Farmers of Alberta (UFA) in 1921. The

UFA was populist in character, and some of its leaders had participated in the American populist movement in the midwestern farm states during the 1890s. This represented a protest against alleged exploitation of the farming population by eastern economic elites. It was also an attempt to break with the major political parties, which were seen as the tools of business and financial interests.[12] Given the large influx of American farmers from the midwestern states at the turn of the century (22 percent of Alberta's population was American-born by 1911), and the similarity of economic and political grievances on both sides of the border, it is not surprising that the populist spirit had a significant impact on rural Alberta. An extended comparison is not required in order to prove this point. The parallels abound. For example, the writings of Henry Wise Wood, the leading figure in Albertan agrarianism for two decades, contain three of the dominant themes of American populist thought: (1) an assumption of a natural harmony of interest among the productive classes, (2) a dualistic (good versus evil) theory of social evolution and (3) a conspiracy theory of history. The major element that was minimized in Wood's writing—the doctrine of the primacy of money—later emerged forcefully in the Social Credit movement in the 1930s and 1940s.[13] American populism contained a definite strain of antisemitism, although its centrality is a subject of debate. Traditionally, to many farmers in western North America, there was a mystical connection between banks and Jews. "To populists the Jew was a non-producer, a mere manipulator of money, a parasite and at the same time representative of the sinister and forbidding power of international finance."[14] In both ideology and organization, the United Farmers of Alberta (UFA) and Social Credit were the descendants of US populism, even if they also were influenced by ideas of political reform from Britain and central Canada.[15] Significantly, antisemitism did not emerge in the UFA, but it did so with a vengeance in Alberta's second populist movement, Social Credit.

The contingent of UFA MPs who went to Ottawa in the 1920s included some of the ablest and most radical politicians ever elected in Alberta. These articulate men gave eloquent expression to the frustrations and aspirations of Alberta's farmers and to the cause of the downtrodden across Canada. They included William Irvine and Robert Gardiner, both Scottish immigrants, Edward Garland, an Irish-born orator and farmer, and George Coote, an Ontario-born ex-banker, who was the UFA's economic expert. Occasionally, they spoke out against ethnic discrimination. Social Gospeller William Irvine, for example, a Unitarian minister and the editor of the reformist *Alberta Non-Partisan*, which became the UFA newspaper, emphasized the need for religious tolerance and condemned antisemitism.[16] The UFA MPs believed that the existing banking system was unsuited to the credit needs of western agriculture, and condemned the banks accordingly, but their hostility lacked the anti-Jewish animus that later emerged in Social Credit.[17] There is, then, some irony that it was on UFA initiative that Major C. H. Douglas, an English engineer and the founder of Social Credit, first came to Canada in the 1920s to testify before the House of Commons' Standing Committee on Banking.

Nor did antisemitism find much expression in Alberta's Ku Klux Klan in the late 1920s, despite its presence in the American Klan. The upsurge of support for the Klan in Alberta in the late 1920s came partly in response to a new influx of largely Catholic immigrants from central and eastern Europe. Since government immigration policy discouraged Jewish immigration, and since most Jews went to central Canada in any case, few were among these immigrants. As a result, the Klan focused on Catholics. It grew slowly, achieving a total membership of around 5000, with Klan locals in 50 different communities — mostly in the Anglo-Protestant rural heartland of central and southern Alberta. Anti-Catholicism was its major article of faith: most of its literature and activities were directed against combatting the influence of the Roman Catholic church. Although the Klan did circulate copies of the notorious antisemitic forgery, *Protocols of the Elders of Zion*, antisemitism was a minor aspect of its ideology and activities.[18]

The Depression and Antisemitism

Previous economic and social stresses had led to prejudice against other ethnic and ethno-religious groups in Alberta, but the Jews had been largely ignored. However, the crisis of the 1930s finally precipitated a latent antisemitism which merged with other aspects of Alberta's political culture — hostility to banks, and a tendency to believe in conspiracies by evil forces bent on oppressing the common people.[19] This decade brought the most intense economic depression, the greatest class and political conflict, the most labour and social violence and the greatest agricultural challenges in Alberta's history. Protectionist economic policies and economic disaster in Europe cut off food imports from Canada, causing wheat prices to plunge. Net farm income slid from $102 million in 1928 to only $5 million in 1933, the low point of the Depression. Average per capita income declined from $548 in 1928-29, the third highest in the country, to $212 in 1933, well below the national average. The collapse of prices, coupled with prolonged drought and soil drifting in southern and east central Alberta, was devastating. Many farms were on the brink of disaster. A common prairie spectacle was the lineup at railway sidings of farmers with teams and wagons, waiting to get their dole of hay and grain for their stock, as well as food for themselves. Bread lines, soup kitchens, make-work relief projects, protest marches and confrontations between the police and the unemployed became routine in the cities. Albertans in all walks of life groped for some explanation for the devastation and poverty.[20]

As the Depression deepened, many turned to political panaceas. The UFA, once the bright hope for the future, came to be seen as just another old-line party. Some of the working class flirted with the Communists, while radical farm leaders tried to take the remains of the UFA into the socialist CCF. However, the political sensation of the era was Social Credit, a new and dynamic movement pledged to cure a sick economy, with a leader, William Aberhart, whose charismatic qualities matched the needs of a people hungry for authoritative guidance. Aberhart was simultaneously a Calgary high school principal, an extremely successful radio preacher and the founder and head of a successful Bible school. Social Credit embraced a monetary theory which explained the inner workings of capitalism and offered a remedy for its unsatisfactory functioning in periods of international depression. According to C. H. Douglas, the paradox of "poverty in the midst of plenty" could be ended by printing and distributing "social dividends." This would keep purchasing power and productive capacity in balance. Since commerce was carried on by means of credit, he believed that the power to issue or withhold credit entailed control over the commerce of the world. This power was currently in the hands of a small band of bankers and international financiers, and therefore had to be recaptured by "the people." Social Credit, as an alternative to both socialism and capitalism, appealed to almost all sectors of the population. Douglas did not advocate the overthrow of capitalism, but its reformation. This enabled him (and Aberhart) to uphold the principles of private ownership and enterprise, while denouncing those aspects of the system (such as the concentration of economic power) that were widely disliked by farmers, as well as the urban middle and working classes. In August 1935, Social Credit swept to power in Alberta, winning 56 of 63 seats and 54 percent of the popular vote. By October 1935, the sweep was complete. Campaigning on the proposition that "Social Credit absolutely demands that the power of the banker and the financier be broken," the federal branch of the party returned 15 members (out of a possible 17) to the House of Commons from Alberta.[21]

Antisemitism was not central in party propaganda. However, prompted by Douglas's writings and the American populist legacy, it emerged in one wing of the movement. Major Douglas himself was an arch-antisemite. His books and articles referred approvingly to the notorious antisemitic forgery, the *Protocols of the Elders of Zion*, which told of a Jewish plot to achieve world domination. When he claimed that the Jews were the evil force behind both Bolshevism and the capitalist system, he struck a sympathetic chord among some of the Alberta faithful. The economic devastation of the Depression, the need for scapegoats, the mythological link between Jews and money and the virtual absence of "real" Jews in much of rural Alberta were all conducive to the rise of antisemitism. Although not crucial to Douglas at the beginning, his reputation certainly gave it a new legitimacy; after all, for many Albertans, he was the man who had cast light on the mystery of the world economic system and its disorders.[22] In this manner, Social Credit helped to precipitate antisemitism in the province and also to legitimize and spread it.

Antisemitism in rural Alberta was ideological rather than personal. Since only a handful of the 4000 provincial Jews lived in rural areas at this time, the Jewish presence there was primarily figurative. For most farmers, the Jew was a character from the Bible and folklore, not a real person. Urban antisemitism, on the other hand, bore little resemblance to slogans and beer parlour and café folklore. As in cities across North America, it was primarily an upper-middle-class phenomenon. Exclusive social and sports clubs preserved their selectivity by barring allegedly brash, aggressive and materialistic Jewish businessmen and professionals in Edmonton and Calgary, where over 70 percent of the provincial Jewish population resided. However, probably due to their relatively small number, there were no quotas in Alberta's professional schools, such as existed elsewhere in Canada, especially in Ontario and Manitoba.[23]

Aberhart

Only three weeks after his party had swept to power, Premier Aberhart went to Detroit to discuss economics with two American folk heroes and economic reformers who were also notorious antisemites—Father Charles Coughlin and Henry Ford. Coughlin was a Catholic priest who had built up a huge radio following during the early 1930s with a combination of Christian radicalism, economic reform and denunciations of Jewish bankers. Henry Ford, the famous American car manufacturer, had been responsible for the English-language publication and distribution of the *Protocols of the Elders of Zion* (retitled *The International Jew*). Aberhart also was in touch with an important fundamentalist in the United States, William Bell Riley, whose books and sermons were loaded with anti-Jewish sentiments. Given his own fundamentalist background, Social Credit ideology, limited intellectual horizons and contact with known antisemites, the new premier seemed an almost natural proponent of the same obsession. As the most influential and charismatic politician in Alberta's history and the leader of its strongest social movement, he could have turned antisemitism into a dangerous political dogma. Instead, he publicly denounced anti-Jewish attitudes, and warned their perpetrators of divine judgment. Why?[24]

Since Aberhart never supplied any coherent overview of his ideas about Jews, we are left to piece them together from occasional references in sermons, statements to the press and personal correspondence. That he was aware of the national and international political issues surrounding the Jews cannot be doubted; he received a good deal of pro-Jewish literature from the Canadian Jewish Congress and considerable antisemitic literature from Canadian and American fascist organizations. His own beliefs were ambivalent and complex, and therefore difficult to characterize (or perhaps not so much ambivalent as, like other questions he dealt with, simply a bundle of contradictions).[25] The premier had little actual contact with Jews, but many preconceived notions. On the personal level, he had one close Jewish friend, Abe Schnitka, a Calgary printer. Schnitka was a perennial chess companion whom Aberhart appointed as King's Printer. On the theological level, Aberhart's religious convictions, in the main, predisposed him toward a positive view. Although he hoped that the Jews would eventually accept Christ as their saviour, he had a special place for them in his heart. After all, they were the people of God. Daniel, the Old Testament prophet, was one of his favorite references in his prophetic teaching. In 1926, before becoming involved with politics, he wrote: "The Christian should be interested in the Jewish race. Our Saviour was a Jew. The Jews have been the chosen people." In a letter to the editor of the *Western Jewish News* in 1936, Aberhart, then premier, sent a New Year's message that summarized his feelings:

> This event serves to carry us back through 5697 years of Jewish history and tradition. It reminds us of the lasting gifts which Jewish civilization has given to the world. The wisdom and understanding of the great Jewish leaders whose experiences are recorded in the Old Testament have been a constant source of guidance and inspiration throughout the centuries down to modern times.[26]

The Jewish people also played an important part in his eschatology.[27] His lifelong interest in Zionism was based on the fulfillment of prophecy, with paradoxical results. That the Jews would become unwitting dupes of the anti-Christ in the last days and that the anti-Christ himself would be the illegitimate offspring of Satan and an apostate Jewess might be interpreted as latent antisemitism. On the other hand, Aberhart believed that, in God's final judgment, whole nations would be judged on the basis of how they had treated the Jews. He told a radio audience in 1937 that:

> When the son of Man shall come in his glory with all the Holy Angels with him, then shall he sit upon the throne of his glory, and before him shall be gathered all nations, — not all individuals, — all nations, and he shall separate them one from another as a shepherd divideth his sheep from his goats. . . . He is going to judge nations. He's going to say to Russia, "What did you do to the least of these, my brethren. Who are your brethren? Israel. My brethren you know. I am of the tribe of

Judah. What did you do to them?"
"Well, we persecuted them."
"You step over here."
"What did you do Great Britain, to these my brethren?"
"Oh we helped them along."
"You come over here."
And He'll separate the nations. Those nations that treated the breth-
ren, Israel, in the way they have treated them. You better read some of
the pogroms of Europe and you'll see that history has been recording
this judgement all down the ages and the final judgement will come
when they shall be separated when the Christ returns to this earth.[28]

Aberhart was regarded as sufficiently friendly by the Calgary Jewish community to be invited to speak at the opening of the conference of the western division of the Canadian Jewish Congress in August 1939. He
expressed sympathy to the delegates with respect to the Jewish plight in
Europe: "There will never be more than a temporary solution to the problems facing the Jewish race until you find a place to seek your destiny in
freedom."[29] Moreover, a prominent Calgary Jewish lawyer, Abraham
Shumiatcher, publicly supported Social Credit. As Aberhart's lawyer during the 1940 provincial election, he rounded up several Calgary Jews to
sign the premier's nomination papers on that occasion.[30]

On the negative side, Aberhart's adoption of Social Credit ideas must
have inevitably coloured his views of Jews and Judaism; however, he did
not espouse the virulent antisemitism of Major Douglas. In statements to
the press and in his correspondence, the premier repeatedly denied that he
was antisemitic. Nor, in his view, was Alberta Social Credit. In September
1938, when Major Douglas attacked the Jews as a menace to Western civilization because, in his eyes, they controlled trade and were "parasites,"
Aberhart issued a statement disassociating his party from this allegation: "I
should like our people to know the Social Credit movement as we understand it, is not only opposed to anti-Semitism but condemns it in the
strongest possible terms." Furthermore, in a letter to a Jewish Social
Crediter in Saskatchewan, Aberhart wrote, "You will really see that I am
bitterly opposed to anti-Semitism. . . . I can assure you that the Social
Credit principles we are adopting here in Alberta make no distinction
between religion or race of any kind. We believe in the live and let live
doctrine."[31]

Yet, with each denial, Aberhart managed to include comments with an
antisemitic ring. In the same letter cited above, the premier wrote: "What
surprises me is the inability of some splendid fellows, who are Jewish by
birth, to discern the people who are opposed to them. . . . You must
surely be aware that much of the persecution in other lands is due to the
oppression by members of your own race." Similarly, in the press state-

ment in which he denied that Social Credit was antisemitic, he pointed to
Anglo-Saxon and Jewish bankers as the root of the world tyranny that kept
people enslaved, arguing that he did not oppose Jews per se, but simply
Jewish financiers. He also inserted an original explanation of the persecutions in Europe with decided antisemitic overtones:

> This dominating control of the financial system is exercised by two
> main groups of money barons—the Jewish group and the Anglo-Sax-
> ons. And it is in connection with the activities of these forces that this
> Jewish question has gained its prominence. Anyone who has followed
> the history of the rise to power of the Jewish group of financiers and of
> the activities and ramifications of its American head will have no illu-
> sions as to the objective which this financial octopus has steadily pur-
> sued, but the Anglo-Saxon group of financiers, which is non-Jewish, is
> just as sinister in regard to its activities. Personally, I have little doubt
> that in working through Jews, the Jewish financial group has sacrificed
> its own people on the altar of its greed for power and this group is pre-
> eminently responsible for the poisonous anti-Semitism which is ram-
> pant in the world today.
>
> The history of the persecution and abuse to which Jews have been
> subjected for centuries makes it easy for these unscrupulous financiers
> who are feeling the resentment which is being directed toward them on
> account of their activities everywhere to direct this resentment into
> channels of diabolical persecution of the innocent Jewish people in
> many countries.[32]

Despite these problematic statements, it is doubtful that Aberhart was
being hypocritical in claiming that he was not an antisemite. Instead, like
many ideologues, he was adroit at juggling contradictory assumptions and
at dividing his mind into watertight compartments. While his fundamentalist and Social Credit beliefs gave his opinions about Jews a particular
form, his overall ambivalence reflected public attitudes in Alberta. In the
final analysis, the most important thing is that he publicly repudiated antisemitism. His belief in biblical eschatology and the religious significance
of the Jews was too strong for him to become deeply involved in this
social evil. Moreover, Aberhart had a highly developed sense of social justice, possibly because of his affinity for the Hebrew prophets. He also
nursed an intense personal dislike of Major Douglas, who had publicly
questioned his understanding of Social Credit. The banks, the federal government and his political opponents in Alberta were scapegoats enough to
explain the Depression and his government's inability to solve its
dilemmas. The premier played no part in the federal cabinet's determination to keep the number of Jewish refugees who came to Canada during
the 1930s to an absolute minimum. Also, he largely muffled the antisemitic voices in the Alberta Social Credit movement, and refused to join those

federal Social Credit MPs who followed Major Douglas down a more open and blatant path.

The Shape of Things to Come: Social Credit and Antisemitism during the 1940s

The heightened nationalism of the World War II years was instrumental in furthering antisemitic attitudes among some Social Credit politicians. At first glance, this seems surprising; Social Crediters certainly had no sympathy for National Socialism, and were nearly unanimous in their support of Canada's war effort against Nazi Germany.[33] The resurgence, then, of antisemitism in Alberta during the war years must have been induced by Social Credit orthodoxy in England, where Major Douglas was still the dominant figure. Douglas was alarmed by the growth of state regimentation. With paranoid clarity, he saw the war as a tool employed by international finance to gain complete world power and undermine freedom. He was adamant that these "world plotters" had to be unmasked. At the centre ". . . were the leaders of World Jewry; the plot was a relentless Judaic conspiracy against Christian civilization. International Jewry controlled both international finance and bolshevism." The Social Credit theoretician also implicated the Freemasons and the Nazis in the massive conspiracy—no ordinary feat, considering that Hitler took exactly the same view of 'international Jewry' in *Mein Kampf*![34] One wing of the Social Credit movement in Alberta followed Major Douglas in these antisemitic fantasies, convincing itself that there was indeed a perennial conspiracy against economic freedom, national sovereignty and Christianity. The main proponents of this Douglasite obsession were the members of the Alberta Social Credit Board, Norman Jaques (MP for Wetaskiwin) and the newspaper organ of the national Social Credit movement, the *Canadian Social Crediter*.

The Alberta Social Credit Board was established by Aberhart as an 'educational' arm of the movement in 1937 to mollify backbenchers who were threatening an open break over his failure to implement Social Credit policies.[35] Originally, this organization had been staffed mostly with insurgents from the backbenchers' revolt, who were advised by L. D. Byrne and G. F. Powell, Douglasite experts brought from England. Its composition changed only slightly later, so that it became increasingly a vehicle for unmodified Douglasite views. The first explicit antisemitic innuendoes came in its 1942 annual report. After attacking the "Union Now" movement in Great Britain as an "evil plot" which would lead to financial dictatorship, and the "subjugation of the British Empire and the United States to International Finance . . . ," the Board warned that such a move toward world government would surrender "control" to an "alien international authority" composed of men "probably not even British." Although its publications did not use the word "Jews" to identify the world plotters, the arguments were so predictable and familiar and the names (those who were "exposed") so identifiably and overwhelmingly Jewish, that no reader could fail to conclude that Jews were the backbone of the cabal.[36]

Throughout the war, according to Douglas and his followers, the world plot continued to mushroom; consequently the antisemitic content of the Board's reports became more and more overt. In 1946 the message began ominously:

> In previous Reports we have drawn attention to the existence of a delib-
> erate conspiracy to establish a World Slave State to be maintained by
> overwhelming force concentrated in the hands of a ruthless and closely
> knit international junta. We have named many of the conspirators and
> the organizations which these World Plotters have harnessed in their
> service. We have shown that their chief weapons have been economic
> power exercised through a centralized financial system and political
> power exercised by permeating every sphere of human activity with the
> materialistic Marxian-socialist doctrines. We have supplied a mass of
> irrefutable evidence of the existence of this World Plot and its paralyz-
> ing development. The events of the past year provide further evidence
> of a rapidly developing and preconceived plan for world domination,
> whose bold outlines are now so plain that many who formerly doubted
> are now thoroughly alarmed at the emerging pattern of the shape of
> things to come.[37]

The Board maintained that the conspiracy was aimed at complete world monopoly, to be achieved through "state monopoly" as advocated by communists and socialists. The notion of an international communist conspiracy dedicated to the destruction of freedom was destined to gain wide acceptance in the future Cold War era; however, the Social Credit Board made an early contribution to this scenario by seeing all the international bodies created at the war's close as part of a general plot. By focusing on international finance as the chief conspirator among an interlocking array of strategists, and by identifying individual Jews as the main actors in this machination, its members made certain that the plot was seen as Jewish. With the help of Douglasite propaganda, they identified such people as "Lord Rothschild, who is one of the wealthiest men in the world and who occupies a prominent place in the inner circle of International High Finance . . ." and "the advisor of all Presidents, Bernard Baruch," as being among those who were bringing international finance and socialism together to achieve world domination. Jewish financiers and economists, needless to say, provided the key liaison between the super capitalists and socialists.[38] Evidence for these claims was provided by a detailed, but highly selective, analysis of late nineteenth- and early twentieth-century history, designed to show the control exercised by Jews over the major financial institutions in Great Britain and the United States, as well as their roles in the Russian Revolution, World War I and the Great Depression. Naturally, they had also played a major part in the outbreak of World War II.

> The totalitarian nations were being heavily financed in their prepara-
> tions for war and ultimate world domination by alien bankers with
> headquarters in the United States and England. . . . [These same] ruth-
> less internationalists deliberately [created] an economic crisis in 1929
> which plunged the world into an era of needless suffering climaxed by a
> world war.[39]

The Board maintained that the world plotters were behind the establishment of international organizations, since national authority would be
undermined and state regimentation imposed. WIth public money being
used to promote such a distorted view of world history, it is little wonder
that one opposition member of the legislature described the Social Credit
Board as "going around the country having nightmares."[40]

Norman Jaques et al.

In addition to this organization, the Douglas worldview had an outspoken
champion in Norman Jaques, the Social Credit MP for Wetaskiwin from
1935 to 1949. Until his death, Jaques delivered annual speeches in the
House of Commons denouncing the international financial conspiracy.
Other Social Credit MPs also warned of the dangers of international
finance, socialism and international organizations. Some (Such as John
Blackmore, MP for Lethbridge) indulged in antisemitic analyses.[41] But
Jaques was the most open in identifying Jews as the common denomina-
tor in the sinister coalition of forces attempting to achieve world domination. Since he had the House of Commons (and Hansard) at his disposal,
he could propagate his views to a wider audience than the Social Credit
Board ever enjoyed. An outspoken man, Jaques did not hesitate to name
names; for example, in 1943, he created an uproar in the House when he
attempted to read from *Protocols of the Elders of Zion*. Ironically, because one
of his persistent concerns was the national press's indifference to Social
Credit ideas, he resented the widespread (negative) attention which such
speeches received. Certain that he was not antisemitic, he felt that Social
Credit was "misunderstood" and unfairly represented by journalists.[42]

Jaques's background and personality did not conform to the stereotype
of a rural, populist Social Credit politician. Born in London, England, in
1880, he was educated at Eastbourne College prior to coming to Canada
in 1901. He took up a homestead in central Alberta and eventually became
a successful horse farmer before the Depression wiped him out financially. Jaques had been attracted to Social Credit ideas prior to the rise of

Aberhart through the New Age Club, which brought together students of Social Credit theory throughout the province during the early 1930s. (Incidentally, New Age Club members resented Aberhart's attempt to take over the Social Credit movement in Alberta, since he deviated from the strict Douglas line.) Jaques maintained close ties with the Douglas secretariat in London, and knew Major Douglas personally.[43] The Member of Parliament's manner was that of a cultured English gentleman, rather than an antisemitic demagogue. Indeed, in background, style and ideas, he was almost a clone of Douglas himself. His speeches in the House of Commons, like the speeches of his mentor, were not harangues, but carefully reasoned lectures supported by long excerpts from political and economic "authorities." Despite this appeal to reason, however, Jaques was obsessed by the notion of a world plot and its alleged Jewish instigation. As described by another Social Credit MP in a parliamentary debate "he lives and moves and has his being in this particular subject and pays little attention to anything else that goes on in the House."[44]

Both in his speeches and in the pages of the two national Social Credit newspapers of the 1940s, *Today and Tomorrow* and its successor, *The Canadian Social Crediter*, Jaques outlined the Douglasite view of history defended by the Social Credit Board. International finance had created the Depression and the conditions leading to World War II. The plot for world domination was multifaceted and could be seen almost everywhere; it was evident in the attempt to return to the gold standard and in efforts to establish international organizations that, according to Jaques, would undermine national sovereignty as well as the British Empire.[45] He used a variety of terms that were common currency among professional antisemites: for example, "international racketeers," "moneylenders" and "German-American-Jewish financiers." To the Social Credit MP, these dangerous people were the descendants, both practically and philosophically, of "Shylock, Ricardo and Marx." He was quite specific about the identity of the "world plotters," naming 20 different Jewish and German bankers, and asking rhetorically, "How many French names are in that list, how many British, how many Christians?" Nor was the supposed connection between Jews and international finance the only thing that troubled him; he was equally concerned about the connection between Jews and socialism. "Fascism you can describe as gentile communism, and communism you can describe as Jewish fascism."[46] The Member for Wetaskiwin presented an even more elaborate world plot than the Social Credit Board had depicted by linking Zionism to an already massive conspiracy. In a number of lengthy addresses given in 1945, 1946, 1947 and 1948, Jaques attempted to discredit the Jewish movement by charging it, in collusion with the left, with attempting to undermine British authority and prestige, and with manipulating the United Nations to that end. He saw the struggle "for the control of Palestine" as "the key to world control." In August 1946, he informed the House of Commons that "all the terrible convulsions and troubles and upheavals in the world is [sic] the result of aliens seeking to impose their atheistic Oriental collectivism upon national cultures of individualism."[47]

The editors of *The Canadian Social Crediter* were in agreement and were pleased to have Jaques elaborate his insights in their paper; for example, in 1947 they published his attack on the development of international economic and political organizations in which he contended that:

> The controlling, if hidden hands behind all these world organizations are those of International Finance, International Political Zionism and International Socialism. The evidence is complete and irrefutable. Therefore, there can be but one answer to the question as to who is planning the "one World." The answer is SHYLOCK AND MARX, the pagan internationalists who indelibly identify themselves and their plans by smearing Christian Nationalists with anti-Semitism.

The paper also alleged an alliance between Jews and Communists. In one edition, *The Canadian Social Crediter* disclaimed antisemitism, but went on to declare that ". . . the prophets and priests of the Marxist revolution were racially at one with the master usurers and animated by much the same hidden purpose."[48]

Jaques denied repeatedly that he was an antisemite, and attempted to refute such charges by pointing out that Social Credit had been one of the first supporters of conscription at the outbreak of the war against Nazism. Such denials, however, were less than convincing, since they were usually accompanied by blatantly antisemitic remarks; in fact, one such denial was simultaneous with his recitation from *Protocols of the Elders of Zion*! His worst fears were vindicated when radio stations in Edmonton refused to broadcast his antisemitic speeches and when Premier Manning purged his Douglasite friends from the editorship of the Social Credit newspaper. To Jaques, these nefarious actions were attempts by Zionists to stifle the significant "revelations" he was making. When he died suddenly (of a heart attack) in 1949, his Social Credit colleagues stated that the strain associated with his crusading activities had undoubtedly contributed to his early demise. Some of his more zealous supporters even went so far as to suggest that perhaps his death had not been natural, but assisted by his allegedly pro-Zionist doctors.[49]

The view of world history promulgated by the Social Credit Board, Norman Jaques and the *Canadian Social Crediter* was based on classic formulations of ideological antisemitism; it amalgamated all the major foes of Social Credit — international finance, socialism and internationalism — and identified them as either predominantly or exclusively Jewish. This conspiratorial vision was similar to the one portrayed in the *Protocols*, although the Douglasites attempted to provide an up-to-date account of things. For such persons only a master plot could make sense of a chaotic world marked by wars, depression and the growth of totalitarian states. However, it should be emphasized that this form of antisemitism was different in some respects from its German counterpart. While sharing Hitler's identification of the Jews with communism and international finance, Social Credit antisemitism made no assumption of Aryan racial superiority and Jewish racial inferiority. It was preoccupied exclusively with international Jewish bankers, and paid almost no attention to Canadian Jewry.

Social Credit's religious connection raises a question about the role of religion in the growth of antisemitism in the Douglasite faction. Undoubtedly, religion supplied some of its energy. Jaques, for example, spoke of "Christian nationalists" and their opponents. For other Social Crediters, the presumed relationship between their movement and Christianity was a decided impetus:

> ... the movement was distinctly constructed on the presupposition that its goals and ideology were not only consistent with Christianity, but were in some way a frontline defence of the vital elements of a decadent Christianity. In this sense, Social Credit was thought to have a special role to play in the world which would begin in Alberta. . . . The battle for a way of life of which Christianity was conceived as its anchor. . . . Social Credit was thus a secular expression of the on-going battle between "good" and "evil" and between Christian and anti-Christian forces that were being waged in the world.[50]

If one saw the world as a battleground between titanic anti-Christian forces on the one hand, and "the people" on the other, it was easy to turn to antisemitism. However, the real link between Social Credit and antisemitism did *not* come through Protestant fundamentalism. None of the eight Social Credit MLAs who served on the Social Credit Board belonged to fundamentalist sects: two were Catholics, four belonged to the United Church and two identified themselves as non-denominational Protestants. Norman Jaques was a nominal Anglican. On the other hand, the two fundamentalists, Aberhart and Manning, became increasingly critical of the antisemitic elements in the party, and Manning eventually silenced the Douglasites.

Manning, the Douglasites and Antisemitism

The confrontation between Ernest Manning and the Douglasites in the late 1940s was significant, revealing several important political and religious currents in Alberta. The internal clash, in addition to demonstrating the changing balance of forces within the movement, also measured the strength of antisemitism in the province and further clarified its relationship with religious fundamentalism. Disharmony did not begin with Manning. Aberhart, despite his growing attraction during the early war years to certain aspects of the cult of British Israel (which was tainted by Anglo-Saxon racism), continued his denunciations. For example, the *Prophetic Voice*, the organ of the Prophetic Bible Institute which he had established, and over which he maintained tight control, warned that antisemitism was "a devilish thing, to which no true-hearted man can lend himself. . . . Woe betide the Jew-hater. . . . God grant that the Christian People of this land will refuse to be swept away by the rising tide of this perilous, blasphemous anti-Semitism." Another article in the *Prophetic Voice*, which appeared shortly after Aberhart's death, proclaimed that "Anti-Semitism is a thing of a the devil; cowardly, unmanly, inhuman, brutal, hateful, illogical, ungrateful and barbaric. Let no child of God be ensnared into this vile and monstrous thing! Let us instead bless the nation that gave us the Blessed Book!"[51]

After the premier's death in May 1943, Manning was left to deal with the Douglasites and their increasingly outspoken anti-Jewish sentiments that were blackening the reputation of Social Credit. Since most of his religious, economic and political education had been under Aberhart's direction, it is not surprising that he adopted the latter's position on this issue. Manning belonged to the Canadian Palestine Committee, which promoted the idea of a Jewish state, and, in November 1943, publicly lauded the Zionist cause.

> The Balfour Declaration is a milestone in the efforts of the Jewish people to gain a foothold in their Homeland . . . that is so rightfully theirs. It is in Britain's interests to recognize the rights and justice of the Jewish people. Further, there was a Divine promise that the Jews would someday hold the title deeds of Palestine. They are the only people in the world who had such a promise.[52]

In October 1945, Manning joined other political leaders, civic officials and religious leaders in a public meeting in Edmonton calling for the abrogation of the British White Paper which restricted Jewish immigration to Palestine, and for the opening of its doors to Jewish immigrants.[53]

Before long, the new premier was forced to take a public stand on the proclamations of the Douglasites. Not only did Manning's theological views conflict with their views on the Jews, but also his political astuteness warned him that Social Credit dogmatism would exact a heavy political price. His perception of where the threat to freedom actually lay was more circumscribed and respectable than that of Douglas. For Manning, socialism was the prime ideological and political foe. When the provincial CCF tried to publicize the antisemitic remarks of some Social Crediters in order to discredit the party, Manning heatedly denied such accusations in the official Social Credit newspaper:

> In establishing a properly functioning democracy we have overcome the divisions of party politics, religion and racial origin which have been deliberately fostered by those who wish to enslave the people. In this crusade for human liberation, there is no place for anti-Christianity, anti-Semitism, anti-Catholicism, or anti-anything else. Tolerance and co-operation must be the foundation upon which we build.[54]

Given the dissonance between this statement and the blatant views of the Douglasites, who were in control of the Social Credit Board, Manning's hand was forced. The inevitable purge came in 1947, after the Board's 1946 Annual Report, which was released in March. Its naked antisemitism was the final straw as far as the public and the politicians were concerned (for several years, public expenditure for the Board had been a sore point). An uproar was precipitated in the legislature. The report was clearly an embarrassment to the government. Manning quickly issued a statement denying that Social Credit was antisemitic and dissociating the movement from "any statements or publications which are incompatible with the established British ideals of democratic freedom or which endorse, excuse or incite anti-Semitism or racial or religious intolerance in any form." Then, with the endorsement of the next convention of the Social Credit League, which met in November 1947, Manning announced the abolition of the Social Credit Board. Upon meeting with members of the executive of the Canadian Jewish Congress shortly thereafter, the premier also announced a new editorial policy for *The Canadian Social Crediter*, stipulating "that in identifying the enemies of the people it should hold no creed or race up in ridicule." Articles by Norman Jaques were banned, and the editor and assistant editor of the newspaper were forced to resign. Manning had been unhappy for some time with *The Canadian Social Crediter*, warning one national Social Credit executive member in May 1947 that "no one is going to get behind a publication which contains little but negative and destructive criticism flavored with 'Jewbaiting.' "[55]

The premier went further in February 1948 and fired Education Minister R. D. Ansley and Social Credit Board technical advisor L. D. Byrne, who were both known for their staunch Douglasite views.[56] Byrne, who had been brought over from England as one of Major Douglas's emissaries in 1937, was Deputy Minister of Economic Affairs and chief advisor to the Social Credit Board, whose report he had publicly defended. Ansley was fired because he had defended both the report and Byrne's defence of the report. The cabinet also purged Douglasites from the caucus by making certain that they did not win renomination. Ultimately, as J. A. Irving has put it, "the failure of the Douglasites to win a popular following made it easy for the realists (supporters of Manning's position) to eliminate all but one of them from the Alberta legislature by 1952."[57]

What significance can be attached to this major party split? In actuality, Manning's expulsion of the Douglasites had many causes and was not simply a reaction to their antisemitism. Some of the latter had criticized his government for its failure to implement Social Credit policies, thereby challenging his leadership from within the party. In addition, the Social Credit Board's 1946 report was not only more openly antisemitic than previous reports, but it also followed Major Douglas in criticizing the secret ballot, advocating an open, signed ballot which would limit the citizen's financial liability to schemes for which he had voted. Combined with these notions, the Board's antisemitism appeared to be one more aspect of an ideology already veering toward fascism. Furthermore, Douglasite opposition to Zionism, as expressed by Norman Jaques, was incompatible with the worldview of many Alberta Protestants, who saw the return of the Jews to Palestine as a fulfillment of prophecy and one of the key "signs of the times" foretelling the imminence of Christ's second coming. Finally, after the revelation in 1946 of the mass destruction of Jews by Nazi Germany, antisemitism became both incompatible with the sympathies of the democratic countries, and intolerable in itself.[58]

The extent to which the Douglasite faction sealed its fate within the Social Credit movement is unknown; one can, however, conclude that there were definite limits to antisemitic rhetoric in Alberta. In retrospect, antisemitism seems to have been confined primarily to the most fervent disciples of Major Douglas; outside the Social Credit party, it was regarded as a crank phenomenon, and within it as an embarrassment. Thus Manning's purge and the death of Norman Jaques largely silenced its overt expressions in the party rank and file.[59]

The purge of the Douglasites illuminates the relationship of religious fundamentalism to antisemitism. Although Alberta's image as a Bible belt occasionally has been used to explain anti-Jewish animosity in the province, it is clear that this explanation must be qualified. Alberta's most important fundamentalist leaders in the political arena, Aberhart and Manning, eschewed antisemitism. In addition, two national leaders of the Social Credit party during the 1940s and 1950s, John Blackmore and Solon Low, were both Mormons, and their pro-Jewish Mormon religious views seem to have restrained their support for orthodox Douglasite antisemitism. To the Mormons, the Jews had been God's elect, and their own history was, in many ways, the re-enactment of the history of the earlier chosen people. Thus, their trek westward in the United States in the nineteenth century replayed the flight from Egypt; they saw their new home as Zion and even referred to non-Mormons as "gentiles." They also saw the return of the Jews to Israel as the fulfillment of biblical prophecy. These religious views inhibited, if they did not prevent, the spread of Douglasite ideas among Mormon Social Crediters.[60]

Both Blackmore and Low were ambivalent on the subject of Jews, and their views changed over time. In the early 1940s, they belonged to the Canadian Palestine Committee. Blackmore told the House of Commons in 1944 that he supported a Jewish state:

> Many years ago the Jews, responding to a religious and national, as well as a natural impulse, sought for themselves a new home in their old home in Palestine. English-speaking democracy encouraged the Jew to hope; they promised him support. That promise came before the Hitlerian massacres. The Jew, with millions of his countrymen tortured and dead, still hopes and looks to us to make his hopes come true.
>
> Where in democracy are our charity and justice? Where is our Christianity if we let the Jew now hope in vain? ... The homeless Jew is a challenge to all the decencies that make what we are pleased to call our English-speaking civilization.... This house should recognize this truth and this duty by an appropriate resolution and should give leadership to all nations along the path of justice and fair play through the fulfillment of the long cherished dream of the establishment in Palestine of a national homeland for the Jews.[61]

Blackmore, however, still saw the Jews as connected to a world financial conspiracy and, during the early 1950s, to the world communist conspiracy. In his pro-Joe McCarthy, anti-communist crusade of the 1950s, he recommended to his correspondents that they read radical right-wing American anti-communist literature that contained antisemitic allegations.[62] Yet, like Jaques, he denied heatedly charges that he was an antisemite. "I am not anti-semitic, neither is any Social Crediter," he declared, going on to say "... I and all Latter Day Saints believe that the Jews are to go back to Palestine — that is far from being anti-Jewish. Many passages in the Bible clearly promise that the Jews are to go back to Palestine, the Promised Land; certainly I will not be entertaining any beliefs contrary to the Scriptures."[63]

Solon Low's views on Jews combined Social Credit theory, Mormonism and, like Aberhart, an interest in British Israel ideas. His support of Zionism in the early 1940s changed to criticism in the late 1940s. In a memorandum to Blackmore in the mid-1950s, Low outlined the evolution of his opinions. He stated that, as a member of the External Affairs Committee of the House of Commons in 1946, he had listened to the views of both Jewish and Arab groups and had concluded (as he stated publicly on the CBC in December 1946) that there was a close relationship between international communism, international finance and international political Zionism.

I spoke of these things honestly as *policies*. At no time have I ever referred to them as Jewish organizations. But, those who for political advantage want to do me harm have used that speech and have interpreted it in such a way as to try to make the unwary and uninformed believe that I am anti-Jewish.

Low pointed to anti-Zionist American Jews as evidence that opposition to "political Zionism" did not make one antisemitic; he also argued that his action as provincial treasurer in Alberta in appointing a Jew to the position of purchasing agent for the provincial government was a clear sign that he was not personally antisemitic.[64] Blackmore's and Low's denials do not, of course, absolve them of the accusations, but it is clear that they were less extreme than Jaques. In 1956, Low publicly condemned the Quebec wing of his party, *L'Union des Électeurs*, for being antisemitic.[65]

This discussion is not meant to imply that antisemitism did not exist in sectarian circles in Alberta. It did. However, the real causes of antisemitism within Social Credit and within Alberta lay in the economic and social conditions of a debtor region isolated from the centres of economic and political power, not in the pulpits of sectarian religious groups. Fundamentalist and non-conformist Christianity restrained rather than encouraged it.

Other Factors

A discussion of antisemitism during and shortly after World War II cannot be limited to an analysis of its manifestation in one wing of the Social Credit movement, since it appeared in other contexts. Paradoxically, public opinion polls in the United States revealed an increase in hostility toward Jews during World War II. Jews were seem as less patriotic than other citizens and "... were more often charged than any other ethnic group with shirking their share of the war effort." Although the charge had no factual basis, it was raised in Canada nonetheless, and occasionally in Alberta. For example, in rural Alberta, an official of the Gleichen Branch of the Canadian Legion expressed his misgivings in the local paper:

> In spite of the terrible persecution which the Jews have suffered it seems strange that they still do not seem to realize that if we lose the war they are done. We have no statistics but would guess that each province in Canada could easily raise a battalion of Jews and financed by Jews alone. We do not hesitate to warn them that if we lose the war that bad as our lot would be theirs would be worse and most of us will at least have the consolation of firing a shot or two in our own defence.

Similarly, in Calgary in February 1944 *The Herald* carried an extended exchange of correspondence as to whether Jews in Canada were doing their part to aid the war effort. Although these criticisms were considerably more restrained than the charges laid by some Social Crediters, they shared the assumption that Jewish loyalty ultimately was not to the nation.[66]

In order to understand the increase of prejudice during the war years, a more complete study is required of the social tensions in Alberta that generated ethnic hostility. Many factors were conducive to the development of ideological antisemitism during the 1930s and 1940s. Political upheavals on a worldwide scale cried out for explanation; the limited success of Social Credit outside of Alberta had to be interpreted in a way that would maintain the self-esteem of ardent and therefore frustrated party faithful. In addition, the Great Depression, the beginnings of massive urbanization and the war itself left many Albertans with a profound sense of social insecurity and dislocation — a feeling that could be eased only by finding a scapegoat. It should also be remembered that, during the 1930s and 1940s, the information explosion that later expanded the intellectual horizons and ideological options of rural Albertans had not yet occurred. Most people did not have access to a plethora of viewpoints, and were consequently susceptible to the distortions of panacean and single-cause interpretations.

In addition to Manning's suppression of antisemitism within the ranks of Social Credit, there were two further indications of its limits in Alberta: (1) a growing acceptance of Jews within urban community life; and (2) considerable public support at the end of the war for Zionism. The upward mobility of Jews in Alberta's urban centres surpassed that of all other non-British immigrant groups, and the war and immediate post-war period brought a number of "firsts" for Alberta Jewry. For example, Abe Fratkin, a Russian-born musician who owned a music store, started the Edmonton symphony and became its first conductor in 1943. Moses Lieberman, an Ontario-born lawyer and football fan, helped establish the Edmonton Eskimos in 1949 and served as director of the club. A. W. Miller, a lawyer, was elected to Edmonton City Council in 1951. John Dower, a prominent businessman and driving force in the Edmonton Chamber of Commerce, and Dr. M. Weinlos, who taught at the University of Alberta's Faculty of Medicine, were each chosen as Edmonton's "Citizen of the Year."[67]

The other indication was political. The major urban dailies supported Jewish immigration to Palestine, and criticized British efforts to restrict Jewish immigration.[68] At the end of the war, the Canadian Palestine Committee, which was established to show non-Jewish support for Zionism, had 144 members across Canada, of whom 40 were from Alberta. They included politicians from all political parties and prominent clergymen and business leaders. The Christian Council for Palestine, founded during the war with the financial support of Jewish organizations in order to rally Christian support for a Jewish national home, had 205 clergymen as members, including 14 Anglican, United and Presbyterian ministers in Alberta.[69] At a public meeting in Calgary in October 1945, 400 Calgarians, including some of the city's most influential lawyers and ministers (United Church and Anglican), met to protest Britain's restriction of Jewish immigration into Palestine and urge the Canadian government to "set an example to the rest of the world by opening its doors to Jews to the extent that they can be assimilated into the country. . . ."[70]

Obviously, then, in the Alberta of the 1940s, antisemitism was not the only, or even the prevailing, attitude toward Jews. Nevertheless, negative images did surface to a significant degree. Their emergence precisely when the world was becoming aware of the grim harvest of mass murder in Nazi Germany can only be explained by the persistence of the conspiratorial cast of mind.

Conclusion

By the 1950s, antisemitism in Alberta was fading fast. Social Credit ideologies became increasingly isolated, and Albertans stopped reading Major Douglas. The oil-induced prosperity of the 1950s and 1960s removed the economic stresses that required explanations and scapegoats. Although the war had changed Alberta, massive oil and gas discoveries, beginning in 1947 and continuing throughout the 1950s and into the 1960s, totally transformed the provincial economy, hastening social and political change. This new prosperity brought immigration, urbanization and a more consumer-oriented society dominated by American popular culture. Alberta grew dramatically, changing from a predominantly rural agricultural economy to an urban society dominated by the oil and gas industry. In 1951, just over half of the population was urban; by 1961 almost 70 percent was urban. As Alberta, like the rest of Canada, became more urban, the Jews became less threatening as symbols of urban life.[71] As Albertans themselves became better educated, and as business values came to dominate the political culture, the former seemed much less distinctive than previously. A predominantly Alberta-born generation excelled in education, the professions and the arts, winning respect for their accomplishments. Writer Henry Kriesel, theatre impresario Joe Schoctor, university president Max Wyman, publisher Mel Hurtig, patrons of the arts such as Martha Cohen and Jack Singer, and Tory politician Ron Ghitter helped break down unidimensional stereotypes. During the 1970s and early 1980s, the economic, social and political resentments of western society were directed against central Canada, the Liberals and Pierre Trudeau rather than against international Jewish bankers. Antisemitism no longer fitted into the prevailing political scheme of things.

The lingering antisemitism in rural society exposed during the Keegstra affair did not mean an upsurge in the province as a whole; rather, it was mostly a reflection of the vestiges of Social Credit ideology. Keegstra's fervent belief in the teachings of Major Douglas and his ties with extremist groups such as the Canadian League of Rights (which also has Social Credit roots through its founder, Ron Gostick) provide the real key to his antisemitism.[72] But the doctrines of right-wing extremists are now clearly marginal in Alberta politics. Social Credit, whether of the Douglasite or Aberhart variety, is totally dead as a political force in the province. Antisemites are no longer elected to parliament. The contrast between Keegstra's well-deserved obscurity, working in a garage in small-town Alberta, and the political success of Social Credit MPs like Jaques during the 1940s, reflects important changes in the political culture and the appeal of antisemitism to the populace.

Notes

1 Charles Glock and Rodney Stark, *Religious Belief and Anti-Semitism* (New York: Harper, 1966).

2 Max Rubin, "Alberta's Jews: The Long Journey," in *Peoples of Alberta*, ed. Howard and Tamara Palmer (Saskatoon: Western Producer, 1985), chap. 14, and Henry Klassen, "Enterprise in Business: The Jewish Factor in Calgary, 1888-1930," *The Jewish Star*, December 2-15, 1988.

3 *The* (Calgary) *Herald*, July 5, 1893.

4 Public Archives of Canada, Department of Interior, J. George Jessup to Commissioner, Dominion Lands, Winnipeg, April 23, 1894.

5 Rubin, "Alberta's Jews," pp. 332-35.

6 H. Palmer, *Patterns of Prejudice: A History of Nativism in Alberta* (Toronto: McClelland & Stewart, 1982), pp. 27-31.

7 Ibid., chap. 1.

8 *Calgary Herald*, February 24, 1987; February 15, 1908; *Calgary Albertan*, April 24, 1911; September 11, 1912.

9 *Calgary Herald*, December 4 and 22, 1905.

10 June 14, 1919.

11 Provincial Archives of Alberta, oral history interviews with Jack Saslow, Harry Bloomfield, Sam Slutker and Simon Simons.

12 For parallels between the American and Canadian farm revolts, see Paul Sharp, *The Agrarian Revolt in Western Canada* (Minneapolis: University of Minnesota, 1948). For the most recent study of American populism, which downplays antisemitism as a key ingredient of populism, see Lawrence Goodwyn, *The Populist Moment* (New York: Oxford University Press, 1978).

13 The themes of American populism referred to above are drawn from Richard Hofstadter's analysis in *The Age of Reform* (New York: Knopf, 1955), chap. 2. For an overview of the scholarly debate concerning the nature of populism and its relationship to nativism, see entire issue of *Agricultural History* (October 1965), and W. T. K. Nugent, *The Tolerant Populists* (Chicago: University of Chicago Press, 1963). For a discussion

of Henry Wise Wood, see W. L. Morton, "The Social Philosohy of Henry Wise Wood," *Agricultural History* 22 (1948).

14 Irwin Unger, "Critique of Norman Pollack's 'Fear of Man,'" *Agricultural History* 39, 4 (1965): 75-80.

15 For a discussion of the UFA and Social Credit as populist movements, see L. B. Pashak, "The Populist Characteristics of the Early Social Credit Movement in Alberta" (M.A. thesis, University of Calgary, 1971).

16 H. Palmer, "William Irvine and the Emergence of Political Radicalism in Calgary, 1916-1921," *Fort Calgary Quarterly* 7, 2 (Spring 1987): 1-19.

17 W. L. Morton, *The Progressive Party in Canada* (Toronto: University of Toronto Press, 1950), pp. 186-87.

18 Palmer, *Patterns of Prejudice*, pp. 100-108.

19 For background on Albertans' attitudes toward banks and bankers see T. D. Regehr, "Bankers and Farmers in Western Canada, 1900-1939," in *The Developing West*, ed. John Foster (Edmonton: University of Alberta Press, 1983), pp. 303-36, and David Jones, "An Exceedingly Risky and Unremunerative Partnership: Farmers and the Financial Interests Amid the Collapse of Southern Alberta," in *Building Beyond the Homestead*, ed. D. Jones and I. McPherson (Calgary: University of Calgary Press, 1985), pp. 207-28.

20 For the best account of the economic and social climate which led to the rise of Social Credit, see John Irving, *The Social Credit Movement in Alberta* (Toronto: University of Toronto Press, 1959).

21 Irving, *Social Credit Movement in Alberta*, and David Elliott and Iris Miller, *Bible Bill* (Edmonton: Reidmore, 1987).

22 For statements by Major Douglas on the "Jewish question," see C. H. Douglas, *Social Credit* (London: 1933), pp. 30, 146, 153.

23 Oral history interviews cited in Palmer, *Patterns of Prejudice*, p. 210.

24 For background on fundamentalist support for Zionism, see Ernest Sandeen, *The Roots of Fundamentalism: British and American Millennarianism, 1800-1930* (Chicago: University of Chicago Press, 1970), pp. 9, 20-22, 67, 93, 99, 215. For a discussion of the antisemitic views of Coughlin and Ford see Sheldon Marcus, *Father Coughlin* (Boston: Little, Brown, 1973), and John Higham, *Strangers in the Land* (New York: Atheneum, 1967), pp. 282-85.

25 David Elliott, "Anti-thetical Elements in William Aberhart's Theology and Political Ideology," *Canadian Historical Review* 59, 1 (1978): 38-58.

26 *The Prophetic Voice*, December 1926, p. 8, and Provincial Archives of Alberta (PAA), Aberhart Papers, Letter to the Editor, *Western Jewish News*, August 24, 1936.

27 David Elliott, "The Devil and William Aberhart: The Nature and Function of His Eschatology," *Studies in Religion* 9 (Summer 1980): 325-37.

28 For Aberhart's view of Zionism see the publication of the Calgary Prophetic Bible Conference, "God's Great Prophecies," Lecture 5, p. 14, Glenbow Archives. Quotation from radio broadcast in Public Archives of Canada, Sound Division, Aberhart Recordings, September 12, 1937. See also, Walter Norman Smith Papers, Transcript of Aberhart's radio talk on CFCN, April 14, 1935, Glenbow Archives.

29 A. I. Shumiatcher Papers, file 44, "Minutes of the Second Session of the Third Regional Congress Conference," Glenbow Archives, *Calgary Herald*, August 7, 1939.

30 Shumiatcher Papers, file 199 "Nomination Papers," and Shumiatcher to Aberhart, March 7, 1940, Glenbow Archives.

31 *Edmonton Journal*, September 22, 1938, PAA, Premier's Papers, Aberhart to Henry Brachman, October 27, 1938.

32 PAA, Premier's Papers, Aberhart to Henry Brachman, October 27, 1938, and *Edmonton Journal*, September 22, 1938. For an excellent discussion of ambivalent attitudes toward Jews in the United States, see John Higham, *Send These to Me: Jews and Other Immigrants in Urban America* (New York: Atheneum, 1975), chaps. 7, 8.

33 H. J. Schultz points out that "Probably no public figure supported the war effort more readily or more regularly than Aberhart," ("Portrait of a Premier: William Aberhart," in *Politics of Discontent*, ed. Ramsey Cook [Toronto: University of Toronto Press, 1967], p. 21). For the federal Social Credit stand on conscription and support for the war effort, see Mary Hallett, "The Social Credit Party and the New Democracy Movement: 1939-1940," *Canadian Historical Review* (December 1966): 301-25.

34 C. B. Macpherson, *Democracy in Alberta* (Toronto: University of Toronto Press, 1953), p. 182; J. L. Finlay, *Social Credit: The English Origins* (Montreal: McGill-Queens University Press, 1972), pp. 103-104; and David Elliott, "Anti-Semitism and the Social Credit Movement: The Intellectual Roots of the Keegstra Affair," *Canadian Ethnic Studies* 17, 1 (1985): 81.

35 Elliott and Miller, *Bible Bill*, chap. 17.

36 In his analysis of the Social Credit Board's role in the expression of extreme Douglasite views, John Barr suggests that their involvement was a result of their having little concrete work to do because of the disallowance of Social Credit legislation and the onset of the war. He also suggests that they were increasingly frustrated by being further and further removed from the centre of Social Credit power within the province: "They continued to be cut off from the important decision-making in the government. And so the board turned to the cultivation of greener ideological pastures. Partly in an attempt to explain why it had failed to produce a workable plan for reform, partly because it had too much time on its hands, the board began to delve into some of the more bizarre world-plot theories Major Douglas had hatched in the old country" (John Barr, *The Dynasty* [Toronto: McClelland & Stewart, 1974], p. 127). For a complete text, see *Annual Report*, Social Credit Board, 1942, p. 11.

37 *Annual Report*, Alberta Social Credit Board, 1946, p. 3.

38 Ibid., p. 12.

39 Ibid.

40 Opposition member cited in *The Herald* (Calgary), April 25, 1947.

41 For Blackmore's sustained analysis of the need for monetary reform which discusses the plot of hidden bankers to control the world, see *Money the Master Key* (n.p., n.p., 1939).

42 See *Debates*, House of Commons, July 12, 1943, pp. 4661-64, 5396-98.

43 On Jaques's New Age activities, see Irving, *Social Credit Movement*, p. 85; biographical details on Jaques from Canadian Parliamentary Guide and interviews, Frank Thorn, Secretary of Wetaskiwin constituency association during the 1930s and 1940s, Wetaskiwin, April 21, 1979; and Nanette Jaques McKay, Calgary, 1979.

44 Quotation from E. G. Hansell, *Debates*, House of Commons, July 24, 1943, p. 5398, and interview, James Gray, Calgary, March 1979.

45 *Debates*, House of Commons, June 13, 1940, p. 763; August 6, 1940, p. 2603; and February 24, 1941, p. 1208.

46 Jaques's reference to the "nefarious trio" appears in *Debates*, House of Commons, March 24, 1943, p. 1532. For Jaques's assertion about the left, see ibid., July 17, 1946, p. 3553.

47 Ibid., December 17, 1945, pp. 3706-10, 5744-48. Jaques's summary statement appears in ibid., August 31, 1946, p. 5747.

48 *The Canadian Social Crediter*, October 9, 1947, and *Today and Tomorrow* 4 (1943).

49 Tribute to Norman Jaques in *Debates*, House of Commons, January 31, 1949, p. 50. Interview, Frank Thorn.

50 Harry Hiller, "Religion, Populism and Social Credit in Alberta" (Ph.D. thesis, McMaster University, 1972), p. 435.

51 Aberhart was attracted to the British Israelite belief that the Anglo-Saxon peoples were the descendants of the 10 lost tribes of Israel, and that the second coming of Christ would be associated with the triumph of the British Empire. In his radio broadcasts, Aberhart explained that without "any shadow of doubt" the members of the Anglo-Saxon race were favoured of God and were the descendants of the Old Testament Israelites. These beliefs enabled Aberhart to provide a firm theological base for the Allied war effort. The guarantee of Allied victory rested on the conviction that the British Commonwealth and the United States were instruments in God's hand. But Aberhart was either not aware of, or ignored, the fact that the British Israel movement in eastern Canada and the United States was distributing copies of the *Protocols of the Elders of Zion* and publishing antisemitic tracts. See Lita-Rose Betcherman, *The Swastika and the Maple Leaf* (Toronto: Fitzhenry & Whiteside, 1975), p. 141, and Ralph Roy, *Apostles of Discord* (Boston: Beacon Press, 1953), chap. 5. For the denunciations of antisemitism, see *Prophetic Voice*, September 1942, pp. 2-3, and January 1944, p. 4.

52 Quoted in "Canadian Public Opinion Speaks Out on the Palestine Issue," Blackmore Papers, file 167, Glenbow Archives.

53 Ibid.

54 For the CCF's accusations that Social Credit was antisemitic, see *People's Weekly*, July 22, 1944 and January 26, 1946. For Manning's views, see *Today and Tomorrow*, March 2, 1944.

55 Manning's letter quoted in PAA, Premier's papers, file 1476, Manning to Jukes, May 20, 1947.

56 For further discussion of the purge of the Douglasites, see Alvin Finckel, *The Social Credit Phenomenon in Alberta* (Toronto: University of Toronto Press, 1989), p. 105.

57 For evidence of growing criticism of the Social Credit Board, both from within and without the Social Credit movement, see *Edmonton Journal*, March 18, 1943; March 1, 1946; March 21, 1946, and *Edmonton Bulletin*, March 20, 1945; March 21, 1946. For Manning's statement of dissociation, see *Edmonton Bulletin*, April 1, 1947. For the announcement of the Board's abolition, see *Edmonton Bulletin*, November 5, 1947. Stipulations of the new editorial policy for *The Canadian Social Crediter* quoted in Hugh Halleday, "Social Credit as a National Party in Canada" (M.A. thesis, Carleton University, 1966), p. 86. Quotation from J. A. Irving, unpublished manuscript on Social Credit, University of Toronto, Victoria College Archives, p. 42.

58 For evidence of attitudes toward the Douglasite faction, see *Calgary Herald*, April 25, 1947, and November 12, 24, 25, 1948.

59 Antisemitism lingered, however, among the committed Douglasites. For example, Ron Gostick, former secretary-treasurer of the Social Credit Association of Canada, published a right-wing newspaper, *The Canadian Intelligence Service*, which imbibes antisemitism from radical right-wing publications in the United States. In 1989, Gostick moved his operation from Flesherton, Ontario, to High River, Alberta.

60 The subject of Mormon attitudes toward Jews is complicated. For Mormon views of themselves as the new chosen people which provides the context for their attitudes toward Jews, see Jan Shipps, *Mormonism: The Story of a New Religious Tradition* (Urbana: University of Illinois, 1985), and Klaus Hansen, *Mormonism and the American Experience* (Chicago: University of Chicago Press, 1981). On the generally positive relationship between Jews and Mormons in Utah, see Jack Goodman, "Jews in Zion," in *The Peoples of Utah*, ed. Helen Papanikolas (Salt Lake City: Utah State Historical Society, 1976). For "official" theological statements of Mormon attitudes toward Jews and Zionism, see Bruce R. McConkie, *Mormon Doctrine* (Salt Lake City: Bookcraft, 1958). The discussion of the way Mormon views limited the appeal of Douglasite antisemitism in the Mormon communities in southern Alberta is based on interviews with Mormon leaders in Lethbridge.

61 *Debates*, House of Commons, January 31, 1944, p. 45.

62 Blackmore Papers, file 310, Blackmore to Glen Gorius, January 22, 1954, Glenbow Archives.

63 Blackmore Papers, file 378, Blackmore to Luana Blackmore, November 29, 1957, Glenbow Archives.

64 Low Papers, file 21, "Memorandum for Mr. Blackmore on Charges of Anti-Semitism," n.d., Glenbow Archives.

65 *Jewish Standard*, June 1, 1956, and Hugh Halleday, "Social Credit as a National Party in Canada" (M.A. thesis, Carleton University, 1966), pp. 80-87.

66 For an analysis of increased antisemitism in the United States during World War II, see Charles Herbert Stember, et al., *Jews in the Mind of America* (New York: American Jewish Committee, 1966), p. 215. For evidence of Jewish support of the war effort, see *Canadian Jews in World War II*, ed. David Rome, vol. 1, 2 (Montreal: Canadian Jewish Congress, 1947, 1948). The legion official's statement is found in the *Gleichen Call*, July 10, 1940. See also ibid., January 17, 1940.

67 APA, Oral History Tapes. Interviews with Abe Fratkin, March 2, 1975, and Moses Lieberman, April 16, 1975. See also Mel Fenson, "A History of the Jews in Alberta," *Canadian Jewish Reference Book and Directory*, p. 284.

68 *Calgary Herald*, November 13, 1943; *Edmonton Journal*, August 21, 1945; *Edmonton Bulletin*, August 29, 1945; and *Lethbridge Herald*, August 27, 1945.

69 Blackmore Papers, file 167, Glenbow Archives. For background on the Canadian Palestine Committee and the Christian Council for Palestine, see David Bercuson, *Canada and the Birth of Israel* (Toronto: University of Toronto Press, 1985), pp. 21-22, 25.

70 For an account of the Calgary meeting see *Calgary Herald*, October 10, 1945.

71 On the decline of American antisemitism in the post-war period, see Higham, *Send These to Me*, pp. 192-95. Studies of contemporary antisemitism in Canada show that

antisemitism is stronger in central Canada than the west, including Alberta. See League for Human Rights, of B'nai B'rith, *The Review of Anti-Semitism in Canada*, 1986, pp. 15, 16.

72 Ron Gostick is the son of Social Credit MLA and provincial librarian Edith Gostick and was involved in the national Social Credit organization. His publications were the source of many of Keegstra's radical right ideas. See Stanley Barrett, *Is God a Racist?* (Toronto: University of Toronto Press, 1987), pp. 204-11, 215-61. Barrett himself emphasized the religious origins of Keegstra's antisemitism, but his own evidence suggests the importance of the Social Credit connection. "By the time he had graduated from university, he had read most of Douglas' writings on social credit. Twice in the 1970s, and again in 1984, he ran for public office under the Social Credit banner" (ibid., p. 244).

8

The Shadow of Evil: Nazism and Canadian Protestantism

Marilyn F. Nefsky

"The future of humanity lies in the recognition of the shadow."[1] During the 1930s, Nazism cast an ominous shadow over many nations, including Canada. Many Canadians, overcome with inertia, xenophobia or nativism, were affected by its presence. During this period, neither the images nor issues were clearly delineated. Once war was declared, and Canada entered the battle on the side of the British, they could no longer remain inert; the war touched them personally and drew their commitment to defeat the Nazi foe. Although Canada played an admirable role in the war effort, Canadians, in general, were slow to recognize the ultimate significance of the Nazi phenomenon; they were also slow to recognize the true dimensions of the Jewish plight and the refugee crisis.

To what extent did the Christian churches of Canada, supposed defenders of truth and justice, succeed in understanding and responding to this colossal challenge to the human conscience? According to Irving Abella and Harold Troper in their ground-breaking study, *None Is Too Many*, the Canadian churches as a whole succeeded hardly better than the nation at large. During the Nazi era, when Jews suffered terrible persecution, leading ultimately to the Holocaust, no salvation came forth from Christian Canada; "the churches remained silent."[2] Are Abella and Troper correct? How silent, in fact, were the churches during this critical period in world history, particularly the Protestant churches? If they were indeed silent, how is their silence to be explained? Apathy? Antisemitism? Other factors? Was their silence excusable or morally reprehensible? What does silence mean in the face of something so vast?

Notes for Chapter 8 are on pp. 215-25.

In order to consider these questions, a certain amount of historical reconstruction is necessary. The social situation in Canada is relevant, since the socio-economic conditions that brought Hitler to power in Germany were not totally without their Canadian parallels. The reaction of the churches to these conditions undoubtedly affected their reaction to National Socialism, Nazi persecution and the refugee crisis. German Christian views of Jews and Judaism also had their parallels in Canada and also affected Canadian responses to contemporary events in Europe. The period between 1933, when Hitler became Chancellor of Germany, and 1945, when Nazism was defeated, will be examined under the following headings: the Third Reich; Nazi antisemitism and persecution; the refugee crisis; socio-economic conditions in Canada; Jews and Judaism. While the denominations were by no means consistent, even within themselves, certain indelible impressions emerge from their newspapers and journals.

The Third Reich

As early as 1933, Canadian Protestants were attentive to events in Germany. Most reacted to Hitler's appointment as chancellor with surprise and alarm, recognizing him as "a petty prophet, proclaiming a Messianic hope," inflaming the Germans with the spirit of militaristic nationalism.[3] Even the initial commentaries in *L'Action catholique* (Quebec) expressed certain apprehensions regarding the new chancellor's German chauvinism.[4] Non-Catholic Canadian Christians wondered how the more respectable people of Germany could support a man such as Hitler. Perhaps, they pondered, the Germans were "so weary of the unending struggle that they will tamely acquiesce in whatever is done by the Nazi chief."[5] Millions of Germans were unemployed, and millions more were paid below subsistence levels; the nation was suffering, and Hitler offered hope. The masses regarded him as a modern messiah "who has arisen to redeem his people from the intolerable shackles — the spiritual and physical — imposed by the Allies in 1919."[6] While some Canadians believed that Hitler's expressed desire for peace was sincere, blaming his underlings for the acts of terrorism, others found it incredible that he would offer a nation steeped in a thousand years of Christian religion and civilization a new paganism as a spiritual solution to its troubles. How long would the German people endure such a travesty?[7]

Not all references to Nazi Germany and Hitler expressed apprehension, however; in some instances, the church press and its correspondents turned to rationalization and even approval. After the German dictator concluded the Concordat with the pope in August 1933, he gained a greater degree of sympathy from some of the French Catholic journals.[8] He also gained some sympathy in Protestant circles. A Baptist commentator of the day, the Reverend J. Gordon Jones, commended the determination of the Germans "to do anything to change the present conditions."[9] Unlike Canadians, he added reprovingly, the Germans were at least doing something to ameliorate their difficulties. An obviously Germanophile United Church minister, the Reverend Harold B. Hendershot, who had studied in Marburg, insisted that, despite a few injustices, Hitler's goals were beyond reproach, and Canadians ought to recognize this fact.[10] Irrespective of his methods, a later (1935) United Church article declared, the German ruler at least had saved his country from a disaster worse than any he had inflicted and, to his credit, had created an ordered society.[11] As late as 1939, some Protestants in Canada still admired the manner in which "from a defeated and starving people, the Germans had been brought to a position of tremendous power and fitness."[12] That this transformation had been forced upon them seemed of little consequence. In the same year an eminent Baptist, Dr. Watson Kirkconnell, declared, half approvingly, in his presidential address to the Baptist Union of Western Canada, that National Socialism had given the German people a new meaning in life; it had restored pride in their country, their race and themselves; it had given them a sense of direction and destiny.[13] Such remarks did not go unchallenged, however. Another United Churchman, the Reverend Claris E. Silcox, annoyed at Hendershot's Germanophilia, denounced what he called the "German Psychosis," while another Canadian Baptist, J. C. Carlisle, disputed a German Baptist's recent glowing account of Nazi Germany's so-called "freedom of religion."[14]

In the early pre-war period, there was a tendency to excuse the rise of National Socialism because of the Treaty of Versailles, an agreement conceived in bitterness and vengeance. A full-page article in a United Church periodical entitled "The Challenge of Germany" argued that the treaty created conditions "in which no nation could remain sane."[15] Even the Reverend Richard Roberts of Toronto, one of the denomination's great preachers, acknowledged that the situation in Germany was not due wholly to "the perversity of the German people."[16] Rather, Hitlerism was the last resort of a nation caught in a desperate plight of the Allies' making. Some continued to blame the Versailles Treaty, even after evidence of Nazi cruelties appeared in the religious press. A 1936 Anglican periodical reported the Very Reverend W. R. Inge, Dean of St. Paul's, London, England, as claiming that the treaty was responsible for the indignity and humiliation suffered by the Germans.[17] Yet, the belief that the treaty was mainly responsible for subsequent events was by no means universal. Other commentators pointed out that the Germans were flouting its provisions, violating every pledge they had made since 1918.[18]

With Hitler's invasion of Poland in 1939 came a sudden change of mood. Now convinced that there was little good about National Socialism, much of the church press attempted to justify Canada's engagement in the war. It was noticed that "the Nazis were not in the least interested in equality, justice or peace."[19] As news of successive German victories swept the Western world, Nazi Germany was perceived increasingly as less a military foe than as a form of evil incarnate sweeping across Europe like a cyclone: "After the last conflict the world had thought it knew the infamy and cruelty of the Germans; it was mistaken, for the present struggle has revealed depths of iniquity hitherto unsuspected.[20] Appalled by the atrocities perpetrated by the German forces, some church leaders argued that the church must condemn Nazi rule as intrinsically diabolical. Still more horrific, wrote Dorothy Sayers, a contemporary British novelist, playwright and contributor to Anglican periodicals, was that what the church considered evil, Nazi Germany considered good – a direct repudiation of the fundamental beliefs of Christianity.[21] Confirming this view, the Archbishop of York, Cyril Garbett, was quoted in *The Canadian Churchman* as saying that the trouble with the Nazis "is not the telling of lies; it is what Plato called the lie in the soul."[22]

As the war clouds grew darker, the sense of evil running amuck grew more overwhelming. In 1941, the United Church press cited Reinhold Niebuhr, a renowned American theologian, as saying that a Nazi triumph would mean not a return to the barbarism of the Dark Ages, but "the creation of something new and altogether worse than the world has ever seen."[23] No longer were typical church editorialists denigrating the Treaty of Versailles as the source of the Nazi plague; instead, they were moving to its defence. The treaty, they argued, had become the *bête noire* of world conditions primarily through successful German propaganda.[24] True, it contained no spirit of forgiveness, but, as a Baptist writer, the Reverend T. N. Tattersall, declared, neither had the Germans any spirit of repentance, and "forgiveness without repentance is unknown in any moral order."[25] The Germans, in fact, had suffered very lightly compared with the sufferings they were now inflicting on others. In a self-reproving analysis, Archbishop Garbett noted in 1942 that the Allies had been slow to act because they could not believe that such a perversion of civilization was possible: "We thought Hitler was deplorable rather than damnable, and that is our condemnation."[26] The archbishop was not alone in this sentiment. During the war years, its corollary was reiterated constantly in Protestant publications: the imperative need to defeat the Third Reich. However, victory alone was not the final goal. Defeating Hitler would not save the world in itself, for the Nazi tyrant embodied "all the malaise of the pre-war world: loss of direction, loss of soul, sense of impotence, man-worship . . . devil worship."[27] Defeating Hitlerism required destroying the roots from which the evil had sprung, as well as the soil of despair, resentment and wounded pride in which it had been nurtured.

The Protestant churches came to regard Nazism as more than a political configuration; it was seen as a pagan faith antithetical to Christianity – a

pagan faith on a crusade. It sought to replace "the tortured pain-torn figure of the crucified Christ" with a racist Teutonic spirit.[28] Already the
Germans had shown themselves to be fanatically committed to its ban-
ners. Whether or not they liked the programs of their leaders, the fact
remained that the latter "always have been executed."[29] A few church editorialists argued that a conscious distinction must be made between Nazi
Germany and the German people. An element of compassion prevailed:
the German people were described as generally apathetic, loyal, disciplined
and most of all desirous of peace.[30] It was difficult, however, for the lay
public to accept this view, especially when, at the end of 1942, 11 governments released a joint declaration confirming the reports of the Nazi
atrocities. On the whole, the churches continued to equate the German
state with evil incarnate. A patriotic as well as a religious fervour prevailed.

As the war advanced, the Christian denominations were frequently
reminded that their fight was not merely *against* Nazism but also *for* religious liberty and freedom. There were still calls for compassion for the
Germans, whatever the extent of their guilt: surely "countless numbers . . . were innocently hurtled along by a demoniac and dynamic mass
movement."[31] Few delusions, however, were entertained about the
dimensions to which this demonism could grow. The Nazis both practised what they preached, and preached what they practised.[32] Despite the
depths to which the Third Reich had plunged, the Canadian churches
universally agreed that Germany must be treated with Christian forbearance, though they also recognized that this would be no mean task. It
required assuaging feelings of hatred and revenge and overcoming fears of
recurring war. While restrictions and controls would be necessary after the
conflagration, the German people had to be given the opportunity to
recover spiritually as well as materially.[33] However, the mood of Christian
forbearance was not uniform. Whereas the United Church insisted that
the German people ought not to be condemned collectively for the Nazi
crimes, the Baptists seemed to feel that the suffering which Germany had
brought upon itself was thoroughly deserved, and that "this generation of
Germans will bear some of the economic, political and cultural marks of it
to their dying day."[34]

On the whole, the Canadian churches did not blame Germany alone
for the European fiasco. Hitler could never have succeeded "had we not
provided the tools — those fears and antipathies — which he so cunningly
used to divide and immobilize us."[35] As usual, however, Baptist opinion
was less self-incriminating in its evaluation of Nazi Germany, arguing that
from the beginning the German people were "drunk with the wine of
conquest."[36] More than other Canadian Christians, the Baptists refused to
diminish the responsibility of the German Christian population for the
success of National Socialism. While many European Protestants, as well

as Catholics and Orthodox Christians, were determined adversaries of Nazism, "many — perhaps a majority of Protestant Christians yielded to the totalitarian pressure and sought deviously to rationalize their faith in conformity with the nazi ideology. . . ."[37] Whatever their defence, they allowed Nazism to grow and flourish, failing to oppose it while it was still formative and capable of control.

Nazi Antisemitism and Persecution

How did the churches respond to reports of antisemitism and the persecution of the Jews under the Third Reich? As soon as the anti-Jewish boycotts were instituted in April 1933, Canadian Christians acknowledged the reality and seriousness of the Jewish plight. The Protestant churches called forth bitter condemnation. Following the implementation of the Aryan laws, these churches and their publications continued to report intermittently on the intensifying program of antisemitic oppression.[38] Nazi activities were condemned as neither Christian nor decent; the Baptists, in particular, called (ineffectually) for a concerted effort on the part of the Christian community to protest against the outrages.[39] Some church leaders asserted that it was high time to arouse public opinion in Canada.[40] In 1936, *The Presbyterian Record* published a series of articles dealing with Nazi Germany. One of these articles considered the information revealed by the former High Commissioner for Refugees, James G. McDonald, in his letter of resignation. Resigning in order to make the world see "the horror and tragedy of it all," McDonald explained the true nature of the Jewish persecution: the Nazi regulations were designed not only to rob Jews of their human rights but actually to destroy the Jewish population.[41] With a note of desperation, he pleaded that "world opinion move to avert the existing and impending tragedies."[42] Two years later, the United Church referred to these tragedies as "organized, cold-blooded terrorism."[43] In February 1939, Dr. Conrad Hoffman, Secretary of the Committee on the Christian Approach to the Jew (from the International Missionary Council), declared that Hitler was determined to cleanse Germany of all Jewishness through a slow process of annihilation.[44] Underscoring the situation, a Presbyterian commentator, the Reverend D. M. MacMillan, wrote that Christians should take to heart that "hundreds of thousands of human beings have been ruthlessly persecuted for no other reason than they have been born Jews."[45]

Despite these and other voices, it was difficult from the beginning for Canadian Christians at large to believe that the stories of Jewish persecution were true. Some clergy were predisposed to disbelieve such tales because of their own Germanophilia; a few even professed to understand how Germany could harbour such a deep distrust and hatred of the Jews. H. B. Hendershot, for example, accusing the Jews of having "unfairly pushed themselves to too great prominence during a period of dislocation and unrest," found the current situation in Germany a rather natural reaction to the "Jewish problem."[46] As aliens in Germany, the Jews had been neither wise nor grateful to their host country.[47] Throughout the pre-war period, articles of this type appeared occasionally in the church press. Thus, Dr. C. Kerr, a Presbyterian, suggested that the Germans were only treating "the Jews exactly as the Jews once treated other peoples they thought might contaminate them.... [T]hey set out to exterminate them."[48] The Baptist World Alliance Congress, which had met in Berlin in 1934, implicitly denied the persecution rumours, suggesting that, while some excesses and atrocious deeds had been committed against the Jews, the situation was not one tenth as horrible as they had been *made* to believe.[49] In the eyes of these pro-German (and pro-German Christian) commentators many of the victims of Nazi crimes thoroughly deserved their blows.[50] But these views did not predominate. For the most part, during this troubled era, there was a visible measure of sympathy for Hitler's victims.

Once war was declared, reports on the persecution of the Jews began to dwindle; nevertheless some church writers continued to address the issue. Pointing to older patterns in German history, especially during times of turmoil, they suggested that Jewish persecution should have come as a surprise to no one. *Mein Kampf*, they declared, showed a remarkable continuity of purpose: "the extirpation of the Jews and the enlargement of the Third Reich."[51] In a 1940 address, Dr. Adolph Keller, the Secretary of the Central Bureau for the Relief of the Evangelical churches, reported that there was no end to the destitution and despair in Europe; the Jews went homeless and forsaken for utterly irrational reasons: "a demonic power decrees to these people who are like ourselves: 'Die! There is no place for you among mankind!' "[52] As soon as news of the systematic mass destruction of the Jewish population arrived in Canada late in 1942, the churches began to report it, but with dubious results. The greater the horror, the more inconceivable it became to the Canadian imagination.

Some, however, managed to conceive the inconceivable. In October 1942, an eminent United Church minister, the Reverend Ernest Marshall Howse, addressed a public meeting in Winnipeg with outrage at the "degenerate ferocity" with which the Nazis were destroying the Jews.[53] In December of the same year, the Anglican Church published a speech by the Archbishop of Canterbury, William Temple, which drew the conclusion that extermination was the true purpose of the Nazi anti-Jewish fury, and that to believe otherwise was to deny reality.[54] The same church paper also quoted the Archbishop of York, who drew attention to the fact that the ghastly cruelties and atrocities in Nazi-occupied lands were "committed not only by a small handful of sadists, but by thousands of Germans and . . . not a protest has been raised either by those who are ordered to commit them or by the people of Germany who must have some knowledge of what is done in their name."[55] A prophetic statement in the 1942 Christmas issue of *The Canadian Churchman* indicates that, before the end of 1942, the churches were informed about and reporting to their constituencies not only military events but also — though certainly to a lesser degree — what was happening to the Jews: "It is unlikely that more than a remnant of the Jewish population will survive."[56] For many church leaders, it was not until this time that the real significance of the Jewish persecution began to dawn.

As World War II moved towards its denouement, the German nation's culpability for the fate of the Jews, along with other Nazi crimes, received growing attention. One view regarded Hitler as solely responsible, excusing the average German citizen as "a dupe of a master mind."[57] Another view, emphasizing the prolonged persecution of Poles, Czechs and Jews of all nations,[58] reminded Germany that it would have to face the consequences of its actions. During this debate, the church press presented few but nevertheless significant reports of the Nazi mass murders. Recognizing the apparent boundlessness of Hitler's hatred of the Jews, a few Christian writers condemned the "barbarous and inhuman" Nazi policy of "cold-blooded extermination."[59] By the middle of 1943, the graphic details of 'life' in the concentration camps found their way into Canadian journals. A reprinted address of Archbishop Garbett (of York) vividly portrayed the unique horror reserved for Hitler's victims, depicting the "starvation; exportation in 'trains of death'; wholesale massacre by shooting and poison gas." In his words, it was an unparalleled "bloodbath on a gigantic scale."[60] Toward the end of 1944, the United Church editors admitted, perhaps on behalf of all the churches in Canada, that they had been reluctant for a long time to accept at face value the accounts of Nazi atrocities. Apparently, Jewish reports alone were insufficient to convince sceptical churchmen. However, eyewitness accounts by reputable American correspondents had finally verified "the scientifically brutal way in which men, women and little children were destroyed in mass murder gas chambers."[61] The hour of truth had arrived, and the evidence could no longer be fudged. Yet, to the discerning, the Jewish plight had been visible from the beginning. What remedies were proposed?

The Refugee Crisis

Despite the accounts of Jewish persecution and the expressions of sympathy in the early period, the churches offered few practical solutions to the problem. From 1935 onward, certain prominent church leaders made conscious and conscientious attempts to inform their constituencies about the Jewish refugees. By 1936, the seriousness of the refugee crisis began to dawn on the churches at large. Fifty representatives of the major Protestant denominations drew up a manifesto in response to James McDonald's letter of resignation and distributed it to all members of Parliament and throughout Canada. The manifesto not only protested against the Nazi treatment of Jews and other non-Aryans, but also declared that the churches could no longer remain silent on this issue. It declared: "Should the flow of exiles from Germany not cease, we feel that Canada should share with other countries the responsibility of providing a haven for at least a reasonable number of selected refugees."[62] Clearly, "a *reasonable* number of *selected* refugees" was not a call for all-out rescue; nevertheless, the manifesto embodied an increasing sensitivity to the Jewish situation and indicated a willingness by a few Christians to pressure the Canadian government through appeal to public opinion. However, it did not precipitate effective national action. As Dr. Conrad Hoffman commented in the same year, "Christian agencies have so far done little in the way of relief — they have contented themselves with protests."[63]

By 1938, some Canadian churches and churchmen were issuing further appeals. The United Church, emphasizing the need to assist both Jewish and Christian refugees, urged the Canadian Christian community on behalf of the International Council of the World Alliance for International Friendship to make every effort to assist and relieve Hitler's victims.[64] In the September prior to *Kristallnacht* (November 9-11, 1938), the Anglican Church Council for Social Services passed a resolution urging the Canadian government to "continue to explore the possibilities for the Immigration [*sic*] of selected groups of Jewish people and non-Aryan Christians from Austria and Germany, so far as is possible and desirable, and . . . [to] assume a share of the responsibility of finding a home for these unfortunate victims of political aggression."[65] In the aftermath of *Kristallnacht*, the Reverend W. T. Steven of the Moose Jaw Baptist Church, Moose Jaw, Saskatchewan, penned a resolution suggesting that his denomination offer refuge to "those persecuted people" on the ground that such persecution was "entirely opposed to the principles of Christianity, democracy and freedom which are dear to the hearts of Canadians."[66] The resolution passed by the Baptist Convention of Ontario and Quebec urged the Dominion government to admit to Canada "carefully selected individuals or groups of refugees, as being desirable not only from human and ethical standpoints, but also because such immigration would prove a valuable addition to our national economy. . . ."[67] When it became apparent that these resolutions and exhortations were falling short of effective action, concerned church leaders intensified their efforts. An editorial in *The Presbyterian Record* of January 1939 reprinted a plea issued on behalf of the Archbishop of Canterbury, the Moderator of the Church of Scotland, the Moderator of the Federal Council of Evangelical Free churches and other non-Canadian religious dignitaries that "in the name both of our Christian faith and of common humanity ... [Dominion governments] open their doors generously to refugees before it is too late. ..."[68] In March, the editor of *The Presbyterian Record*, W. M. Rochester, referred to the indescribable misery of those seeking asylum. Denouncing the Canadian government's closed-door policy, he argued that, as a Christian nation, Canada should not be daunted by material considerations: "Help is needed. Let us give it and at once."[69]

As the impending war approached, those in the Canadian churches concerned with the European Jews expressed little confidence in the government; "there is every sign that the Canadian Government, if it acts at all, will act with discreditable hesitation."[70] Excluding refugees from a country so large and sparsely settled was as unconscionable as the crude immoralism of the Nazis; the ostensibly Machiavellian conduct of the federal cabinet remained unfathomable to Christians involved in the issue. When humanitarian appeals proved ineffectual in moving public opinion, these individuals appealed to material considerations, assuring the populace that unanticipated benefits would come to a country offering a haven to refugees, although a truly Christian nation has the moral obligation to help the needy apart from self-interest.[71] In the winter of 1938, representatives of the churches, together with other Canada-wide groups, joined together in Ottawa to form the Canadian National Committee on Refugees and Victims of Political Persecution under the auspices of the League of Nations Society in Canada.[72] Various organizations passed further resolutions urging that the Canadian government adopt a wise and well-controlled immigration policy.[73] One Anglican member severely criticized the "half-hearted" resolutions passed by most churches. With the emphasis on "selected refugees," and on the benefits accruing to Canada from the latter, he argued, "we seem to be far more interested in what we can get from the refugees than what we can give them."[74] Canon W. W. Judd, General Secretary of the General Council for Social Service, while concurring with these sentiments, suggested that demanding an open door policy from the current government would serve in fact to seal it shut. If, on the other hand, the government could be persuaded to yield even a few inches, at least some of the Nazi victims would be saved.[75]

In a radio lecture on the refugee crisis, Dr. Kirkconnell, now president of the Baptist Union of Western Canada, argued that if Canada as a Christian nation coldly allowed the refugees to "perish on the doorstep of the world," it would be just as guilty as the Nazis for their persecution and suffering.[76] Acknowledging, in spite of his admiration for German "direction and destiny," the indescribable brutality of the Nazi regime, Dr. Kirkconnell, like others, felt it necessary to point out that fewer than 50 percent of the victims of the Third Reich were Jewish. In order to succeed in their appeal for refugee aid, concerned churchmen took pains to impress this fact upon the nation.[77] The churches were well aware of the sheer indifference of a large section of the Canadian public to the entire crisis. They were also aware of the presence of antisemitism in Canada. That so many of the victims were Jews was cause enough to do nothing. This was epitomized in the lack of public outcry at the Canadian government's refusal to allow the desperate Jews on the ocean liner S.S. *St. Louis* (*Voyage of the Damned*) to land on Canadian soil in June 1939.[78] The Quaker G. Raymond Booth encapsulated the attitude of much of Canadian society toward such refugees: "Between Nazism which drives them forth and a certain kind of Canadianism which seeks to bar their coming, there isn't much to choose from morally."[79]

Once war was declared, matters became desperate. In a 1940 address, Dr. Adolph Keller argued that unless Canadian Christians raised their voices for justice and extended their hands in mercy, the refugees would not survive the current persecution.[80] The Executive Committee of the Council for Social Service of the Anglican Church deplored the public indifference to the refugee crisis.[81] In 1940, the Baptist Convention of Ontario and Quebec passed a more extensive resolution, urging the Canadian government to receive the victims of the Nazi terror.[82] A few church leaders, determined to stir the Christian conscience, implored Canadians to accept responsibility for the refugees, and to demand their admission to Canada en masse. Yet despite these resolutions and motions urging the Canadian government to participate in refugee relief, "the streams of Christian sympathy and love" were more like rivulets, hardly able to dent the "barriers of Canadian national selfishness."[83] Canada was second on the list of countries offering the least aid to Nazi refugees; first was Soviet Russia, a country that ideologically repudiated Christianity. Some Canadian Christians were not proud of this record.[84] Toward the end of 1943, when the evidence of the Holocaust could no longer be ignored, the General Synod of the Anglican Church passed a motion urging the federal government "to welcome victims of political persecution regardless of race or creed."[85] Emphasizing that millions of human beings were being tortured to death in Nazi camps, one United Church writer implored the nation to save these victims before they were totally destroyed.[86] The Presbyterian Church, following the example of its counterparts, suggested urging the government to open its doors "to a *fair share* of the refugees," and to provide as far as possible for their immediate necessities.[87] Unfortunately, Christian charity was not universal among the churches. Such was the temper of the times that the Presbyterian Board considered the issue "a knotty point," requiring extensive consideration.[88] Although reduced in number, reports on the murders continued to be published in the church press. Referring to the thousands of people, especially Jews, being "packed into cattle cars and taken to Poland to be shot," *The*

United Church Observer appealed again for unlocked national doors.[89] One correspondent indicted the integrity and morality of Canadian Christians: had they become so callous that the fate of millions of people failed to stir them to action?[90]

Socio-Economic Conditions in Canada

The pre-war decade was one of the most devastating eras Canadians ever had to face. Early in this decade, the Canadian industrial machine came to a virtual halt. Almost 20 percent of the Canadian labour force was unemployed; economic recovery was slow and uneven. Although the downswing ended in 1933, a severe recession in 1937-38 retarded recovery, which was still far from complete when the war broke out in 1939.[91] Natural disasters contributed to the economic decline. A drought that had struck the Canadian prairies in 1929 continued in some areas long after. Swarms of grasshoppers attacked the vegetation, and rust spores destroyed young heads of wheat. Farming was impossible. Many western Canadians attempted to wait out the drought; others looked elsewhere for subsistence. The churches were preoccupied with social, economic and political issues arising from these problems. Except for the provisions supplied by congregations in the east, the problems in the west would have continued unabated.[92]

In addition to the economic crisis, the 1930s was "a period of controversy and confrontation." Despite the insoluble nature of the Depression, Canadians demanded immediate political action. The Bennett and King governments' ineptitude in dealing with the crisis undermined the stability of the social order. Mistrust in the democratic process was intensified by the apparent corruption of the Liberal government in Quebec, and the suppression of the press in Alberta.[93] The pre-war period produced psychological as well as economic depression. Psychologically, the 1930s induced loss of faith in personal security as well as political democracy; a generation learned painfully that the independence reaped from employment was largely illusory.[94] Many Canadians started to look at other political systems for solace and succour. This loss of faith was particularly distressing to Protestants of British origin, who placed the concept of political democracy at the root of their heritage. In general, an exceedingly suspicious and xenophobic mindset prevailed in much of the country.

Pro-British feelings, traditional in Anglo-Canada, grew more intense. Although little more than half the population was British in origin, British ideas and institutions were considered the spiritual as well as racial heritage of the nation.[95] There were also strong emotional ties with Britain, especially for some of Canada's socio-economic policy-makers. At their worst, these pro-British attitudes degenerated into an Anglo-Saxon nativism which aggravated the cultural divisions within Canadian society by railing against so-called foreign elements: European immigrants, French-Canadian Catholics and Canadian Jews. These strong anti-alien attitudes played a significant role in keeping immigration and refugee numbers low.[96] At their best, they elevated the principles of Anglo-Saxon democracy above narrow racial concerns. Initially, Nazism was perceived as just another foreign nationalistic movement. While Canadians had never been greatly interested in international affairs or international diplomacy, they became increasingly introverted during the 1930s. With plenty of trouble at home, European events seemed very remote indeed; like earthquakes or famines, "they made the headlines but . . . were soon forgotten."[97] When they did turn their attention abroad, those Canadians sympathetic to Hitler's victims were fearful that criticism of Germany would cause the Nazis to escalate their persecution. Moreover, until war became inevitable, they also feared the consequences of too much criticism for Canada itself. Would the nation be drawn closer to the impending conflict?[98]

In addition to national economic problems, there was the perennial problem of regional disparity. The cleavage was particularly pronounced between French and English Canada. Industrialization, by bringing rural Catholic Quebec out of its isolation and into contact with the alien ethos of urban, Protestant society, had created new tensions. Unionization had contributed to the growing split, since management tended to be English-speaking, and labour French-speaking. Threatened with the loss of their social identity and cultural integrity, French Canadians accentuated above all their language, religion and provincial autonomy, thereby enlarging the division between the two solitudes.[99] In response to the crisis of the social order, some Canadians flirted with fascism and socialism; others developed an exaggerated fear of communism. When Pope Pius XI condemned communism for destroying the family and economy, Francophone antipathy grew still stronger, and fascism became more attractive.[100] In Quebec, the *Parti national social chrétien* appeared, combining elements of Italian and German fascism. The leaders of French Canada feared that an open-door refugee policy would mean an increase in the number of Anglo-Saxon Protestants, thereby threatening to reduce the Francophone, largely Catholic population to a powerless minority. They also feared that Jewish refugees might take over the business and wealth of the province, leaving French Canadians unemployed and impoverished. Largely for these reasons, Quebec adamantly opposed opening the door to refugees, especially Jews.[101] Worried by evidence of Liberal party corruption in the province, Prime Minister King, for whom power was a paramount concern, believed that he had to retain the French-Canadian vote for the Liberals at all costs. Since the rest of Canada was relatively silent on the issue of Jewish refugees, it was easy for the federal cabinet to adopt the popular line and keep the doors tightly shut.[102] In fact, the refugee question was suppressed as much as possible.

Canadian Christendom, therefore, if, by Christendom, we mean the nation as a whole rather than a vocal minority in the institutional churches, had little to say on this burning issue. Most Christians in Canada were simply indifferent; a few were actually hostile. Indeed, as we have seen, some pre-war clergy—Protestant and Catholic—were either pro-German or sympathetic to fascism in any case and thus disinclined to criticize Nazi policies: e.g., the English Anglican Bishop, A. C. Headlam (frequently quoted in Canada), Harold Hendershot of the United Church, Dr. C. Kerr of the Presbyterian Church and the influential nationalistic Quebec Catholic, Abbé Lionel Groulx.[103] But, as we have seen, many of these pro-German and pro-fascist comments were refuted in church publications by other churchmen. For this reason, it would be inaccurate to suggest that the general silence of Canadian Christendom— after all, Canada was overwhelmingly a Christian nation—stemmed from a tacit approval of Jewish persecution. It is considerably more accurate to conclude that this silence came in large measure from apathy, preoccupation with other problems and the general xenophobia of the day.

Jews and Judaism

In spite of the foregoing, antisemitism did play a part in public policy. Indeed, according to the Reverend Claris E. Silcox, some of the indifference to the refugees was due to "the existence throughout Canada . . . of a latent antisemitism."[104] Silcox, of course, was speaking of the respectable, as well as of the cruder elements in Canadian society: Christians who would never have mistreated Jews themselves nor have approved of those who did, but who were content to leave the status quo and its injustices intact, without troubling themselves to rescue aliens from foreign perils. Beneath the surface of their religion lingered "uncrystallized but negative feelings about Jews" in general.[105] This latent antisemitism would normally have had little effect, but during the Nazi era it meant that a large number of otherwise decent and considerate people were predisposed to indifference. Some denominational leaders were aware of the problem of antisemitism in their midst.

During the 1930s, the churches posited a traditional belief in the inferiority of Judaism to Christianity. For French Catholics, this inferiority was rooted in a view of the Jew as a stranger, unassimilable, mercantile and totally removed from any religious sensitivity.[106] For Anglo-Protestants it was rooted in pietistic and evangelical views which envisioned the need to convert Jews to the true religion.[107] Whereas much of the French-Catholic literature in Quebec was replete with explicit anti-Jewish theological sentiments, the literature of the other Canadian churches contained a more implicit antisemitism. The Pharisaic ancestors of contemporary Jews were seen as burdened and blinded by the Mosaic law; they were conceived as a suspicious and envious lot, self-righteous and hypocritical. Even as the shadow of persecution began to fall, the church press typically continued to refer to the Pharisees as having been "utterly perverted by arid legalism and a rigorism that made them merciless and blind."[108] While these epithets were attached to first-century Jews, there was little commentary to suggest that contemporary Jews were other than a modern version of their spiritually withered ancestors. The reader was left to draw his own conclusions. Nor did wartime atrocity stories change matters. The same besmirched image persisted: the Pharisees were like "white sepulchres, beautiful on the outside but rotten on the inside."[109] They were tied and bound in their own pride and spiritual stupidity. Because they thought in terms of Jewish domination, they failed to recognize Jesus as the messiah. Even when the true state of affairs in Nazi-occupied Europe was being reported in both the religious and secular press, some church members were still capable of describing the Jews as the cause of their own suffering, having so wickedly crucified "Christ."[110] As late as February 1945, a radio address cast the Pharisees as virtuous individuals who "became men of closed minds and enemies of Jesus."[111] Not even a knowledge of the death camps caused some churchmen to refrain from denouncing Jews and Judaism in this fashion.

However, these negative views, the culmination of centuries of religious antisemitism, were not unqualified among Canadian Christians. A number of sermons and articles acknowledged the great contributions made by Jewish saints and prophets. Christians were reminded that Jesus was born a Jew, that all the apostles were Jews, and that most of the New Testament was written by Jews. As a United Church writer, C. A. Lawson, remarked, "We never would have had our Christianity in its present form if it had not been for the Jews who loved Christ."[112] One book reviewer maintained that, if Christians thought of Judaism as a sterile religion, they might "be startled to find here a devotion to religious principles coupled with a recognition of the constant expansion of the idea of divine revelation. . . ."[113] Nor were the Pharisees always depicted as hypocrites and sinners; while excessively and meticulously careful about ritualistic requirements, wrote the Reverend H. Beverly Ketchen, a Presbyterian, the Pharisees at least took their religion seriously, unlike the far from righteous Christian community of the present day.[114] For the evangelizing churches especially, the Jewish personality was far from irremediable. The Presbyterians and Anglicans pursued the task of Jewish evangelization throughout the entire Nazi era. Jewish missions were maintained and staffed, often with ordained converts, and progress reports were regularly submitted for publication. Improved Jewish-Christian relations were cer-

tainly encouraged, but conversion was always the goal. Identifying an ear-
nest yearning among Jews for spiritual satisfaction, the Reverend John
Stuart Conning stated that Christians owed them kindness and goodwill;
in "no other way can the estrangement of Jews to the Christian faith be
overcome."[115] In 1938, the Anglican Archbishop of Toronto, who was also
the Primate of Canada, concluded a Good Friday pastoral letter on the
sufferings and injustices endured by the Jewish people by saying that "this
distress also lends urgency to the need of evangelism among them. . . ."[116]
As the war grew more intense, these evangelical Christians continued to
regard Jewish persecution as a rare opportunity to present the gospel.[117]

Such Christians naively believed that conversion to Christianity would
cure not only the spiritual but also the material problems of the Jews,
especially the menace of antisemitism. Referring to German "Neo-paganism," the Montreal Jewish Mission proclaimed as its underlying principle
the belief that "Christ alone is the final solution" for the Jews[118] — a phrase
the ironic significance of which could not have been known to its authors.
However, these attempts at Jewish evangelization proved mostly unsuccessful, leading to occasional complaints about Jews who "instinctively
know where to find their profit and readily avail themselves of it."[119] Neither the recognition of neo-paganism nor an interest in saving Jewish
souls served to eradicate antisemitism, either prior to or during World War
II, even in the churches themselves. Wondering what it would be like to be
a Jew, a writer in *The Canadian Baptist* admitted the many "insults and
penalties that a Christian world is heaping . . . on [Jewish] heads."[120]
Those involved in Jewish evangelization considered antisemitism among
Christians a form of "vile, anti-Christian teaching," but were willing to
capitalize on the vulnerability of its victims nevertheless.[121] Continuing
reports of Jewish persecution in Nazi-occupied lands brought few Canadian Christians to a condemnation of anti-Jewish discrimination in Canada itself.[122] The onset of the war did little to stem its rising tide. Referring
to antisemitism as an "ever-recurring plague," a letter to *The Canadian
Churchman* inquired why Canadians damned the fascists and the Nazis,
when Christendom itself bore so much responsibility for the current situation.[123]

The recognition of antisemitism in their midst, of course, was the first
step to its eradication in the Christian churches, but this cause had little
success during the Nazi era. The traditional choice offered to Jews was
conversion, which would have marked their virtual disappearance as Jews,
or the preservation of their religious and national identity, which inevitably involved persecution.[124] In 1936, Dr. Conrad Hoffman remarked that
"one would almost think sometimes that there was some peculiar inhibi-
tion that tended to prevent Christian people in general from making their
religion really practical."[125] Many who did not directly contribute to Jew-

ish misery did nothing to protest against it.[126] Urging an open-door policy just prior to the war, a politically astute writer reasoned that the Canadian government would admit Jewish refugees only if *public opinion* favoured such a policy, but public opinion was not favourable. Hitler, the article pointed out, showed acute insight when he ridiculed the West for a "concern in refugees which led to no concrete action."[127] Throughout the war years, a few highly placed church leaders continually condemned Christendom for its lack of any great concern for Jewish refugees. The still greater tragedy was that some professed Christians "shouted out against allowing any Jews to find sanctuary among us."[128] Describing the indifference of the Christian populace in 1944, one United Church commentator grieved: "if they (the Jews) had been cattle, they would have been welcomed anywhere. As human beings they were wanted nowhere!"[129] Perhaps the American theologian, Reinhold Niebuhr, captured the Canadian, as well as American Christian attitude toward an open-door refugee policy most accurately: "We hate the horrors the Nazis perpetrated against the Jews . . . but still we don't want too many of them to come to America because we fear it would increase the anti-semitism . . . [which is] too strong already."[130] This antisemitic feeling was evident as late as 1944, when G. G. Harris, a United Church adherent and correspondent, adamantly argued that Christians must refrain from friendship with Jews "so long as they stubbornly deny that Christ was born of Bethlehem"[131] — clearly not an attitude conducive to public sympathy for refugees.

Conclusion

As early as 1933, the Canadian Protestant churches regarded Hitler's rise to power with apprehension. By the time war was declared, it had become evident that Nazism had touched the German soul in a deep and demonic fashion. Nazi Germany had to be defeated, not because it had stretched its grasp over the whole of Europe, nor because it had denied the most fundamental human rights, nor even because of its cruel and barbaric treatment of the Jews, but because everything it did and said was totally unchristian and anti-Christian.[132] Jewish persecution was not ignored by Canadian Protestantism. The major phases in the Nazi roundup of the Jews were reported, even if these reports were superseded for the most part by accounts of the European campaign. During the 1930s, the church press described the upheavals resulting from the Aryan laws, their increased intensity in subsequent years, the widespread pogrom of *Kristallnacht*, the massacres by the *Einsatzgruppen* and, finally, the deportation and planned extermination of the Jews across Europe. Of course, as Deborah E. Lipstadt points out in her study of the American press during the same period, *how* the news is presented is just as important as the fact of its presentation.[133] Items buried in back pages or in larger stories attract little attention, and all too often the fate of the Jews was minimized, even when it was reported, by this means. Throughout the Nazi era, a few highly placed Christian leaders and activists lodged protests against the persecutions, and various church organizations passed resolutions urging an open-door policy for Jews and other victims of Nazi terror. Are Abella and Troper correct, then, when they claim that the Canadian churches remained silent? If they mean that the latter said little or did nothing about the Jewish plight in their synods, presbyteries and publications, they are incorrect. Silence did not prevail. The Protestant churches were neither speechless nor inactive and, therefore, can be exonerated of this charge. Whether they said as much as they should have said, and did as much as they should have done, of course, is another question.

Prevailing wartime conditions led to questions of credibility. News was carefully censored; confirming evidence from governments was non-existent; press reports were inconsistent in numbers and details. Since the Nazi government used euphemisms to convey relevant information, suspicion arose over the reliability of what was reported. Given the fabricated atrocity stories circulated during World War I, accounts of Jewish persecution were greeted with public scepticism. Church members, believing that civilized people could not act in so uncivilized a manner, assumed that they were exaggerated. In the words of the Archbishop of York, it was difficult "to believe that such a perversion of civilization was possible."[134] When Christian opinion failed to respond, it was partly for this reason. Even when the churches did respond, they did not speak in a united voice. Indeed, they could not. The non-Catholic churches in Canada had no operative mechanism that would have enabled them to speak as one. They voiced their concerns through their presbyteries, synods, councils and the like, along denominational lines. Unfortunately, the lack of co-ordination gravely weakened their attempts to influence the government and public opinion on behalf of the Jewish refugees.[135]

That prominent church leaders and members did speak out, and a number of ecclesiastical bodies passed resolutions, does not preclude the fact that their constituencies as a whole did not follow their example. There was no mass outcry, no moral outrage from the Christian public at large, that is to say, from the vast numbers of Canadians who were nominal Christians. Moreover, how representative of the general public were men such as Silcox, Howse and Judd? Were they more representative than those on the opposite side — Hendershot, Kerr and Groulx? How much was the Christian conscience in Canada *really* touched by what these men wrote, said and did about the Jewish plight? Did not "the voices that were raised" make the "general stillness louder."[136] In this larger sense, Abella and Troper are correct.

The general silence of the nation did not stem from a lack of information regarding events in Nazi-occupied Europe. By 1943, the Jewish plight was widely reported in the secular as well as the religious press, and, at times, was the focus of public addresses by leading secular as well as religious figures. Rather, apathy, a preoccupation with other problems, as well as a mood of xenophobia in Canada itself, coloured public perceptions. Most Canadians, like most people everywhere, worried about "themselves and their families first and about others — especially if . . . alien — later, if at all."[137] The difficult socio-economic conditions of both the pre-war and war eras did not encourage altruism. In the case of the Jewish refugees, a not always latent antisemitism tied the tongues of far too many Canadian Christians, nominal and otherwise — tongues that otherwise might have spoken. In this regard, the 'Christian' nation was not without guilt.

Those steps that were taken — occasional rallies, protests, speeches, sermons, resolutions — were insufficient to achieve much success in changing the flow of the stream. No widespread moral indignation was generated.[138] Would it have mattered? The Archbishop of Canterbury maintained that "it would be mere blindness to realities to suppose that the heart of the present rulers of Germany could have been changed by any Christian plea, or that non-resistance to their acts could have changed it."[139] Perhaps it is wishful thinking to conceive of Canadian Christendom halting Hitler in his tracks. Nevertheless, one cannot excuse the indifference and callousness that led a Christian nation and its government to acquiesce far too much in the face of transparent evil, allowing the "possibility of good on earth . . . to slip through our fingers and turn into dust."[140] Had Christian opinion in Canada been mobilized fully, it might have succeeded in extracting effective action from a reluctant cabinet. If Canada had offered the Jews sanctuary, perhaps other nations would have followed. Had any one nation acted decisively, perhaps the Nazis would not have attempted to solve the "Jewish problem" with such confidence and determination.[141] Canadian Christendom, not merely its religious leaders, had a moral imperative to shame the Canadian government into doing everything that possibly could have been done to save the victims of Nazi persecution. If its collective voice had been louder, "silence" would not be its indictment — an indictment in which failure is writ large: a failure to truly recognize the shadow.

Notes

1 This paraphrases the statement made by Carl G. Jung in a letter to Victor White, December 31, 1949: "The future of mankind very much depends upon the recognition of the shadow" (*Letters*, vol. 1 [Princeton: Princeton University Press, 1973], p. 541).

2 See Irving Abella and Harold Troper, *None Is Too Many: Canada and the Jews of Europe 1933-1948* (Toronto: Lester & Orpen Dennys, 1982), p. 284.

3 "The German Venture," *The New Outlook*, February 8, 1933, p. 123, and "When Liberty Dies, Death Stalks," *The Canadian Baptist*, July 12, 1934, p. 2.

4 For the Québécois Catholic response, see Eugène L'Heureux, "Petites notes," *L'Action catholique*, March 27, 1933; Jules Dorion remarked about the rather brutal methods of Hitler in "Autour de Hitler et de ce qui se passe sous nos yeux," ibid., May 20, 1933, editorial. However, in all *L'Action catholique* editorials on Hitler "but" becomes a key word. See Richard Jones, *L'Idéologie de L'Action catholique* (Laval: Les Presses de l'Université Laval, 1974), pp. 159-60, 160, n. 65.

5 "Is Hitler Master of Germany?" *The New Outlook*, March 15, 1933, p. 235, and "The German Peril," ibid., March 22, 1933, p. 251.

6 "Hitler's Germany," *The New Outlook*, May 29, 1935, p. 560, and "London Letter," *The Canadian Churchman*, November 30, 1933, p. 726.

7 "The World Crisis," *The Montreal Churchman*, May 1937, p. 18.

8 Jones, *L'Idéologie*, p. 87; see also David Rome, *Clouds in the Thirties: On Anti-Semitism in Canada 1929-1939* (Montreal: Canadian Jewish Congress, Section 6, 1978), p. 26.

9 Reverend J. Gordon Jones, "What Can We Do About It?" *The Canadian Baptist*, December 7, 1933, p. 14. He added that if Canadian Christians were half as devoted to the principles of Christ as the Nazis were to those of Hitler, there would be a sincere change in their attitude toward the present conditions in Canada and "we would be that much nearer to realizing the Kingdom of God."

10 "The German Point of View," *The New Outlook*, August 9, 1933, p. 584. Eugène L'Heureux put forth the same view in "Le concordat allemand," *L'Action catholique*, August 31, 1933, editorial; see also Louis-Philippe Roy, "En Europe," ibid., November 16, 1938, editorial.

11 "Hitler's Germany," p. 560.

12 Reverend J. E. Ward, "Democracy," *The Canadian Churchman*, February 9, 1939, p. 84.

13 "The Price of Christian Liberty," *The Canadian Baptist*, August 17-24, 1939, p. 5.

14 C. E. Silcox, "German Psychosis," *The New Outlook*, August 16, 1933, p. 598, and J. C. Carlisle, "Freedom of Religion in Germany," *The Canadian Baptist*, September 15, 1938, p. 5.

15 "The Challenge of Germany," *The New Outlook*, November 22, 1933, p. 825; see "The Holy Church Throughout the World," *The Canadian Churchman*, November 30, 1933, p. 725 which expressed similar sentiments.

16 Dr. R. Roberts, "If Jesus Went to Germany," *The New Outlook*, November 15, 1933, p. 805; reproduced with the same title in *The Canadian Baptist*, February 1, 1934, p. 4.

17 "Nazism," *The Canadian Churchman*, May 7, 1936, p. 292.

18 "I See in the Papers," *The Canadian Baptist*, April 11, 1935, p. 2; ibid., September 17, 1935, p. 2; and "Never Forget," *The New Outlook*, July 12, 1933, p. 519.

19 Ernest Bogart, "America in a World War," *The Canadian Churchman*, February 12, 1942, p. 111. "The Baptist Youth," *The Canadian Baptist*, February 15, 1940, p. 11 argued that Germany "has lied, broken her word repeatedly, stolen other's property and killed mercilessly." Even before the war the Baptist press argued: "You cannot deal with mad war dogs" ("Munich and After," *The Canadian Baptist*, May 25, 1939, p. 13).

20 "Our Empire in Fateful Fear," *The Canadian Baptist*, June 15, 1940, p. 3.

21 "Ministry of Information — Religious Division," *The Canadian Churchman*, June 6, 1940, p. 358. Others expressed similar sentiments: see "Columbia," *The Canadian Churchman*, March 7, 1940, p. 157; "Round About," ibid., p. 228. "Never was it more certain that we who oppose Nazi Germany are standing, a living barrier between the incarnate spirit of evil and all that is God-begotten and God-honoring in the life of man" ("The Allies See It Through," *The Canadian Baptist*, June 15, 1940, p. 10). See the Reverend John Pitts, "Is Hitler Anti-Christ?" *The Presbyterian Record*, September 1940, pp. 265-66.

22 "Freedom, Justice and Truth," *The Canadian Churchman*, February 5, 1941, p. 84, "Freedom, Justice and Truth," *The United Church Observer*, February 15, 1941, p. 27.

23 "We Must Believe in Divine Providence, Says Reinhold Niebuhr," *The United Church Observer*, June 15, 1941, p. 1; "God in Our Time," *The Canadian Churchman*, September 4, 1941, p. 483; and "The Powers Behind Hitler," *The Canadian Baptist*, October 1, 1940, p. 4.

24 Roman Collar, "As I See It," *The United Church Observer*, February 15, 1940, p. 14. There were still those who felt that the Allies had made mistakes at Versailles. See "Christmas While Cannons Roar Across the Battle Fields," *The Canadian Baptist*, December 15, 1939, p. 3; "German Mentality," ibid., April 15, 1940, p. 14; and "The Treat of Versailles — Another Point of View," *The United Church Observer*, July 1, 1940, p. 17.

25 Reverend T. N. Tattersall, "War and God's Judgment," *The Canadian Baptist*, February 1, 1940, p. 7.

26 Archbishop Cyril Garbett, *The United Church Observer*, March 1, 1942, pp. 3, 30. See also "Thinking It Over," ibid., May 15, 1940, p. 43, and "Agrees with Roman Collar," ibid., June 15, 1940, p. 17.

27 "Round About," *The Canadian Churchman*, November 30, 1940, p. 661; see also "God's Peace Not Hitler's," *The Canadian Baptist*, June 1, 1940, p. 3; and "The Peace Terms," ibid., March 1, 1941, p. 3.

28 "Dreams of Christian Humanity," *The Canadian Baptist*, April 1, 1942, p. 3; "The Swastika to Replace Cross," ibid., January 15, 1942, p. 5; *Mein Kampf* was to supersede the Bible as the greatest written work, maintaining the highest ideals and code of ethics for the German people. See also "Is Hitler Anti-Christ?" *The Presbyterian Record*, September 1940, p. 266. "What Has the Church Done?" *The United Church Observer*, September 1, 1940, p. 10, referring to Nazism: "Its philosophy, its ideas, its professed teachings, are the most anti-Christian that have appeared on this earth since our Lord was crucified."

29 "Germany's Black Record," *The Presbyterian Record*, March 1942, p. 71, and "War's Dilemma," *The Canadian Baptist*, January 1, 1941, regarding the British blockade against the German people, "for the war is their responsibility as well as Hitler's" (p. 3). See "Opinions of British Christians Unanimous Against Reprisals," *The United Church Observer*, November 15, 1940, pp. 1, 26, and "Days That Shook the World in Flanders Field," ibid., June 15, 1940, p. 5.

30 "Ecumenical Mission of the Church Today," *The Canadian Churchman*, June 12, 1941, p. 377.

31 "Out of the Ashes—What?" *The Canadian Baptist*, June 15, 1945, p. 3, and "The Spiritual Outlook in Germany," *The United Church Observer*, July 15, 1945, p. 5, referred to the Germans as "a people dumb, dull, apathetic, living still, but not alive."

32 Quoted from the Archbishop of Canterbury's book, *The Church Looks Forward*, in "These War Thoughts," *The Canadian Baptist*, May 1, 1945, p. 8; cf. "Dr. Oldham Warns of Wrong Approach to Germany," *The United Church Observer*, December 1, 1944, p. 1.

33 "Sir Stafford Cripps on Treatment of Germany," *The Canadian Churchman*, July 5, 1945, p. 386, and "Religion in Colleges," *The Canadian Baptist*, September 15, 1945, p. 3.

34 "Attitudes of Christians to Germans Today," *The Canadian Baptist*, September 1, 1945, p. 8, and *The United Church Observer*, July 5, 1945, p. 5.

35 "Am I My Brother's Keeper?" *The United Church Observer*, February 1, 1944, p. 11, and "What Shall We Do with Germany?" *The Presbyterian Record*, April 1945, p. 100.

36 "Thanks Be to God," *The Canadian Baptist*, May 15, 1945, p. 3; the allusion to wine is particularly salient given the strong temperance movement in the Baptist tradition. Cf. "Transitory and Abiding," ibid., June 15, 1945, p. 3 which discussed the Nazi obsession with the belief in their racial superiority, an obsession which created "strong animals without conscience, pity or imagination."

37 "Out of the Ashes—What?" p. 3; "European Churches and German Nazism," ibid., October 1, 1945, p. 8; and "Germany's Regeneration," ibid., October 15, 1945, p. 8.

38 "Anti-Jewish Bigotry," *The New Outlook*, March 29, 1933, p. 267; "Germany and the Jews," *The Canadian Baptist*, April 6, 1933, p. 3; *The New Outlook*, April 12, 1933, p. 299; May 17, 1933, p. 387; "The Jews and the World Crisis," *The Montreal Churchman*, December 1941, p. 20; and "Ill Treatment of the Jews," *The Canadian Baptist*, April 27, 1933, p. 5. Note the somewhat reserved fashion with which Nazi persecutions were reported in *L'Action catholique* as cited in Jones, *L'Idéologie*, p. 91.

39 *The Canadian Baptist*, September 28, 1933, p. 584.

40 See, for example, "A Chat with the Editor," *The Canadian Churchman*, January 23, 1936, p. 50.

41 "Germany and the Jews," *The Presbyterian Record*, May 1936, p. 132.

42 Ibid.

43 "Overshadowed Austria," *The New Outlook*, May 27, 1938, p. 507; see also "When Liberty Dies, Death Stalks," p. 2.

44 Dr. Conrad Hoffman, "The German Refugees," *The Canadian Baptist*, February 2, 1939, p. 7.

45 Reverend D. M. MacMillan, "The Sovereignty of God," *The Presbyterian Record*, July 1939, pp. 217-19; cf. ibid., January 1939, pp. 4-5, and March 1939, p. 67. See also "Healthy Instincts," *The New Outlook*, November 18, 1938, p. 1095.

46 Reverend H. B. Hendershot, "The German Point of View," *The New Outlook*, August 9, 1933, p. 584. See also "Editorial in Brief," *The New Outlook*, April 12, 1933, p. 301; "La Juiverie 'manoeuvre' le monde chrétien," *L'Action catholique*, November 28, 1938, editorial; also Jones, *L'Idéologie*, chap. 3, "La juiverie," pp. 69-91.

47 Cf. Right Reverend A. C. Headlam, Bishop of Gloucester, in "Holy Church Throughout the World," *The Canadian Churchman*, October 19, 1933, p. 631. See

also M. K. O'Meara, "In Germany This Summer," ibid., October 5, 1933, p. 60, who likewise questions the validity of the persecution reports, having seen "Jews dressed as well as anyone else, with perhaps more fondness for jewelry."

48 Dr. C. Kerr, "The Light of the World," *The Presbyterian Record*, December 1936, p. 367.

49 "Berlin, 1934," *The Canadian Baptist*, September 6, 1934, p. 3; italics added. This attitude tended to be more representative of German Baptist reporting than of the Canadian Baptist press in general. See, for example, Dr. Hans Luckey, "Freedom of Religion in Germany," ibid., September 15, 1938, p. 5.

50 See reference to the Right Reverend A. C. Headlam, note 48 supra.

51 Review of "The Moral Issues of War," *The Canadian Baptist*, May 1, 1940, p. 2, and "The Powers Behind Hitler," ibid., October 1, 1940, p. 4. See also "Hitler Tells the World," *The New Outlook*, February 3, 1939, p. 99; "Canadian Post-Mortem on Refugees," *Social Welfare* (Spring 1939): 83; and "Liberty," *The Canadian Churchman*, January 23, 1940, p. 82, where it referred to the treatment of the Jews as "the refinement of cruelty. It reduced them to lower than slaves, even than beasts." See also, "War May Days," *The United Church Observer*, June 1, 1940, p. 5.

52 "Central Bureau for Relief of Evangelical Churches in Europe, Foreign Affairs Bulletin," *The Presbyterian Record*, March 1940, p. 85.

53 Reverend Ernest Marshall Howse, "I Speak for the Jew," October 11, 1942, unpublished manuscript.

54 "Too Horrible to Think About," *The Canadian Churchman*, December 24, 1942, p. 754.

55 "From Over and Across," *The Canadian Churchman*, September 10, 1942, p. 509.

56 "The Church Overseas — The Church in Poland," *The Canadian Churchman*, December 31, 1942, p. 771.

57 "Hitler Not Entirely to Blame," *The Canadian Churchman*, May 6, 1943, p. 287. Should one "identify the Nazi wolves with the German sheep?" asked the Reverend C. J. St. Clair Jeans, in "What Shall We Do With Germany?" p. 100.

58 "Bombing Policy," *The Canadian Baptist*, August 16, 1943, p. 11. See also "The Germans Must Be Punished," *The Canadian Churchman*, October 12, 1944, p. 564, and "Nazi War Monuments," *The Canadian Baptist*, August 1, 1945, p. 12. Compare with "Passionate Believers," ibid., June 15, 1944, p. 1, where it stated that the Germans "believed in their Fuhrer as an incarnation of God. They believed in blood and soil and saw a world prostrate at the Teuton's foot. . . . Because they believed, they conquered."

59 "From Over and Across," *The Canadian Churchman*, January 14, 1943, p. 25, and "The Empire as Refuge from Massacre," ibid., February 25, 1943, p. 121.

60 "The Persecution of the Jews," *The Canadian Churchman*, April 15, 1943, p. 230, and "Conference on the Post War Role of Religion," *The United Church Observer*, May 1, 1943, p. 26.

61 "Atrocities," *The United Church Observer*, September 15, 1944, p. 4. The article continued with a story of Lublin's concentration camp which "is too brutal and horrifying beyond description."

62 "Canadian Churches and German Refugees," *Social Welfare* (March 1936): 25-26, and "The Manifesto on German Refugees," *Social Welfare* (September 1936): 93.

63 "Practical Christianity," *The New Outlook*, March 11, 1936, p. 236.

64 "The World of Religion," *The New Outlook*, October 7, 1938, p. 958, and "The Cry of Man's Anguish," ibid., December 16, 1938, pp. 1224-25.

65 "Anglican Action on the Refugees," *Social Welfare* (Winter 1939): 64. See also the resolution passed by the International Council of the World Alliance for International Fellowship through the Churches in *Social Welfare* (September 1939): 32 which sought to do all they could to awaken public opinion to "the great evils involved in the systematic ostracism and persecution of the Jewish race and thousands of Christians who have kinship with the Jews."

66 "Moose Jaw and the Jews," *The Canadian Baptist*, December 1, 1938, p. 12.

67 "The Convention Resolutions: 'European Refugees,'" *The Canadian Baptist*, June 29, 1939, p. 11.

68 W. M. Rochester, "Germany and the Jews," *The Presbyterian Record*, January 1939, pp. 4-5. The editorial ended with a critique that "Canada as a nation must not be wanting at this time in such a grave crisis. . . ."

69 W. M. Rochester, "Without a Country," *The Presbyterian Record*, March 1939, pp. 67-68.

70 "Is It Nothing to You?" *The New Outlook*, February 10, 1939, p. 120; cf. "Is It Nothing to You?" *The Canadian Churchman*, March 2, 1939, p. 130.

71 "A Chat with the Editor—Political Refugees," *The Canadian Churchman*, February 2, 1939, p. 66.

72 *Twenty-Fourth Annual Report*, The Council for Social Services of the Church of England in Canada, 1939, pp. 18-19. Both Christian and Jewish organizations were involved, including such notables as the United Churchman Reverend Claris E. Silcox, the Anglican Canon W. W. Judd and the Roman Catholic Archbishop of Toronto James Charles McGuigan. No Francophone organization was represented; see Abella and Troper, *None Is Too Many*, pp. 18, 45, and Rome, *Clouds*, Section 13, 1981, pp. 726-28.

73 The significant word here is "wise," for Abella and Troper have established that the immigration policy of the Canadian government was in fact well controlled but hardly wise. See also "Refugees," *The New Outlook*, July 1, 1939, p. 10; "Let the Church Be the Church," *Fourteenth Annual Report*, Board of Evangelism and Social Service, The Anglican Church of Canada (1938), p. 52. Also "The Convention Resolutions," *The Canadian Baptist*, June 29, 1939, p. 11.

74 J. E. Barrett, "The Open Door for Refugees," *The Canadian Churchman*, February 16, 1939, p. 100.

75 Ibid., February 23, 1939, p. 121.

76 "Canada and the Refugees," *The Canadian Baptist*, May 25, 1939, p. 14.

77 For example, "Editorial in Brief," *The New Outlook*, May 20, 1936, p. 469; "Human Dumping," ibid., July 15, 1938, p. 674; Rochester, "Germany and the Jews," pp. 4-5; "A Chat with the Editor—Political Refugees," p. 66; "Is It Nothing to You?" p. 130.

78 Regarding the Church leaders' response, see "Have We the Courage?" *The Canadian Churchman*, July 27, 1939, p. 442; W. F. Ambrose, "The Wandering Jews," *The Canadian Churchman*, June 15, 1939, p. 378; and *The Canadian Baptist*, June 15, 1939, p. 3.

79 G. Raymond Booth, "The Holy Innocents, 1939,' 'The Canadian Churchman, December 21, 1939, p. 734. See also Booth's "What They Say," reprinted from The American Friend, which treats antisemitism in Canada and the refugee crisis, n.d.

80 "Central Bureau for Relief," The Presbyterian Record, March 1940, p. 85. The United Church Observer discussed the same address but without reference to the Jewish question (February 1, 1940, p. 3).

81 "Canada and the Refugees," The Canadian Churchman, September 7, 1939, p. 489.

82 "Resolutions at Ottawa," The Canadian Baptist, July 1, 1940, p. 2.

83 Diocese of Toronto Synod Journal, Eighty-eighth Session, May 4, 1940, p. 183, Appendix A.

84 "Toronto," The Canadian Churchman, May 30, 1940, p. 350.

85 "What Happened at the General Synod Jubilee — Day by Day," The Canadian Churchman, September 23, 1943, p. 527.

86 "Conference on the Post War Role of Religion," p. 26.

87 "On Behalf of the Jewish Race," The Presbyterian Record, June 1943, p. 147. This article also encouraged the membership to denounce antisemitism wherever it is found and to remember at all times that " 'The Author and Finisher of Our Faith' was born of Mary, a Jewish maid."

88 "On the Rampant — Open Canada to Refugees," The Presbyterian Record, February 1944, p. 41.

89 "Unlock Our Doors to Refugees," The United Church Observer, October 1, 1943, p. 11.

90 Lorna Francis, "A Challenge to Christians," The United Church Observer, March 15, 1944, p. 11.

91 See "Justice and Faith in God," The United Church Observer, March 1, 1942, p. 3; H. Blair Neatby, The Politics of Chaos (Toronto: Macmillan, 1972), p. 46; Lita-Rose Betcherman, The Swastika and the Maple Leaf (Toronto: Fitzhenry & Whiteside, 1975), p. 2; Michael Horn, The Great Depression of the 1930s in Canada (Ottawa: Canadian Historical Association, 1984), pp. 3, 20; and Donald G. Creighton, Dominion of the North: A History of Canada (Boston: Houghton Mifflin, 1944). See Barry Broadfoot, Ten Lost Years (Toronto: Doubleday, 1973) for personal anecdotes of the period.

92 The Canadian Churchman, March 2, 1933, p. 137, and "Rax Me That Bible," The Presbyterian Record, March 1937, p. 87.

93 Neatby, Politics, pp. 30-31, 149; Betcherman, Swastika and the Maple Leaf, p. 2; and The New Outlook, September 20, 1936, p. 910. Prime Minister King's insensitivity to Canadian suffering is illustrated in his remark that "What is needed is not so much a changed social or economic system as a changed heart" (The New Outlook, March 15, 1933, p. 238).

94 Horn, Depression, p. 20, and Neatby, Politics, p. 22.

95 Howard Palmer, Patterns of Prejudice (Toronto: McClelland & Stewart, 1982) on Anglo-Saxon nativism in Canada; Neatby, Politics, p. 166; cf. Robert Bothwell, Ian Drummond and John English, Canada 1900-1945 (Toronto: University of Toronto Press, 1987), pp. 299, 312-13.

96 Betcherman, Swastika and the Maple Leaf, pp.45-47, and David S. Wyman, The Abandonment of the Jews (New York: Pantheon Books, 1984), p. 7.

97 Neatby, Politics, pp. 163-64.

98 See, for example, "Canadian Christians and German Refugees," *Social Welfare* (March 1935): 25-26. This dread stemmed from remembrance of the role Canada played in World War I and the great loss of lives in the war to end all wars.

99 Neatby, *Politics*, pp. 41-47.

100 Alan Davies and Marilyn F. Nefsky, "The United Church and the Jewish Plight During the Nazi Era, 1933-1945," *Canadian Jewish Historical Society Journal* 8, 2 (Fall 1984): 56-57, and Betcherman, *Swastika and the Maple Leaf*, pp. 2, 81-87. See also *The New Outlook*, April 22, 1938, p. 388; *The United Church Observer*, July 1, 1939, pp. 15, 32; and *The Canadian Churchman*, May 5, 1938, p. 291.

101 Quebec papers such as *La Nation*, *L'Action catholique*, *L'Action nationale* frequently published vicious antisemitic statements. See "At the Montreal Synod," *The Canadian Churchman*, May 12, 1938, p. 301, which describes these antisemitic sentiments as "neither Christian nor British." See Jones, *L'Idéologie*, chap. 11, "La Hantise de L'Immigration . . . Surtout Juive," pp. 269-81. Also Victor Teboul, "Antisémitisme: Mythe et Images du Juif au Québec," *Voix et Images du Pays* 9 (1975): 105-12; "Les Jeux de la politique," *L'Action nationale* 13, 1 (1939): 50; Anatole Vanier, "L'Antisémitisme," *L'Action nationale*, February 1934, p. 87. Early in 1939 the Société St. Jean-Baptiste de Quebec submitted a petition of 127 000 signatures to the Dominion government protesting against any immigration in general, but against Jewish immigration in particular (see Rome, *Clouds*, Section 12, 1980, pp. 684-85, 712).

102 "The astute Mackenzie King knew that there were no votes to be gained in admitting Jews; there were, however, many to be lost" (Abella and Troper, *None Is Too Many*, pp. 281-82). See also "Unlock Our Doors to Refugees," pp. 11, 26. Palmer maintains that "the combination of anti-Semitic feeling in key areas of the civil service and in his own cabinet, as well as in the general public, kept him [Prime Minister King] from acting on his privately held humanitarian concerns" (p. 151). For a different view of King and his cabinet, see Abella and Troper, *None Is Too Many*, passim. It is worth noting that the Leader of the Opposition, Robert Manion, also opposed entry of refugees on the grounds of the high rate of unemployment in Canada.

103 Until 1938, when Hitler began to attack the Catholic Church in Germany, little condemnation of his rampage against the Jews came from Francophone Catholicism (Rome, *Clouds*, Section 1, 1977, pp. 66, 80-82). See, for example, Canon Cyrille Labrecque, who maintained that Francophones were wise to protect themselves from the corrupt and anti-Christian Jews (*La Semaine religieuse de Québec* [October 4, 1934], cited in Rome, *Clouds*, Section 3, 1977, p. 102). After the disenchantment with Hitler, Jules Dorion turned to unqualified condemnation of Hitler's persecution of the Jews; see "The Jews and Germany," *L'Action catholique* (November 14, 1938), editorial. Mention must be made of the Francophone Catholic, Father Stéphane Valiquette, who struggled unceasingly to overcome the antisemitism he perceived in Quebec. See Betcherman, *Swastika and the Maple Leaf*, pp. 32-33 on Abbé Groulx.

104 From an address, "Canadian Post-Mortem on Refugees," given at Convocation Hall, University of Toronto, March 21, 1939 (United Church Archives, Claris E. Silcox, Speeches). Reverend Gordon Domm of the Bathurst United Church,

Toronto, commented about the dormant but excessive antisemitism among Canadians of all ranks, which if the stage were set cleverly, would threaten the whole land (*The Globe and Mail*, 1938, cited in Rome, *Clouds*, Section 4, pp. 5-6).

105 Wyman, *Abandonment*, pp. 12, 13; Louise Smith Harvey, "To the casual spectator, there is never any feeling against the Jewish people, but scratch the surface and see what happens" (*Canadian Forum*, 1935, cited in Rome, *Clouds*, Section 7, 1979, p. 3). Reverend Norman Chappel of the Saskatoon United Church also warned of the growing antisemitism in Canada (*Saskatoon Phoenix*, October 31, 1938).

106 Teboul, *Antisémitisme*, pp. 93, 95, 99, and Mgr. Gfoellner, "Lettre pastorale," *L'Action nationale*, June 1933, p. 381, where he referred to the extremely pernicious influence of the Jews in all areas of civilization.

107 Davies and Nefsky, "United Church and Jewish Plight," p. 57. See "Editorial — All Things New," *The Montreal Churchman*, January 1935, p. 5, which argued that "the Jewish religion passed into backwater."

108 See, for example, Rev. P. K. Dayfoot, "Our Bible Lesson — The Pharisees," *The Canadian Baptist*, January 19, 1933, p. 12, May 3, 1934, p. 12; "Christ and Religion," ibid., August 1, 1935, p. 6. See also Rev. J. B. Maclean, "Proportional Giving," *The Presbyterian Record*, January 1933, p. 5, January 1934, p. 28; Lord Tweedsmuir, Governor-General, "Address," ibid., January 1938, p. 12; and "Our Spiritual Need," ibid., April 1945. Also, "With Other Editors," *The New Outlook*, December 2, 1936, p. 1102, and "Comment on Religion and Life," ibid., May 21, 1937, p. 465. Also, "The Great Commandment," *The Canadian Churchman*, March 30, 1933, p. 67; Rev. C. B. Mortlock, "The Christian Revolution," ibid., December 3, 1936; "A Chat with the Editor," ibid., February 11, 1937, p. 82; "A Chat with the Editor," ibid., July 7, 1938, p. 422.

109 "A Chat with the Editor," *The Canadian Churchman*, January 18, 1940, p. 34.

110 Rev. H. R. Hunt, "Wherein Lies Freedom?" *The Canadian Churchman*, November 26, 1942, p. 51, and Hunt, "Comfortable Words," ibid., January 28, 1943, p. 51. See Rev. John Pitts, "Is Hitler Anti-Christ?" *The Presbyterian Record*, September 1940, pp. 264-66. Also Rev. F. D. V. Narborough, "The Danger of Pharisaism," *The Canadian Churchman*, February 11, 1943, p. 83; W. H. Colclough, "Gentile Only," *The United Church Observer*, March 15, 1943, p. 10; R. H. Baxter, "Challenges Rabbi's Statement," ibid., October 1, 1944, p. 13; "Surely the Jew Was the Killer of Christ"; Dr. F. W. Boreham, "He Cam' Unto His Ain Folk," *The Canadian Baptist*, February 15, 1945, p. 1; and "The Three Crowns," ibid., August 15, 1945, p. 1, which refers to "Jesus whom the Jews so wickedly crucified." Rev. John Inkster of Toronto's Knox Presbyterian Church argued that "The Jews' denial and crucifixion of Christ was the reason why God's curse rested on them and why they will continue to suffer even more in the future . . ." (*The Globe and Mail*, December 5, 1938, p. 4). See also Father Albert St.-Pierre, "Les Juifs et les premiers chrétiens," *Revue dominicaine* (February 1935): 85-97; Father Raymond-Marie Martineau, "Les Juifs et la Chrétienté," ibid., March 1935, pp. 167-85, which justified the violence against the Jews by rooting it in theology (cited in Rome, *Clouds*, Section 3, 1977, p. 117).

111 J. B. Skene, "Our Spiritual Need," CBR Radio Vancouver, February 1945, reprinted in *The Presbyterian Record*, April 1945, p. 118.

112 C. A. Lawson, "Christianity's Debt to Judaism," *The United Church Observer*, January 1, 1942, p. 11; cf. "The Jewish New Year, 5694," *The New Outlook*, September 13, 1933, p. 660; and Rev. Lewis Sutherland, "The Empty Tomb," *The Presbyterian Record*, March 1937, p. 68. See also Reverend John Stuart Conning, "Palestine and the Jews," *The Presbyterian Record*, September 1939, p. 262.

113 C. E. S., "Book Reviews," *Social Welfare* (September 1928): 25; "Rax Me That Bible," p. 87, a missionary play which maintains that the gospel was first proclaimed "to the Jews, a people of real genius, dwelling at the heart of the civilized world."

114 Reverend H. B. Ketchen, "The Courageous Candor of Jesus," *The Presbyterian Record*, August 1942, pp. 249-50; in a review of "Render Unto Caesar," the writer commented "when Jesus inculcated loyalty to the state he did not break with the Jewish tradition, His sympathies in this instance were more Pharisaic than Zealot" ("The Book Shelf," *The Canadian Churchman*, May 30, 1940, p. 346).

115 Rev. John S. Conning, "The Presbyterian Church and the Jews," *The Presbyterian Record*, March 1935, p. 87.

116 *Mission to the Jews*, Missionary Society of the Church of Canada, Good Friday 1938.

117 "The Yiddish New Testament," *The Presbyterian Record*, October 1941, pp. 303-304.

118 "Report of the Montreal Jewish Mission," *Diocese of the Montreal Synod Journal* (April 1935): 100.

119 "Presbyterian Mission to the Jews," *Acts and Proceedings* (June 1942): 25. This remark seems to have been directed more at the former director of the mission than at Jews in general.

120 "If I Were a Jew . . . ?" *The Canadian Baptist*, March 8, 1934, p. 4. The article concludes: "If I were a Jew today I might wonder how one who professed to love Jesus, the Hebrew, could treat my race so despicably."

121 Rev. M. Zeidman, "The Jews," *The Presbyterian Record*, February 1938, p. 39; Rev. J. S. Conning, "The Presbyterian Church and the Jews," *The Presbyterian Record*, March 1935, p. 87; *Mission to the Jews*, Missionary Society of the Church of Canada, Good Friday 1938; and "Report of the Montreal Jewish Mission," p. 100.

122 "Pharisaism," *The Montreal Churchman*, July 1938, p. 14. An example of the ongoing Jew-baiting were the billboards at lakes and rivers inviting "Gentiles Only"; see concern regarding this in "I See in the Papers," *The Canadian Baptist*, December 1, 1938, p. 2.

123 "The Book Shelf," *The Canadian Churchman*, September 28, 1939, p. 545, and "The Question Box," ibid., August 8, 1940, p. 456.

124 "As Others See It," *The New Outlook*, May 30, 1934, p. 403.

125 "Practical Christianity," *The New Outlook*, March 11, 1936, p. 236.

126 "Good Friday and Missions to the Jews," *The Montreal Churchman*, April 1938, p. 8.

127 "Refugees," *The United Church Observer*, July 1, 1939, p. 10, and "Hitler Tells the World," *The New Outlook*, February 3, 1939, p. 99.

128 Rev. Claris E. Silcox, "Let My People Go!" *The United Church Observer*, April 15, 1943, p. 11.

129 "Jesus — A Refugee!" *The United Church Observer*, January 15, 1944, pp. 11, 26.

130 "Niebuhr Demands Christians Face Problems 'Practically,' " *The Canadian Churchman*, September 28, 1944, p. 539.

131 G. G. Harris, "Letter to the Editor: Christian Toleration," *The United Church Observer*, September 1, 1944, p. 17.

132 Robert W. Ross (*So It Was True!* [Minneapolis: University of Minnesota Press, 1980], p. 289) describes the failure of World War II to intervene on behalf of the Jews. The war was fought to defeat Nazism; there were no side endeavours to free or save the Jews or even to inform them that they had not been forgotten. For reasons why no rescue attempts were made, see Wyman, *Abandonment*, pp. 335-38.

Regarding the Church's attitude, see "The Church and Political Problems of Our Day," *The United Church Observer*, June 1, 1940, p. 8, and "The Foundations of Morals," ibid., September 15, 1942, pp. 11, 27. See "Niemöller's Warning," *The Canadian Churchman*, November 16, 1944, p. 643: "I approved when Hitler attacked the Jews for I thought that they were detrimental to German culture. I likewise approved when Hitler liquidated the trade unions for I thought they were detrimental to our economic life. It was only when the Nazis attacked the Churches, and my own Church in particular, that I realized what Nazism really was."

133 Deborah E. Lipstadt, *Beyond Belief: The American Press and the Coming of the Holocaust 1933-1945* (New York: The Free Press, 1986), p. 9.

134 "Justice and Faith in God," *The United Church Observer*, March 1, 1942, p. 3.

135 An example of this lack of co-ordination is supplied by a 1943 motion of the Saskatoon Presbytery of the Presbyterian Church that deplored the persecution of the "Jewish race" and expressed sympathy and a desire to help. The motion concluded that, as far as the presbytery was aware, no other Canadian church had taken a similar stand. But this was not the case. See "On Behalf of the Jewish Race," *Acts and Proceedings of the Presbyterian Church* 22 (June 1943): 147; emphasis in the original.

136 Alice L. and Roy Eckardt, "Again, Silence in the Churches," *The Christian Century* (July 26-August 2, 1967): 970; see also Kenneth Leslie, "Anti-Semitism — Fascism's 'Christian' Weapon," address given at the Fellowship for a Christian Social Order Conference, May 15, 1943: "those who remain silent . . . as all Christendom remained silent — and still remains silent or murmurs its polite sighs of regret which are an even greater insult to its founder. . . ."

137 J. K. Roth, "On the Impossibility and Necessity of Being a Christian: Reflections on Mending the World," *American Journal of Theology and Philosophy* 9, 1 and 2 (January-May 1988): 79.

138 Ross, *It Was True*, pp. 287-88, 291.

139 "A Call to Repentance and Trust," *The Canadian Churchman*, October 26, 1939, p. 599; see also Roth, "Reflections," p. 87.

140 Pierre Sauvage, a distinguished filmmaker, whose words were quoted in Roth, "Reflections," p. 97.

141 Wyman, *Abandonment*, p. 334, and Abella and Troper, *None Is Too Many*, pp. 32, 280.

9

The Keegstra Affair

Alan Davies

The salient facts are simple: on April 9, 1985, James Keegstra, a small-town, high school social studies teacher in Alberta, was brought to trial in Red Deer for wilfully promoting "hatred against . . . the Jewish people . . . while teaching students at Eckville High School" between September 1978 and December 1982, under Section 281.2 of the Criminal Code of Canada. Following an acrimonious and well-publicized trial, the defendant was convicted, only to have his conviction overthrown in 1988 by the Alberta Court of Appeal on the ground that the law under which Keegstra was prosecuted violated freedom-of-speech guarantees in the newly promulgated Canadian Charter of Rights and Freedoms. The Crown then appealed to the Supreme Court of Canada, which upheld the constitutionality of the law in question. Subsequently, in 1991, the Alberta government decided that Keegstra must stand trial a second time; his second trial began on March 2, 1992, also in Red Deer; at its conclusion Keegstra was again found guilty (an appeal has been launched). The legal niceties surrounding the case constitute a subject in itself, and have been discussed in at least one published account.[1]

Keegstra was defended by Douglas Christie, who had also defended Ernst Zündel in Toronto earlier in 1985 for the dissemination of lies concerning the Holocaust, and was to defend him once again in 1988.[2] The lawyer did his best on both occasions to turn the two defendants into political martyrs by making the right of free speech the hinge of both trials.[3] Whether or not such radical libertarianism is morally defensible in an age of mass propaganda transcends even legal considerations; in the final analysis, it is an article of faith that depends on convictions rather less plausible today than when Oliver Wendell Holmes delivered his famous

---

Notes for Chapter 9 are on pp. 245-47.

Supreme Court verdict in the United States, or when John Stuart Mill wrote *On Liberty* or John Milton, *Areopagitica*.[4] Not freedom of speech, but Jew-hatred, is the heart of the Keegstra affair.

The Man

The son of immigrants from the Netherlands, James Keegstra was born in Vulcan, Alberta, in 1934,[5] as a child of the Depression. Radical movements of every description were spawned on this breeding ground, including Social Credit, with its curious combination of economic and religious prescriptions for the ills of the age. Antisemitism, moreover, was embedded in this new political *Zeitgeist* from the beginning. Keegstra was also a child of conservative Christianity. Protestant fundamentalism in one form or another was popular on the prairies, and, since the Keegstras, with their Dutch Calvinist background, were devout in any case, they—and their youngest son—were susceptible to its appeal. The young James Keegstra attended William (later Premier) Aberhart's Bible Institute in Calgary and joined the latter's Social Credit party. Disdaining the farm, he became an auto mechanic and subsequently pursued a Bachelor of Education degree in industrial arts at the University of Alberta (Calgary), with the intention of becoming a high school teacher. During this formative period, he was employed by a series of schools, including the fundamentalist Hillcrest Christian College in Medicine Hat. In 1968 he settled in Eckville, initially to teach in his chosen field, but soon to devote himself to other subjects as well, such as history (fashionably disguised as "social studies" in the Alberta educational curriculum). An affable individual, at least on the surface, Keegstra was popular with most of his students—he was adept at fixing their cars—and with enough of the local population to win the office of mayor by acclamation. His rigid moralistic views, however, did not make the non-smoking, non-drinking, anti-dancing, anti-card-playing, Bible-believing Christian a favourite with everyone in town.

The trouble erupted when the teacher's anti-Jewish (and, incidentally, anti-Catholic) views attracted complaints from certain Eckville parents, thereby inviting the intervention of the district school superintendent, Robert David, in 1981. A train of events was launched that finally led to Keegstra's dismissal and subsequent indictment. The details have been described elsewhere, and need not be retold here.[6] Instead, I wish to examine the man and his ideas in light of the history of antisemitism. Although Keegstra was only a bit player in the ancient drama of Jew-hatred, his case is important. Not only does it expose the antisemitic mind in all of its nakedness, but it also reveals the intellectual, religious and social sources from which Keegstra drew, together with their roots in the Canadian milieu. Both Keegstra himself and his world view deserve careful attention. We will begin with the man on the witness stand.

The anti-Semite is afraid of discovering that the world is ill conceived, for then it would be necessary for him to invent and modify, with the result that man would be found to be the master of his own destinies, burdened with an agonizing and infinite responsibility. Thus he localizes all the evil of the universe in the Jew. . . . Anti-Semitism is thus seen to be at bottom a form of Manichaeism. It explains the course of the world by the struggle of the principle of Good with the principle of Evil. Between these two principles no reconciliation is conceivable; one of them must triumph and the other be annihilated. . . . Knight-errant of the good, the anti-Semite is a holy man.[7]

These Sartrean lines, written in France in the aftermath of the Holocaust and French complicity in the murder of the European Jews, could have been composed in Eckville several decades later; they describe Keegstra perfectly.[8] A thoroughgoing dualist—Manichaeism was an ancient dualistic religion—the defendant in the Red Deer courtroom knew exactly how to identify the evil powers, and those on the devil's side. Indeed, any true Christian, he seemed to believe, can do the same, since the Bible leaves no room for doubt on the matter, and no one can argue with God's Word. The Bible declares that the Jews are the children of the devil, and that the devil is the father of lies (John 8:44); consequently, no other opinion is acceptable. One is either for Christ or against him, and, since the Jews are obviously against him, they must be for the devil, which means that they favour the destruction of the Christian church and Christian society—in short, the destruction of everything that Keegstra deemed precious and good. Judaism, it follows, is an evil religion, premised on a hatred of Christ and Christianity, so that Jews who take Judaism seriously must also be evil. The Talmud, moreover, is an evil book, since, Keegstra believed, it has instilled and continues to instill in Jewish souls these feelings of hatred for the Son of God, as well as teaching Jews to cheat and perhaps even to murder Christians.

This alleged Jewish hatred was a crucial element in the defendant's scheme of things, one that he returned to again and again during his trial. Not even the disclosure under cross-examination that he had never studied Jewish history, and that he knew nothing or next to nothing about rabbinic thought except what he had read in blatantly antisemitic writings, could shake his convictions. Good 'Christian' friends, the court was told, had supplied him with reliable books that revealed the *real* truth about the Talmud, Jews and Judaism. (Later, these good Christian friends were identified as agents in an obscure antisemitic and right-wing literary organization located in Flesherton, Ontario.[9]) Since Keegstra trusted his friends, there was no reason for him not to trust their books. Conversely, since he did not trust Jews, who, by definition, were liars, he certainly did not trust Jewish books. Furthermore, he had even read, or, to be more exact, had arranged for one of his friends to read for him, some of the terrible things said about Christ and Christians in an English (Soncino) translation of the Talmud. So he knew that the charges were true. In the mind of this knight-errant of the good, the powers of darkness and their earthly allies were not difficult to name.

Jews, however, according to Keegstra, are not the only liars, although they are undoubtedly the devil's most important allies in the cosmic struggle between good and evil. University professors, he informed the court, also tell lies, especially historians, who are fearful of losing their positions should they publish unconventional views. The latter, of course, are secretly censured and controlled behind the scenes by their Jewish masters, the hidden rulers of the age.

As a university graduate himself, Keegstra believed that he was in a good position to evaluate academics. In fact, his entire philosophy of education rested on the conviction that everyone should learn to think autonomously without regard for orthodox opinion. On his own account, he had learned early to think for himself, engaging in his own independent research; hence, as a teacher, his main concern was to see that his students adopted the same principle. It was his Christian responsibility to make certain that no one fell victim to the conventional interpretations of Jewish-intimidated historians who were afraid to tell the real truth about past and current events. It was his Christian responsibility to make certain that his young charges received a well-rounded education by setting the record straight. It was his Christian responsibility to expose the deceitful professors and their mainstream publishers, together with the other liars of the age. It was his Christian duty to resist the powers of evil that are seeking through socialism, communism, international capitalism, etc. — all of which in one way or another are extensions of Talmudic Judaism — to gain total domination over the world.

Socialism, communism and international capitalism, in spite of their seeming differences, all represent millennialism, or the attempt to establish a radical new world order; for Keegstra, such a project was anathema. Not only did it smack of a seditious Jewish utopia, but also it could be constructed only on the ashes of Christendom. Although a Christian fundamentalist, Keegstra was not (unlike many fundamentalists) a millennialist, for millennialism was too Jewish for his taste. War and revolution, especially revolution, are the means through which this brave new world — a Jewish totalitarianism — is to come to pass. When Keegstra studied history in one or two survey courses at the University of Alberta, it did not take him long to realize that his instructors were not providing the 'real' reasons for the wars and revolutions of the modern era. He, James Keegstra, the man who believed in thinking for himself, would make good this deficiency.

Revolutions, Jews and Illuminati

Revolution was his forte, especially the French Revolution of 1789. The following excerpts from student essays are representative:

(A) *The World Menace since 1776*

The best place to start will be with a ruthless cutthroat known to the world as Adam Weishapt [*sic*]. He ... was a jesuit but disliked the church so he broke away from it when he was 25-30 years old. In 1771 Adam Weishapt disappeared mysteriously until May 1st 1776. (Incidently [*sic*] this date is said to be Satan's birthday). During these five years Adam Weishapt had been writing a plan in which he was going to take over the world with. In order to get this plan he had sold his soal [*sic*] to Satan. This plan was based on deseption [*sic*] and was made up of five points. These five points are as follows:

(a) destruction of all Monarchy & legal government

(b) destroy all religions — especially Christianity

(c) abolish marriage (children raised by the state)

(d) abolish private property (land) and all inheritances

(e) abolish all loyalty and allegiance

This plan is now the plan of all socialist and communist countries. It is the plan being followed behind the presant [*sic*] day Iron curtain.

Adam Weishapt, after announcing his plan organized a secret society. This organization was called the "Illuminaty" [*sic*] which means the enlightenment. His symbol for this organization is the same symbol used for communist countries. The five pointed Red star. It was the Illuminaty which was behind the French Revolution.

In 1789 was the first revolution started by the jews to set up this new world order under a one world government. This uprising was the French revolution headed by Weishapts Illuminaty. The entire revolution was conducted by a pack of Jewish leckies [*sic*] who went under the name of Jacobins. It was these bushrats that came up with the (Guillotine?) to butcher innocent people with. This revolution was far from bloodless. The Jacobins would ride around in packs and bash in childrens heads, rape the women and then drown them. They would also cut open the stomaches [*sic*] of men and let them bleed to death. This by the way was all done to follow Weishapts first point in his plan ...

This essay shows how the Jews are conspiring to take over the world. And when they do they will set up a New World order under a One world gov't. I have shown in this essay since 1776, with Adam Weishapts five point plan, the Jews have been causing anarchy & chaos throughout the world. I have also shown that where ever the communist rule it was set up by the Jews. In my opinion this must come to a dead halt. We must get rid of every jew in existence so we may live in peace & freedom.

(B) *Judaism in the World since 1776*

To start Judaism in the world since 1776, I'll start off with Weishaupt. On May 1, 1776, the birthday of Baal, a wicked man named Adam Weishaupt, comes out of five years of hiding. During hiding he formed a group called the Illuminati and a five point plan. . . .

Weishaputs [*sic*] plan was based on the Talmud. This plan was to bring in a One World Government though [*sic*] the NEW WORLD ORDER.

One of the first steps of the NEW WORLD ORDER was the French Revolution. Naturally the first Act in the revolution was Emancipation of the Jews. On July 14, 1789 the conspirators tricked the French people. They forged the kings [*sic*] signature and made the proclamation to the peasants to storm the Bastille. Trust these Jews to do something like that. The people wouldn't turn violent unless these was planned agitation. . . .

The revolution was so bloody yet the people weren't violent. It was the Jews who carried out such horrors as smashing babies heads against rocks or abusing young girls and then drowning them. The sickest one yet is known as the "Feast of Reason". These nerds killed Christian girls and poured their blood on a naked prostitute, thus honoring the prostitute. This symbolizes the Jews destruction of all good. After hearing of some of these Sadistic acts, I thought the guillotine to almost be a blessing. . . .

The unknown men behind this bloody revolution were Clootz, (a member of the German Jew Company) and Mirabeau who said "It matters not to me if I walk knee deep in Gentile blood". Now it take a pretty far gone man to say something like that. . . .

It's sad to think that people are actually out to destroy this beautiful world that God created. Now that these conspirators are close to reaching their goals, the only thing we can do is to have faith in God and realize that he'll protect his people. I'm sure that the people who laugh at the truth of the Jews will find out. If only there was a way of informing the people, if only they would believe. But time goes on and people continue laughing and ignoring the Jews and the Jews get their One World Government while everyone is laughing. It's awful isn't it?[10]

Virtually every essay submitted to Keegstra on modern history repeated this strange thesis. Indeed, as a few unsympathetic ex-students testified at the trial, *not* to explain the French Revolution and subsequent wars and revolutions (especially the Russian Revolution) in terms of the Faustian Adam Weishaupt, the evil Illuminati, the still more evil Jews and their devil-connection, was to flirt with academic danger. It meant that one was not thinking for oneself, but simply regurgitating misinformation from mainstream historians who were merely puppets dancing to the strings of Jewish puppeteers. Hence, most of Keegstra's students wrote what they knew their teacher wished them to write; in this, they were similar to students everywhere. However, many of them also believed him. The few who did not were easily intimidated, since Keegstra was a stern disciplinarian, and since the principal, Edwin Olsen, was unlikely to come to their defence. No one really questioned his authority until the novelty of his views and their bizarre implications aroused some Eckville parents to instigate his downfall. Finally, in a criminal court with a new audience, in fact, with half the nation as his audience, he had the opportunity to elaborate on Adam Weishaupt, the Illuminati, the Jacobins and the Jews to his heart's content. Conspiracy was his subject, and the French Revolution was only the beginning.

Nesta Webster

Keegstra did not invent this account of modern history; he had mentors. Foremost among them was Nesta Webster, a now forgotten English writer who specialized in conspiracy theories during the World War I era, and whose books at one time even influenced Winston Churchill, a point that Keegstra did not neglect.[11] A morbidly romantic woman with a clairvoyant turn of mind, Mrs. Webster evidently regarded herself as the reincarnation of a French countess of the era of the 1789 revolution and therefore in a position to describe this violent upheaval from, so to speak, an inside perspective.[12] She was also intensely antisemitic and, in her later years, an ardent supporter of British fascism.[13] Her book, *Secret Societies and Subversive Movements* (1924), was impounded by the RCMP from Keegstra's private library and, judging from the numerous marginal notations, was a favourite text in the defendant's halcyon days. Erudite, brilliantly written, almost spell-binding in places, its thesis certainly commands attention.

According to Mrs. Webster, a series of conspiracies that really constitute a single vast conspiracy account for the great political upheavals in European and world history. In different ages this conspiracy has assumed different forms — ancient gnostics, Syrian assassins, Jewish Cabbalists, medieval Knights Templar, Freemasons, Illuminati, etc. — and its true leaders are both virtually unknown and endowed with superhuman powers. Ultimately, they represent an "occult power" in league with the "powers of darkness"; hence, they are both cosmic and Satanic. Their constant aim is to overthrow the existing social order, especially Christianity and its realms, in order to establish a totalitarian empire, wholly evil in character. The main historic roots of the conspiracy lie in the Jewish Cabbala, and, while Jews were never the sole conspirators, they were always the archconspirators as far as Mrs. Webster was concerned. (Her final chapter is entitled "The Jewish Peril.") However, the conspiracy is extremely complicated, consisting of many levels, of plots within plots and secret societies within secret societies whose deepest inner recesses remain mysterious and unfathomable. The surface of things is never to be trusted, for that which lies concealed is more important than that which meets the eye; since it is concealed, moreover, no one, not even Mrs. Webster herself, has plumbed its depths fully, so that her book cannot reveal the complete truth. Nevertheless, like Virgil guiding Dante through the circles of Hell, the author undertook to expose as much of this dangerous terrain as possible. Not surprisingly, her allegations possess a fantastic quality. Everything is explained in terms of a single idea, reflecting the peculiar mood of the war and post-war periods when spies, conspiracies, assassinations and revolutions were in the air, and when the Bolshevik conquest of Russia was fresh and menacing. In particular, Mrs. Webster was obsessed with conspiracy against Britain and the British empire, and she was not alone in this obsession. She also imbibed the popular antisemitism of the day, especially in upper-class British society.[14]

In spite of her attack on occult powers, her book displays a peculiar fascination with both the occult and the Orient whose "inscrutable character" she regards as the "cradle of secret societies." The conclusion is a suitable depiction of her mental universe:

> For behind the concrete forces of revolution—whether Pan-German, Judaic, or Illuminist—beyond that invisible secret circle which perhaps directs them all, is there not yet another force, still more potent, that must be taken into account? In looking back over the centuries at the dark episodes that have marked the history of the human race from its earliest origins—strange and horrible cults, waves of witchcraft, blasphemies, and desecrations—how is it possible to ignore the existence of an Occult Power at work in the world? Individuals, sects, or races fired with the desire of world-domination, have provided the fighting forces of destruction, but behind them are the veritable powers of darkness in eternal conflict with the powers of light.[15]

Keegstra was impressed. The notion of a cosmic conspiracy certainly explained the otherwise puzzling disturbances of history, making sense out of things in a satisfactory manner. Nesta Webster's conspiracy, moreover, was grounded in Judaism: an added appeal. The Alberta teacher could detect nothing implausible in her argument; as far as he was concerned, her reading of history and reconstruction of old religions and religious brotherhoods was devoid of error.

Indeed, few untutored readers, even today, would recognize the far from reputable character of many of Mrs. Webster's sources or their historic roots in the negative experiences of a particular section of European society during the nineteenth century. The losers in the French Revolution and in its later political manifestations—anti-Masonic, anti-Jewish right-wing Catholics, usually either clerics (including some converted Jews) or aristocrats—together with other reactionary elements in France and Germany—were her favourite authorities. Festering in constant resentment against the new political and social order in France and its seismic effects on other nations, and especially resentful of the emancipation of the Jews, these alienated older writers railed against anything and

everything that resembled democracy or liberalism.[16] Drawing on medieval ideas, they tended to demonize (a) the French Revolution, (b) all later
revolutions and (c) everyone allegedly responsible for these nefarious
events. Hence, they fell on the French Freemasons and their supposed
allies, the Bavarian Illuminati, as well as the French Protestants and, of
course, eventually the Jews, shifting responsibility for the 'devil-instigated'
revolution away from the old regime and the church. Thus arose the
strange notion of a Jewish-Masonic conspiracy—the Protestants managed
to drop out of the equation—against 'Christian,' i.e., Catholic France, or
against Christendom itself, that modern antisemites never weary of invok-
ing.

For some reason, perhaps because of her own preoccupation with the
occult, Mrs. Webster paid special attention to the insignificant and short-
lived Illuminati, and their founder, Adam Weishaupt. This explains why
Keegstra's students heard so much about the latter. Weishaupt was a
somewhat enigmatic figure, but scarcely the evil genius that his calumnia-
tors imagined, although his social and political ideas were undoubtedly
radical.[17]

Many of these old books mixed up religious and racial language along
dualistic lines—good Christians (French, Aryans, Catholics) versus bad
Jews (non-French, Semites, Talmud-believers)—especially after 1870, the
defeat of Napoleon III at Sedan, when France sank into an angry and
xenophobic mood, with treason in the air. Characteristically, the right-
wing authors regarded themselves as pious and moral individuals at war
with the devil and his agents. Without exception, they believed in simple
cosmologies that eliminated ambiguity from history, explaining everything
in clear and absolute terms. They wanted the Jews and Freemasons eliminated from public life in France and Germany (where, by the 1870s, the
Jews had also achieved emancipation) and the European clock turned back
to pre-1789 time. No progress was possible; everything had to be frozen
exactly as it was in pre-revolutionary times. Modernity signified change,
and change was evil. Since the Jews in particular were identified with
modernity (democracy, capitalism, socialism, communism), they, too,
were obviously evil and had to be returned to their medieval ghettos
before they succeeded in contaminating the entire Christian world.

The full extent of this contamination, and the ideological purpose that it
served, has been analyzed by Stephen Wilson in his study of antisemitism
in France during the Third Republic.[18] In order to hold the perils of
modernity at bay, the French reactionaries incorporated nationalist, racist
and antisemitic slogans into an anti-modern world view in which the
'Christian' values of the past—an idealized past that never really existed
except in their own imaginations—were contrasted antithetically with the
'anti-Christian' values of the present. Considering themselves to be the

custodians of the nation's moral and spiritual treasures, these men invested 'Christian' France, the France that once had been and was no more, except in their hearts, with all of the virtues that were deemed to have disappeared from the contemporary republic. Rural society, for example, was exalted over urban society, or the pure Christian country over the corrupt Jewish city; pre-capitalist industry was exalted over industrial capitalism, or the peasant/artisan over the factory proletarian; order, hierarchy and authority were exalted over disorder, egalitarianism and relativism, or a system with firm moral boundaries over a system in which change and revolution were endemic. The emancipation of women, especially sexual liberation and the dissolution of the patriarchal family, were feared. In short, the right-wing Catholics turned to visions of a pre-modern Christian utopia—a type of paradise lost—and insisted that society conform to their static and rigid model, with its medieval and authoritarian principles; otherwise, the anti-Christ would prevail. This was not conservatism, but total reaction. It also supplied the foundations for a future French fascism.

No revolution has ever occurred on Canadian soil; however, a definite fear of revolution haunted Canada during the Depression era.[19] Keegstra, a Protestant rather than a Catholic, nevertheless revealed with every word he uttered the same pathological fear of liberalism, rationalism and modernity as the nineteenth-century Europeans whose ideas he absorbed through Nesta Webster, and the same desire to turn the hands of the clock in a backward direction, fixing them in past time. A man cast in the same psychological mould, his personal and social values were also absolute and monolithic, as indeed his concept of 'truth,' which he emphasized so strongly in the classroom, demonstrates clearly.

Truth, according to Keegstra, contains no tension or paradoxes; it is unambiguous and undialectical and can only be opposed by total error: "He who is not for me is against me," as Scripture declares. The nineteenth-century right-wing ideologues thought likewise. As they had sought to make France (and Germany) 'Christian' again, Keegstra, it became apparent during his testimony, was motivated by a burning desire to make Canada 'Christian' again. His politics no less than his religion were characterized by a decidedly right-wing flavour. An ardent member of the Social Credit party, he not only stood for Parliament while awaiting trial (he was defeated resoundingly), but he also stood for the party leadership (a contest which he also lost) following his conviction. Social Credit philosophy was one of the cornerstones of his peculiar vision of reality.

Social Credit and the Jews

The Social Credit party in Alberta was born during the Great Depression as a kind of Christian response to the crisis of the age. Its theory, as formulated by Major C. H. Douglas, the English architect of the new movement, sought to diagnose the ills of modern capitalism and to prescribe for their cure.[20] What was amiss in the present arose from the fact that control over financial credit had fallen into the hands of a cabal of international bankers who manipulated the system for private gain. As a result, it was necessary for the state to regain control of the monetary system from these bankers in order to restore economic justice. This would be accomplished by issuing 'social credit' in the form of a dividend for every citizen, permitting a recovery of individual purchasing power. To prevent inflation, however, a medieval style 'just price' would be established for all products. In this fashion, both financial security and personal freedom would be guaranteed without resorting to socialism or collectivism, which the movement opposed fiercely.

Moreover, the Social Credit way of life was deemed to be both moral and biblical; in fact, it was identified with the true Christian social order. In Alberta, largely through the evangelical fervour of William Aberhart, a fundamentalist preacher and teacher, it soon acquired both a populist and anti-eastern flavour, feeding on western distrust of the remote federal government in Ottawa, the ally of the rapacious international bankers who liked to bully poor farmers. Naturally, Aberhart's main appeal was to rural, small-town audiences, where religious revivals were commonplace, and where the sufferings of the Depression were felt most keenly. In 1934, the party swept to victory, inaugurating a new era in provincial history.

With doctrines of this description, it is not difficult to understand the existence of a certain degree of antisemitism in the Social Credit rank-and-file, especially at a time when antisemitic ideas were in vogue across the Atlantic. Major Douglas himself was an arch-antisemite, convinced of the existence of a Jewish-instigated conspiracy linked with international finance and bent on achieving world domination. "While all international Financiers are not Jews, many are, and the observable policy of these Jews and of Freemasonry is that of the Talmud."[21] Interestingly, his paranoiac tract *The Big Idea* refers approvingly to Nesta Webster.[22] Such antisemitic myths blended easily with the Social Credit world view. The dreaded bankers, moreover, with their links to the "occult" — a term that Douglas borrowed from Webster — were largely easterners from Toronto and Montreal, and both of these cities, as everyone knew, were home to substantial Jewish immigrant communities. In this way, anti-eastern, anti-immigrant and anti-Jewish feelings were employed as a means of mutual enhancement, each inflaming the other.

The Social Credit tendency to identify itself with Christian values (the just price theory) and Christian civilization also agreed with a homogeneous view of society opposed to all religious, cultural and ethnic pluralism. This in turn was consistent with the prevailing racial ideology of Anglo-

Saxondom in English-speaking Canada, which had its own reasons for distrusting Jewish immigrants and other strangers. The Social Credit party, however, unlike some other right-wing parties of the day, never adopted an antisemitic plan in its platform, and its leaders, especially Aberhart's successor Ernest Manning, bore down hard on the antisemites. Nevertheless, the antisemitic strain endured, at least in the federal branch, surfacing among some Social Credit members of the House of Commons during the war and post-war periods.[23] As Keegstra himself illustrates, it disclosed itself among the orthodox Douglasites in the twilight years of the movement, long after the party's political demise outside of British Columbia.

Whether Keegstra adopted Social Credit ideas because of their compatibility with antisemitism, or antisemitic ideas because of their compatibility with Social Credit, is hard to determine; almost certainly, both passions took hold early in his life. Perhaps they crystallized simultaneously. At any rate, Keegstra, in spite of his professed dedication to the classroom and the teaching arts, was a man with a political agenda. Otherwise, he would never have offered himself for elected office. However, the political agenda was muted during the trial. On the stand, the defendant portrayed himself as a peaceful citizen who abhorred violence and wished no harm to befall anyone either through his words or actions. Possibly he sincerely regarded himself in this light. But conspiracies are necessarily dangerous, especially international and diabolical conspiracies designed to destroy the treasured symbols and values of the true religion in favour of an Orwellian tyranny (*1984*) linked to the power of darkness.

Time, moreover, was short, for Jews were already beginning to Judaize Canada, for example, by changing the hate laws and bringing prophets such as Keegstra to trial. In the face of this peril, the teacher clearly did not wish his students to ignore the call to arms. To discover the 'real' nature of Judaism and sit idly while the poison spreads is surely immoral. To worship Christ and watch complacently while the body of Christ is devoured by God's enemies is surely immoral. To unmask the sinister operations of the still extant Illuminati and their hidden masters without seeking to block their path is surely immoral. Anti-Jewish legislation of some description was the logical next step for the Social Credit politician, although fate and the Canadian public cheated Keegstra of this opportunity. Edifying hints of speeches he might have made in the House of Commons were dropped during his testimony, and the testimony of various witnesses, for example, his thoughts on Joe Clark, Douglas Roche, Peter Lougheed and Pierre Trudeau. All, it seems, are entangled in the conspiracy: Clark because he had once declared his support for a 'new world order,' Roche because of his desire to reduce the military arsenal of the West, Lougheed because he had helped bring Keegstra to trial (although a more unlikely disciple of Adam Weishaupt in Canadian politics would be hard to imagine), and Trudeau who, horror of horrors, actually wore a *red* rose in his lapel!

Anti-Talmudism

Conspiracy, then, is the clue to history, and once this clue has been grasped, the Christian is required as a matter of duty to expose and thwart the conspirators at every turn. While not all the conspirators are Jews, and while not all Jews are conspirators — about 8 percent, Keegstra seemed to believe — it still follows that a sufficient number are implicated in order to cast suspicion on the remainder. It is a wise precaution, therefore, to suspect all Jews, at least until they demonstrate to the satisfaction of the Christian community that they are *not* involved in the conspiracy. Conversion to Christianity would be the most convincing sign of personal innocence, and, like so many antisemites, Keegstra seemed to know one or two 'good' Jews of this kind. The worst Jews are Talmudic Jews, although 'atheistical' Jews such as Leon Trotsky, the arch-plotter of the Russian Revolution, also stirred the defendant's ire because, in spite of their atheism, they still managed perversely to cling to the Talmud. Trotsky was anti-Christian; consequently, according to Keegstra's logic, he must have possessed a Talmudic mind. Anti-Talmudism is an old, although not the oldest motif in Christian anti-Judaism and antisemitism, extending back to the Middle Ages when, under the instigation of apostate Jews, the church sought to destroy — sometimes literally — the rabbinic books in order to clear the path for conversion.[24] The notion that rabbinic literature is laden with anti-Christian texts and that Judaism is a religion obsessed with hatred of gentiles found classic expression in Johan Eisenmenger's famous work *Entdecktes Judenthum* (1700), and in its subsequent imitations, i.e., August Rohling's *Der Talmudjude* (1871) and I. B. Pranaitis's *The Talmud Unmasked* (1892). A copy of the latter was impounded from Keegstra's private library. Unquestionably, it played an important role in the construction of his world view.

In this assembly of citations, subtitled *The Secret Rabbinical Teachings Concerning Christians*, Talmudic and other ancient Jewish writings are raked for anti-Jesus, anti-Christian and alleged anti-Christian passages, all of which are interpreted in the worst possible light, without mitigation or discrimination. That some of these sayings are anti-pagan rather than anti-Christian, and that the obviously anti-Christian ones most likely were prompted by Christian hostility toward Judaism after the Christianization of the Roman empire in the fourth century, is not acknowledged.[25] That all of them together represent only a tiny fraction of a huge collection of Jewish lore and law is also not acknowledged; rather, the impression is deliberately created that they form the core of rabbinic faith and practice, and that Judaism, for this reason, is intrinsically foolish and wicked. That a number of them, notably the verses employed to document the charge that the Talmud commands the extermination of Christians,[26] simply do not mean anything of the kind, receives no recognition. Even when Pranaitis is correct in his depiction of an anti-Christian sentiment, for example, the claim that Jesus was born out of wedlock of dubious parentage,[27] his failure to recognize that he is dealing with legend and folklore rather than with serious theology invalidates his conclusions. Neither the author of *The Talmud Unmasked* nor his older mentors understood the character of rabbinic reasoning and its dialectical temper; they thought that Jews read their sacred books in the same fashion as orthodox Christians usually read the Bible, i.e., in wooden, literal and absolute terms. They thought that everything in the Talmud, like everything in the Bible, was an article of faith. The result, as Jacob Katz has pointed out, is a savage parody of Judaism.[28] But Keegstra, a Christian fundamentalist already predisposed to believe the worst of Jews and Judaism, accepted Pranaitis as he had accepted Nesta Webster. In his testimony, he returned repeatedly to anti-Talmudic themes. Obviously, such allegations as the following had made a deep impression on his mind:

> nothing more abominable can be imagined than what they (the Jews) have to say about Christians. They say that they are idolators, the worst kind of people, much worse than the Turks, murderers, fornicators, impure animals, like dirt, unworthy to be called men, beasts in human form, worthy of the name of beasts, cows, asses, pigs, dogs, worse than dogs; that they propagate after the manner of beasts, that they have diabolic origin, that their souls came from the devil and return to the devil in hell after death; and that even the body of a dead Christian is nothing different from that of an animal.[29]

In reality, this catalogue is a more accurate description of the extreme forms of Christian anti-Jewish slander, for example, the fourth-century diatribes of St. John Chrysostom, than the reverse.[30]

Keegstra, however, missed this irony. Blinded by his misconceptions, he could see only one thing: the presence of anti-Jesus and anti-Christian tales in the rabbinic corpus. Having seen only one thing, he knew only one thing: the Talmud had to be evil because it said evil things. Hence the rabbis who composed the Talmud must have been evil, and thus also their spiritual descendants. Not only did they defame Christ, but they instilled every conceivable vice in the hearts of their followers, especially greed, deception, exploitation and murder. Such notions were Keegstra's daily bread; his students made them their daily bread as well.

Khazars and Zionists

Among the assorted antisemitica impounded from the defendant's private library was a non-antisemitic writing by the famed ex-communist Jewish writer Arthur Koestler entitled *The Thirteenth Tribe*. This historical study argues that the majority of "surviving" (i.e., post-Holocaust) Jews in the world are of east European, mainly Khazar racial origin. Hence, ". . . their ancestors came not from the Jordan but from the Volga, not from Canaan but from the Caucasus, once believed to be the cradle of the Aryan race; . . . genetically they are more closely related to the Hun, Uigur and Magyar tribes than to the seed of Abraham, Isaac and Jacob."[31]

Who were the Khazars? The Kingdom of Khazaria stretched between the Black and Caspian Seas on the steppes north of the Caucasian mountains from the seventh century until its eventual disintegration in the twelfth or thirteenth century (the date of its demise is unclear). During the eighth century, the Khazar king (Bulan) and his court adopted Judaism as the state religion, probably—so Salo Baron suggests—as a declaration of neutrality between the Christian and Muslim empires, since conversion to either Christianity or Islam would have involved the kingdom in political subservience to either Byzantium or Baghdad.[32] The new official religion, however, was syncretistic in character, and rather minimal.[33] Nevertheless, Khazaria became a Jewish haven, and the subject of romantic tales. Before its final destruction, according to Baron, its Jewish inhabitants "sent many offshoots into the unsubdued Slavonic lands, helping ultimately to build up the great Jewish centers of eastern Europe."[34] It was the descendants of these offshoots who, in Koestler's thesis, became the 'thirteenth tribe'—the *Ashkenazic* (but not *Sephardic*) Jews of the modern world. Most Jews, therefore, are not 'Semites,' i.e., the descendants of the biblical Hebrews; hence, Koestler declares, the term 'antisemitism' is meaningless, "a misapprehension shared by both the killers and their victims."[35] However, this conclusion, in his opinion, must not be "maliciously misinterpreted as a denial of the State of Israel's right to exist," for the latter rests on international law, not racial origins.[36] Thus the author sensed the danger in his own argument and attempted to neutralize it. His attempt was in vain.

Keegstra grasped the possibilities of Koestler's thesis, and he made certain that his students grasped them as well. Repeatedly, class essays introduced the Khazars into the broad sweep of history in exactly the manner that Koestler feared the most; lines such as the following are endemic: "The Khazzars wanted to get control of the Zionist sect and get Palestine as a homeland for the Jews." "Nicholas I (of Russia) . . . announced that he would threw [*sic*] a constitution. He attempt failed because of Kazzar Jews assassinating high gov't officials in charge of this constitution." "In eastern Russia, Jews (Kazars) put tremendous pressure on the Czars. Their goal was to fame [sic], and smear to get rid of the Czar. Collective Slaughtering, by Zionist organizations started in France, by 1886 Herzle." "Chaim Weisman said that he would get the U.S.A. into the war on England's side if England would promise him something in return. This is what they had to promise . . . they had to break their promise to the Arabs and give Palestine to the Khazzar Jews."[37] Judging from these citations, there were two lessons to be learned in social studies at Eckville High School: (1) as descendants of the Khazars, modern *Ashkenazic* Jews possess no valid claim to middle-eastern soil in the twentieth century; consequently, Zionism is based on a Jewish fraud; (2) as descendants of the Khazars, a Hunnish, Mongolian people with savage instincts, modern *Ashkenazic* Jews possess the racial traits of their ancestors and must not be trusted in Christian society. They are Khazars still, and Zionism is a Khazar movement, aimed at the displacement and destruction of the (semitic) Arabs. Israel, therefore, has no right to exist, and its existence should be terminated. A nasty book, the Talmud, and a nasty race, the Khazars, truly deserve each other, and together explain why the Jews act like Jews, that is to say, why they prey on gentiles. In Keegstra's eyes, the Zionists—there are many references to Herzl in the student materials—constituted the Jewish menace par excellence, the highest pitch of malevolence.

The Holocaust was another Jewish-Zionist-Khazar fraud as far as Keegstra was concerned, a fraud calculated to win sympathy for the Jews in order to assist them in achieving their nefarious ends. Although historical revisionism was not his personal hobby, he certainly found it congenial. Along with many other publications of either an eccentric or a vicious nature,[38] Arthur Butz's *The Hoax of the Twentieth Century*, a work that has acquired the status of a new antisemitic classic, was impounded from Keegstra's private library. According to this revisionist text, Jews invent monstrous lies about mass murders because of their Talmudic mentalities; they were always liars, and the Holocaust hoax was only the latest, most reprehensible example of this deeply ingrained instinct.[39] Once again, the Talmud was found at fault. Consequently, for Keegstra, there were no gas chambers and ovens at Auschwitz, nor any Nazi extermination program. These themes found a favourable response among his students, to wit: "Modern day historians have tried to tell us that Hitler exterminated many Jews. True, Hitler hated the Jew [sic] but he emigrated them, not exterminated them." "Jews today cry of persecution in World War II, but there is a lot of people right here in Canada who know different and no one listens. Those piles of dead bodies that the Bolshevik Press says were Jews were really probably (1) Dead Germans from typhus (2) Bodies from when Stalin massacred 5,000,000 DP's (3) Bodies of the

9,000,000 Prussians that were killed when they had to march back to West Germany."[40] Obviously, the teacher had succeeded in making his point.

Conclusion

Keegstra did not take kindly to the charge of antisemitism. Antisemitism, in his view, was still another Jewish fraud: a smoke screen invented by Jews in order to cloud the real issues and divert public attention from the truth. "TRUTH – THE FINAL SOLUTION" screamed the large buttons that his friends and supporters, especially the members of the so-called Christian Defence League sported in the corridors as the trial dragged on. It is not antisemitic to tell the truth, and the truth is not hard to discern, at least not for Bible-believing Christians. The holy man on the stand, his voice ringing with sincerity, seemed to be surrounded by his own peculiar cloud of witnesses: John Chrysostom, Tomás Torquemada, Johannes Pfefferkorn, Martin Luther (whose anti-Jewish tracts Keegstra cited from time to time), Edouard Drumont, August Rohling, Adolf Hitler and many others. All the Jew-haters of the Christian ages were gathered in the shadows of the Alberta courtroom. Figuratively speaking, not Keegstra alone, but the entire Christian *adversus Judaeos* tradition stood on trial with him in Red Deer.

However, Keegstra's antisemitism was not merely the reiteration of an old religious fanaticism. It possessed certain modern components as well, notably a terrible fear of even the slightest alteration in familiar symbols and mores lest the entire scheme of things crumble into ruin. Time, at all costs, has to be arrested in its dangerous course, for the insecure psyche can endure only so many blows, and every day spawns new wars and rumours of wars. Keegstra, the son of immigrant parents, and therefore the child of both insecurity and poverty, born in the Depression and raised during the war era, puzzled and troubled by the ravages and perils that encircled his life in rural Alberta, haunted, like so many others of his generation, by the mystery of evil, was apparently in search of some form of absolute reassurance. He found it in an extremist ideology that managed to clarify all the existential questions to his inner satisfaction. A perfectly sane man — mental aberration in the clinical sense was not a factor in his case — he lacked nevertheless the self-knowledge, critical acumen and wisdom that a more intelligent assessment of both his internal feelings and the external world would have required. Keegstra, in other words, the man who prided himself on his mental originality, could not think at all; instead, like Adolf Eichmann in Hannah Arendt's famous description, his mind ran only in clichés.[41] As a result, his case supports Arendt's contention, elaborated in her posthumously published philosophical reflections, that socially oppressive attitudes and actions have something to do with an absence of thought, i.e., with an inability or a refusal to move beyond convention into an authentic encounter with the problems and dilemmas of life itself.[42] "Clichés, stock phrases, adherence to conventional, standardized codes of expression and conduct have the socially recognized function of protecting us against reality, that is, against the claim on our thinking attention that all events and facts make by virtue of their existence."[43]

For this reason, Keegstra was impervious to alternative explanations of both the meaning of Scripture and the events of history, and it was useless to instruct him. Conspirators, he informed the court, write with long meaningless words, or beyond his comprehension; hence, anything intellectual (do not intellectuals usually write with long meaningless words?) had a conspiratorial ring. Unable to engage in serious and genuine reflection on theology and history, he could only interpret the struggle between good and evil in simple dualistic terms, since dualism does not necessitate thought, only belief. Dualism, as Reinhold Niebuhr once wrote, is the religion of immaturity rather than maturity, and leads naturally to the demonization of one's foes: "The child-man, unable to understand the relation of things to each other, ascribes an ultimate source to every natural event, thus peopling his world with spirits, monsters, gods, devils and other mysterious potencies."[44] In the end, Keegstra, Sartre's "Knight-errant of the good" if there ever was one, emerged as a pathetic, if not a tragic, figure. He was too small to be tragic. So obviously mediocre, a nobody who wanted desperately to be a somebody, he chose a foolish path to fame. Unlearned, he attempted to pass himself off as learned; unintelligent, he attempted to pass himself off as intelligent; unimportant, he attempted to pass himself off as important. In spite of everything, it was difficult not to feel sorry for him as he toppled from his pedestal.

The pathos must not be exaggerated; Keegstra thoroughly deserved his public humiliation. An obscure figure to begin with, he has since sunk back into obscurity, although his second trial may restore him briefly to the limelight. This, in itself, reveals a lack of significant support in his own province, not to mention the nation at large. The times are not auspicious for such extreme ideas, especially with the decline of Social Credit orthodoxy, the political womb of his antisemitism. The times can change again, but, at the moment, ideological antisemitism of this variety is out of joint with the social, religious and political climate of Canadian society. Keegstra drew most of his support either from old-fashioned Douglasite diehards or from European immigrants in rural Alberta already predisposed to a certain measure of anti-Jewish prejudice. Despite his own fundamentalist beliefs, he drew relatively little support from Christian fundamentalists in the vast Bible-belt of the prairies, a hopeful sign. While he should not be dismissed as a total anomaly—after all, antisemitism has persistent roots in both Anglo- and French Canada—he should not be regarded as representative. Other Keegstras may yet arise—in fact, one, Malcolm

Ross, has arisen already in New Brunswick[45] — but they will not be representative either.

Notes

Abbreviated versions of this chapter have been published under the following titles: "Keegstra in Red Deer," *Touchstone* 5 (January 1987): 33-39, and "The Queen versus James Keegstra: Reflections on Christian Antisemitism in Canada," *American Journal of Theology and Philosophy* 9, 1 and 2 (January-May 1988): 99-116.

1 Cf. David Bercuson and Douglas Wertheimer, *A Trust Betrayed: The Keegstra Affair* (Toronto: McClelland-Bantam, 1985). For a more journalistic account, see Steve Mertl and John Ward, *Keegstra: The Issues, the Trial, the Consequences* (Saskatoon: Western Producer Prairie Books, 1985). For a description of Keegstra based on personal interviews, see Stanley R. Barrett, *Is God a Racist?* (Toronto: University of Toronto Press, 1987), pp. 215-60.

2 *R. v. Ernst Zündel, Criminal Code of Canada*, 177. Note that Zündel was tried under a different section of the Criminal Code than Keegstra.

3 See Douglas Christie, *The Zundel Trial and Free Speech* (n.p.: C-FAR Press, n.d.).

4 Cf. Alan Davies, "Freedom of Speech," *The Ecumenist* 26, 3 (March-April 1988): 44-47.

5 For a fuller biographical account, see Bercuson and Wertheimer, *Trust Betrayed*, pp. 6f.

6 Ibid., chap. 5, and Mertl and Ward, *Keegstra: The Issues*, passim.

7 Jean-Paul Sartre, *Anti-Semite and Jew*, trans. George J. Becker (New York: Schocken Books, 1948), pp. 40-43.

8 Having been issued a subpoena by the Crown as an expert witness in the history of antisemitism, I spent almost two weeks in court listening to Keegstra's testimony as well as observing the defendant and his claque at close range. My observations and comments are based on personal recollections and impressions during this period, which I recorded in written form. As matters transpired, I was not required to take the stand after all, nor was the expert in rabbinic literature, also subpoenaed by the Crown. Keegstra spoke freely, and revealed a great deal about himself in the course of cross-examination. He convicted himself entirely out of his own mouth.

9 Ron Gostick, Pat Walsh. Their organization is called "The Canadian League of Rights."

10 From RCMP files. I have suppressed the names of the student authors of these and other papers cited in this study. The spelling mistakes have been left uncorrected.

11 In an article published in the *Illustrated Sunday Herald*, February 8, 1940, entitled "Zioninsm versus Bolshevism: A Struggle for the Soul of The Jewish People." This article, which I believe the older Churchill would have repudiated, reveals that, like many others of his day, the British statesman was influenced by conspiracy theories and the myth of the 'international Jew'. In other respects, however, it is strongly pro-Jewish — a fact that Keegstra neglected to mention during his testimony — and pro-Zionist. For Churchill at the time, 'national Jews' and 'Zionist Jews' were radically different from 'international Jews'.

12 For a rather unsatisfactory description of Nesta Webster and her life, see Richard M. Gilman, *Behind World Revolution: The Strange Career of Nesta H. Webster*, vol. 1 (Ann Arbor: Insight Books, 1982).

13 Ibid.

14 For descriptions of British antisemitism in Nesta Webster's day, see Colin Holmes, *Anti-Semitism in British Society 1876-1931* (London: Edward Arnold, 1979), and Gisela C. Lebzelter, *Political Anti-Semitism in England 1918-1939* (New York: Holmes & Meier, 1978). These studies analyze fully such movements as the "Britons," the "Imperial Fascist League" and the "British Union of Fascists" and their peculiar pathology. Both books contain references to Nesta Webster.

15 Nesta Webster, *Secret Societies and Subversive Movements* (London: Boswell Publishing, 1924; republished by the Christian Book Club of America), pp. 405-406.

16 Cf. August Barruel, *Mémoire pour servir à l'histoire de jacobinisme* (1797); John Robison, *Proofs of a Conspiracy against all the Religions and Governments of Europe, carried on in the Secret Meetings of Freemasons, Illuminati and Reading Societies* (1797); P. L. B. Drach, *De l'Harmonie entre l'église et la synagogue* (1844); Emil Eckert, *Der Freimaurer-Orden in seiner wahren Bedeutung* (trans. French 1854); Alphonse de Toussenel, *Les juifs rois de l'époque* (1846); Henri Gougenot des Mousseaux, *Le Juif, le judaisme et la judaisation des peuples chrétiens* (1869); E. N. Chabauty, *Francs-Maçons et Juifs, sixième age de l'église d'après l'Apocalypse* (1880); and Joseph Lémann, *L'entrée des Israelites dans la société française et les états chrétiens* (1886). Some of the above were cited by Mrs. Webster.

17 Weishaupt seems to have been a political and social idealist whose vision of a new world order was more utopian than realistic. His order (Illuminati) was suppressed by the Bavarian Elector in 1784, and Weishaupt was forced to flee. An unsuccessful attempt to revive the order was made in Germany by Leopold Engel about 1904-1906. Weishaupt was demonized by the anti-revolutionary Abbé August Barruel and the Scottish anti-Mason John Robison (see n. 16). For further references, see Klaus Epstein, *The Genesis of German Conservatism* (Princeton: Princeton University Press, 1966), and J. M. Roberts, *The Mythology of the Secret Societies* (London: Secker & Warburg, 1972).

18 Stephen Wilson, *Ideology and Experience: Antisemitism in France at the Time of the Dreyfus Affair* (Teaneck, NJ: Fairleigh Dickinson University Press, 1982), chaps. 14 and 16.

19 Cf. H. Blair Neatby, *The Politics of Chaos: Canada in the Thirties* (Toronto: Macmillan, 1972), p. 34.

20 For a good exposition of Social Credit theory, see John A. Irving, *The Social Credit Movement in Alberta* (Toronto: University of Toronto Press, 1959).

21 Major C. H. Douglas, *The Big Idea* (London: K.R.P. Publications, 1942), p. 49.

22 Ibid., pp. 10, 17.

23 See the essay by Howard Palmer ("Politics, Religion and Antisemitism in Alberta, 1880-1950") in this volume.

24 Cf. Jeremy Cohen, *The Friars and the Jews: The Evolution of Mediaeval Anti-Judaism* (Ithaca: Cornell University Press, 1982).

25 Cf. Clemens Thoma, *A Christian Theology of Judaism*, trans. Helga Croner (New York: Paulist Press, 1980), pp. 89-90.

26 For example, Pranaitis writes as follows: "Even a Christian who is found studying the Law of Israel merits death. In *Sanhedrin* (59a) it says 'Rabbi Jochanan says: A *Goi* who

pries into the Law is guilty of death'" (I. B. Pranaitis, *The Talmud Unmasked: The Secret Rabbinical Teachings Concerning Christians* [St. Petersburg: n.p., 1892; reprinted in English, New York: E. N. Sanctuary, 1939], p. 77). Pranaitis assumes that this verse is tantamount to a direct death sentence. However, in Talmudic usage, the statement is metaphorical only, and implies no more than a severe denunciation; it has nothing to do with capital punishment, and was never read as such by Jews. It belongs, moreover, to an early age, and is hardly applicable today. It also refers to pagans (idolators) rather than Christians. Clearly the ancient rabbis were offended by the spectacle of idol-worshippers mocking their laws.

27 See R. Travers Herford, *Christianity in Talmud and Midrash* (London: Williams & Norgate, 1903), pp. 35-41.

28 Jacob Katz, *From Prejudice to Destruction: Anti-Semitism, 1700-1933* (Cambridge: Harvard University Press, 1980), p. 20.

29 Pranaitis, *Talmud Unmasked*, p. 46.

30 John Chrysostom, *Homilies Against the Jews* (Antioch, 386-87 C.E.).

31 Arthur Koestler, *The Thirteenth Tribe: The Khazar Empire and Its Heritage* (London: Hutchinson, 1976), p. 17.

32 Salo Wittmayer Baron, *A Social and Religious History of the Jews*, vol. 3, 2nd ed. (New York: Columbia University Press, 1957), p. 198.

33 Ibid., pp. 200 f.

34 Ibid., p. 206.

35 Koestler, *The Thirteenth Tribe*, p. 17.

36 Ibid., p. 223.

37 RCMP files.

38 E.g., Philip Mauro, *The Hope of Israel*; Rev. Clarence Kelly, *Conspiracy Against God and Man*; Col. Curtis B. Dall, *Israel's Five Trillian Dollar Secret*; John Stormer, *None Dare Call It Treason*; Michael J. Goy, *The Missing Dimension and World Affairs*; and Ivor Benson, *This Worldwide Conspiracy*, etc.

39 Arthur R. Butz, *The Hoax of the Twentieth Century* (Chapel Ascote: Historical Review Press, 1976), pp. 246-47.

40 RCMP files.

41 Hannah Arendt, *Eichmann in Jerusalem: A Report on the Banality of Evil* (New York: Viking Press, 1963), p. 55. Unlike Eichmann, however, Keegstra is not a murderer. There is no sign that he ever plotted the *physical* extermination of the Jews, in spite of his rhetoric. In this sense, his antisemitism is not modern at all.

42 Hannah Arendt, *The Life of the Mind* (New York: Harcourt, Brace, Jovanovich, 1971), Section 1.

43 Ibid., p. 4.

44 Reinhold Niebuhr, *Beyond Tragedy: Essays on the Christian Interpretation of History* (New York: Scribner's 1937), pp. 135-36.

45 Malcolm Ross, a New Brunswick mathematics teacher and the author of revisionist and antisemitic tracts, has been removed from the classroom by the Moncton School Board following a human-rights inquiry. Unlike Keegstra, however, Ross does not seem to have introduced his antisemitic views into his lessons.

10

The Zündel Affair

Manuel Prutschi

Introduction

On November 18, 1983, Mrs. Sabina Citron of the Canadian Holocaust Remembrance Association went before a justice of the peace to swear out charges against Ernst Zündel under the "false news" section of Canada's Criminal Code.[1] This section makes it a crime to produce and disseminate wilfully material which is false, known to be false, and damaging to a public interest. The action began as a private complaint; however, the Crown took the case over in January 1984. By the time of the preliminary hearing in June, the indictment involved two separate charges: (1) the publication of a four-page letter entitled "The West, War and Islam" advancing the notion of a conspiracy by Zionists, bankers, communists and Freemasons to control the world; (2) the publication of a 30-page pamphlet entitled *Did Six Million Really Die?* stigmatizing the Holocaust as a "colossal piece of fiction and the most successful of deceptions."[2] The Crown also specified the affected public interest as that of social and racial tolerance.

Ernst Zündel was already familiar to the Jewish community as a hatemonger. Moreover, government officials, both federal and provincial, had become aware of him and had explored various legal avenues long before criminal charges were actually laid. The Canadian Holocaust Remembrance Association had played a significant role in the imposition of an interim mail ban on November 13, 1981, a prohibitory order that was repealed almost a year later.[3] Mrs. Citron's group, as well as other Jewish organizations, had also pressed the attorney general of Ontario, Roy McMurtry, to prosecute Zündel under Canada's 1970 anti-hate law, which makes it a crime to advocate genocide or wilfully to promote hatred

---

Notes for Chapter 10 are on pp. 272-77.

against an identifiable group as defined by race, colour, ethnicity or religion.[4] McMurtry was sensitive to Jewish concerns, but hesitated in pressing charges because he feared that some of the provisions in the Criminal
Code might allow Zündel to escape with an acquittal. Mrs. Citron, impa-
tient with the lack of action, decided to lay a private charge under the
"false news" section, which did not require the consent of the attorney
general. Although he had the power to stay this charge, McMurtry chose
instead to take control of the case. To have stayed the charge would have
been tantamount to granting Zündel a second triumph, after his initial
victory in the postal-ban hearing. A private prosecution would have been
highly unusual in Canada and would have shown a less than forceful attitude toward the merchants of hate. Furthermore, there were "reasonable
grounds" for proceeding, and these were sufficient.

Mrs. Citron, in effect, had forced the hand of the attorney general. A
Holocaust survivor herself, she regarded individuals such as Zündel as
responsible for her own personal tragedy. Almost certainly, the object of
her attention understood why she was bound by past obligations to "slay
the Nazi dragon on Carlton Street."[5] Zündel was far from perturbed at
the legal action initiated against him. He had expected it and, indeed,
eagerly anticipated it. In fact, it is possible that he printed the Holocaust
denial pamphlet *Did Six Million Really Die?* as a deliberate toss of the
gauntlet. He promised to fight the case all the way to the Supreme Court.[6]

Trials and Appeals

Zündel, from the beginning, demonstrated a remarkable flair for theatri-
cality. He always arrived at court sporting a bullet-proof vest, making himself even stockier and more portly in appearance: a figure reminiscent of
Mussolini rather than Hitler. His balding head sported a blue hardhat
with the motto "Freedom of Speech." His entrances and exits were
attended by a retinue of male followers with yellow hardhats. Arriving to
be sentenced after his first trial, he appeared "with a blackened face
(because whites cannot receive justice in Canada) carrying a cross, like
Jesus on his way to Calgary. The cross bore the inscription 'Freedom of
Speech'; not only was Zündel, like Jesus, being crucified by an evil society,
but freedom of speech was being crucified as well."[7] All of this, of course,
was for the benefit of the television cameras. Since, however, courts do
not brook such antics, nor allow their proceedings to be photographed or
filmed, the Zündelists had to surrender their props (and the cameramen
their equipment) on entry.

As his defence counsel, Zündel retained the Victoria-based attorney
Douglas Christie, whom he met in 1984 during a brief visit to Alberta to
support James Keegstra during the latter's preliminary hearing. Not only
has Christie remained Zündel's lawyer, but he has emerged as the peren-

nial legal defender of Canadian antisemites, acting also for the long-time Toronto Nazi, John Ross Taylor, and Imre Finta, a Hungarian-born Toronto restaurateur charged with war crimes.[8] A vigorous advocate of western separatism, Christie founded the Western Canada Concept Party, and ran unsuccessfully as an independent twice in federal elections.

Zündel's first trial lasted eight weeks. On February 28, 1985, the jury delivered its verdict, acquitting him on the charge connected with "The West, War and Islam," but finding him guilty of spreading false news about the Holocaust. One can only speculate on the reasons for the jury's acquittal on the first charge. Perhaps it was regarded as less important, since scarcely any time was devoted to it during the trial. Perhaps the jury reasoned that, since the letter at issue was mailed abroad only (to 1200 addresses in the Middle East), it was unlikely to have prejudiced a public interest in Canada. The acquittal might also have been another example of the Canadian penchant for compromise; having convicted Zündel on the second and more significant charge, the jurors were able to afford some measure of magnanimity. On March 25, he was sentenced to 15 months in prison, but freed on bail pending an appeal.

To prove the Holocaust denial charge, the Crown had to establish the falsity of the tract Did Six Million Really Die? To achieve this, the truth of the Holocaust had to be established. For this reason, Dr. Raul Hilberg of the University of Vermont, one of the world's foremost authorities on the subject, was called as an expert witness, as well as a number of survivors. In accordance with a practice sometimes employed in judicial proceedings, the Crown also requested that judicial notice of the Holocaust be taken. (In other words, the court was asked to accept certain matters germane to the case without actually having to prove them. Such judicial notice can be sought when the facts are so well-known "in the community" that they cannot "reasonably be questioned," or when the facts are capable of determination by readily available evidence of indisputable accuracy.)[9] The prosecutor requested judicial notice of the fact that, between 1933 and 1945, millions of Jews were annihilated deliberately by Nazi Germany, and that this annihilation was accomplished by various means, including starvation, deprivation, mass shootings and gassing. The prosecutor refrained from making this request until after the conclusion of the case against Zündel, but repeated it after the defence had called all its witnesses. On both occasions, however, the presiding judge chose to reject the application, believing that the taking of such notice would hinder a proper defence, as well as lifting a burden off the prosecution. The Crown also sought to convince the jury that Zündel did not believe his own assertions about the falsity of the Holocaust. This was done by suggesting, particularly during cross-examination, that the defendant, far from being the disinterested researcher that he claimed to be, was in fact an ardent neo-

Nazi. Thus, Zündel simply selected material that seemed to support his claims, dismissing the massive evidence to the contrary. Holocaust denial was really a scheme to rehabilitate the Third Reich. Finally, the Crown argued that a campaign branding the Jews as liars and swindlers was not conducive to social and racial harmony in Canada and was therefore injurious to the public interest.

The defence chose to raise radical questions about the Holocaust itself. Christie engaged in brutal cross-examinations of survivor witnesses, seeking to undermine their testimony, cast doubt on their suffering and deprive their experiences of any real significance. The defence also called 'expert' witnesses of its own in the form of various notorious Holocaust deniers, not unlike Zündel himself. The media, in its coverage, tended to focus on the sensational and provocative suggestions of the defence counsel, as well as on the testimony of his witnesses. The Holocaust itself was not news; however, the suggestion that the murders were a hoax was news. Hence, the front-page headline in *The Globe and Mail* of January 12, 1985, read: "Lawyer Challenges Crematoria Theory." Christie also tried to establish that Zündel honestly believed the Holocaust denial views that he promoted. If the jury could be convinced of his sincerity, it was bound to find him innocent under the law. The jury, however, was not convinced, returning a verdict of guilty. Zündel was defiant and unrepentant. At what has been described as "an impromptu press conference held from the prisoner's dock in the courtroom,"[10] he declared that the trial had gained him "one million dollars worth of publicity."[11] However, this bold claim was without foundation. In fact, the only change of public attitude as a result of the trial was one of greater sympathy for the Jewish community.[12] Ironically, the sector of the population most sympathetic to antisemitism was also the sector least responsive to media reports; even the converted did not listen.

The defendant launched an appeal, which was heard in September 1986, by a panel of five judges of the Ontario Court of Appeal. His lawyer argued that the "false news" law was unconstitutional, violating the freedom of expression provisions of the Charter of Rights and Freedoms. He also argued that the Judge had made numerous errors, depriving his client of a fair trial. The Appeal Court rendered its decision in January 1987. It found the law constitutional, declaring that certain modes of expression, e.g., "spreading falsehoods knowingly," were not protected by Charter guarantees of free speech. It also declared that social and racial tolerance constituted a paramount public interest. However, the court ordered a new trial, agreeing that fundamental errors had been committed during the proceedings. The defence counsel, for example, should have been allowed to question prospective jurors. The court acknowledged that some of the questions that Christie sought to ask were improper, but felt that the judge should have allowed him to formulate more acceptable questions. More importantly, the court found that the judge had equated Zündel's "knowledge" of the falsity of the pamphlet *Did Six Million Really Die?* with "an absence of honest belief" in the truth of its claims.[13] However, the 'false news' law demands proof beyond a reasonable doubt of "guilty knowledge" on the part of the accused – a standard that is one significant notch higher than absence of honest belief. This confusion, together with the jury selection errors, warranted a retrial. The Crown unsuccessfully sought leave to appeal the court's decision to the Supreme Court of Canada. Zündel's second trial began on January 11, 1988, almost three years later.

The second trial was in many ways a replay of the first, but with some significant differences. The Crown found a new expert, Professor Christopher Browning, a prominent Holocaust historian at Pacific Lutheran University. No survivors were called. Moreover, judicial notice of the Holocaust was obtained. This "bare bones" (as the Crown later referred to it) judicial recognition of the historical character of the mass murders still permitted the defence to raise questions regarding the intent of Nazi policy, the means employed and the number of victims. As a consequence, the rights of the accused were protected. The defence strategy was unchanged, although Zündel did not take the stand this time. Some new faces were added to the roster of witnesses, the most significant being that of the ultra-nationalistic English historian, David Irving. Irving had not denied the historicity of the Holocaust initially but, in his book *Hitler's War*, had suggested that the murders were not Hitler's personal work. Indeed, he had once offered a £1000 reward to anyone who could produce a written order from the Führer for the destruction of European Jewry. More and more willing to associate openly with Holocaust deniers, he chose to identify himself publicly with their position at Zündel's second trial. Another difference between the two trials lay in the more sensitive and restrained nature of the media coverage. The camera footage rarely, if ever, appeared on the television news, so that Zündel's antics passed unnoticed as far as the public was concerned.

The defendant was found guilty again by a jury of his peers and sentenced to nine months in prison. His appeal was heard by a three-judge panel of the Ontario Court of Appeal in September 1989. In February 1990, the court upheld both the conviction and the sentence. At the time of writing, his legal fate remains unresolved, pending a final appeal to the Supreme Court of Canada.

Background and Beginnings

Ernst Christof Friedrich Zündel was born on April 24, 1939, in the village of Calmbach, in the Black Forest region of Germany. He was barely six when the war ended in 1945, too young to have joined the *Hitler-Jugend*

(Hitler Youth) or to have been involved in anything serious in the Nazi period.[14] Ernst was one of three siblings; if his account is to be believed, his sister became a Christian missionary in Africa and his brother a lawyer in the United States.[15] His father was a woodcutter who had served as a medic during World War II; his mother was of peasant stock. Both his parents were apolitical. The family is said to have lived on the same farm for 300 years. In his autobiography, Zündel writes that, from this inconspicuous background, he emerged with boyhood memories of personal suffering during Germany's defeat—"hunger, cold and sickness" under the French military occupation.[16] Moroccan and Algerian troops occupying the local schoolhouse forced him and his friends to attend classes in the Protestant church. In 1953, he enrolled in a trade school, obtaining a diploma as a photo retoucher three years later. This became his later vocation in Toronto. After graduating, he lived and worked for a while in north Germany. In 1958, at the age of 19, he emigrated to Canada, bringing a letter of recommendation from his last German employer which described him as excellent at his trade and a person whom everyone liked: Germany's loss was Canada's gain! The immigrant first settled in Montreal, where he married Jeannick LaRouche, a French-Canadian girl from the Lac St. Jean region. The couple had two sons, Pierre Ernst and Hans.

Continuing his education, Zündel studied history and political science at Sir George Williams University (he was later to credit these studies with his "general historical background" to the Holocaust).[17] However, it was outside the university walls that Zündel received the education that mattered the most to his subsequent career. His teacher was Adrien Arcand, Canada's quintessential Nazi who, in the early 1960s, was living out his last years in Montreal. In his autobiography, Zündel devotes space to what he regards as the sad story of Arcand's arrest and imprisonment without trial for the duration of World War II as "Canada's Hitler."[18] He bewails this injustice, especially since Arcand never received a penny of restitution. The master's fate, according to his youthful admirer, was no different from that of thousands of Germans, Italians and Japanese. "Not a soul writes about (them) in Canada today and no monuments have been erected and no Holocaust film has been produced about them."[19] Arcand himself was a philo-German who spoke German fluently. Taking Zündel under his wing, he made his private library of 4000 books, including many German pre-war monographs, available to his disciple. Arcand also introduced Zündel to, or placed him in touch with, his friends and contacts in Canada, the United States and Europe. This network included noted antisemites such as Paul Rassinier, Henry Coston, Admiral Sir Barry Domville, Sir Oswald Mosley and others. As a result of these contacts, Zündel writes, his "life was enriched."[20] The aged fascist played mentor to the young immigrant, much as the old Houston Stewart Chamberlain once played mentor to the young Adolf Hitler. Zündel credits Arcand with bringing "order into my confused mind"[21] (elsewhere, he declares that Hitler brought order to a confused Germany[22]). Summing up his entire apprenticeship, Zündel states that "in distant Canada he (Arcand) made a German out of me."[23] Indeed, his autobiography proudly reproduces two photographs of the two men sitting together.

In the mid-1960s, Zündel left Montreal and settled with his family in Toronto, a city that, from 1963 to the end of the decade, was passing through a visible phase of neo-Nazi activism. A youthful David Stanley from suburban Scarborough was its first catalyst. When Stanley repudiated neo-Nazism after having read Eric Hoffer's *The True Believer*, he was replaced by a not much older John Beattie as local leader. Not surprisingly, Zündel began to associate with the various Toronto neo-Nazi groups, including Stanley's and Beattie's. He already possessed the largest private collection of Nazi memorabilia in Canada, including books, portraits, insignia, etc. — a collection conceivably enhanced by his rumoured inheritance of Arcand's vast library of antisemitica. However, he avoided leadership roles, preferring to stay on the fringe; he had the leadership of another party in mind. Taking his first stab at stardom, Zündel, despite his German citizenship, placed his name in the 1968 leadership contest of the federal Liberal party (credential arrangements at Canadian political conventions were rather loose at that time). He described himself as a dark horse candidate, representing what he referred to as "the third element,"[24] i.e., ethnic groups whose ancestry was neither British nor French. Zündel also portrayed himself as a staunch anti-Communist, making, of course, no mention of his neo-Nazi views and associations; since he was not known publicly in this capacity — in fact, he was not known at all — neither did anyone else. In his autobiography, he speaks of his candidacy as though it had constituted the sensation of the day. "I was therefore the only non-Minister and outsider, the youngest candidate and also the first immigrant and German Canadian in Canada's history who had achieved this. This gave me the image of a maverick, a Skorzeny figure of politics."[25] In reality, no one cared who he was, his nomination attracted almost no attention, and he received not a single vote. Immediately forgotten, he returned to obscurity in his double life.

During this period, Zündel had also been busy with his professional and business career. In this pursuit, he was successful and soon owned his own advertising agency and commercial studio. As an artist, he worked for such national magazines as *Maclean's, Homemaker's* and *Quest*: in December 1973, his name appeared in a full-page advertisement, together with the names of other "writers, illustrators and photographers" who had "all helped make *Homemaker's* and *Quest* Canada's most successful new magazines."[26] Also, Zündel twice won awards for his work from the Art Directors' Club of Toronto. While enjoying these plaudits, however, he continued and intensified his neo-Nazi activities, especially his literary endeavours. Nor was he loath to employ his artistic talents for the cause. In 1976, a series of multi-coloured, multi-lingual leaflets appeared, calling for the release of Rudolf Hess from prison. They bore a Verdun, Quebec, postal box number and were attributed to something called the Western Unity Movement. The quality of the art suggested the work of a professional. As no Western Unity Movement existed in Verdun or elsewhere, the leaflets were soon traced back to Zündel, who had simply rented a Verdun postal box as a drop for his propaganda campaign. In 1977, he demonstrated his originality by producing some tracts claiming that UFOs (unidentified flying objects) were Hitler's secret weapon: a weapon still in use and being refined in secret bases in the Antarctic and below the earth's surface. A flyer advertising these extraterrestrial claims described them (rightly) as "a radical departure from all previous UFO literature in the English-speaking world."[27] The claims reported in the tracts, it seems, "were researched in many languages on four continents, and present a continuing story dating back to the middle of the 1930s, when the first Nazi saucers were planned, right up to the present day."[28] Zündel penned this material under his quasi-pseudonym of Christof Friedrich. With characteristic puffery, his flyer described himself, i.e., Friedrich, as "the multilingual-globetrotting author" who was "in great demand as a lecturer and panelist on UFO and psychic matters."[29]

Zündel did not limit his literary efforts to the outer edges of neo-Nazi research; he also made substantial contributions to the more traditional themes of antisemitism and white supremacy under the same nom de plume. Thus, in a 1976 issue of *The Liberty Bell* entitled "Four Books That Shook the World," he presented a two-page synopsis of antisemitic articles from the 1920s that had first appeared in Henry Ford's *Dearborn Independent*. In the January 1970 edition of "White Power Report," another product of White Power Publications, he published an article entitled "Our New Emblem — The Best of Both Worlds." This particular edition also described the activities of Don Andrews and the small fascist organization that styled itself the Western Guard (Andrews, a Balkan-born, Canada-raised antisemite and white supremacist, was at the forefront of neo-Nazi agitation in Toronto in the mid-1970s).

Obviously, Zündel had maintained his association with the various Toronto neo-Nazi groups, as well as with John Ross Taylor, the neo-Nazi elder statesman in Canada. He was also present at a public meeting of Ron Gostick's Canadian League of Rights in the Royal York Hotel in Toronto in December 1977. During this time, Zündel began to acquire a personal following, with meetings in his home attended by guests in the dozens. Known neo-Nazis who gravitated to him included Walter (or Wolfgang)

Droege, an associate of Andrews, as well as David Astle and Jack Prins, former associates of John Beattie. In late 1977, Zündel organized his own group, "Omega," in association with the Hungarian Geza Matrai, the man who had "jumped" Premier Kosygin of the Soviet Union in 1971. This group absorbed Droege as well as Armand Syksna. To distribute his neo-Nazi materials and handbills, however, Zündel usually recruited hangers-on from the entourages of Don Andrews and John Ross Taylor.

This Jekyll-and-Hyde existence was not without its personal toll. In 1975, his wife left him, fearful of death threats, as Zündel explained in an interview in *The Globe and Mail*.[30] Since his own profile was relatively low at the time, it is more likely that his wife simply tired of his obsessions, and of the somewhat unsavoury company that he kept. On the whole, Zündel managed to keep his dual identity intact. There were occasional lapses, as, for example, when Jewish businessmen dealing with him in a professional capacity received hate propaganda by mistake, rather than the material under contract. One client, on entering Zündel's shop in mid-1976, found "a huge rock-iron swastika on the wall, surrounded by portraits of Hitler and other Nazis."[31] Still, these incidents were exceptions, and few outsiders knew of his neo-Nazi persona. Hence, it was possible in 1976 for Hanoch Borda to write a rather straight story in *The Toronto Star* daily feature "Whatever Became of . . . ?" about the anti-Communist, ethnic candidate in the Liberal party leadership race in 1968.[32] Noting that "Ernest Zuendel" had now dropped the "e" from his first and last names, Borda did not realize that his subject had simply returned to the original German spelling. The article raised the possibility that Zündel might seek political office again: "I am still young!"

The screening of the television miniseries "Holocaust" in April 1978 provided Zündel with a new opportunity for publicity and notoriety. Under the cover of his newly launched front organization, "Concerned Parents of German Descent," he picketed the screening of the series and denounced its serialization in the press. The revelation, in Mark Bonokoski's column in *The Toronto Sun* (1978), of Zündel's outright neo-Nazism hardly deterred the self-appointed champion of German national honour at all. A few months later, in October 1978, together with his followers, he staged a series of pickets in Toronto, Hamilton and Oshawa against the film *The Boys From Brazil*. The protagonist in this film is Joseph Mengele, the "Angel of Death" of Auschwitz, responsible for sending hundreds of thousands to the crematoria, and infamous for his brutal medical experiments. Mengele is portrayed as attempting to revive Nazism through a variety of means, including the cloning of Adolf Hitler. In objecting to the film, Zündel declared: "It is unfortunate that German people are either depicted as bungling Colonel Klinks with a monocle or killers."[33] Subsequently, in January of 1979, he organized a series of poorly attended demonstrations before the Israeli Consulate, the West German Consulate and other German agencies and businesses to protest the screening of the "Holocaust" series in Germany. In his flyer, Zündel referred to East Germany, West Germany and Austria as "the three German puppet States," and the government of West Germany as the "West German Occupation Regime."[34] Significantly, the flyer bore the name of Ernst Christof Friedrich Zündel: at last, he had decided to cast off his double life and devote himself openly to the cause.

The Cause

Zündel utilized at least two postal drops: in Verdun, Quebec, and in Buffalo, New York. He relied on the latter particularly during the year when his postal privileges were suspended in Canada. His principal centre of operation, however, which served as headquarters, office and residence, was his house on Carlton Street, on the edge of downtown Toronto. An old, somewhat neglected, Victorian structure, it listed four different occupants on the front shingle: *Samisdat Publications; Carlton Galleries; Idea Centre, Zündel Studios*. They were, of course, one and the same. Other organizations could have been listed as well, e.g., "Western Unity Movement" and "Concerned Parents of German Descent" and, in 1981, "The German-Jewish Historical Commission." Zündel, in a classic image inversion, named his principal publishing organ "Samisdat" — the term used by Soviet dissidents to describe their underground publications. "Idea Centre" no doubt referred to his firm, "Great Ideas Advertising." What great ideas emanated from this Canadian Carlton underground?

The central idea is simple enough: the Holocaust never took place, being a monumental fabrication by Jews or Zionists (two terms used interchangeably) to extract reparation money from Germany for themselves and for the state of Israel. The German people constitute the principal group victimized by this Jewish scam. Not only is the Holocaust described as a "legend," but its alleged victims, as well as those engaged in a so-called remembrance, are characterized as "holocaust racketeers."[35] The Holocaust, Zündel asserts, is

> a gigantic hoax which cynically and diabolically aims at blackmailing the German people all over the world. . . . There were no "six million holocaust victims." There was no Nazi genocide programme. There were no gas chambers for "exterminating" Jews or anybody else. The Second World War caused tremendous suffering on all sides — German and Jew, Axis and Allied. None were the victors; all were the victims. But I repeat THERE WAS NO JEWISH HOLOCAUST.[36]

This claim is elaborated elsewhere: "My conclusion . . . is that no such extermination programme ever existed and that it is wartime hate propaganda masquerading as history."[37] Zündel is thus among the proponents of historical revisionism, or Holocaust denial – the new antisemitism of the late twentieth century. Integral to this allegation is the view that World War II was basically a conflict between two peoples, the Germans and the Jews, each with its own constellation of allies. In one of his flyers, this notion is explicit: "We do not deny that many Jews and their allies suffered and even died in World War II, nor do we omit to mention the fact that many millions of Germans and their allies suffered and died in that conflict."[38]

The apposition of Germans and Jews is, of course, misleading. "Germans" really stand in this context for Nazi Germany, a powerful, technologically advanced, fully armed, modern state, whereas the Jews in the Nazi era constituted an unarmed, defenceless, civilian population in a number of states where their status and security was more or less uncertain. Yet, in one sense, the apposition is not misleading; it reflects the brutal fact that, between 1939 and 1945, Nazi German did indeed fight two wars, World War II and a special war against the Jews. Zündel and other deniers regard the Jews as having "started the Hatemongering which led directly to World War II," and as having "declared a 'holy war' against Germany" in late March of 1933.[39] Ironically, this charge was inspired by an old headline in the London *Daily Express*, "Judea declares war on Germany";[40] the latter, however, referred to Jewish reactions outside of Germany to Nazi-inspired Jew-baiting after Hitler's accession to power in 1933, i.e., demonstrations and calls for the boycott of German goods.

According to Zündel, therefore, the Jews brought the war on themselves: this theme is recurrent. Thus, the Jews are blamed for *Kristallnacht* in November 1938: "Mysterious people wearing SS uniforms suddenly appeared out of nowhere, set fire to the synagogues and just as suddenly and mysteriously vanished. The same tactics as the Zionists used against Germany as partisans, maquis and as members of the Jewish Brigade: false uniforms, false documents, etc."[41] One truth is absolute as far as the propagandist is concerned: whatever happened to the Jews in the Nazi era, the Third Reich was not responsible: "in the Hitler period thousands of Jews emigrated to Palestine with the knowledge and assistance of the German authorities in co-operation with the Zionists ... [T]he German breakdown brought with it the breakdown of Jewish emigration."[42] In other words, all was well under Hitler; matters only took a turn for the worse when the Nazi order collapsed. After the war, as nature's ingrates, the Jews were consumed by a bloodthirsty passion for vengeance against Germans. "I must kill a German in cold blood and I must rape a German girl" are the words Zündel puts into Jewish mouths.[43] It was the Jews, he suggests in one of his newsletters, who tried to assassinate Konrad Adenauer in 1952.[44] Indeed, as well as concocting the Holocaust, the Jews, at once capitalists, communists and Freemasons, have been busy manipulating world events and the media for their own ends. Working directly, or through agents, they direct hate propaganda against the Islamic nations and eastern Europeans, as well as the Germans and the Japanese. "Zionists never stop at words. Their words of hate always precede their hateful deeds."[45] As Satanic assassins and murderers, they are responsible for mass tortures, deportations, murders, and all imaginable kinds of calamities — indeed, as one commentator has put it, "for evils that could be generated only by the four horsemen of the Apocalypse or by a full regiment of apocalyptic cavalry."[46] According to Zündel, they have well nigh achieved the destruction of the West and represent a constant danger to world peace. In one of his publications, *Samisdat Battletips*, he writes that, at times, Jewish deeds do compel Germans "to use fighting methods that are not exactly according to the rules of German chivalry, honesty and fairness."[47]

While "Jew" and "Zionist" are used interchangeably, "Zionist" is usually preferred for at least two reasons: (1) It can be more easily employed to denote something evil, e.g., as the "liars-for-hire," "pogrom-propagandists," and "Zion-nazis," whereas the term "Jew" includes Jewish groups, such as the hasidic Neturei Karta, as well as certain individuals, such as Alfred Lilienthal and Richard Arens, who are useful because they oppose the State of Israel on principle;[48] (2) "Zionist" is also preferable because the Canadian anti-hate law specifically limits the types of groups protected from victimization.[49] Zündel writes: "Zionism is a political movement, not a racial movement. . . . [T]herefore any criticism of Zionist policy cannot be 'racism'."[50] As, moreover, "no Zionist is 'a member of an identifiable group' under the Criminal Code, anymore than Liberals or Conservatives, can such criticism constitute "hate" under the Criminal Code?"[51] This awareness of the ambiguities of the law is evident elsewhere as well. "The so-called 'Holocaust' is a historical topic, not a 'race' or 'religion' and the condemnation of the one implies in no way a condemnation of the others."[52] Moreover, his plea continues, "dissent is not 'hate' and disagreement is not 'genocide', nor are my intentions 'hateful' or 'murderous'."[53] In a circular making a sales pitch for books and cassette tapes, he disassociates himself and one of his organizations expressly from part of the content: "although these items do not always reflect the viewpoints of the members or officers of Concerned Parents of German Descent, they have been selected for their generally informative and topical content."[54]

The proposition that no mass murder of Jews ever took place implies that there were no war criminals. It follows, therefore, that such persons found after the war must be defended against judicial action at all costs. The case of Albert Rauca is a good illustration. Rauca was accused of the murder of over 11 000 Lithuanian Jews in the ghetto of Kovno. In late 1982, he was extradited from Canada to West Germany, but died before standing trial. To Zündel, he was an innocent man persecuted by the media: "TRIAL BY MEDIA – MURDER BY MEDIA" is how Rauca's plight was described. The case of John Demjanjuk, an American citizen accused of having been "Ivan the Terrible," a sadistic and murderous guard at Treblinka, is another illustration. In late 1985, Demjanjuk's extradition to Israel to face trial was ordered. To Zündel, Demjanjuk is merely another innocent victim of a Jewish smear. His SS uniform was a fake, and his identification card as an SS concentration camp guard was "crudely forged, Soviet KGB-supplied."[55] Past political inaction regarding suspected Nazi war criminals is exploited to hinder any future action. "In Canada, almost a dozen Solicitor Generals and nearly half as many Prime Ministers treated Zionist agitation about 'war crimes' with the extreme caution the issue deserves. Were these men all derelict in their duties or were all these Canadians secret Nazi sympathizers?"[56] The extradition of Rauca under Solicitor General Robert Kaplan – a Jew – is ascribed to "Zionist pressure" in order "to turn his ministry into branch office for Simon Wiesenthal."[57] In Zündel's view, these alleged offenders are innocent, elderly persons, often anti-Communist, who only wish to live out their lives peacefully in the country of their adoption. "Individuals who have resided in Canada for 36 years without having run afoul of the law, many of them contributing valuable knowledge of Communism's inner workings and evil designs to Canada's defence, are now to be dragged out of retirement and old people's homes."[58] Such sacrificial lambs to a Jewish-instigated "war crimes hysteria" should be protected by responsible Canadians.

Zündel's other favourite passion is the glorification of the Third Reich. "We stand fast, true to our past and to our people," he proclaims to his German-language audience.[59] Which past he means is not in doubt. "The generation of our fathers had their Horst Wessel and Leo Schlageter! They sacrificed their life for our people. Can we do less?"[60] Wessel, a pimp and thug who died in a beer-cellar brawl, was immortalized in the Nazi hymn, "The Horst Wessel song"; Schlageter was no better.

Propaganda Techniques and Activities

Most of Zündel's material takes the form of circulars, leaflets and letters, including letters to the editor; occasionally, he also issues questionnaires. Some of his organizations have distinctive letterheads, e.g., Concerned Parents of German Descent, which features a pre-adolescent blonde girl against a dark background, curled up, fragile and fearful, with a teardrop descending from each eye. The pathos-inspiring caption underneath reads, "HELP US." The German-Jewish Historical Commission sports an imperial eagle in the top left corner and a Star of David on the right.

Zündel's style is also distinctive: a tightly packed text, sometimes with press clippings and commentaries appended. His mail-order operation purveys books, pamphlets, tapes, video cassettes, films, records and art. There are homemade audio-visual productions, as well as tapes of media interviews in which the self-appointed defender of Germany's honour is the star attraction. Fantasy in space, as well as fantasy in history, is included, with such titles as UFO's — Nazi Secret Weapon? or Little Known UFO Sightings from Around the World. The catalogue also shows that Samisdat serves as a clearing-house for Holocaust denial publications from all over the world. Authors represented are the Americans, Arthur Butz, with his The Hoax of the Twentieth Century, and Austin J. App, with his The Six Million Swindle; the Briton Richard Harwood, with his pamphlet Did Six Million Really Die?; the Germans, Udo Walendy, with (among other titles) Truth for Germany: The Guilt Question of the Second World War and Thies Christophersen, with his Auschwitz: Truth or Lie; the Frenchman Robert Faurisson, with his taped presentation ("in slide show form") on the 'fraudulent' character of the gas chambers; and the Swede Ditlieb Felderer on videotape with The Anne Frank Diary Hoax. For US$10, one can obtain South Africa Today, in which life in the last white bastion in Africa is described as it "really is."[61]

A great deal of Nazi material can be ordered, especially tapes of Hitler's speeches with a "simultaneous English-language translation." One can hear "the man whose voice captured the hearts and minds of millions of enthusiastic supporters." Other Nazi offerings include the movie Triumph of the Will, which is advertised as "The Third Reich's Version of the Woodstock Festival." For only $10, one can purchase Hitler Declares War on Poland or Hitler Declares War on America; one can also purchase "Hitler's sad but powerfully prophetic final broadcast from Berlin on January 1 1945." Besides Nazi speeches, the Music of the Third Reich can be obtained, offering "old favourites" like the "Horst Wessel Lied," and the "Badenweiler March," described as "Hitler's favourite." One can further assuage one's penchant for Nazi melodies with "Black shirt and Brown shirt Stormtrooper Songs and Marches." Art is also available; the Nazi aficionado can obtain for two dollars "large, beautiful illustrations of Nazi Secret Weapons suitable for framing." Devising a symbol based on the old runic form of the letter "Z," the ingenious artist-entrepreneur has marketed his own creation as "Thor's Warrior Belt Buckle," which comes with an "embossed Lightning Bolt of Thor," and the "Amulet of Thor," depicting "Thor's Lightning Bolt within the Sacred Sun Symbol." In both cases, the lightning bolt is the letter "Z."

Canadian politicians, both federal and provincial, were bombarded incessantly by Zündel. Elections provided special opportunities to canvass both incumbents and other candidates hungry for office. Another favourite target group was the media; on the whole, however, Zündel has been unsuccessful in his efforts to employ the media as a vehicle for the promulgation of his views. From time to time, he enjoyed modest success, usually in one of the smaller outlets. Thus, for example, in October 1979, a substantial letter to the editor from the tireless propagandist was printed in *The Mirror* of Middleton, Nova Scotia. This prompted a reply from an expatriate American living in Annapolis Royal, Nova Scotia, Ms. Barbara Bachrach Taylor, who questioned the editorial decision to publish Zündel, characterizing his letter as "very disturbing in many ways to many people in the community," and proceeded to answer it.[62] On another occasion, in June 1981, a Niagara Falls radio station put him on a three-hour phone-in program.

Zündel also distributed his material to libraries and schools across Canada. Invariably, the recipients contacted the Canadian Jewish Congress with expressions of concern. In late 1978, when a copy of Butz's *The Hoax of the Twentieth Century* was mailed to a junior high school principal in Toronto, and when it was discovered that other mailings were being planned, the Toronto Board of Education alerted all elementary and high school principals under its jurisdiction. Apart from sundry individuals and organizations, Zündel acquired a steady list of subscribers numbering between 700 and 800 in Canada.[63] His Canadian mailing list, however, pales in comparison to his infiltration of the antisemitic market in the United States. Here alone, he claims a mailing list of 29 000, although it is unclear as to whether this includes about 10 000 radio and TV stations. As part of his North American promotion campaign, he has placed full-page advertisements for Samisdat Publications in such magazines as *Soldier of Fortune* and *Saga*; he advertised also in *Marvel Comics*, until its pages were closed to him.[64]

Outside of North America, West Germany constitutes his principal target, where (as in Canada) his mass mailings are aimed at parliamentarians. In December 1983, he sent the book *Allied War Crimes* to all members of the West German parliament, acquiring in his homeland an ideologically sympathetic clientele for his mail order business. In December 1980, the Parliamentary Secretary of State for the Federal Ministry of Finance announced in the *Bundestag* that, between January 1, 1978 and December 30, 1979, "200 shipments of a right wing extremist and neo-Nazi content . . . books, periodicals, symbols, decorations, films, cassettes, records . . . came overwhelmingly from Canada."[65] He added that, as a result of similar shipments during the first half of 1980, prosecutions were being considered. On April 23, 1981, in a letter to the Canadian Jewish Congress, an official of the Ministry of Finance in Bonn identified the source of these materials as "Samisdat Publishers, 206 Carlton Street, Toronto, Ontario, Canada M5A 2L1."[66] A story on Simon Wiesenthal in

the *New York Times Magazine* of May 3, 1981, provides a particularly telling example of how Zündel's mailings filter through German society and
beyond. A Dutch tourist, vacationing in Upper Austria, was supplied with
antisemitic material by a gas station attendant, who, in turn, had obtained
the writings from a friend who was a Samisdat subscriber.[67]

Canada, the United States, Germany and Europe do not comprise the
limits of Zündel's reach; Australia is also within his orbit, as is the Middle
East. In the summer of 1981, 400 tapes in the Arabic language apparently
were shipped to opinion-makers in Arab Lands.[68] Zündel's claim to be in
touch with people in 45 to 47 countries in at least 14 different languages is
not impossible: an impressive operation indeed! This propaganda mill is
by no means an altruistic enterprise. While much of the material is mailed
unsolicited, much of it, together with his vast mail order enterprise, gen-
erates funds. Police sources estimate that a steady income ranging between
$60 000-100 000 per annum comes from his empire. Moreover, he has
frequently appealed directly for money. A report of the West German
Ministry of the Interior reveals that, in one fund-raising campaign in
1980, Zündel raised close to 100 000 German marks (the equivalent of
$50 000).[69] Even this estimate may be too modest. In one of his own pub-
lications in 1981, he pooh-poohed the German magazine *Der Spiegel* for
guessing that his total annual budget amounted to 100 000 marks, count-
ering indignantly that "Samisdat has long ago exceeded the figure . . . for
no organization that spans the world and reaches forty-five countries can
manage with so low a budget."[70]

An enterprising and ambitious man, Zündel regards himself not only as
a businessman and publisher, but also as an intellectual and author. Certainly, he is not unintelligent. His mission is both practical and theoretical,
combining his flair for organization with his flair for drama and exhibitionism. One forms an impression of an impresario—a P. T. Barnum of
Holocaust denial. Various circuses are staged at his home, grandiloquently
described in publicity literature as "Samisdat Lecture Hall." His guest per-
formers have included R. G. Dommerque (or Dommergue) from France
and J. J. Burg from West Germany. Other speakers have been Frank
Walus from the United States and Mrs. Rost Von Toningen, described as
the "wife of the former financial genius and Finance Minister of Hol-
land."[71] Zündel both arranged their public appearances and acted as publicity agent, setting up media interviews, etc.

Zündel's activities as an impresario are not restricted to Canada. As
early as the late summer of 1979, he was engaged (as Ernst Christof
Friedrich Zündel) in organizing a North American speaking tour and a
"historical symposium" for what he referred to as his "Samisdat Truth
Squad."[72] The projected itinerary was ambitious, including Los Angeles,
Las Vegas, Flagstaff, Denver, Topeka, Kansas City, St. Louis, Chicago,

Detroit, Buffalo, New York, Philadelphia and Washington. There is no indication that it ever took place, but Zündel, undaunted, planned a similar venture for his "flying 'truth-squads'" through his German-Jewish Historical Commission several years later.[73] Although the impresario might appear more comic than criminal, the image of buffoon is undoubtedly a device to disarm. It is evident that Zündel's ideas are toxic, his modus operandi carefully conceived, his connections in Canada and elsewhere most unsavoury and the consequences of his presence and his activities potentially dangerous.

An inkling of this danger was unearthed on March 24, 1981, in what *The Toronto Star* described as "the biggest crackdown on neo-Nazis since West Germany was founded in 1949."[74] West German police, raiding hundreds of homes of German neo-Nazis, discovered weapons, ammunition and explosives, as well as tens of thousands of copies of Zündel-type and Zündel-produced material, including, among other things, the diary of the top neo-Nazi leader, Manfred Roeder. Roeder, an ex-lawyer incarcerated in West Germany as a terrorist killer, claimed an organized network of radical right adherents stretching across 35 countries. His diary mentions Zündel. The report of the Ministry of the Interior in West Germany identified Gary Rex Lauck, George Dietz and Ernst Zündel as important North American contacts of the West German radical right and its principal suppliers of neo-Nazi and antisemitic propaganda. Lauck, of Lincoln, Nebraska, is the leader of the American Nazi party; Dietz, of Reedy, West Virginia, is a leading American white supremacist; Zündel, of course, has published in Dietz's publications, and has admitted that Dietz has visited his Toronto home.[75] There is a sinister aspect to these connections. As the propagandist himself has reported, he was once visited by the police who, in his words, "were looking for persons who might be on my mailing list who were wanted for murdering a certain person of Hungarian birth in Missouri. The murdered man was a National Socialist and possessed many of my writings."[76]

The Nielsen Incident

In late 1980, Zündel launched an attack on History 398Y, the Holocaust course taught at the University of Toronto by two Jewish history professors, Jacques Kornberg and Michael Marrus, using his follower, Ernst Nielsen. In a Zündel pamphlet, Nielsen is described as having been born in pre-war Germany, and having served during the war as "an air-sea rescue pilot."[77] Shot down on July 1, 1940, he was imprisoned in England, and subsequently in Canada. In the early 1950s, Nielsen came to Canada as an immigrant, no doubt emulating other German prisoners of war who had found their wartime imprisonment in Canada not particularly harsh and had seen the nation as a land of opportunity. In Zündel's account, however, Nielsen's settlement is portrayed as some kind of noble act for which Canadians should be profoundly thankful, rather than a piece of obvious opportunism. "Mr. Nielsen is not a man to bear grudges," the pamphlet states, "so he returned to Canada in the early 1950s and went to work as a productive member of our society."[78]

In the 1979-80 academic year, Nielsen audited History 398Y; in 1980-81, he enrolled formally in the course. It is quite clear that his purpose was not the pursuit of knowledge but to instruct the instructors and the rest of the class that the Holocaust was a hoax and a fraud. His tactics consisted of constant interruption and harassment. As a result, he was asked to withdraw from the course in both years. On November 10, 1980, in a letter to Professor William Callahan, Chairman of the Department of History, Nielsen appealed his second removal. His two-page letter, a précis of Holocaust denial, describes the books on the class reading list as "nothing but hate literature." The works "are not factual, but are Zionist incitements to hatred of Germans — living, dead, and yet unborn." Most of the authors cited in the course are "virulently anti-German, Zionist fiction writers, not historians."[79] Nielsen further argued that a professor teaching a course on this subject should "not be a member of any ethnic group or organization directly concerned with the Holocaust legend," adding that "no teacher be a Jew or a German, a Zionist or a Nazi."[80] (The apposition and the equation of Zionist and Nazi is significant.) The letter also provides a list of notorious Holocaust deniers in the guise of "recognized scientific authorities," adding the suggestion that the University of Toronto sponsor a 'Holocaust Symposium.' Nielsen concluded by offering to procure a number of his "authorities" for the benefit of the university community.

This offer, as well as the entire affair, was almost certainly masterminded by Zündel; Nielsen was merely his mouthpiece and agent provocateur. Indeed, Nielsen's letter to Callahan, both in form and content, is typical of Zündel's style and method. Nielsen, for example, wrote that he had "been assured of the backing of several local and international German ethnic organizations," but the only organization actually mentioned is the German-Jewish Historical Commission — one of Zündel's fronts.[81] Furthermore, another of Zündel's fronts, Concerned Parents of German Descent, avidly took up his defence. In a pamphlet titled *Holocaust Course Stirs Controversy,* Zündel referred to the professors in History 398Y as "Biased, predatory and mendacious Zionist advocates who write Holocaust fiction for profit," and railed against the "misallocation of . . . tax dollars."[82] Declaring that "the abuse of our University system through the inclusion of hateful, biased, unscrupulous Zionist propaganda posing as history must be halted," he listed the names and telephone numbers of a number of university officers and administrators, urging his supporters to phone in protest even on weekends.[83] The incident, however, although unpleasant for the instructors, as well as for the Jewish students in the class, only confirmed the importance of the course by providing an in-class illustration of the pathological antisemitism and nationalism that had kindled the flames of the Final Solution in the first place. As far as Zündel and Nielsen were concerned, their efforts were an exercise in futility.

Zündel and the Jewish Community

In the spring of 1981, Zündel applied to the Canadian Jewish Congress for the advertised position of director of the Holocaust Documentation Bank Project (designed to document extensively the memories of Canadian survivors). He penned his application on April 10, barely two weeks after the media had identified him as a major manufacturer and exporter of neo-Nazi and Holocaust denial literature. In his application (which, incidentally, contains his full name), he described himself as "the ideal candidate" for the position. He was, in his own words, "extremely knowledgeable and sensitive in regard to the Holocaust issue," and possessed "a good understanding of... Yiddish."[84] The applicant also generously offered the project his "substantial Holocaust archives."[85] The Congress sent Zündel a standard reply indicating that his application had arrived too late for consideration and that a director had been appointed already.

In 1981, Zündel announced that his German-Jewish Historical Commission was organizing a series of Holocaust symposia to begin in November or December of the same year. To raise funds, he addressed himself to Canadian business people, seeking minimum donations of $250. "Minimum donors" were to be granted "the German-Jewish Historical Commission's Community Fellowship Award," while "donors of $500 or more" were to be honoured at a "Symposium Celebrity Banquet."[86] Prominent Jewish scholars were asked to participate. Rabbi Gunther Plaut, for example, was invited to present his "Holocaustological viewpoints,"[87] and Michael Marrus, whom he had castigated as a mendacious Zionist during the Nielsen incident, was also invited: Zündel indicated that he knew that Marrus understood the "tremendous" educational value of "such a meeting of minds."[88] His needling of the Jewish community knew no bounds. On September 28, 1981, in the classified section of *The Toronto Star* carrying Rosh Hashanah greetings for that year, there was an entry from Ernst Zündel and Samisdat Publishers Limited wishing a "Happy New Year to all our Jewish friends."

Another favourite theme was his avowed intention to meet with representatives of the Jewish community, allegedly to work things out. He articulated that intention in a 1981 letter to Rabbi Plaut and repeated it in a letter of November 4, 1982, to the Canadian Jewish Congress, referring

(among other things) to the "rapidly-eroding Holocaust Legend" and the
"wild claims of mass-gassings."[89] In the later letter, he described himself
as "the only person in Canada who can virtually guarantee the Jewish
community a smooth transition from hysterical World War II hate propaganda to historical fact. . . ."[90] Obviously, nothing could and nothing did
come of such overtures, although this foregone conclusion did not
dampen his zeal. In February 1983, under his Concerned Parents of German Descent letterhead, he mailed a six-page letter to rabbis and Jewish
community leaders across Canada. Opening with "Shalom," he called
once more for dialogue, declaring that, because his previous gestures were
turned down by "senior members of certain influential Jewish community
organizations," he had chosen to go above their heads to communicate
directly with Jewish leaders in different parts of the country.[91] He offered
himself as a speaker to synagogues and Jewish Community Centres (for a
fee, of course) ending with the pious hope that the lies separating Jews and
Germans would be put to rest, and that the "liars" would be anathema-
tized.[92] In making his point, he actually referred to the Talmud, citing a
phrase which he paraphrased as stating "that a lie kills three persons — the
person lied about, the person who believes the lie and finally, the liar himself."[93]

   Predictably, the Jewish community was angered by these provocations,
which rubbed salt in wounds already opened by Zündel's neo-Nazi and
Holocaust denial activities. His tactics constituted a brutal assault on Jewish sensibilities, as well as a desecration of Hitler's victims. Through his
characterization of the Holocaust as a political-financial swindle, he also
defamed the Jewish people. Hence, he became another name on a list of
Canadian antisemites from whom redress was sought through legal
means. The search for legal protection against antisemitism in particular,
and racism in general, led finally to his indictment and trials.

Zündel's Creed

The Hitler We Loved and Why is the title of a 120-page (text and photographs) soft-cover book co-authored by a certain Christof Friedrich, who,
of course, was none other than Ernst Zündel. The journalist Mark
Bonokoski blew Zündel's cover in a *Toronto Sun* column of April 19, 1978,
showing that Zündel, using his middle names Christof Friedrich, had produced, with Eric Thomson, this panegyric work, published by White
Power Publications, of Reedy, West Virginia. White Power is headed by
George Dietz, who is also the editor and publisher of *The Liberty Bell*.
Zündel, in his interview with Bonokoski, neither confirmed nor denied
that he was Christof Friedrich, but Dietz definitely told Bonokoski that
Zündel and Friedrich were one and the same. Furthermore, on the day
after Bonokoski's column appeared, Zündel openly admitted that he was

Christof Friedrich in an interview with David Schatsky on CBC radio.[94] In February 1977, *The Liberty Bell* reviewed *The Hitler We Loved and Why* as follows: "(Friedrich) leaves no doubt about it. Hitler was well loved and loved in return, but this relationship between the Leader and his people was not the gushy, sickly-sweet effusion of an obese Jewish mother for her pimply, draft-dodging son. This was Aryan love. Strong, steady and uplifting."[95] Hitler is portrayed as a revered saint and holy man, a godly messiah who had rescued Germany with the salvationist ideology of white supremacy. Out of the rubble of a nation laid waste by the Jews, the Führer built an orderly, corruption-free, economically vibrant, and morally pure society in which "our men were manly and our women feminine," and "nutrition came before profit; quality before quantity."[96] Everyone was properly cared for in this Nazi utopia, including the animals (even in wartime, it seems, there were ration cards for dogs as well as people). The disabled, however, did not fare as well, since Hitler devised a eugenic solution for them. Nor, according to 'Friedrich,' "were idiots, morons and imbeciles possible under National Socialism, simply because such sorry specimens were not allowed to reproduce."[97] Unashamedly, medical certificates of fitness or unfitness for child-bearing in the Third Reich are reproduced. "For... National Socialism is simply the application of Nature's Laws to politics," and "Hitler, the artist and designer, designed a society for loving human beings, not plastic dummies."[98] Through this great struggle, the white Germanic messiah prevented "the end of White Civilization." Even in defeat, therefore, "we loved him because his spiritual presence prevented our sufferings and sorrows from overwhelming us."[99]

Friedrich's book concludes on a lofty note. Today, Hitler's spirit "soars beyond the shores of the White Man's home in Europe. Wherever we are, he is with us. WE LOVE YOU, ADOLPH HITLER!" Hitler has transcended death. He is a type of risen German Christ, a faith-figure in the eyes of his disciples. To have loved him in the past is to love him in the present and future, since Hitler is the same yesterday, today and forever. *The Hitler We Loved and Why* is Zündel's personal creed and a revelation of his soul. It provides us with a spiritual clue to the inner man.

The Man

What caused the post-Hitler, post-Nazi, apolitical youth to become an ardent neo-Nazi? What led the professional photo retoucher to become an amateur retoucher of history? It is not inconceivable that the answer to this question involves the troubling effect that a uni-dimensional portraiture of Germans in post-war literature had on an impressionable young mind. Zündel disclosed as much in an interview with Michael Tenstzen of *The Globe and Mail* (December 6, 1983). Male adventure magazines of the 1950s and 1960s, with their focus on German atrocity stories, left a mark on his psyche. "I said, this is ridiculous. I knew German soldiers in our village, my father and his brother were ones and they never talked about stories like this."[100] His concern with the negative stereotyping of Germans as "goose-stepping mass murderers or stupid figures of fun" is, in fact, shared by mainstream German Canadians. Many of the latter have been genuinely disturbed by the persistent focus of the media, film industry and popular literature with that narrow, albeit momentous, era in German history known as the Third Reich. For the most part, however, these German Canadians have acknowledged and confronted the reality of the Holocaust. Believing that there is no cause for shame in ethnic origin, since there is no such thing as collective guilt, they are proud of their heritage and their achievements in this country. Russell Doern, for example, a member of the Manitoba legislature, declared in an article in *Maclean's* magazine: "I, too, am angered, sickened and horrified by the terrible crimes committed by the Nazis—which the world must never forget." However, in his view, "German-Canadians must stand proud as an intelligent, industrious and sensitive people who have made a significant contribution to Canadian society since the first Germans came here 227 years ago. Only then will our history be placed in proper perspective."[101] In reply to a letter from Zündel, Reuben C. Baetz, Minister of Culture and Recreation for Ontario, wrote as follows (December 31, 1981)

> Stereotypes feed on ignorance. If the public knew the story of the German community, if it were aware of the contributions Canadians of German origins have made to all aspects of our life, if it were sensitive to the achievements of all that is best and finest in the German intellect and spirit, the kinds of objectionable materials you cite would lose both their credibility and their audience. In the long run this is the best solution, I believe.[102]

Zündel, however, for a variety of reasons, could never bring himself to take this approach. For one thing, he could not adopt the achievements of German Canadians because he refused to become one, never having taken out Canadian citizenship. To be sure, he did anglicize his name to "Ernest Zuendel" when he arrived first in Canada, but this did not last; indeed, sometime in the 1970s, he reaffirmed his Germanness by returning to the original spelling. If he could not bring himself to emulate German Canadians, he could have emulated the post-war German generation, that generation that confronted Nazi criminality, turned its back on Nazism, and built a new, vibrant and democratic society. He also could have emulated authentic German heroes, such as the anti-Nazi martyrs who died at Hitler's hands for their opposition to the dictatorship and its murderous policies. But he did not, The only Germany Zündel saw was a "vanquished and divided German nation"[103]—one he could neither associate with nor accept. Burdened by guilt, his pride and self-esteem injured, unable to honestly face the past and thereby transcend it, he opted to deny it. Since, moreover, Holocaust denial is but one side of a coin whose other side includes the glorification of the Third Reich, opposition to justice for Nazi war criminals and a desire to found a white supremacist Fourth Reich – in short, neo-Nazism – Zündel made the mental and emotional transition from a post-Hitler youth to a post-Hitler Hitlerite.

Certain personal character traits also played a part in his conversion, notably a strong capacity to suspend belief. The same irrationalism that allows him to ignore scientific evidence pointing to the non-existence of flying saucers allows him to ignore historical evidence pointing to one of the best-attested facts of all time: the Holocaust. Of course, it is likely that Zündel does not believe in flying saucers at all and these stories are merely for effect. It is also likely, as the court found in two trials, that he does not believe in his own propaganda claims, despite the immense psychological power of wilful self-deception. Holocaust denial is employed as the key device in marketing neo-Nazism. "If there was never any crime of mass murder then there are no mass murderers. Nazism and the Third Reich are whitewashed and made once again respectable and, what is most important . . . attractive."[104] There is also considerable evidence of egomania and exhibitionism. Zündel regards himself, and wants to be seen, as a man of substance, a leader, as the sort of pre-eminent individual described in his autobiography. He does not only love Hitler, he wishes to emulate him. This passion surely makes him design new neo-Nazi symbols, incorporating the initial of his own name. Apparently, he sees himself as a budding Führer; indeed, he described himself to *The Toronto Star* (October 3, 1978) as the "Führer of Concerned Parents of German Descent."[105] Another factor that may have affected his Nazi metamorphosis is a peculiar sense of shame about what he claims was his original pacifism. In his interview with Tenstzen of *The Globe*, he indicated that he "chose Canada because he knew the country did not have peacetime conscription."[106] Perhaps his militaristic neo-Nazism is in part a classic overcompensation for an earlier non-violent (religious?) ethic. Such things are not unknown. In any case, the ex-pacifist had marketed depictions of Nazi weapons and "warrior belt buckles," telling Dick Chapman of *The Toronto Sun* (in a March 25, 1981, interview) that, once the Bonn government is overthrown, "we [will] . . . certainly execute several hundred of the current crop of leaders in West Germany."[107] If Zündel was ever a pacifist, those days are clearly far behind.

Conclusion

Zündel did not emerge from a vacuum. Rather than constituting a new phenomenon, he belongs an an antisemitic continuum with pre-war roots — a continuum only temporarily interrupted in the early 1940s when Canada fought the Axis powers. After all, Adrien Arcand was his personal mentor: the Nazi, so to speak, fathered the neo-Nazi. Throughout his career, moreover, Zündel has been at the centre of a number of circles composed either of antisemites or the 'fellow travellers' of bigotry, all of which have intersected and continue to intersect at various points. The lines between such groups are often blurred, and there is a great deal of cross-fertilization. Zündel's special contribution to antisemitism in Canada has been the popularization of Holocaust denial, inspiring other Canadian antisemites, not merely the neo-Nazis, to adopt this ideology as their stock in trade. In addition, by means of his mailings overseas, he has placed Canada on the global map as a major exporter of neo-Nazi material, developing a large network of worldwide contacts. Probably more than any other Canadian antisemite, Zündel has been able to avail himself of these connections to expose his clientele to the broadest conceivable range of international antisemitic influence. Thus, as a premier antisemite both locally and internationally, he has deparochialized Canadian antisemitism, and made it 'world class.'

Notes

1 Formerly S. 177, now S. 181, *Criminal Code of Canada*.

2 Richard Harwood [alias Richard Verrall], *Did Six Million Really Die?* (Toronto: Samisdat, n.d.), p. 4.

3 See the "Report of the Board of Review Appointed to Inquire into the Facts and Circumstances Surrounding the Interim Prohibitory Order" on Samisdat Publishers Ltd., October 18, 1982, in Toronto Jewish Congress/Canadian Jewish Congress, Ontario Region Archives, JCRC papers MG8/S-Ernst Zündel (hereafter referred to as TJC-JCRC-Zündel).

4 Formerly S. 281.1-281.3, now Ss. 318, 319 and 320 of the *Criminal Code of Canada*.

5 Cal Millar, "Man Who Claims Holocaust Never Happened Facing Charge," *The Toronto Star*, December 7, 1983, in TJC-JCRC-Zündel.

6 Michael Tenstzen, "Man Charged by Auschwitz Survivor," *The Globe and Mail*, December 7, 1983, p. 3. Kelly McParland, "Weak Laws Let Hate Peddlers Flourish, Critics Say," *The Toronto Star*, October 13, 1983, p. A24. Both in TJC-JCRC-Zündel.

7 Alan Davies, "A Tale of Two Trials: Antisemitism in Canada 1985," *Holocaust and Genocide Studies* 4, 1 (1989): 77.

8 Letter to the editor from Zündel to *Canadian Lawyer* (May 1986): 5, in TJC-JCRC-Zündel. At the time of writing Christie had most recently appeared before the Supreme Court of Canada, representing Ross in late November and Taylor and Keegstra in early December 1989. Finta was acquitted at his trial.

9 See, for example, Peter K. McWilliams, *Canadian Criminal Evidence*, 3rd ed. (Aurora, ON: Canada Law Book, 1988), p. 24-1; *R. v. Zündel*, in *Criminal Reports*, 3rd series,

vol. 56, editor-in-chief Don Stuart (Toronto: Carswell, 1987), p. 55; and Ronald Joseph Delisle, *Evidence: Principles and Problems* (Toronto: Carswell, 1984), p. 90.

10 Paul Lungen, "Zundel: 'I Won', Despite Conviction," *The Canadian Jewish News*, March 7, 1985.

11 Kirk Makin, "Zundel Guilty, but Unrepentant," *The Globe and Mail*, March 1, 1985.

12 See Gabriel Weimann and Conrad Winn, *Hate on Trial: The Zündel Affair, The Media and Public Opinion in Canada* (Oakville: Mosaic Press, 1986).

13 See Manuel Prutschi, "Zündel Verdict Validated Use of 'False News' Law," *The Canadian Jewish News*, February 19, 1987.

14 Ernst Zündel graphic arts/photo retouching grade record (March 23), diploma (March 31, 1956), attached to his application to Canadian Jewish Congress (CJC) for position of Director of Holocaust Documentation Bank Project, all attached to CJCmemo, with enclosures. Rebecca Rosenberg (National Holocaust Remembrance Committee) to Ben Kayfetz, May 11, 1981, in TJC-JCRC-Zündel. Zündel's *The Hitler We Loved and Why* is inappropriately titled, since he had no real personal experience of Hitler at all. At his first trial, he claimed that he only provided the photographs.

15 Michael Tenstzen, "Hate Literature Factory in a Congenial Setting," *The Globe and Mail*, December 6, 1983, in TJC-JCRC-Zündel.

16 Two-page memo from B. G. Kayfetz to Rabbi Jordan Pearlson summarizing "Zündel's autobiography," including a number of direct quotations, January 25, 1982. Kayfetz had received a copy of the 64-page Zündel autobiography from Canada Post, for analysis, in TJC-JCRC-Zündel.

17 Zündel letter of application (April 10, 1981), re Directorship Holocaust Bank Documentation Project (see n. 14, above).

18 Memo, Kayfetz to Pearlson, "Zündel's autobiography" (n. 16, above).

19 Ibid.

20 Ibid.

21 Ibid.

22 Christof Friedrich and Eric Thomson, *The Hitler We Loved and Why* (Reedy, WV: White Power Publications, 1977), pp. 20, 23, in TJC-JCRC-Zündel.

23 Memo, Kayfetz to Pearlson, "Zündel autobiography."

24 *The Toronto Star*, daily feature "What Ever Became of . . . ?" by Hanoch Borda, attached to memo, B. G. Kayfetz to J. C. Horwitz and Rabbi Jordan Pearlson, "Re: Ernst Zündel" July 20, 1976, in TJC-JCRC-Zündel.

25 Memo, Kayfetz to Pearlson, "Zündel autobiography."

26 Photocopy of advertisement submitted as part of his curriculum vitae by Zündel to CJCre job application, Holocaust Documentation Bank Project (see n. 14, above).

27 Zündel flyer "Truth-Declassified," addressed to "Dear UFO Researcher." Part of enclosures re letter from B. G. Kayfetz to Morris Saltzman (CJC Vancouver) March 29, 1977, in TJC-JCRC-Zündel.

28 Ibid.

29 Ibid.

30 Tenstzen, "Hate Literature Factory."

31 Mark Bonokoski, "Neo Nazi Leads Protest," *The Toronto Sun*, April 19, 1978, p. 16, in TJC-JCRC-Zündel.

32 Borda, "What Ever Became of . . . ?"

33 Unidentified newspaper article reproduced in Zündel flyer headed "Achtung: Act Now—Prevent Pogroms Later," and attached to a letter to a subscriber from Eric Murray, an official with Concerned Parents of German Descent, March 14, 1979 in TJC-JCRC-Zündel.

34 Zündel flyer addressed to "Comrades," and beneath his signature he refers to his organization as SAMISDAT/COMBAT GROUP ZÜNDEL," in TJC-JCRC-Zündel.

35 See, for but one example, flyer headlined "Dear Member of Parliament you are being lied to . . . ," and flyer, "Dissent is not hate. The 'Holocaust' is a hoax!" both part of a packet of Zündel materials attached to memo, Bob Willmot (Canada Israel Committee) to Mark Silverberg (CJC Vancouver), cc'd to Ben Kayfetz, Ottawa, April 19, 1984, in TJC-JCRC-Zündel.

36 Zündel flyer on letterhead of Concerned Parents of German Descent addressed "To Our Fellow Canadians" [1979?], in TJC-JCRC-Zündel.

37 Zündel flyer addressed "To the People of Canada" and headlined "Attorney General Attempts Cover-Up and Censorship," attached to memo from B. G. Kayfetz to Morley Wolfe re "Zündel," December 3, 1979, in TJC-JCRC-Zündel.

38 Zündel flyer titled "Is This 'Racism' or 'Hate'?" addressed to politicians, media, clergy and educators as "A Final Appeal for Help!" attached to memo, Kayfetz to M. Wolfe re "Zündel," ibid.

39 Zündel flyer headlined "Who Are the Hatemongers, Agitators and Terrorists in Toronto?" p. 4, responding to an anti-Zündel march by the Jewish community, May 31, 1981, in TJC-JCRC-Zündel.

40 Ibid.

41 Memo, B. G. Kayfetz to Rabbi Jordan Pearlson and four others, re "Zündel's German Material," June 10, 1981, p. 2. It is a "précis" with, in some cases, "direct translation" by Kayfetz of four Zündel items, all bearing the title "*Samisdat*" in one form or another, made available to CJC by West German Consulate. Covering memo plus six pages of text in TJC-JCRC-Zündel.

42 Ibid.

43 Ibid.

44 Ibid.

45 Rene Jean Ravault, "A Content Analysis of Two Mailed 'Messages' Written by Mr. Ernst Zündel (Samisdat)," February 1982, p. 16, in TJC-JCRC-Zündel. Ravault is quoting from p. 1 of *Backlash*. The other publication analyzed was *The West, War and Islam*. Dr. Ravault, a Professor of Communications at the University of Quebec in Montreal did the analysis for Canada Post re the hearings into Zündel's mail ban, February-March, 1982.

46 Ibid., p. 11.

47 Ibid., p. 28.

48 However, these Jews are far from denying the Holocaust. Thus Richard Ahrens, in a press clipping that Zündel himself has reproduced, refers to "the massacre of Jews under Hitler in World War II," and declares unequivocally: "I saw some of the death camps." Yet Zündel, unfazed, includes this press clipping as part of a Holocaust denial mailing!

49 See p. 2. For a text of the law, refer to *Pocket Criminal Code 1990*, ed. Gary P. Rodrigues (Toronto: Carswell, 1989), pp. 166-68.

50 Zündel flyer, attached to memo, Kayfetz to M. Wolfe re "Zündel," December 3, 1979 (see above, n. 37).

51 Ibid.

52 Zündel flyer, "Let's Take a Closer Look," addressed to politicians, p. 4, headlined "Battle Royal Between Zündel and Zionists?" in TJC-JCRC-Zündel.

53 Third page of flyer "Dissent Is Not Hate," etc., part of packet attached to memo from Willmot to Silverberg, cc'd to Kayfetz (see above, n. 35).

54 P. 2 of Zündel circular headlined: "Kaplan: Justice, Vengeance or Hate?" attached to note from J. S. Midanik, Q.C. to Ben Kayfetz, July 7, 1980, in TJC-JCRC-Zündel.

55 Reverse side of flyer on letterhead of The German-Jewish Historical Commission titled "A Challenge to Simon Wiesenthal!" in TJC-JCRC-Zündel. The question of Demjanjuk's identity has not been settled by the Israeli courts.

56 Zündel flyer with Star of David on one side and symbol for poison on the other, titled "Hate, the 'New' Poison," p. 6 [late 1983], in TJC-JCRC-Zündel.

57 Ibid.

58 Ibid., p. 10.

59 Memo, Kayfetz to Pearlson et al., "Zündel's German mat'l," June 10, 1981, p. 5 (see above, n. 41).

60 Ibid., p. 3

61 Copy of six-page catalogue offerings from Samisdat Publishers, attached to letter from a University of Chicago Professor of Medicine (who received the material unsolicited) to the FBI in Washington, and cc'd to B'nai B'rith Anti-Defamation League, in TJC-JCRC-Zündel.

62 *The Mirror*, October 10, 1979, copy of press clipping attached to letter from Shirlee Fox (Atlantic Jewish Council) to Ben Kayfetz, November 30, 1979, in TJC-JCRC-Zündel.

63 So reported Shelley Kesselman, when covering Zündel's postal hearing for the *Ottawa Jewish Bulletin and Review*, March 19, 1982, p. 2.

64 Pat Cunningham, "Mail-Order Fascism Rewrites History," in *The Toronto Clarion*, November 28-December 11 [1979?], in TJC-JCRC-Zündel.

65 Text of exchange in the *Bundestag* as translated by Ben Kayfetz, attached to memo from Ben Kayfetz to Rabbi Jordan Pearlson re "Zündel," May 11, 1981, in TJC-JCRC-Zündel.

66 Copy of letter, as translated by Ben Kayfetz, attached to ibid.

67 Paul Hofman, "Austria's Jewish Question," in the *New York Times Magazine*, May 3, 1981, p. 144. Attached to memo from Ben Kayfetz to Jordan Pearlson, June 16, 1981, in TJC-JCRC-Zündel.

68 In "Zündel's German material," p. 4, attached to memo from Kayfetz to Pearlson, et al., June 10, 1981 (see above, n. 41).

69 George Jahn, "Bonn Fears Extremists Being Supported from Abroad," *The Globe and Mail*, October 30, 1981, p. 16, in TJC-JCRC-Zündel.

70 In "Zundel's German Mat'l," p. 5, attached to memo, Kayfetz to Pearlson, et al. (see above, n. 41).

71 Zündel flyer/invitation in German, on obverse side announcing program for June 4 and 5, 1983, attached to English translation by Ben Kayfetz, in TJC-JCRC-Zündel.

72 See Zündel flyer attached to memo from B. G. Kayfetz to Rabbi J. Pearlson and R. L. Ronson re "Zündel," August 20, 1979 and exchange of correspondence between Kayfetz and Milton Ellerin (American Jewish Committee), August 8 and 15, 1979, in TJC-JCRC-Zündel.

73 Zündel flyer on letterhead of The German-Jewish Historical Commission announcing the Commission's founding, with Zündel as "Director and Spokesman" and "Prof." R. G. Dommerque as "Research Analyst (France)." For specific reference see reverse side of flyer. In TJC-JCRC-Zündel.

74 "German Raids Find Metro Nazi Propaganda," *The Toronto Star*, March 25, 1981, p. A25 (UPI wire story), in TJC-JCRC-Zündel.

75 Ibid.; Dick Chapman, "Metro Man Branded a Nazi," *The Toronto Sun*, March 25, 1981, p. 22; "City Man Link to Nazis," *The Toronto Sun*, March 30, 1981, p. 27; Jahn, "Bonn Fears Extremists," p. 16; and Bonokoski, "Neo Nazi Leads Toronto Protest."

76 In Zündel's German material, p. 4, attached to memo, Kayfetz to Pearlson et al., June 10, 1981 (see above, n. 41).

77 Letter from Ernst Nielsen, "Student of History," to William J. Callahan, Chairman, Department of History, University of Toronto, November 10, 1980, turned into Zündel flyer headlined "Race Hatred Taught at University of Toronto," p. 2, attached to letter from Ray D. Wolfe to Ben Kayfetz, January 13, 1981, in TJC-JCRC-Zündel.

78 Ibid.

79 Ibid., p. 1.

80 Ibid., p. 2.

81 Ibid., p. 1.

82 Zündel flyer likewise attached to letter from R. D. Wolfe to Kayfetz, January 13, 1981 (see above, n. 77).

83 Ibid.

84 Zündel letter of application, April 10, 1981, re Holocaust Documentation Bank Project.

85 Ibid.

86 Zündel letter on German-Jewish Historical Commission letterhead, September 14, 1981, in TJC-JCRC-Zündel.

87 Zündel letter on German-Jewish Historical Commission letterhead, with attachments, to Rabbi W. Gunther Plaut, c/o *The Canadian Jewish News*, September 1, 1981, in TJC-JCRC-Zündel.

88 Zündel letter on German-Jewish Historical Commission letterhead with attachments, to Professor M. Marrus, c/o History Department, University of Toronto, September 14, 1981, attached to letter from Michael M. Marrus to Ben Kayfetz, September 24, 1981, in TJC-JCRC-Zündel.

89 Zündel letter in German to Rabbi Plaut [probably June 1981] on plain white paper and signed "the non-hater." Zündel letter on plain white paper to "The Directors," The Canadian Jewish Congress, November 4, 1982, in TJC-JCRC-Zündel.

90 Ibid.

91 Zündel letter attached to blue covering note sent by a recipient to Ben Kayfetz, p. 1, in TJC-JCRC-Zündel.

92 Ibid., p. 6.

93 Ibid.

94 Copy of a letter from B. G. Kayfetz to Mark Silverberg in Edmonton, April 16, 1979, in TJC-JCRC-Zündel.

95 Bonokoski, "Neo-Nazi Leads Toronto Protest."

96 Friedrich and Thomson, *The Hitler We Loved and Why*, pp. 72, 78.

97 Ibid., p. 83.

98 Ibid., pp. 77, 86.

99 Ibid., p. 116.

100 Tenstzen, "Hate Literature Factory."

101 Reproduced on a Zündel flyer, the obverse side of which bears the letterhead of the "Western Unity Movement" and the inscription "There is a world to be conquered together, or to be lost alone!" in TJC-JCRC-Zündel.

102 Reproduced on Zündel flyer, the obverse side of which has the letterhead of Concerned Parents of German Descent and the inscription at the foot of it "Only the Blind Can't See," in TJC-JCRC-Zündel.

103 Second page of flyer, "Dissent Is Not Hate," etc., part of packet attached to memo, Willmot to Silverberg, April 19, 1984 (see above, n. 35).

104 Manuel Prutschi, "Holocaust Denial Today," in *Canadian Jewry Today: Who's Who in Canadian Jewry*, ed. Edmond Y. Lipsitz (Downsview, ON: J.E.S.L. Educational Product, 1989), p. 31.

105 Reproduced in a Zündel flyer attached to letter from Eric Murray of Concerned Parents of German Descent to a subscriber, March 14, 1979 (see above, n. 33).

106 Tenstzen, "Hate Literature Factory."

107 Chapman, "Metro Man Branded a Nazi."

11

Jewish-Ukrainian Relations in Canada Since World War II and the Nazi War Criminal Issue

Harold Troper and Morton Weinfeld

In 1971 the Government of Canada declared its support for multiculturalism. This policy bestowed symbolic recognition on ethnicity as a positive
value in the evolution of the Canadian identity. Some observers belittled
the move as a cynical appeal to the Euro-ethnic vote; others saw it as an
attempt to undermine a burgeoning French-Canadian nationalism by
reducing the latter to the Quebec variant of a larger ethnic revival across
Canada; still others saw it as a legitimate effort to reassure Canadians of all
origins that their heritages were truly appreciated. Whatever its reasons,
the Canadian government promised to assist the ethnic communities in
preserving their cultures and traditions.[1] However, culture is not just
song, dance and food. It can also encompass attitudes incompatible with
Canadian social mores. Not the least of these pertain to intergroup hostility, for example, antisemitism, and the reactive feelings of animosity generated among Jews. What happens to old antipathies when they migrate to
liberal democracies? Do they persist? Do old-world conflicts serve a useful purpose in new-world diasporas? How are they acted out by those who
maintain them?

The encounter between Jews and Ukrainians in Canada during the past
40 years offers several clues. A residue of negative sentiment from their
400-year-old relationship with each other still infects the folk memory of
both peoples. Moreover, this sentiment encrusts the historical legacy precious to each as part of the cement that bonds its members together. All
ethnic bonding requires a sense of history, either real or imagined. His-

Notes for Chapter 11 are on pp. 297-300.

tory, according to D. V. Grawronski, "is the interpretive study of the recorded fact of bygone human beings and societies, the purpose of which is to develop an understanding of human actions, not only in the past but for the present as well."[2] As E. H. Carr has noted, the "facts of history cannot be purely objective, since they become facts of history by virtue of the significance attached to them by the historian."[3] What history reveals depends on where one digs for evidence, and where one digs depends on the questions one wants answered. The same events are interpreted differently by Jewish and Ukrainian historians with separate, if overlapping, visions of the past and its meaning for today.

The Jews and Ukrainians share a common geographic origin in eastern Europe. However, they do not share a common perspective. The central tenet of Ukrainian historical self-awareness defines the Ukrainians as an oppressed people, dispossessed of political sovereignty and struggling for national realization against foreign imperial might — Polish, Austro-Hungarian, Russian, German, Soviet — and their local agents. This *Nasha Pravda*, or community truth, and the sense of mission it engenders, is essential to understanding Ukrainian nationalism. It is also crucial to future survival. Canadian Jews also attach priority to collective survival, but their historical narrative — rooted in the same soil — is not a tale of the suppression of national aspiration, but of a long spiral of antisemitism leading eventually to the Holocaust.

Two Narratives

Jews and Ukrainians play a role in each other's narratives. To the Ukrainians, the Jews in the Ukraine were not attached to the land but to their own marginality. Either for profit or security, they joined those suppressing the legitimate aspirations of Ukrainian nationhood, serving as intermediaries between the Ukrainians and their enemies. They were the tax collectors, liquor dealers, innkeepers, estate managers and moneylenders who benefitted from oppression. To the Jews, on the other hand, the Ukrainians were the oppressors, squeezing the Jews between a tyrannical regime and the violence of local peasants. The ground was forever shifting under Jewish feet. They yearned for security, but rare was the Jewish generation that did not feel the edge of the sword.[4]

Like ghosts stalking the landscape of historical memory, these divergent visions haunt the two worlds today. For Ukrainians, the 1648 rebellion led by Bohdan Khmelnytsky was an early chapter in the struggle for national self-determination. That it ultimately failed does not detract from Khmelnytsky's place in the pantheon of national heroes. For Jews, however, his name is cursed. His rebellion is associated with wholesale slaughter, and he is regarded as a spiritual forefather of Hitler.[5] In the same vein, for Ukrainians, the flickering light of an independent nation glowed briefly with the short-lived Ukrainian National Republic, 1917-21 — a glorious national rebirth smothered in its infancy by Soviet power. The Petlura government, in Ukrainian memory, not only sought to realize these aspirations, but also to ensure the security of its Jewish minority. It legislated an end to discrimination, and welcomed full Jewish participation in the state, while encouraging Jewish communal life. Once again, Jewish historical memory differs. The Petlura regime is recalled as an era of savage pogroms. Its model Jewish legislation was never enforced, and, far from encouraging Jewish communal life, the government silently approved attacks by an antisemitic populace. Instead of a moment of enlightenment, the 1917-21 republic is a black mark in Jewish annals — another step down the road to mass destruction.[6]

World War II also divides Jews and Ukrainians. For the former, the Holocaust could not have happened without the wilful participation of local populations. Nowhere, many Jews believe, was that more readily given than in the Ukraine; nowhere were local people more brutal; nowhere do they bear so great a responsibility for the murder of millions. The Nazis only licensed a longstanding and ferocious Ukrainian antisemitism. The Ukrainian narrative is different. At least the Jews could identify their enemies. For the Ukrainians, trapped between Soviet and Nazi armies, each threatening to grind them to dust, the choice was painful. For some, active or passive collaboration with the Nazis offered a better chance of physical and national survival than with the dreaded Soviets, to whom the Jews looked for salvation. If some Jews collaborated with the Soviets against their Ukrainian neighbours, a few Ukrainian "criminals," it is conceded, participated in the Holocaust. Others, led in spirit and deed by the Ukrainian Catholic Metropolitan, A. Sheptytsky, risked their own lives to save Jews. Sheptytsky instructed his church officials to hide local Jews, while issuing pastoral letters against Ukrainian cooperation in anti-Jewish actions and protesting directly to Himmler. This, the Ukrainians note, is far more than was done by the Vatican.[7] Despite Sheptytsky's efforts, however, few Jewish survivors recall the churches of the Ukraine, both Catholic and Orthodox, as friendly. (As secular institutions had been repressed, the churches had become centres of nationalist and, all too often, antisemitic activity.)

Canada

Today, in Canada, far removed from the Ukraine, these two separate and incompatible narratives still determine diaspora Ukrainian and Jewish self-definitions. For (arguably) the two most survivalist ethnic communities in the country, the inheritance of historical pain — for Ukrainians, the denial of a legitimate homeland and, for Jews, the experience of physical annihilation, the last act in an age-old antisemitic drama — acts as a power-

ful psychological and social bond. Although memory is blurred for Canadian-born generations, the natural conviction that each people was an
instrument of the other's suffering remains ingrained. However, in a liberal and democratic society, such antipathies cannot be uttered publicly.
Hence, these grievances have not caused conflict until recently. For the
most part, the communities have remained two solitudes: a result, in part,
of separate immigration patterns. While both peoples entered Canada soon
after the turn of the century, each found a separate niche. Until World
War II, the Ukrainians were predominately rural and western, whereas the
Jews congregated in eastern cities. There was some Ukrainian contact
with Jewish merchants on the prairies, and Jewish contact with Ukrainians in the immigrant north-end of Winnipeg, but institutional encounter
was rare.

After 1945, the character of both communities changed. Newly arrived
survivors from Europe, the decline of antisemitism in the larger civic culture, widespread economic prosperity, professionalization, social mobility
and pride in the rebirth of a Jewish national state after the European catas-
trophe reshaped and re-invigorated Canadian Jewish life. Today, Canada's
300 000 Jews (about 66 percent Canadian born) enjoy the highest standard
of living of any Canadian group and support the most elaborate network
of intra-ethnic organizational structures in Canada. The post-war era also
reshaped Ukrainian Canadian life. Post-war arrivals, largely 'displaced
persons', introduced a new ideological fervour and nationalist sentiment
into the community, now about 600 000 strong. Once settled in Canada,
they renewed their communal tie with, and concern for, the Ukraine.
Many were committed to a militant anti-communism, combined with a
strong commitment to their own culture. Moreover, these post-war
Ukrainians located in the large urban centres of eastern Canada, already
settled by Jews. Through organizational skill and nationalist zeal, they
soon influenced, if not dominated, the entire Canadian-Ukrainian community, making their agenda, to a greater or lesser degree, its agenda.[8]
Survival was paramount, as it was for the Jewish community, since assimilation (more advanced among the Ukrainians) was a common danger. The
Ukrainians have found it more difficult to persuade their constituency —
now more than 90 percent Canadian born — to assume communal burdens as well as to retain the old language and other loyalties. Nevertheless,
they are second only to Canadian Jews in this respect. All threats to collective identity are to be opposed.

In 1985, the integrity and good name of the community and the sanctity
of its nationalist struggle suddenly faced a new crisis. The issue of Nazi
war criminals in Canada came to the surface, and the smouldering embers
of historical antipathy from the old world suddenly ignited again in the
new. In fact, they had been burning since the 1950s.

The Nazi Issue

Nothing illustrates Jewish-Ukrainian sensitivities as well as the case of the Galicia Division. Late in 1943, as the Nazis sought to stem the tide of Soviet advance, Berlin authorized the organization of a Ukrainian *Waffen* S.S. unit. By the time it was ready for its "counter insurgency" duties, the military needs of the eastern front took precedence. In 1944 the unit was deployed to confront seasoned Red Army troops, only to be decimated at the Battle of Brody. Of the almost 11 000 troops who went into combat, barely 3000 survived. The Nazis, now in full retreat, brought the ragtag remnant back to division strength by pressing into its ranks other Ukrainians, including men who had assisted the Nazi occupation in various capacities and were retreating westward with their masters. However, before the reconstituted Galicia could be tested again on the battlefield, it surrendered en masse to British forces.[9] The division underwent routine security investigation in prisoner-of-war camps in northern Italy and received a clean bill of health. Soviet authorities attempted to secure its return; almost to a man, the Galicia members refused. They claimed not to be Nazis, but local nationalists who had enlisted to fight the hated Russians. Furthermore, they had expected to become the core of the new army of an independent Ukrainian state that would arise Phoenix-like out of the ashes of war. As a Nazi military unit, the Galicia was ineligible for displaced persons' status, and, as part of the S.S., its members were also ineligible for most overseas resettlement programs. The prisoners were transferred to Britain, where they attracted the attention of the Ukrainian-Canadian community. After assuming responsibility for the comfort needs of the ex-soldiers, the latter quietly lobbied the Canadian government to allow them to enter Canada. At first, the government resisted; having belonged to the notorious S.S., Galicia members automatically were barred. However, in July 1950, as the nation was opening its doors wider to European immigration, especially that of displaced persons, the cabinet exempted the Galicia from this prohibition.[10]

The Jewish community was stunned. Its organizational umbrella, the Canadian Jewish Congress, protested the federal move as a moral outrage. Its leaders reminded the government that the S.S. had been designated by the Allies as a criminal unit. With the direct role played in the mass murder of Polish and Ukrainian Jewry by the S.S. and local collaborators, there was no doubt in Jewish minds that the Galicia had blood on its hands.[11] The government, taken aback by the Jewish reaction and negative press coverage, offered a compromise. It would forestall the admission of Galicia members temporarily in order to allow the Congress sufficient time to present hard evidence of criminal acts implicating specific individuals.

The delay was welcomed; at first the position was taken that it should be sufficient to show that the Galicia, as an integral part of the S.S. (made up entirely of volunteers), forfeited eligibility for immigration for that reason. This argument failed because of the cabinet ruling. If individuals were to be prohibited, evidence of criminal acts had to be provided. The Congress tapped every source available, but came up empty. Perhaps because of the poor state of available records in the early 1950s or perhaps because no wrong-doing had transpired, the Jewish network produced neither evidence implicating the Galicia as a unit in specific criminal acts nor evidence against individual Galicia members. Out of patience with Jewish requests for further delays, and under continued pressure from the Ukrainian community, the government authorized immigration.[12]

The Jewish Congress was defeated, but not converted. Doubts persisted. A number of Jews believed that many unrepentant Nazi sympathizers, if not actual war criminals, were among both the Galicia members and other east European displaced persons entering Canada at the time, including many Ukrainians. Spokesmen for the Ukrainian community, in turn, saw Jewish agitation as little more than age-old Ukrainian-baiting. As Ukrainian organizational life in Canada became ever more nationalist and anti-Soviet, accusations that Jews would stop at nothing to undermine the Ukrainian national cause grew more shrill. Relations between Jewish and east European communal organizations — at best, cool, formal and distant, especially with the Ukrainians — began to deteriorate. During the 1950s and 1960s, new periodic eruptions charged the atmosphere further. In 1957, for example, when the Ukrainian nationalist leader, Andreii Melynk, was scheduled to visit Canada to celebrate the twenty-fifth anniversary of the birth of his movement, the editor of an independent Winnipeg Jewish newspaper lashed out against one "famous in Poland as a ruthless anti-Semite," and an active Nazi agent involved in the ruthless murder of Ukrainian Jews.[13] As these charges spilled into the public press, the Ukrainian community leaders responded with anger. Fearing the Melynk visit would be spoiled and, indeed, their national cause placed under a cloud of suspicion, they demanded an apology.[14] Holocaust survivers bristled at this notion, and Congress leaders again scrambled to determine whether or not the accusations against Melynk contained any truth. If so, the charge would stand. If, however, no proof was found, there would have to be an apology, no matter how unpalatable. No incriminating evidence emerged, and, in the end, the editor was forced to retract and apologize.[15]

The incident receded into memory. There were others, but not many. This was not because Jews and Ukrainians found cause for cooperation, but because their institutional relations were so restricted that even frictions were rare. Through the 1960s, each community, uneasily aware of the other, kept its distance.

Rapprochement

In the 1970s, some desire, albeit one-sided, arose for rapprochement, largely at Ukrainian initiative. In part, this was a reflection of demographic shifts. A new generation of Canadian-born, urban and educated Ukrainian and Jewish professionals were gradually making their weight felt within their respective community councils. Some, especially some Ukrainians, were ready for detente. The younger leaders were not immune to old-world feelings, nor did the older generation readily step aside in their favour, but many saw much to gain from better relations. Among the Ukrainians, the desire for some measure of reconciliation arose in part out of a fear that they were being turned into historical villains. Unfortunately, their *Nasha Pravda*, or community truth, collided with the Western understanding of the Holocaust and its roots in European antisemitism. Increasingly, the Ukrainian national drama and its vale of tears was overshadowed in Canada by a more popular reading of the past transfixed on Jewish suffering. Not only was their national struggle ignored, but the Ukrainians found themselves regarded in an unsavoury light: something they resented greatly. The more the Holocaust captured the public and scholarly imagination, the more their self-assertion was dismissed as a licence to murder Jewish men, women and children, with their heroes vilified as collaborators and murderers. To a community fighting to keep its collective identity alive, this trend had to be resisted. Holocaust denial was out of the question; however, if common cause could be established with the Jewish community in areas of mutual interest—interethnic relations in Canada, the Soviet question, joint approaches to government—the heat might be reduced.

There were also social and economic reasons to enlist Jewish cooperation. The art of survival was an art in which Jews were thoroughly versed, having lived as a diaspora minority for two millennia. The Ukrainian diaspora, by contrast, was barely a century old. Furthermore, the Jews had blazed a successful path through North American urban business and professional life. As more Ukrainians began to emulate this example during the 1970s, one-to-one contacts increased, along with an appreciation of the Jewish model of social mobility. The fact that their rivals had managed to carve a place for themselves without sacrificing Jewish continuity added to its appeal. Economic and political security, pride in local cultural enrichment and in the Jewish national homeland, all invigorated the Jewish diaspora—a feeling that Israel's electrifying victory in the 1967 'six day war' did nothing to dissipate. This was not lost on the Ukrainians. That diaspora Jewry could celebrate the rebirth of political independence after 2000 years of statelessness stood as a beacon of hope to a Ukrainian diaspora dispossessed of its homeland. Moreover, if the Jews (and Israelis) could reach an accommodation with Germany and the Germans, why not with the Ukrainians? Some Ukrainians also believed that they could offer reciprocity in forgiveness; after all, in their own eyes, they had much to forgive.

However, nothing could have been more remote from Canadian Jewry than this notion. Nor did most Jews understand, let alone sympathize with, the problems of Ukrainian ethnic survival; they knew little or nothing of the agonies of Ukrainian history, whether in the Ukraine itself or in the diaspora. If anything, Jewish leaders regarded the Ukrainian community as among the most powerful voices in Canada, if not through organizational strength, then through the sheer weight of numbers. They felt frustrated in their own lobbying efforts, even regarding such basic matters as anti-boycott legislation (to prohibit foreign firms or governments from demanding discrimination against Canadian Jews or other Canadian citizens as a business precondition, particularly in the Middle East).[16] Ukrainian pressure, on the other hand, seemed to produce the federal policy of multiculturalism — an achievement which the Jewish polity, for all its supposed influence, could not match. If the Jewish leaders needed additional proof of the surging strength of the Ukrainian polity, it arrived on October 9, 1971, the day after the formal announcement of the multiculturalism policy in the House of Commons. The prime minister had flown to Winnipeg to address the tenth tri-annual congress of the Ukrainian Canadian Committee (UCC), the Ukrainian-Canadian umbrella organization. In his banquet speech, he congratulated Ukrainians for helping to reshape Canadian social policy — in other words, multiculturalism! His platitudinous words, however, were less important than his presence. By *reporting in* to the UCC, so to speak, he had lent credence to the notion that a new era of ethnic political influence, especially Ukrainian, was dawning in Canada.[17]

Consequently, better Ukrainian-Jewish relations were not an easy task. Modest efforts were launched in Winnipeg, where the Jewish community was dwarfed in size and political weight. In Toronto as well, the seat of Ukrainian nationalist sentiment, several attempts at bridge-building were started. In the autumn of 1974, the head of the UCC in Ontario invited members of the Canadian Jewish Congress executive in Toronto to dinner. "Our discussion" a Congress staff member recorded later, "ranged across the whole spectrum of Jewish-Ukrainian concerns. We touched, of course, on the animosity and suspicion that persists in certain quarters on both sides. It was felt this might be to some extent a form of generation gap which may diminish in the course of time." In the meantime, it was agreed, informal contacts should continue in spite of the negative feelings such contacts might generate among militant factions in both communities.[18]

Hostility could arise even on safe issues, such as Soviet violations of human rights. The Jewish position called for Soviet adherence to freedom of religion and freedom to migrate, as set down in the Soviet Constitution. Thus, Congress officials publicly supported the release of the imprisoned Ukrainian activist Valentin Moroz in 1974. Yet even this symbolic gesture raised ire in the Jewish community, predominantly that of Holocaust survivors for whom memories of Jewish maltreatment in the Ukraine remained fresh.[19] A Jewish statement of support for Moroz's human rights made common cause with organizations regarded by some Jews as little more than a collection of unreconstructed fascists and Nazi sympathizers.[20] However, the Moroz statement managed to still several of the more strident anti-Jewish voices in the Ukrainian community. Alex Epstein, a Toronto Jewish lawyer with personal contacts, regarded it as an excellent first step in the direction of better relations. Ukrainians, he informed the Jewish Congress, "were deeply moved by this expression of sympathy and support from the Jewish community." The gesture could not but help the "young and liberal" leadership coming to the fore "in stifling anti-Semitic remarks and statements made by other Ukrainians."[21]

The War Criminal Issue

One issue, however, derailed these modest steps toward better working relations: the problem of Nazi war criminals. Their presence in Canada was long a Jewish concern. With the entry of Galicia Division members in 1951 and the mass immigration of displaced persons, Canadian Jews were convinced that some — nobody knew exactly how many — Nazi activists, collaborators and war criminals had managed to conceal themselves in the nation. All efforts to enlist government cooperation in a manhunt, or even to interest the Canadian public, had failed. When pressed on the matter, Canadian authorities always responded that they lacked a legal framework for action, but the suspicion that the government did not care could not be suppressed. Jewish demands were easily ignored; there was no groundswell of public outrage to support them. The Holocaust, it seemed, was a Jewish obsession, and war criminals a parochial Jewish concern.[22] Not surprisingly, this indifference had an inverse effect. As anger that such individuals should go unpunished grew stronger in the Jewish community, the cause of prosecution rose higher on its agenda. A series of events served to intensify this feeling. In May 1960, the State of Israel announced the apprehension of the Nazi arch-murderer Adolf Eichmann. His trial in Jerusalem for "crimes against humanity," and, under Israeli law, "crimes against the Jewish people," exposed Jews and non-Jews alike to the reality of the Holocaust as no other event had done. Eichmann's trial was a crucial first step in turning a private Jewish agony into part of the Western historical legacy: an event of monumental proportions destined to plague historians, moral philosophers and the human conscience. After the trial, thoughtful persons could no longer dismiss the Final Solution as a momentary excess of a few extremists; it was established now as the centrepiece of a political and racial ideology with deep historical roots, commanding the loyalty of millions. It was also a labour-intensive venture conducted with the wilful cooperation of a seemingly endless supply of assistants, German and non-German alike.[23]

In 1964, shortly after Eichmann's execution, world Jewry, including Canadian Jewry, was galvanized by the news that the West German statute of limitations would soon halt all war crimes prosecutions in Germany. The Canadian Jewish leadership prevailed on the Canadian government to intercede with the West German authorities, reminding the prime minister that Canada had "no statute of limitations whatever for crimes involving murder or, for that matter, other homicidal crimes." Pearson agreed, and Canada lent its voice to the world outcry. West Germany responded with a 10-year moratorium on the implementation of its statute of limitations in the case of war crimes. However, despite this victory, the sad irony remained that it was easier to get Canadian officials to protest against legal sanctuary for Nazi war criminals in West Germany than to act against alleged Nazi war criminals in Canada.[24] The matter was exacerbated in 1965, when a small band of self-styled Canadian Nazis organized a series of public outdoor rallies in Toronto and Montreal. They gathered in a Toronto park replete with Nazi regalia and swastika flags, gaining attention from the press and television. Jewish community reaction was swift. Backed by civic, media, labour and church leaders, the Canadian Jewish Congress demanded appropriate legal action from the civic authorities. Some Jews, especially Holocaust survivors, demanded more. The latter constituted an important voice in Jewish life, commanding immense moral authority. They organized counter-demonstrations, which occasionally spilled over into violence; also, youthful Jewish self-defence groups sprang up. One self-defence group, N34 (named for Newton's Third Law: for every action there is an equal and opposite reaction) joined with the survivors to confront the neo-Nazis.[25] Newly founded survivor organizations won popular support for the memorialization of the Holocaust, Holocaust education in the schools, and renewed pressure on the government to deal with the war criminals question.[26]

In 1967, during the six-day Arab-Israeli war, Canadian Jewry again envisioned an apocalypse. For two weeks, the worst was feared. Was it possible that, for the second time in a quarter century, a major Jewish community faced annihilation? The lightning Israeli victory removed the immediate threat, but the episode touched Canadian Jewry as had no other post-war event. What might have happened cemented bonds between Canadian Jewry and Israel, as terrible memories were rekindled.

Renewed demands that Nazi war criminals living in Canada be brought to justice followed naturally. Yet all efforts to persuade the government to investigate its resident criminals failed; even efforts to build a broad coalition of Canadian groups in support of remedial action failed. Canada was an insecure nation with a fragile collective identity, preoccupied with national unity. The Nazi war criminal issue was simply too foreign, too reminiscent of things better forgotten and too disassociated from the prosperous calm of civil life to engage the country in a crusade.

In the United States Jewish lobbying had had more impact. Following the 1973 deportation to West Germany of Hermine Braunsteinner Ryan, the "mare of Maidanek," American immigration and justice officials took steps leading to the creation in 1979 of the Office of Special Investigation (OSI) within the Department of Justice to root out Nazi war criminals and to remove them from the country. Canadian Jewish leaders applauded the American initiatives and demanded that Canada follow suit.[27] No sooner had the OSI begun investigating several post-war Ukrainian immigrants to the United States, however, when trouble erupted. Leaders of the American Ukrainian community began attacking the OSI as anti-Ukrainian, suggesting that it was in bed with the Soviets. Ukrainian Canadians also took alarm. They doubted that their own government would follow the American example, but the Jewish campaign remained a source of concern.

In the spring of 1977, at a luncheon in Toronto of officials of the Canadian Jewish Congress and the World Congress of Free Ukrainians, the Ukrainian secretary-general assured his Jewish counterparts "that his organization would not harbour war criminals knowingly and he was interested in seeing a positive policy on this question was enacted."[28] The pledge seemed unequivocal, but it required little to test it. Several months later, an anonymous flyer was mailed to Ukrainian organizations across Canada requesting information on an individual said to have been a ranking Ukrainian police official accused in the death of several hundred Jews, and to be living in Canada. "It is hoped" the flyer stated, "people in Ukrainian circles will be able to find Solhan." Any information was to be sent to Wiesenthal's documentation centre in Vienna. The flyer was signed "a concerned Canadian."[29] Perhaps smarting at the suggestion that Ukrainians could snap their fingers and deliver up Nazi war criminals, the secretary-general, in a letter to a Congress staff member who had attended the earlier luncheon, affirmed Ukrainian cooperation "in bringing to justice any individual who has been responsible for premeditated murder," but also noted "a number of mistaken accusations against innocent individuals which were legally challenged and withdrawn." As the accuser remained nameless, the accused could not defend himself. Hinting that the CJC was either behind the flyer, or knew who was, the secretary-general demanded that henceforth Jewish officials communicate directly and openly with "the numerous central organizations of our community in the world, rather than by anonymous channels."[30]

Congress officials were taken aback by the charge that they were behind the anonymous flyer and amazed at the notion that a word could rein in its authors. This monolithic view was as misleading with respect to the Jewish community as it was with respect to the Ukrainian. Furthermore, was not the Ukrainian protest somewhat disingenuous?[31] The offending flyer was a request for information rather than an accusation of guilt. What of the ringing declaration of support for bringing war criminals to justice? "On reading of the (secretary-general's) letter," one Congress staff member concluded, "I see it is something less than that."[32]

The war criminal issue concerned both communities. However, the Jewish effort to spark government action was not succeeding. To various delegations, petitions, protest resolutions and personal representations, the answer was consistent: as there was no legal framework in Canadian law under which to act, there was no justification for police investigations or for court proceedings.

Legal and Political Considerations

One door remained open. If another country should request the extradition of a Canadian resident, the Canadian legal and administrative machinery could oblige. However, even here, there were limits. Canada could not initiate action, but merely respond. Nor could all countries apply. The list of nations with which Canada had negotiated extradition treaties was restricted, and it was extremely unlikely that the government would respond favourably to a request from, for example, the Soviet Union, with its dubious system of justice. Hence, eastern Europeans were fairly safe in this respect.[33] In the late 1970s, after years of attempting to sway federal authorities by emphasizing the moral injustice of allowing Nazi war criminals to live freely in Canada, the Canadian Jewish Congress shifted its strategy, challenging the government's long-standing position that Canadian law contained no remedy. It was determined to show the availability of a series of legal options. In so doing, it also hoped to prove that a lack of political will, not a lack of legal means, sheltered the war criminals from prosecution. If, indeed, this was true, why was it true? Had not the Holocaust become part of Western history? Did not Canadian Jewry enjoy a high profile in the Canadian social mosaic? Did not individual Jews enjoy previously undreamed of positions of authority, prestige and responsibility in Canadian society? Was not the Canadian Jewish lobby the envy of other ethnic communities?

The answer has several parts. The Liberal government of the day was the creature of Pierre Trudeau. While Trudeau's personal interest in the war criminal issue has not been fully determined,[34] there is little doubt that the prime minister, a student of history, drew a sharp line between the past and the present. The man who had opened the window of opportunity to Jews in public service as no other prime minister had ever done — appointing a Jewish chief justice of the Supreme Court of Canada, appointing three Jews to his last cabinet, appointing a Jewish ambassador in Washington, and peppering his personal staff with Jews — had little patience with the special pleading of the Jewish community (or, for that matter of other ethnic lobbies). He did not oppose ethnic continuity, nor did he reject the right of any group to petition for the relief of grievances, but, from his point of view, the national interest came first, and few, if any, ethnic interests were one with the national interest. If he ever considered the war criminal issue, probably he regarded it as a parochial Jewish concern with little broad support in the nation; if pursued, it could even undermine national harmony. How? Perhaps Trudeau felt that raising the matter might dredge up the complicity of previous governments, as well as that of prominent individuals and institutions, in the admission and harbouring of Nazis. Certainly the prime minister, a shrewd politician, understood the dangers of inflaming interethnic tensions in Canada. If a new consensus for federal unity was his goal, then the potentially divisive Nazi issue should be avoided. Setting Jews and eastern Europeans, notably Ukrainians, on a collision course — even in the name of justice — was not in the national interest. However, the issue would not go away, and the Jewish community was determined to make its case — a legal case — more forcefully. In the spring of 1982, as Congress officials were preparing a legal brief, their cause received several unexpected boosts.

The Rauca Case

Albert Helmut Rauca, a 73-year-old suburban Torontonian, was taken into custody by the RCMP on a West German extradition warrant. He stood accused of direct involvement in the murder of thousands of Lithuanian Jews during World War II. The Congress leaders were delighted. Not only did the proceedings promise the removal from Canada of an accused Nazi mass murderer, but they also attracted national attention. However, the hearings had an ironic result. Rauca's lawyer argued in favour of domestic prosecution, forcing the Congress to hold back its brief at least temporarily, lest it seem to support the accused.[35] Meanwhile, its staff in Toronto made their knowledge of foreign archives and other war crimes-related material available to the Justice Department lawyer acting for the Crown in the extradition proceedings.[36] In fact, Rauca was extradited, but died in Germany before his trial.

The tumult raised the public awareness of wanted war criminals and the possibility that more were ensconced in Canada. In late August 1982,

Today Magazine published an article about Harold Puntulis, who, like Rauca, had lived quietly in suburban Toronto for many years, after (allegedly) having participated in the murder of thousands of Jews and Gypsies in the Baltic area during World War II.[37] Puntulis, however, also like Rauca, died. Public sensitization grew again in September 1982, when the book *None Is Too Many*, by Irving Abella and Harold Troper, was published. This study of the Canadian response to the plight of European Jewry during the Nazi era described in detail the rigid Canadian rejection of Jewish refugees during the long night of terror, nurturing the idea that Canada had given haven, perhaps unwittingly, to some of their murderers after the war. The wide publicity left many Canadians with a sense of profound shame regarding past immigration policies. It further stiffened the resolve of Canadian Jewry to demand action.[38]

Perhaps because of this heightened public awareness, perhaps because Jewish legal arguments at last were having the desired effect, perhaps because Trudeau, slumping in popularity polls, gave signs of stepping down, leaving his ministers to jockey for support in an impending leadership race, a softening seemed to occur on the war crimes issue. Guarded hints were dropped that the government might be prepared to bring charges against several resident Nazi war criminals. Some Jewish leaders interpreted these as a commitment.[39]

A New Government

Before its resolve could be tested, the Liberal government received a crushing electoral blow. On September 17, 1984, a Progressive Conservative cabinet under Brian Mulroney was sworn into office with the largest majority ever awarded a Canadian political party. For the Jewish community, the change was troubling. Trudeau had not been sympathetic to its agenda, but its leaders had enjoyed access to his government. However, Jewish connections with the new Conservative political machine were limited, and Mulroney himself was largely unknown. Only one Jew now sat on the government benches. On the other hand, several Ukrainians— traditional supporters of the Conservative party—were included in the new cabinet. The Jewish establishment felt locked out.[40] Who would speak for their interests now? However, the Jewish voice managed to make itself heard. Sol Littman, a retired journalist who represented the Simon Wiesenthal Center in Los Angeles, was the author of an article in *Saturday Night* exploring Canadian complicity in the post-war admission of alleged war criminals, illustrating his point with Galicia Division members.[41] If the Ukrainians were unhappy at being included in an article on Nazi war criminals, they were livid at Littman's assertion that the division had been assigned guard duty at concentration camps and had participated in putting down the 1943 Warsaw ghetto uprising, at the cost of thousands of Jewish lives. Their veterans protested that their unit was innocent of anti-Jewish activities, and that the Warsaw ghetto uprising had been crushed before the Galicia was organized. A libel suit was filed against Littman and *Saturday Night*. As a result, the offending sentences in the manuscript of his forthcoming book on the subject, *War Criminals on Trial*, were expunged with a publisher's note stating that the material in *Saturday Night* had appeared in "somewhat different form."

Littman and the Simon Wiesenthal Center were outside the Canadian Jewish Congress. Yet, robed in Wiesenthal's mantle, Littman was granted an interview with Mulroney's new minister of justice, succeeding where the Congress had failed. As a bewildered Jewish leadership looked on, he arrived in Ottawa, accompanied by several spokesmen for the California-based organization. Impervious to past failures, the Center pressed its own agenda. The minister reassured the delegation of his concern and hinted that some plan of action was in the air.[42] Several weeks later, Littman received an urgent call from California informing him that the Center had obtained certain documents, under American freedom of information legislation, indicating, among other things, that in 1962 a Dr. Joseph Menke had applied to the Canadian embassy in Buenos Aires for admission to Canada. His request had been referred to the Canadian visa control office in Cologne, Germany, which, in turn, had requested information on Menke from Allied intelligence authorities in Europe. According to the documentation, Canadian authorities had been advised that Joseph Menke was a known alias used by the notorious Dr. Joseph Mengele, the wanted 'angel of death' who had conducted barbaric medical experiments on inmates at Auschwitz. Littman contacted both the Canadian Immigration Service and the RCMP. Neither divulged any record of the Menke application or whether or not it had been rejected. Concluding — incorrectly, as matters transpired — that Menke and Mengele were one and the same, and that, in all probability, the mass murderer actually had arrived in Canada, Littman wrote to the prime minister on December 20, 1984, charging that the nation had been negligent in not following the case, and in not advising the Allied authorities of Mengele's whereabouts at the time. "This," he declared, "leaves us with the frightening possibility that Mengele may actually be living in Canada today."

> If this possibility seems too incredible to credit, let me remind you that former S.S. Master Sergeant Helmut Rauca who was responsible for the death of 9,200 innocent men, women and children in one afternoon, arrived in Canada as an immigrant in 1950 and lived here totally undisturbed until he was finally tracked down by the RCMP in 1982.

He demanded a "release of all documentation" and "an immediate investigation" into the Mengele affair.

> The dimension of Mengele's crimes, and the legacy of his 400,000 victims, demand that no stone remain unturned in the quest to bring this man, who is the personification of evil, before the bar of justice. Only a thorough investigation ordered by your government can ascertain what role Canada played in the bizarre case of Joseph Mengele.[43]

A copy was sent also to the minister of justice, with whom a second meeting was arranged. The minister was not moved particularly by the Mengele revelations, but indicated again that something was in the air; he refused to be more specific.

Almost four weeks later, Littman was informed by the Wiesenthal Center that the *New York Times* now possessed the file on Mengele's alleged Canadian connection. Rather than allow the matter to be submerged in a larger account, he arranged for a press conference in Toronto on January 20, 1985, telling reporters that he planned to reveal the contents of his letter to Mulroney.[44] He also informed the *New York Times* of his Mengele accusations.[45] The media smelled a good story. *Maclean's* telephoned the prime minister's office, taking the officials by surprise; they seemed never to have heard of the letter. Apparently, it had been misplaced in the wave of Christmas greetings during the holiday week. Immediately prior to his scheduled press conference, Littman was contacted by an aide, who apologized and suggested that the press conference be postponed until the prime minister had considered the allegation, but Littman refused, releasing his letter and the accompanying documentation to the press. The story made the headlines the following Monday and was carried even in the *New York Times*.[46]

The controversy placed Ottawa in an uncomfortable situation. Stumbling for an appropriate response — one that would keep the government on the side of the angels, and perhaps, create the impression of decisive action — Mulroney decided on a judicial inquiry. On February 7, 1985, he announced that the respected Quebec Superior Court Justice Jules Deschênes had agreed to conduct an inquiry into the presence of Nazi war criminals in Canada, including Mengele, and to determine if any means existed in Canadian law to deal with them.

The Deschênes Commission

The Conservative caucus and cabinet were surprised. Some MPs huddled together discussing the possible political consequences.[47] The Jewish Congress leaders reacted with disbelief. They had never pressed for an inquiry; indeed, they had never been close enough to Mulroney or his cabinet to press for anything. While welcoming the federal initiative publicly, they were uneasy in private, not knowing what the prime minister really intended. Were the long-awaited test cases a dead issue?[48] Since the Mengele letter was the most apparent factor prompting the establishment of the Deschênes Commission, the attendant publicity would cause the public to regard Littman, not the Jewish Congress, as responsible for having forced the government's hand. The Ukrainian community was also galvanized; regarded already as anti-Ukrainian, Littman's earlier allegations against the Galicia Division were seen as part of a larger attack on the Ukrainian diaspora. When he spoke of 3000 eastern European war criminals in Canada, including many Ukrainians, was he not damning implicitly the entire community for sheltering these criminals for decades?[49] To many Ukrainian Canadians, moreover, Littman was not a fringe figure, but a stalking horse for the Canadian Jewish establishment, saying what others believed but did not dare to say.[50]

The federal Conservatives were unprepared for the eruption of Jewish-Ukrainian tensions. For most, the term 'Nazi war criminal' conjured up images of an Eichmann or a Mengele; few thought in terms of non-German collaborators, police officials, concentration camp guards or local bureaucrats. When Ukrainian organizations reacted to the Deschênes Commission as an assault on the Ukrainian diaspora, the government was taken aback, and began to weigh the potential fallout at the ballot box. Whatever goodwill had accrued slowly and painstakingly between Jews and Ukrainians evaporated almost overnight. Jews, applauding the government's decision, collided with Ukrainians increasingly convinced that they were the victim of a smear campaign — a community under siege. Beneath a facade of public civility, old wounds inflicted far away and long ago were reopened. Now the two communities began to scrap in the highly charged atmosphere of the Deschênes hearings.[51] Each, convinced that it occupied the moral high ground, made its case to the media and political leaders. In their private councils, accusations of antisemitism and Ukrainian-baiting were heard with increasing frequency.

However, the Deschênes Commission Report, released on March 12, 1987, had a salutary effect, although its long-term impact cannot be measured. Deschênes found sufficient evident to satisfy himself that 20 Nazi war criminals were living in Canada, and that Canadian law could deal with them.[52] The government immediately declared it would amend the Criminal Code so as to allow for the trial of such persons in Canada, and that legal action would be forthcoming.[53] The Jewish community was pleased; 40 years of federal inaction appeared to be at an end, the long struggle for justice realized, the suffering of Holocaust victims not forgotten, nor their memory betrayed. However, the first of these trials, that of Imre Finta, ended in an acquittal, and charges had to be dropped by the Crown for lack of evidence against the two other men indicted, Michael

Pawlowski and Stephan Reistetter. All three men are residents of Ontario. To date, there have been no further indictments.[54]

The Ukrainian community was also pleased. It, too, had not faltered. It had stood up to the government, public opinion and the Canadian Jewish lobby, seen as the strongest and best organized ethnic voice in the country. Moreover, the Commission had found no evidence linking the Galicia Division with war crimes, and, if rumours proved correct, no Ukrainian Canadians were on the confidential list of war criminals living in Canada that Deschênes had presented to the government with recommendations for legal action. Along with their Jewish counterparts, therefore, the Ukrainian leadership claimed a moral victory, pledging support both for the prosecution of war criminals in Canada and for a new era of rapprochement. However, there are many shadows. The sense of historical victimization that each community has laid at the door of the other was intensified during the Deschênes inquiry. The trial in Israel of the Ukrainian-born American auto mechanic John Demjanjuk, accused of being "Ivan the Terrible," who operated the gas chambers at Treblinka, coincided with the Canadian deliberations. For many Ukrainians in North America, however, Demjanjuk was either the victim of mistaken identity or the object of a Soviet-inspired conspiracy to delegitimize the Ukrainian diaspora in the eyes of the Western world. Canadian Ukrainians raised a substantial pool of money for his defence, raising the ire of Canadian Jews, many of whom had little doubt concerning his guilt. When convicted, his Canadian supporters responded with anger; reportedly, the vice-president of the Demjanjuk defence fund compared the defendant to Christ and the verdict to the crucifixion. "Jewish people paid for that—rightly or wrongly—but they did pay for the crucifixion. I believe this will have similar results in the future for this conviction today."[55]

These remarks were condemned by more temperate voices, and the matter of Demjanjuk's identity is still under court review in Israel. Classic, old-world antisemitic themes have little resonance in modern Canada, although it is still possible for both Judeophobia and Ukrainophobia to stoke passions, notably among older immigrants who lived through World War II. But intercommunal resentments have played themselves out peaceably on the Canadian national stage, without denunciations, violence or pogroms. Instead of bullets and bombs, mailing lists, legal briefs and ballots are the weapons of choice. What some have called the 'new antisemitism' can be interpreted as merely opposition or indifference to Jewish political or public policy interests. Jews, and other minorities following their example, have organized themselves as pressure groups in order to influence the political process—tactics that involve coalition and compromise. Old-world antagonisms, rooted in differing historical narratives, as well as genuine grievances, may never disappear, but with domestication, their hard edges soften. While some Canadian Jews consider governmental inaction on the war crimes issue a manifestation of antisemitism, others do not. If so, it is of a different order than in the past.

Notes

This article is adapted from Harold Troper and Morton Weinfeld, "Jewish-Ukrainian Relations in Canada Since World War II and the Emergence of the Nazi War Criminal Issue," *American Jewish History* 77 (1987): 106-34. The authors' more comprehensive treatment is found in *Old Wounds: Jews, Ukrainians and the Hunt for Nazi War Criminals in Canada* (Toronto: Viking Press, 1988).

1 House of Commons, *Debates*, October 8, 1971; Howard Brotz, "Multiculturalism in Canada: A Muddle," *Canadian Public Policy* 6 (1986): 41-46; Raymond Breton, "From a Different Perspective: French Canada and the Issue of Immigration and Multiculturalism," *TESL Talk* 10, 3 (1979): 45-56; Manoly R. Lupul, "Multiculturalism and Canada's White Ethnics," *Canadian Ethnic Studies* 15 (1983): 99-107. For three separate overviews of the origins of the federal multicultural policy, see Jean Burnet, "Ethnicity: Canadian Experience and Policy," *Sociological Focus* 9 (1976): 199-207; John Porter, "Dilemmas and Contradictions of a Multi-Ethnic Society," *Transactions of the Royal Society of Canada* 10 (1972): 193-205; and Harold Troper, "Nationalism and the History Curriculum in Canada," *History Teacher* 12 (1976): 11-27.

2 D. W. Grawronski, *History: Meaning and Method* (Glenview, IL: Scott, Foreman, 1969), p. 3.

3 E. H. Carr, *What Is History?* 2nd ed. (London: Macmillan, 1986), p. 114.

4 For a discussion of the historical self-understanding of both Jewish and Ukrainian polities, and the place each allots to the other, see Howard Aster and Peter J. Potichnyj, *Jewish-Ukrainian Relations: Two Solitudes* (Oakville, ON: Mosaic Press, 1983).

5 Alternate Ukrainian and Jewish historical views of the 1648 rebellion is the topic of Frank E. Sysyn, "The Jewish Factor in the Khmel'nyts'kyi Uprising," unpublished paper.

6 Historians continue to debate the Petlura government and its Jewish policy. The issue was a matter of heated exchange in the pages of *Jewish Social Studies*. Taras Hunczak, "A Reappraisal of Symon Petliura and Ukrainian Jewish Relations, 1917-1921," *Jewish Social Studies* 31 (1969): 163-83, and Zosa Szajkowski, "'A Reappraisal of Symon Petliura and Ukrainian and Jewish Relations, 1917-1921': A Rebuttal," *Jewish Social Studies* 32 (1970): 246-63. The exchange, with added documentary material, was published. Taras Hunczak, *Symon Petliura and the Jews: A Reappraisal* (Toronto: Ukrainian Historical Association, 1985).

7 The historiography of the Holocaust as it touches the Ukraine continues to grow. A useful overview of World War II in the larger sweep of Ukrainian history is available in Paul R. Magocsis, "Ukraine: An Introductory History," unpublished manuscript. No discussion of the Holocaust in the Ukraine can ignore Philip Friedman, "Ukrainian-Jewish Relations During the Nazi Occupation" (*Yivo Annual* [1958-59]: 259-98) which is the starting point for much later analysis. The failure of Jews, notably Yad Vashem in Israel, to accord Sheptytsky his due as a 'righteous gentile" still

rankles. See Shimon Redlich, "Sheptytsky and the Jews," *Jerusalem Post*, December 21, 1985.

8 Lubomyr Y. Luciuk, "Searching for Place: Ukrainian Refugee Migration to Canada after World War II" (Ph.D. thesis, University of Alberta, 1984).

9 Literature in English on the Galicia Division, also known as the Halychyna Division, is spotty at best. See, for example, Basil Dmytryshyn, "The Nazis and the SS Volunteer Division 'Galicia'," *The American Slavic and Eastern European Review* 15 (1956): 1-10; Wasyl Veryha, "The 'Galicia' Ukrainian Division in Polish and Soviet Literature," *Ukrainian Quarterly* 36 (1980): 253-70; Richard Landewehr, *Fighting for Freedom: The Ukrainian Volunteer Division of the Waffen-SS* (Silver Spring, MD: Bibliophile Legion, 1985); Myroslav Yurkevich, "Galician Ukrainians in German Military Formations and in the German Administration," *Ukraine During World War II: History and Its Aftermath*, ed. Yury Boshyk (Edmonton: Canadian Institute of Ukrainian Studies, 1986), pp. 67-87.

10 The Ukrainian-Canadian lobbying effort on behalf of the Galicia and community support for the Division is detailed in Bohdan Panchuk, *Heroes of Their Day: The Reminiscences of Bohdan Panchuk*, ed. Lubomyr Y. Luciuk (Toronto: MHSO, 1983); see also Reg Whitaker, *Double Standard: The Secret History of Canadian Immigration* (Toronto: Lester & Orpen Dennys, 1987), pp. 129-38.

11 Canadian Jewish Congress Papers, CJC Archives, Montreal (hereafter referred to as the CJC Papers) Ukrainian Galician Division Papers, 1950-51 (Galician Files), memorandum of Rosenberg to Hayes, June 30, 1950, and telegram of Bronfman to Harris, July 4, 1950.

12 CJC Papers, Galician Files. Memorandum of Rosenberg to Hayes, "Halychyna Division," July 26, 1950; memorandum of Rosenberg to Hayes, "Halychyna Division," October 23, 1950; Hayes to Harris, August 2, 1950; Harris to Hayes, November 6, 1950; Harris to Bronfman, November 7, 1950; and Memorandum of Hayes to National Executive, January 10, 1951.

13 *Jewish Post*, May 2, 1957.

14 British United Press Dispatch, May 4, 1957.

15 CJC Papers, Andreii Melynk Files, Frank to Hayes, May 10, 1957; memorandum of Kayfetz to Hayes, May 17, 1957; Frank to Hayes, May 16, 1957; Kochan to Fenson, May 31, 1957; Canadian Jewish Congress Archives, Toronto, Catzman Papers, memorandum of Kayfetz to Hayes, "Meeting with officers of Ukrainian National Federation," May 14, 1957; and *Jewish Post*, May 23, 1957.

16 Yaacov Glickman, "Political Socialization and the Social Protest of Canadian Jewry: Some Historical and Contemporary Perspectives," in *Ethnicity, Power and Politics in Canada*, ed. Jorgen Dahlie and Tissa Fernado (Toronto: Methuen, 1981), pp. 123-50.

17 National Archives of Canada (NAC), Louis Ronson Papers (Ronson Papers), vol. 4, file 7. "Note for Remarks by the Prime Minister to the Ukrainian-Canadian Congress, Winnipeg, Manitoba, October 9, 1971," October 9, 1971.

18 NAC, Ronson Papers, vol. 4, file 7. Memorandum of Levy to Ronson, "Ukrainian Contacts with JCRC," August 5, 1971.

19 Similar sentiments abounded in the American Jewish community. See Abraham Brumberg, "Poland and the Jews," *Tikkun* (July/August 1987): 15-20, 85-90.

20 Canadian Jewish Archives, Toronto (CJC-T), J. C. Hurwitz Papers, File July-December 1974, memorandum of Kayfetz to Hurwitz re: Relations with Ukrainian Canadians, September 9, 1974; File July-December 1974. Minutes, JCRC, Toronto, September 11, 1974, pp. 6-8.

21 CJC-T, J. C. Hurwitz Papers, File July-December 1974, Epstein to Kayfetz, November 5, 1974.

22 See, for example, CJC-T, Catzman Papers, confidential memorandum of Kayfetz to Catzman, et al., September 5, 1958; Kayfetz to Finestone, September 23, 1958.

23 Hannah Arendt, *Eichmann in Jerusalem: A Report on the Banality of Evil* (New York: Viking Press, 1964), and Gideon Hausner, *Justice in Jerusalem* (New York: Harper, 1966).

24 CJC Papers, Submission to L. B. Pearson. Memorandum of Saalheimer to Gelber, March 27, 1964; Prinz to Rusk, March 2, 1984; Garber to Martin, April 13, 1964; Hayes to Coutts, October 1, 1964; and Bronfman to Pearson, October 14, 1964.

25 Interview with Max Chirofsky, May 21, 1986, Toronto.

26 Interview with Ben Kayfetz, August 9, 1986, Toronto.

27 American and international action against Nazis is considered in Tom Bower, *Blind Eye to Murder: Britain, America and the Purging of Nazi Germany A Pledge Betrayed?* (London: A. Deutsch, 1981); Charles R. Allen, Jr., *Nazi War Criminals in America: Facts . . . Action, the Basic Handbook* (New York: Highgate House, 1985); Adalbert Ruckerl, *The Investigation of Nazi War Crimes, 1945-1978, A Documentation* (Heidelberg: C. F. Müller, 1979); Rochelle G. Saidel, *The Outraged Conscience: Seekers of Justice for Nazi War Criminals in America* (Albany: State University of New York Press, 1984); and Allan A. Ryan, Jr., *Quiet Neighbors: Prosecuting Nazi War Criminals in America* (New York: Harcourt Brace Jovanovich, 1984).

28 NAC, Plaut Papers, CJC National JCRC, Memoranda (Pt. 1), 1977, memorandum of Kayfetz to Plaut, et al., re "Ukrainians," August 18, 1977.

29 NAC, Plaut Papers, vol. 4, file 7. Flyer entitled "Nazi Crimes in Przemyls" (Poland), n.d.

30 NAC, Plaut Papers, CJC National JCRC, Memoranda (Pt. 1), 1977. Shymko to Kayfetz, August 8, 1977.

31 This flyer, obviously calculated to cause trouble between the two communities, suggests neo-Nazi origins. I suspect Ernst Zündel (see essay, this volume). [Editor]

32 NAC, Plaut Papers, CJC National JCRC, Memoranda (Pt. 1), 1977, memorandum of Kayfetz to Plaut, et al., re: "Ukrainians," August 18, 1977.

33 In his report on Nazi war criminals in Canada, Justice Jules Deschênes reviews the legal opinions accepted by the government and their flaws. Commission of Inquiry on War Criminals, *Report. Part I: Public* (Ottawa: Queen's Printer, 1986), pp. 85-239.

34 Some light may be shed with the final release of *Nazi War Criminals in Canada: The Historical and Policy Setting from the 1940's to the Present* prepared for the Deschênes Commission of Inquiry on War Criminals by Alti Rodel.

35 Interview with David Matas, March 29, 1986, Toronto. For a study of the Rauca case, see Sol Littman, *War Criminals on Trial: The Rauca Case* (Toronto: Lester & Orpen Dennys, 1983).

36 CJC, Silverstone Papers, War Criminal Correspondence, 1982. Memorandum of Narvey to Amerisinghe re: "Documents in Soviet Archives," August 19, 1982.

37 Jeff Ansell and Paul Appleby, "The War Criminal," *Today Magazine*, August 28, 1982.

38 Irving Abella and Harold Troper, *None Is Too Many: Canada and the Jews of Europe, 1933-1948* (Toronto: Lester & Orpen Dennys, 1982).

39 Interview with David Matas, March 29, 1986, Toronto; interview with Milton Harris, May 10, 1986, Toronto; and Milton Harris Papers, War Crimes File, MacGuigan to Kaplan, December 8, 1983.

40 Milton Harris Papers, War Crimes File, MacKay to Raphael, November 13, 1984; Crosbie to Raphael, November 19, 1984; Raphael to Harris, November 21, 1984; and Harris to Granovsky, January 1985.

41 Sol Littman, "Agent of the Holocaust, The Secret Life of Helmut Rauca," *Saturday Night*, July 1983, pp. 11-23.

42 Interview with Sol Littman, January 21, 1986, Toronto.

43 Commission of Inquiry on War Criminals, Documents, Littman to Mulroney, December 20, 1984.

44 Interview with Sol Littman, May 7, 1986, Toronto.

45 Interview with Arthur Meighen, May 25, 1987, Toronto.

46 Interview with Sol Littman, October 22, 1986, Toronto. *The Toronto Star*, January 23, 1985, and *New York Times*, January 23, 1985.

47 Interview with Geoff Norquay, March 21, 1986, Ottawa.

48 CJC, Silverstone Papers, Deschênes Commission Press Releases, Newspaper Clippings. CJC Press Release, "Canadian Jewish Congress President Says War Criminal Commission Not Enough," February 7, 1985.

49 Commission of Inquiry on War Criminals, *Report, Part I: Public* (Ottawa: Queen's Printer, 1986), pp. 245-48.

50 CJC-T, JCRC papers, Ukrainian File, Epstein to Satok, February 11, 1985; Satok to Epstein, February 13, 1985; interview with John Gregorovich, April 8, 1987, Toronto; and interview with Roman Serbyn, February 18, 1986, Montreal.

51 For a full discussion of Jewish-Ukrainian relations during the Deschênes hearings and their aftermath, see Harold Troper and Morton Weinfeld, *Old Wounds: Jews, Ukrainians and the Hunt for Nazi War Criminals in Canada* (Toronto: Viking Press, 1988), and David Matas and Susan Charendoff, *Justice Delayed: Nazi War Criminals in Canada* (Toronto: Summerhill Press, 1987), pp. 163-208.

52 Commission of Inquiry on War Criminals, *Report, Part I: Public*.

53 House of Commons, *Debates*, March 12, 1987, 4076.

54 Finta, whose trial began in the autumn of 1989, was acquitted on May 25, 1990.

55 *The Toronto Star*, April 19, 1988. This comment was quoted in Alan Dershowitz, "Hour of Truth for 'Ivan the Terrible'," *Chicago Sun Times*, April 27, 1988, and interview with Susan Reid, May 4, 1988, Toronto. The authors are in possession of an audio tape of the April 19, 1988 press conference.

Index